HUEY P. NEWTON

Black Lives series

Elvira Basevich, *W. E. B. Du Bois*
Nigel C. Gibson, *Frantz Fanon*
Jane Hiddleston, *Aimé Césaire*
Denise Lynn, *Claudia Jones*
Utz McKnight, *Frances E. W. Harper*
Joshua Myers, *Cedric Robinson*
Sherrow O. Pinder, *David Walker*
Delio Vásquez, *Huey P. Newton*

Huey P. Newton

I Am We

Delio Vásquez

polity

First published in 2026 by Polity Press Ltd.

Polity Press Ltd.
65 Bridge Street
Cambridge CB2 1UR, UK

Polity Press Ltd.
111 River Street
Hoboken, NJ 07030, USA

ISBN-13: 978-1-5095-4333-5
ISBN-13: 978-1-5095-4334-2 (pb)

A catalogue record for this book is available from the British Library.

Library of Congress Control Number: 2025951466

Typeset in 10.5pt on 14pt Janson by
Cheshire Typesetting Ltd, Cuddington, Cheshire
Printed and bound in Great Britain by CPI Group (UK) Ltd, Croydon

For further information on Polity, visit our website:
politybooks.com

Dedicated to the memory of Asad Haider.
In a sense emancipated, may your mind be at peace.

Contents

Acknowledgments

If you are serious about Black struggle, you know that in many instances you will be stepping out on nothing, hoping to land on something.

bell hooks and Cornel West (1991)[1]

This book is, among other things, an attempt to lend dignity and prestige to the life of Dr. Huey P. Newton. His effort to revolutionize society through the application of his mind continues to shape our world today. This book would not exist without him. Neither would it exist without the past collective labor of all the individuals who, alongside him, directly shaped our history through their willingness to struggle for change. I am thankful to former members of the Black Panther Party and other movement elders who gave their time in interviews and conversations, or simply offered words of encouragement to me over the years: Flores Forbes, Emory Douglas, Phyllis Jackson, Billy X Jennings, George "Bunchy" Crear, Michael Fultz, Ashanti Alston, Tarik Haskins, Richard Brown (RIP), Brother Shep Shakur, Jamal Joseph, Jalil Muntaqim, Sekou Odinga (RIP), Ericka Huggins, Gwen Swackhamer, Joe Blum, and Eve Rosanne. Thank you especially to Flores Forbes, Phyllis Jackson, and Billy X Jennings for feedback on parts of the manuscript. I am particularly grateful as well to the Dr. Huey P. Newton Foundation, Fredrika Newton, and Xavier Buck for their support and affirmation as I completed this project. I also appreciate those faculty and graduate alumni of the University of California Santa Cruz who contributed to my understanding of Newton's experience at the university through conversations, interviews, and correspondence: Bettina Aptheker, Burney Le Boeuf, Robert Meister, Diane Lebow, Barry Katz, and Richard Mahon.

The core of this book came out of disciplined months spent in the stunning archives of the Dr. Huey P. Newton Foundation Inc. collection held at Stanford University's Green Library, where the labor of archivist Tim Noakes and others was invaluable to my understanding of Newton's intellectual life. I am also thankful for the Freedom Archives in Berkeley, CA, where Nathaniel Moore, Claude Marks, and Danielle Nanos-Luz provided resources and advice during the final stretch of the project but also welcomed me years earlier when I was an inexperienced graduate student. I am grateful as well for the labor of the many archivists working with the Special Collections at Emory University (J. Herman Blake and Emily L. Moore Papers), New York University (Philip Agee Papers), and Columbia University (Random House Records, 1925–99). Thank you for your vital work.

I am appreciative of the labor of my editors, past and present, at Polity, with whom I signed a book contract as a graduate student. Thank you in particular to those who collaborated with me during the final year of the project: Julia Davies, Flo Winkley, Olivia Jackson, Evie Deavall, Gregory Miller, and especially copy-editor Tim Clark. I also deeply appreciate the feedback I received from the anonymous reviewers of the manuscript.

Many of the ideas in this book were produced during my years as a postdoctoral researcher. I am thankful for the support of New York University's Provost's Postdoctoral Fellowship Program in collaboration with NYU's Gallatin School of Individualized Study. I am also thankful for the support of American University's Academic Diversity Postdoctoral Fellowship in collaboration with AU's department of Philosophy and Religion. Thank you to each and every individual who made those fellowships possible. I am grateful as well to the many scholars who offered feedback on early versions of this work over the years: my colleagues in NYU's Black Diaspora Cultural Studies research cluster (Emilie Boone, Clifton Boyd, Madina Thiam, and Audrey Celestine, as well as Robyn Spencer-Antoine for joining us as discussant);

the Workshop on Psychological Warfare, Psychiatric Violence, and the Prison Industrial Complex organized by Danielle Carr and Orisanmi Burton through the Livescu Initiative on Neuro, Narrative, and AI; NYU's Urban Democracy Lab, especially organizer Gianpaolo Baiocchi; my many colleagues within NYU's Gallatin School of Individualized Study; the department of Political Science at Johns Hopkins University, especially organizer P. J. Brendese and discussant Emily Lerman; the Society for Phenomenology and Existential Philosophy, especially Kevin Thompson for organizing our panel; the American Studies Association; and the Clara Luper Department of African & African American Studies at the University of Oklahoma.

I would not have been in a position to write a book at all without the past support of several academic advisors over the years. Thank you Rovana Popoff, Jennifer Scappettone, David Marriott, Megan Thomas, Felicity Amaya Schaefer, Ben Read, Nathaniel Deutsch, Andrés Henao Castro, George Schulman, and Vasuki Nesiah for believing in me as a scholar in the first place. Without your support I would never have secured a job in this peculiar profession of ours.

There are many other people in the academy who provided distinct advice, leads, and acts or words of support during the research or writing process. Among them, I am thankful to Bernard Harcourt, Johanna Fernandez, Cornel West, Che Gossett, John Narayan, Quinn Lester, Hannah Gurman, Alejandro Velasco, Perry Zurn, and Brett Gary. I am especially thankful to those in academia who offered advice whom I also count as real friends: Jeffrey Omari, Colin Asher, Jess Whatcott, Isaac Blacksin, Marcelo Hoffman, and Tag. And I am particularly appreciative to those select friends who took on the hard work of reading drafts or who provided help to make the book stronger: James Tracy, Lani Hanna, Ryan Lee, and especially Nara Roberta. In addition, and in all honesty, this book would be a mere shell of its current form if not for the rich discussions I learned from over the years alongside my brilliant students at UC Santa Cruz and at NYU, in my courses "Black Panther Party: History and Theory" and "Huey Newton: Philosopher/Panther." Thank you to each and every one of you, and a special thank you goes to those former students who read drafts of chapters or otherwise contributed to the project: Ava Emilione, Daniel Abelow, Cecilia Innis, Iman Yusuf, Yudi Feng, and Nayla Tozin.

There is, in addition, a special set of people who played fortuitous roles at pivotal junctures in the story of the creation of this book. Thank you, Asad Haider, for referring Polity to me in the first place, and thank you to Ben Mabie for sharing advice on how to navigate dealing with the publishing industry. Thank you, Angel Dominguez, for sharing Newton's graduate student file with me at UC Santa Cruz and for encouraging the project. Thank you, Tyson Amir, for encouraging me seven years ago to publish on the theory of intercommunalism, after we were led to cross paths and meet at that café in Oakland. And thank you, most of all, Orisanmi Burton, for your insights, mentorship, and brotherhood through the worst of the whirlwind. This book would not exist without you.

Writing this book has been, without a doubt, the most difficult task that I have undertaken in my life, in more ways than I can get away with describing. I hope one day to be able to describe it in full. When surveillance and repression came, it was nothing like what I was expecting. When my laptop crashed and I lost a whole draft of the book, or when another major chapter was stolen from a friend's backpack, these were events that set me back, but they were comparatively minor experiences in the broader arc of the dynamic. Little could have prepared me for the experience in the hospital. I would not have been able to make it through without the people who provided psychological, emotional, and spiritual support, despite it all: Pastora Dorlimar Lebrón Malavé and the People's Church in East Harlem, Dr. John Edwards of West Coast Psychotherapy, and Dr. Edena Walden and Melvin George with Reklame Health. I would not have my health without *la fuerza y el querer de mi madre* Ana Gisela Vásquez, the love and tireless care of my partner Bianca Navas, the support of my dear friends Tanzeem Ajmiri and Karan Dhadialla, and the love of my little brother Dioni Vásquez.

I am deeply indebted to the people who sacrificed their well-being so that I could commiserate with them about the madness of "the experience": Orisanmi Burton, Maya Gonzalez, and Asad Haider (RIP). And I owe more than I can say to "my team" at the United States Postal Service, whose training helped me gain perspective and strength when I was considering leaving academia altogether.

Last, but not least, the spirit of resistance within the music and culture of hip-hop has sustained me throughout my life more times than I can count, through struggles against white supremacy, social isolation, depression, hunger, near homelessness, hopelessness, and technologies of madness. Thank you to KRS-One and Rakim, to Nas, Cormega, Ras Kass, and especially to stic and M-1 of dead prez, Can-i-bus, Lupe Fiasco, and MC Zumbi of Zion I (RIP). The *Workout II* LP was a north star. For the culture. And for humanity, so that one day in the future our descendants may be born free.

The Black Panther Party for Self-Defense Ten-Point Program (1966)

What We Want
What We Believe

1. We want freedom. We want power to determine the destiny of our Black community.
We believe that Black people will not be free until we are able to determine our destiny.

2. We want full employment for our people.
We believe that the federal government is responsible and obligated to give every man employment or a guaranteed income. We believe that if the White American businessmen will not give full employment, then the means of production should be taken from the businessmen and placed in the community so that the people of the community can organize and employ all of its people and give a high standard of living.

3. We want an end to the robbery by the capitalists of our Black community.
We believe that this racist government has robbed us, and now we are demanding the overdue debt of forty acres and two mules. Forty acres and two mules were promised 100 years ago as restitution for slave labor and mass murder of Black people. We will accept the payment in currency which will be distributed to our many communities. The Germans are now aiding the Jews in Israel for the genocide of the Jewish people. The Germans murdered six million Jews. The American racist has taken part in the slaughter of over fifty

million Black people; therefore, we feel that this is a modest demand that we make.

4. We want decent housing fit for the shelter of human beings.
We believe that if the White Landlords will not give decent housing to our Black community, then the housing and the land should be made into cooperatives so that our community, with government aid, can build and make decent housing for its people.

5. We want education for our people that exposes the true nature of this decadent American society. We want education that teaches us our true history and our role in the present-day society.
We believe in an educational system that will give to our people a knowledge of self. If a man does not have knowledge of himself and his position in society and the world then he has little chance to relate to anything else.

6. We want all Black men to be exempt from military service.
We believe that Black people should not be forced to fight in the military service to defend a racist government that does not protect us. We will not fight and kill other people of color in the world who, like Black people, are being victimized by the White racist government of America. We will protect ourselves from the force and violence of the racist police and the racist military by whatever means necessary.

7. We want an immediate end to police brutality and the murder of Black people.
We believe we can end police brutality in our Black community by organizing Black self-defense groups that are dedicated to defending our Black community from racist police oppression and brutality. The Second Amendment to the Constitution of the United States gives a right to bear arms. We therefore believe that all Black people should arm themselves for self-defense.

8. We want freedom for all Black men held in federal, state, county and city prisons and jails.
We believe that all Black People should be released from the many jails and prisons because they have not received a fair and impartial trial.

9. We want all Black people when brought to trial to be tried in court by a jury of their peer group or people from their Black communities, as defined by the constitution of the United States.
We believe that the courts should follow the United States Constitution so that Black people will receive fair trials. The Fourteenth Amendment of the U.S. Constitution gives a man a right to be tried by his peer group. A peer is a person from a similar economic, social, religious, geographical, environmental, historical, and racial background. To do this the court will be forced to select a jury from the Black community from which the Black defendant came. We have been, and we are being, tried by all-White juries that have no understanding of the "average reasoning man" of the Black community.

10. We want land, bread, housing, education, clothing, justice and peace.
When, in the course of human events, it becomes necessary for one people to dissolve the political bonds which have connected them with another, and to assume, among the powers of the earth, the separate and equal station to which the laws of nature and nature's God entitle them, a decent respect of the opinions of mankind requires that they should declare the causes which impel them to the separation.

We hold these truths to be self-evident, that all men are created equal; that they are endowed by their Creator with certain inalienable rights; that among these are life, liberty, and the pursuit of happiness. That, to secure these rights, governments are instituted among men, deriving their just powers from the consent of the governed; that, whenever any form of government becomes destructive of these ends, it is the right of the people to alter or abolish it, and to institute a new government, laying its foundation on such principles, and organizing its powers in such form, as to them shall seem most likely to effect their safety and happiness. Prudence, indeed, will dictate that governments long established should not be changed for light and transient causes; and, accordingly, all experience hath shown that mankind are more disposed to suffer, while evils are sufferable, than to right themselves by abolishing the forms to which they are accustomed. But, when a long train of abuses and usurpations, pursuing invariably the same object, evinces a design to reduce them under absolute despotism, it is their right, it is their duty, to throw off such government, and to provide new guards for their future security.

The Black Panther Party Ten-Point Program (1972)

What We Want
What We Believe

1. We want freedom. We want power to determine the destiny of our Black and oppressed communities.
We believe that Black and oppressed people will not be free until we are able to determine our destinies in our own communities ourselves, by fully controlling all the institutions which exist in our communities.

2. We want full employment for our people.
We believe that the federal government is responsible and obligated to give every person employment or a guaranteed income. We believe that if the American businessmen will not give full employment, then the technology and means of production should be taken from the businessmen and placed in the community so that the people of the community can organize and employ all of its people and give a high standard of living.

3. We want an end to the robbery by the capitalists of our Black and oppressed communities.
We believe that this racist government has robbed us and now we are demanding the overdue debt of forty acres and two mules. Forty acres and two mules were promised 100 years ago as restitution for slave labor and mass murder of Black people. We will accept the payment in currency which will be distributed to our many communities. The American racist has

taken part in the slaughter of over fifty million Black people. Therefore, we feel this is a modest demand that we make.

4. We want decent housing, fit for the shelter of human beings.
We believe that if the landlords will not give decent housing to our Black and oppressed communities, then housing and the land should be made into cooperatives so that the people in our communities, with government aid, can build and make decent housing for the people.

5. We want decent education for our people that exposes the true nature of this decadent American society. We want education that teaches us our true history and our role in the present-day society.
We believe in an educational system that will give to our people a knowledge of the self. If you do not have knowledge of yourself and your position in the society and in the world, then you will have little chance to know anything else.

6. We want completely free health care for all Black and oppressed people.
We believe that the government must provide, free of charge, for the people, health facilities which will not only treat our illnesses, most of which have come about because of our oppression, but which will also develop preventive medical programs to guarantee our future survival. We believe that mass health education and research programs must be developed to give all Black and oppressed people access to advanced scientific and medical information, so we may provide ourselves with proper medical attention and care.

7. We want an immediate end to police brutality and murder of Black people, other people of color, all oppressed people inside the United States.
We believe that the racist and fascist government of the United States uses its domestic enforcement agencies to carry out its program of oppression against Black people, other people of color and poor people inside the United States. We believe it

is our right, therefore, to defend ourselves against such armed forces and that all Black and oppressed people should be armed for self-defense of our homes and communities against these fascist police forces.

8. We want an immediate end to all wars of aggression.
We believe that the various conflicts which exist around the world stem directly from the aggressive desire of the United States ruling circle and government to force its domination upon the oppressed people of the world. We believe that if the United States government or its lackeys do not cease these aggressive wars it is the right of the people to defend themselves by any means necessary against their aggressors.

9. We want freedom for all Black and oppressed people now held in U.S. federal, state, county, city and military prisons and jails. We want trials by a jury of peers for all persons charged with so-called crimes under the laws of this country.
We believe that the many Black and poor oppressed people now held in United States prisons and jails have not received fair and impartial trials under a racist and fascist judicial system and should be free from incarceration. We believe in the ultimate elimination of all wretched, inhuman penal institutions, because the masses of men and women imprisoned inside the United States or by the United States military are the victims of oppressive conditions which are the real cause of their imprisonment. We believe that when persons are brought to trial they must be guaranteed, by the United States, juries of their peers, attorneys of their choice and freedom from imprisonment while awaiting trial.

10. We want land, bread, housing, education, clothing, justice, peace, and people's community control of modern technology.
When, during human events, it becomes necessary for one people to dissolve the political bonds which have connected them with another, and to assume, among the powers of the earth, the separate and equal station to which the laws of

nature and nature's God entitle them, a decent respect to the opinions of mankind requires that they should declare the causes which impel them to the separation.

We hold these truths to be self-evident, that all men are created equal; that they are endowed by their Creator with certain unalienable rights; that among these are life, liberty, and the pursuit of happiness. That to secure these rights, governments are instituted among men, deriving their just powers from the consent of the governed; that, whenever any form of government becomes destructive of these ends, it is the right of the people to alter or to abolish it, and to institute a new government, laying its foundation on such principles, and organizing its powers in such form as to them shall seem most likely to affect their safety and happiness. Prudence, indeed, will dictate that governments long established should not be changed for light and transient causes; and, accordingly, all experience hath shown that mankind is most disposed to suffer, while evils are sufferable, then to right themselves by abolishing the forms to which they are accustomed. But, when a long train of abuses and usurpation, pursuing invariably the same object, evinces a design to reduce them under absolute despotism, it is their right, it is their duty, to throw off such government, and to provide new guards for their future security.

1

Consciousness

I want to break down the illusion that there is distance between us, because if everything is matter, then where do I end and you begin? It's all solid here. And if it's all solid here, then I question who I am. I start to believe that I am not "I," I am "we."

Huey P. Newton (1978)[1]

How does consciousness begin? Huey P. Newton believed that it comes slowly. "We grow into consciousness so gradually that it is difficult to pinpoint the exact minute. It's like waking from a deep sleep – the first minute we're somewhat aware and it's only a time after that we're totally aware of things around us."[2] As an infant, Huey already had conscious awareness of the world around him: "I have memories – I can remember things starting before I was one year old, and I knew about racism then."[3]

Huey P. Newton was born in 1942 into a large family in a Louisiana home.[4] His mother Armelia was from Louisiana, his father Walter came from Alabama, and they began their life together in Arkansas. As the baby of the family, when Huey first saw the light of day, he was the youngest of seven. His family left Louisiana for California when he was a toddler, but, he recalls:

> I remember being there, the house that I lived in, clothes that my Mother wore, and I remember her taking me about three doors away to a woman's house to give me medicine because I wouldn't let my Mother give it to me. I used to

wear a little blue coat and blue hat . . . I guess I was about seven, eight, nine months old then. But as I said, my Mother disagrees. She says there's nothing about it that I could possibly remember but I do remember.[5]

Newton was born with a strong ability to both remember and understand his experiences, and he described how events in his life sometimes became "chiseled in [his] memory."[6] His political partner Bobby Seale recalled, later, how Newton was often able to quote arguments from books by paragraph and page number in debates with fellow students at Oakland City College (later renamed Merritt College).[7] Eventually, as a leader in the Black Panther Party for Self-Defense, Newton would just as quickly cite laws, statutes, and legal decisions in street confrontations with police officers, educating and inspiring on-lookers in the process.[8]

How does consciousness begin, for *societies*? Newton believed that, unlike individuals, societies come to new forms of awareness with suddenness and great force. Describing in 1972 the "information explosion" in the "experimental agencies and universities" of the United States, he stated: "Every serious thinker knows that scientific and technological developments do not grow in a straight line. They develop by leaps and bounds."[9] Understanding consciousness as fundamentally affected by technology, Newton nonetheless argued that all advances in technology are products of the labor of the people. He believed that most leaps in consciousness are only possible through "expropriation from the people" – massive thefts of the collective abilities and labor of everyone combined. "After all, the people are the makers of world history and responsible for everything."[10] In Newton's view, the wills of the people get collected into "reservoirs of information" by elites who take the credit.[11] He believed deeply in what he described as "the combined genius of the great oppressed masses of humankind" – the idea that all advances are ultimately ours to control collectively.[12] However, in order to direct the movement of history, we must become conscious of our reality and then make willful choices over it. This was how Huey Newton defined *power* itself. We must, in his famous words, *define the phenomenon and make it act in a desired manner.*[13]

In the United States, our society does not tend to have a strong memory or consciousness of our past. And our recollection of Huey P. Newton is hazy at best. At one time, he was the face of a revolution that was occurring on American soil, our memory of which has since been buried. Remainders from that time today include oversimplified narratives about the Civil Rights Movement and a vague awareness about a cluster of assassinations during an era that took down even a president. It takes digging through clouds of disinformation to realize that the efforts of the Black Panther Party reshaped how our government functions today. There are also several political prisoners from that time still being held in super-maximum security penitentiaries – but most people do not know about them either.[14]

From that era, Newton is most remembered perhaps in the form of a photograph: "seated on an old colonial wicker chair, an African spear in one hand, an American rifle in the other, Panther beret on his head and a serious, straight look on his face."[15] Newton told his friends, however, that he hated that poster.[16] The shot was curated by the Black Panther Party's most famous member at the time, Eldridge Cleaver, later to become Newton's nemesis.[17] Alex Hoffman, a lawyer and friend to Newton, later recalled: "He never wanted the poster published. 'I'm not that poster,' he said. 'That's Eldridge's picture of who I am. That's not me. They're going to expect me to come out of here and be that poster. I can't even speak in public.'"[18]

The limits of images and representation were a problem that the Black Panther Party as a whole struggled with. One major cause was that over two-thirds of mainstream newspaper reports about them were either directly planted or interfered with by the Federal Bureau of Investigation.[19] The FBI's Director J. Edgar Hoover explicitly commanded his agents to "expose, disrupt, misdirect, discredit, or otherwise neutralize" the Party.[20] Moreover, there was also the fact of their Blackness. That is, they found themselves distorted into racist stereotypes at every turn, even as they innovated a highly adaptive, dynamic organization whose strategies changed as it grew. To transform both how they were depicted and the broader world around them, they created their own newspaper. With a peak circulation of 300,000, it became the most widely read Black newspaper in the country.[21] Nonetheless, as Afrodiasporic people, they were constantly being reduced to objects, figments of a fearful white imagination incapable of grasping that their insistence on self-defense was fundamentally about Black people's desire to live freely and with dignity.

As a Black child in school, Newton's desire for dignity was suffocated by the racism of his teachers. "At the time, I did not understand the size or seriousness of the school system's assault on Black people."[22] In his autobiography *Revolutionary Suicide*, Newton described being beaten by teachers and witnessing stories of Black inferiority being forced into the minds of the children: "As I suffered through Sambo and the Black Tar Baby story in *Brer Rabbit* in the early grades, a great weight began to settle on me . . . and in time I cringed at the mention of Black."[23] Newton told a story of being called up to the front of the class by a teacher who believed he was not paying attention. After calling him stupid, she challenged him to spell the word "business" on the blackboard. Despite knowing how to write the word, Newton froze, "unable to form even the first letter. . . . This happened to me time and again, growing worse with repetition. When I was asked to read aloud in class or spell a word, my mind went blank and cold. . . . Even now, when I read to a group of people, I am likely to stumble."[24] The disconnect that Newton experienced between the knowledge his mind held and the inability of his body to respond was a clear sign something was wrong, and we can grasp it today as indicative of a trauma response. Constantly kicked out of classrooms as a youth, Newton remained illiterate nearly into adulthood. Later, his wife Fredrika Newton described the anxiety he continued to experience even when attempting to write a check in public.[25] In the late 1970s, while earning his doctoral degree, Newton would come to theorize modern education "as a process that drives children mad, and, what is more, . . . the process is conscious, persistent and in the service of the power structure of the modern State."[26] "Not one instructor ever awoke in me a desire to learn more or question or explore the worlds of literature, science, and history. All they did was try to rob me of the sense of my own uniqueness and worth, and in the process, they nearly killed my urge to inquire."[27]

Instead of giving up, however, Newton taught himself. At the age of seventeen, he worked his way through *The Republic*, the classic text by the ancient Greek philosopher Plato, sentence by sentence, with the help of a dictionary, until he had learned to read. "Day after day, for eight or nine hours at a time, I worked on that book, going over it page by page, word by word. I had no help from anyone because I did not want it. Embarrassment overwhelmed me."[28] When he began college, he took the same courses with the same professors that his older brother Melvin had, so that he could memorize and rely upon Melvin's notebooks.[29] Reading soon opened "a whole new world" to him.[30] Before, he used to memorize audio recordings of poems and recite them at parties – Omar Khayyam and Shakespeare, Edgar Allen Poe and T. S. Eliot – but now he internalized novels and philosophy.[31] As he learned, he shared the ideas over wine with his friends on the street corners. He loved applying the Socratic method in pleasant debate with the "brothers on the block," asking them questions that would force them to question their own assumptions. One of their favorite philosophical topics was Plato's allegory of the cave, which Newton and his friends called "the story of the cave prisoners."

> One of the prisoners is freed and gets a view of the outside world – objective reality. He returns to the cave to tell the others . . . [but] the prisoners tell the liberated man he is crazy, and he cannot convince them. . . . The allegory seemed very appropriate to our own situation in society. We, too, were in prison and needed to be liberated.[32]

And so, Newton came to grasp, the process through which *societies* gain consciousness is not just sudden but also likely to be painful.

As part of his own learning process, Newton studied Black history, logic and language, Eastern philosophy, and the philosophy of existentialism.[33] Taking part-time classes in college, pondering questions of existence, he became a hippy of sorts: "I began living like an existentialist, hitchhiking to Los Angeles and back, walking into the class dirty, without shoes, and sometimes soaked to the skin from the rain. It was all the same to me."[34] Books like James Joyce's *A Portrait of the Artist as Young Man* and Thomas Wolfe's *Look Homeward, Angel* shaped his personal search for meaning.[35] And he read the Bible, influenced by his father's work as a preacher and assistant pastor.[36] As a child, Newton was a junior deacon and usher boy, often performing in church plays.[37] Perhaps this was why he typically avoided vulgarity and, to many, came across as surprisingly polite.[38] After meeting him in October of 1967, the great Black American writer James Baldwin wrote:

> Huey is a hard man to describe. People surrounded by legend rarely look the parts they've been assigned, but in Huey's case, the Great Casting Director decided to blow everybody's mind. Huey looks like the most scrubbed, most well-bred of adolescents . . . He is old-fashioned in the most remarkable sense, in that he treats everyone with respect, especially his elders.[39]

Bobby Seale, with whom he founded the Black Panther Party, described how Huey Newton would regularly hold doors open for anyone.[40] "He's a kindhearted person. You can't use his kindness, but he'll give it away. . . . Everybody respected Huey's mind and also Huey's guts. He had something about him, that he didn't drive over people, but he would never let anyone drive over him."[41]

From his father Walter, who was infamous for defying white racists in Louisiana, Huey learned to stand up for himself and others.[42] Walter Newton was fiercely protective of his family, setting the tone for the tightly knit household.[43] From his mother Armelia, Huey gained a love for children and a playful, positive spirit.[44] Newton later described it as an "attitude toward life that led us to insight, affection, humor, and understanding with each other."[45] Unfortunately, Newton's natural inclination towards kindness, his small stature, and even his name attracted bullying from other boys in his youth. Taking tips from his father and older brothers, he learned to defend himself and soon developed a reputation for bold defiance and a willingness to fight anybody. "Fighting has always been a big part of my life, as it is in the lives of most poor people. Some find this hard to understand."[46] The way Newton explained it, in the streets, the best way to make sure that no one bothered you was to always be willing to go after the biggest opponent.[47] And, if a fight was imminent, you had to make sure to strike first.[48] In one incident, he famously taunted a whole group: "I'll fight all of you one at a time or all of you at the same time and you won't wait outside for me, I'll be waiting outside for you."[49] For his fearlessness, with his fists or in debates, he was sometimes called "Crazy Huey," and he gained the regard of the young men on the block, just as he would obtain the respect of fellow students and teachers through scholarly study.

Newton learned, too, how to defend himself in a court of law, as necessary. Like many poor people then and today, Newton sustained himself economically in his youth through a combination of poor-paying jobs and black-market hustles. As a part-time thief, burglar, and scam artist, Newton closely studied the California criminal code, buying books and taking night classes at Hastings Law School.[50] Sharpening his knowledge in debate with course instructor Edwin Meese, a conservative junior prosecutor and later Attorney General under President Reagan, Newton was able to convince juries when in court, gain favorable decisions, and often avoid juvenile detention and later adult prison.[51] By his own account, he was successful most of the time.[52]

Newton was an extremely perceptive reader with a habit of memorizing the footnotes of books: "researching the references that any particular author might have made" was a vital practice when engaging in Black study.[53] According to Seale, at Merritt College "Huey gave inspiration to a lot of brothers and sisters to do a lot of in-depth study and realize the need to have knowledge of themselves as black people."[54] At the same time, Newton remained connected to the block and worked to share what he learned in an accessible way. Though never a naturally gifted speaker, he did, however, possess a more basic, interpersonal form of charisma that, combined with his intellect, gained him the ability to be influential in different social spheres.[55] Newton was among the founding members of the Afro-American Association, an organization that Seale described as developing "the first Black nationalist philosophy on the West Coast."[56] He also participated in the Bay Area chapter of the underground Revolutionary Action Movement (RAM), although this chapter was far less active than the founding chapters in Cleveland and Philadelphia.[57]

Newton and Seale would, however, soon leave both groups behind, frustrated by their unwillingness to take practical action to address the immediate needs and problems of poor Black people. Huey Newton lived a life of the mind, but he lived out his philosophies with the people of the streets, turning theory into practice. He and Seale both felt that the most important groups to connect with were precisely the unemployed, underemployed, and criminalized people of the ghetto, and they believed that the students on campus were avoiding this basic fact. In this regard, they were most inspired by the speeches of Malcolm X, himself a convert from street-life to organizer, and the writings of Frantz Fanon, a decolonial theorist who argued for the political importance of the criminalized poor. Newton was also deeply inspired by the revolution in Cuba, and quickly became convinced that any future politics for Black people had to be based on socialism and cooperative solutions.

Using the office supplies at the North Oakland Neighborhood Anti-Poverty Center where they worked part-time, Newton and Seale printed the first copies of the program of the Black Panther Party for Self-Defense in October 1966. "The service centers collected names of people on welfare, elderly people who needed aid. We used those lists to go around and canvass the community in order to find out the desires of the community. So we would go from house to house and explain to people our program."[58] Dressed in powder-blue shirts, black leather jackets, and black berets, they then established traffic stops at dangerous intersections and conducted armed patrols of Oakland police to stop police brutality. They recruited at the Anti-Poverty Center and at bars and clubs, and they were joined by the people they defended. Within a year, they had established several chapters on the West coast by directly serving people's needs. By 1968, they had become leaders in a national movement to connect Black Liberation to an international context, conceiving of Black Americans as a *colonized people* and forming relationships of solidarity with anti-colonial movements in Asia, Africa, and Latin America. In 1969, the Party – by then majority women – provided free breakfasts for school children and free, quality medical care for anyone who needed it. Behind the militant politics of defiance was a deep care for the experiences of the most oppressed and vulnerable. Underlying the popularity of "Black power" was the Party's more universalist slogan, "all power to the people." And driving their call for self-defense was a commitment to preserve Black life.

At the symbolic center of the movement as a whole was Huey P. Newton, as person and figure. In 1968, Seale referred to Newton as the "leader" of the Party and its "philosophical theoretician."[59] Newton was often a leader from a distance, however, spending three years incarcerated during the period of the Party's strongest growth, after an encounter with a police officer that, despite Newton's being unarmed, resulted in the officer's death. Eldridge Cleaver, Minister of Information and leading writer for the organization, and his wife Kathleen (maiden name Neal), the Party's Communications Secretary with a family background in international diplomacy, took the lead in organizing a national campaign to "Free Huey!"[60] In the process, they created an international symbol and hero, despite his absence. Right after the assassination of Martin Luther King Jr. in April 1968, Newton's face was put on the masthead of *The Black Panther* newspaper. Party members read and memorized his writings and tracked his ideas as he continued to develop them from behind bars. It would be of no help that Newton himself grasped clearly the limits of heroization. As he would later write: "Individuals, with all their strengths and weaknesses, make significant differences in the outcome of political struggles; however, their roles are too often romanticized, clouding an understanding of the political forces propelling them into struggle."[61]

The paradox of Huey P. Newton is that, as a thinker and theorist, he was both greater than the US government has allowed us to remember *and* he was built up in his time into a symbol more powerful than he could have ever possibly lived up to. In 1970, thirteen years before the word globalization was coined, Newton had arrived at the conclusion that nation-states had already been rendered obsolete by the interconnectedness of technology, global capitalism, and American military empire. As former Panther and journalist Mumia Abu-Jamal has observed, this theory, which Newton called *intercommunalism*, enabled him to predict the fall of the Soviet Union nineteen years in advance.[62] During his doctoral studies, he produced dozens of essays and books, most of which are still unpublished, ranging impressively over the fields of anthropology, philosophy, political theory, evolutionary biology, theology, and more. These writings, this book argues, constitute a body of work that may one day prove to rival that of any other American thinker of the twentieth century. At the same time, infamously, the organization that Newton invented came to be regarded by the Director of the FBI as "the greatest threat to the internal security" of the United States.[63] In the process, the agency produced *two million* pages of surveillance on Newton, leading one of his later professors to refer to him as "the most hounded man in the history of mankind."[64] Lastly, retired judge Lise Pearlman has described Newton's trial for the murder of a police officer, which drew international attention, as *the* landmark US court trial of the twentieth century for how it reshaped the jury selection process and established the modern right to a jury of one's peers.[65]

And yet despite all this – or perhaps in part because of it – there has been only one scholarly book written about Newton since his time. Published over two decades ago, Judson Jeffries' *Huey P. Newton: The Radical Theorist* remains valuable and too rarely read, though it was released in a racial climate in which its author had to devote considerable space simply to defending the merits of Black intellectual thought.[66] Jeffries was forced also to devote a whole chapter to addressing distortions and popular misconceptions about the Black Panther Party – a problem that persists today.

Another reason that relatively little has been published about Newton as a thinker is that his intellectual legacy has been massively overshadowed by his tragic collapse. This book also argues that, during his time as a political prisoner, without his knowledge, Newton was subjected to unethical psychiatric procedures that altered his brain and behavior. These procedures were part of a range of government experiments conducted on incarcerated Black people, political activists, military personnel, and hospital patients, starting in the 1950s and continuing for decades after. Afterwards, Newton's personality underwent a change for the worse, a problem then exacerbated by severe addictions to drugs and alcohol. While Newton largely retained his rational faculties through the 1970s, and his intellectual productivity even increased during his periods of sobriety, his emotional health crumbled. As a result, so did those around him suffer, as he lashed out with uncharacteristic violence towards his comrades, friends, and loved ones, as well as the people of the community that had inspired him in the first place. At the same time, Newton was subject to persistent surveillance and harassment by government agents, intensifying his paranoia and his mistreatment of those around him. It is a reflection of the intellect and skill of every other member of the Black Panther Party that the organization continued to innovate, persist, and even produce new leaders at the same time that Newton's unwellness caused him to pull the organization down with him. Throughout it all, the sober and rational side of Newton continued to analyze the world and produce powerful new ideas, preserved today in his unpublished works.

Ever since Newton's fall, the lessons that social movement organizations across the left have taken to heart have been precisely those gained from the shortcomings of the Black Panther Party. Avoid idolization of leaders, if you have them at all; organize horizontally; practice self-care and communal care to avoid burn out and manage mental health; beware the pull of drugs; struggle against sexual violence; assume that you are being surveilled but organize despite it. It is also the case that many of the contours of critical thought in the modern academy continue to return to themes first explored by the Black Panther Party, such as the strengths and limits of organization, the relationship between race and class, the inevitability of the criminalization of Blackness, and the political necessity of Black feminism. To understand all of the causes of the fall of Newton and the Black Panther Party is thus to understand how we have arrived at our present.

In 2004, Ericka Huggins, the former head of the Party's liberation school, offered her summation of the life of Huey Newton: "So part of the story is that he was driven; part of the story is that he was driven crazy; and part of the story is that he was crazy and he was driven. The people closest to him knew it and tolerated it because what he was doing was so magnificent in the beginning."[67] In 1973, James Baldwin wrote, "Huey Newton is one of the most important people to have been produced by the American chaos. His fate is very important."[68] This statement rings true through both Newton's victories and his struggles. Aptly, Huey P. Newton believed most of all in the philosophy of *dialectical materialism*, a philosophy that insists upon the inseparability of the positive and the negative. In his own words, "the basic principle of dialectical materialism is that all phenomena involve both positive and negative forces which are combined but which are constantly struggling with each other for dominance."[69] In this regard, Newton would have likely looked back and recognized that even the destruction of his own life must have within it the kernel of a positive aspect, a minor element that will, over time, overcome the negative. This book endeavors to bring forward that positive element out of the tragedy of his targeted destruction.

Written as an intellectual biography and intellectual history, *Huey P. Newton: I Am We* aims to tell the story of Newton's life but, most of all, to reveal the depth and breadth of the ideas he produced. Among his greatest ideas must be included, of course, the Black Panther Party itself. As for his writing and speeches, despite his late entrance into literacy, Newton's intellectual production developed rapidly and his style as an essayist changed over time, from deceptively straightforward works to extraordinarily dense expositions. Over the years, scholars have slowly begun to engage with some of Newton's published works, but these efforts have been relatively rare and piecemeal. This book draws from all of the strongest available scholarship and also offers its own presentation of Newton's system of thought as it developed over time. In the process, quotations, snapshots, and summaries of Newton's unpublished writings are included whenever possible. Another central goal of this book is to illustrate Newton's interdisciplinarity while making the case that the true work of reconstructing his thought must be a collective scholarly project, drawing from the expertise of philosophers, political theorists, cultural theorists, anthropologists, theologians, and more. Lastly, the subtitle of this book, *I Am We*, carries two layers of meaning. The first reflects Newton's belief in the fundamental oneness connecting all of humanity and the universe. The second gestures towards the extent to which the conditions that created Newton's greatest sufferings are in fact akin to our contemporary conditions.

Huey Newton argued that the "American people are a colonized people even more so than the people in developing countries where the military operates."[70] In his view, it is at the center of American empire that the forces of colonial control – "internal" and "external" – are strongest.[71] After World War II, the global struggle for decolonization that began in the Third World, producing independent nation-states in Africa, Asia, and Latin America, would increasingly touch and then breach the centers of global empire in the First World, reaching a peak in the social movements of the 1960s and 1970s. This global struggle for decolonization would eventually stall here, however, and in the wake of its failure new and unimaginable forms of counterinsurgency and social control would be developed. As Newton predicted in his writings, these controls are chains that burden our minds and bodies today. For all those engaged in studies of history, social movements, decolonization, and abolition – of war, imprisonment, and all forms of slavery – Newton affirmed most of all that any project for real social transformation must have behind it the collective force of the people together:

> The people are the real power. They are the ones who will bring about change, not us alone. A vanguard is like the head of a spear, the thing that goes first. But what really hurts is the butt of the spear, because even though the head makes the necessary entrance, the back part is what penetrates. Without the butt, a spear is nothing but a toothpick.[72]

For humanity, together, "the only way out is through."[73]

* * *

Chapter 2 of this book, "The Defense of Life," analyzes Newton's political thought during the first three years of the Black Panther Party's existence (1966–69). In doing so, it works to reframe the history and ideas defining the start of the organization, setting the grounds for Newton's later theoretical innovations. Newton's early experiences living among the poorest and most criminalized sectors of his community, plus his socialist readings from college, shaped his foundational emphasis on empathy for the lives of those most vulnerable to death. Contrary to still pervasive misconceptions, all of Newton's initial ideas for the Black Panther Party – from the creation of a traffic stop to the armed protest at Sacramento – were designed as acts of care and social defense, especially of the youth, to inspire the oppressed to take control of their own communities. However, Newton also understood that these political actions would be distorted into attacks on white society, revealing the underlying contradictions shaping American culture and government in the process. Once Newton was jailed and elevated into a symbol, his call to shift Party tactics to reduce casualties from armed conflicts with police was overruled by others. Only when new Party leaders and members emerged, reinvigorating Newton's initial focus on survival through new programs, did policies revert to what he called the Party's "original vision."

Chapter 3, "The Theory of Intercommunalism," covers the period immediately after Newton's release from prison (1970–71), when he integrated the Party's developments into a new global political-economic theory that he called intercommunalism. According to Newton, nation-states had already been made obsolete by American economic, military, and technological empire. As for the American people, Newton argued that they would soon come to experience rising unemployment and criminalization caused by the rise of automation and new technologies. On the other hand, these same technologies, if redirected, might instead serve as the basis for a revolutionary form of global human connectedness and shared identity. Newton sought to develop a synthesis of Third World decolonial thought with liberal Enlightenment ideas as he conceptualized Americans as a profoundly colonized people, regardless of racial identity.

Chapters 4 and 5 together retrace approximately the same span of time as Chapters 2 and 3, but with a different focus. Chapter 4, "The Soul Breaker" (1964–71), explains Newton's philosophical understanding of reality, inspired most of all by his early experiences overcoming solitary confinement. Newton's radical and existential doubt of reality shaped his willingness to completely rethink the meaning of lived experience, our ability to use reason to navigate it, and the central role of our will in exercising power over it. This chapter demonstrates the extent to which Newton was influenced by the ideas of a range of philosophers, from

Kant, Hume, and Nietzsche, to William James, A. J. Ayer, and Frantz Fanon. In navigating a careful balance between control and release, empiricism and rationalism, and knowledge and uncertainty, Newton applied the method of dialectical materialism. His ultimate aim was to develop a way to channel the very flow and flux of experience towards the exercise of power, in a revolutionary direction. Chapter 5, "The Structured Vehicle and the Revolutionary Defense of Community" (1970–71), describes the practical, local strategy that was designed to connect to his more abstract theories of intercommunalism and lived experience. This plan focused on redirecting the suffering of the poorest into material defense of loving communities within liberated territories, producing a revolutionary culture in the process. This strategy, hidden by Newton due to political necessity, soon clashed with renewed desires among some Party members for immediate armed combat with the state. In 1971, a split arose in the Party, inspired by ideological differences but driven by government disinformation campaigns that drew Newton and other Panthers into paranoid clashes against one another.

Chapter 6 is titled "The Question of the Most Oppressed." It begins with Newton's insights about the relationship between extreme forms of oppression, the experience of Blackness, political pessimism, and the possibility of resistance. After a brief account of Party views on the politics of various social identities, the chapter provides a close analysis of how Newton understood the relationship of queerness to oppression through an examination of his experiences and writings, especially concerning Eldridge Cleaver. The second half of the chapter reconstructs the complete scope of Newton's anthropological, psychoanalytic, and political analysis of gendered oppression. It traces the gradual development of his views on sexism, from his insular concern with the experiences of men and careful avoidance of the discussion of sex, to his robust denunciation of sexual violence and the entanglement of sex and power. The chapter ends in 1974 with his scholarly analysis of the pre-historic rise of patriarchy and the limits of the sex binary. Newton was in the midst of developing a thoroughly feminist politics when his mental health struggles suddenly intensified, resulting in a wave of acts of anti-social and gendered violence.

Chapter 7, "Contradictions of Power" (1971–74), presents the clear political logic driving Newton's organizational strategies through the 1970s. China was a major influence on Newton's emphasis on social programs, as well as his newly collaborative approach towards black capitalism and electoral politics, though China itself would abandon the Black Panther Party in this period. At the same time, Newton's mental health decline was intensified by addictions to drugs and alcohol, undermining the Party's original focus on the well-being of the people. The transformation in Newton's personality in this period requires confronting the overwhelming likelihood that he was subjected to psychiatric procedures while in prison that distorted his mind. Arguably the most important chapter of the book, Chapter 8, "Technology of Madness" (1974–79), brings together the historical evidence for this argument, starting with Newton's own scholarly writings on the matter. Establishing first that the use of manipulative psychiatric procedures – mind control – was indeed real and pervasive in this period, a close examination of testimonies of Newton's behavioral changes is paired with all available contemporary critical-theoretical treatments of the phenomenon. The final portions of the chapter draw from insights in Black studies, mad studies, military studies, and decolonial psychiatry to consider the possibilities for healing and social defense for the affected, then and now.

It is a testament to Newton's intellect and personal strength that, despite the collapse in his emotional health, he in fact intensified his production of philosophical and scholarly writing late in his life. Chapter 9, "Life of the Mind, Politics of the Street," provides an account of his experiences and writings while at the University of California Santa Cruz as an undergraduate and doctoral student (1973–74, 1977–80). Despite personal trials and struggles against institutional racism, Newton's intellectual production was wide-ranging, including mostly still unpublished writings in anthropology, ecology, political theory, education, philosophy, theology, and evolutionary biology. The second half of the chapter provides an account of Newton's mature analyses of reality and oneness, covering themes of consciousness, love, humanism, the limits of language, and Newton's proposals for future forms of leaderless social organization. It ends with an open inquiry into the circumstances surrounding the end of his life in 1989.

Lastly, the Appendix, "The Intellectual Legacy of Huey P. Newton," provides a list of Newton's unpublished works, collected here as a guide for future use by other scholars. Ultimately, the project of firmly establishing Newton in the canon of Black philosophy and modern Western philosophy more broadly must be a collective one, given the wide-ranging breadth of Newton's thought.

Huey P. Newton in a rattan chair.
Used with permission by Dr. Huey P. Newton Foundation.

Huey P. Newton and a lotus flower.
Used with permission by Dr. Huey P. Newton Foundation.

Bobby Seale and Huey P. Newton.
Used with permission by Dr. Huey P. Newton Foundation.

Huey P. Newton and James Baldwin.
Used with permission by Dr. Huey P. Newton Foundation.

2

The Defense of Life

We were embarked on a campaign to change the world, one person at a time. That change begins with rebuilding the character into a revolutionary character, of which the central component is love. That means love for yourself and love of the people.

Safiya Bukhari (1997)[1]

From the Bottom of Society

As a young adult, Huey P. Newton spent most of his time "relating to those who struggled for survival on the block."[2] Oakland, where the population was 38 percent Black, was burdened by mass unemployment.[3] During the 1940s and 1950s, Black workers who had migrated from the South to take up jobs in Oakland's ports and factories during World War II had their jobs systematically displaced by white Americans returning from the war.[4] Left without substantial options, many made a living whatever way they could. As Newton explained in his autobiography: "Many activities defined by the ruling class as criminal are the acts of poor and exploited people, desperate people, who have no access to the channels of opportunity."[5] Newton's understanding of this reality was informed both by his own economic struggles and by those of others around him. The young Newton worked part-time but also stole, patching together different sources of income in order to sustain himself. Specifically, as he explained, he used his wits to steal from businesses that he felt took advantage of the Black community. Targeting stores that offered predatorial credit lines to customers that left them "in perpetual debt," he maintained that these businesses "did not really lose, because they were actually robbing the community blind. They just wrote off the amount and continued their robbing."[6] The young Newton broke the law with discernment and intentionality. "I never scored on Blacks under any condition, but scoring on whites was a strike against injustice."[7] As he became more well-read, through books like Fyodor Dostoevsky's *Crime and Punishment*, Kafka's *The Trial*, and Victor Hugo's *Les Misérables*, his sense of solidarity with all poor people grew.[8] "I never wanted to hurt poor whites, even though I had met some in school who called me 'nigger' and other names. I fought them, but I never took their lunches or money because I knew that they had nothing to start with."[9]

Newton could have taken on a full-time job, but his opposition to doing so was existentially motivated. He did not want to repeat the life of struggle led by his father, who worked constantly to support Newton's mother and their seven children. He was resentful of the lack of personal freedom that wage labor entailed. "I wanted most of all to be free from the life of a servant forced to take those low-paying jobs and looked at with scorn by white bosses."[10] Whenever he was caught stealing, he applied what he learned in law school and defended himself in court. "Although no skilled legal technician, I could make a good defense. If you are an existentialist, defending yourself is another manifestation of freedom."[11] Highly self-aware and consistently reflective, he understood well the massive distance between his lived perspective and that of those in the legal position to judge him. Although he was often able to convince juries composed of middle-class white people because he "knew the law and [was] articulate," he knew that they did not consider him a peer: "The jury is incompetent to judge the accused; it does not understand the circumstances that brought on his actions."[12] Despite expecting little empathy from others about his life, he maintained an inclination towards empathy for the lives of others.

Working part-time at the Anti-Poverty Center, Newton and Seale saw clearly – both through first-hand experience and government records – how inadequate federal services were at addressing the needs of the poorest in their community.[13] Moreover, as students at Merritt College, they were increasingly influenced by the anti-capitalist, socialist, and Marxist ideas that were circulating on campuses at the time. When they established the Black Panther Party for Self-Defense in October of 1966, all of this informed their emphasis on class solidarity among poor people as fundamental. As Seale put it in 1968, in the biggest picture, "our fight is a class struggle and not a race struggle."[14] That said, they were not short-sighted about the power of racism. As Newton explained in his autobiography years later, racism was a more profound and deeply set obstacle than even capitalism:

> In psychological terms, racism could continue to exist even after the economic problems that had created racism had been resolved. Never convinced that destroying capitalism would automatically destroy racism, I felt, however, that we could not destroy racism without wiping out its economic foundation. It was necessary to think much more creatively and independently about these complex interconnections.[15]

Newton's ideas were often not published until later in Party history, in part because of his incarceration between 1967 and 1970, but also in part because of his writing disability. According to Seale, Newton dictated the Ten-Point Program, "word for word," but Seale was the one who wrote it down, offering "suggestions" as they went.[16] Huey's brother Melvin edited it for grammar and then Bobby Seale's wife Artie and Newton's girlfriend LaVerne Williams typed it up. In creating the Ten-Point Program on the spot, Newton had in fact created a revised version of the Nation of Islam's Ten-Point Program and combined it with the Declaration of Independence, drawing upon each part from memory.

Newton's autobiography, *Revolutionary Suicide*, was published in 1973, after the peak of the Party, and grew out of conversations between the imprisoned Newton and the sociologist and Party ally J. Herman Blake.[17] Blake transcribed and then organized dozens of their conversations, and later Melvin Newton and Party allies Donald Freed and Martin Kenner contributed edits. When one compares the published book to the interview transcripts, it becomes clear that Blake managed to transcribe a work that was impressively faithful to Newton's original thought.[18] Newton was encouraged by his mother to produce the book after she expressed concern about an earlier book written about the Party that had distorted her words.[19] When the idea of writing a book was first proposed, Newton reportedly laughed and remarked: "I can't write a book." Accordingly, while *Revolutionary Suicide* is the best source for our understanding of Newton's life, it was also a text shaped by several participants and created to respond to a political need. Party veteran Flores Forbes would later claim that he never saw Newton write down a word.[20] Early Party member Emory Douglas later explained that Newton often had a circle of scholars who transcribed his dictated words, and Newton always verified the final product.[21]

When Eldridge Cleaver joined the Black Panther Party, he was brought in especially for his skills as a writer, since both Newton and Seale felt inadequate in this regard. In his influential pamphlet "On the Ideology of the Black Panther Party," Cleaver opened by framing the essay as "the historical experience ... and wisdom gained by Black people in their 400 year long struggle against the system of racist oppression and economic exploitation ... interpreted through the prism of Marxist-Leninism" and the "teachings of Huey P. Newton."[22] Although Cleaver is listed as author, he described the text as presenting Newton's ideas and praised his "great contributions"; the pamphlet clearly reflects conversations with Newton from before he was imprisoned.[23] "The Ideology" grappled extensively with the relationship between race and class, expressing a clear appreciation of Marxism for its critique of capitalism's inherent violence. The essay also criticized Marxism, however, for its inadequacy in the twentieth-century American context, particularly for Black Americans. "On the subject of racism, Marxism-Leninism offers us very little assistance. In fact, there is much evidence that Marx and Engels were themselves racists – just like their White brothers and sisters of their era, and just as many Marxist-Leninists of our own time are also racists."[24]

Writing in the nineteenth century, Karl Marx was deeply inspired by the struggles of the working classes of his era, but he struggled to extend his empathy to the poorest in his own society. He made a clear distinction between industrial workers, whom he considered well positioned to lead the way in the rapidly transforming world of his day, and everyone else – those who made a living in informal work, were semi-employed, or were unemployed altogether. The first group he referred to as the working-class *proletariat*; the second he called the *lumpen* ("ragged") *proletariat* and disparaged as "social scum," a point Cleaver highlighted in his essay.[25] The working-class proletariat also happened to be mostly male, able-bodied, and living in the First World, thereby conforming more easily to Marx's ideal of the kind of work discipline, respectability, and organization he saw as necessary for a modern society.[26] By contrast, the lumpenproletariat, as Cleaver elaborated, "are all those who have no secure relationship or vested interest in the means of production and the institutions of capitalist society."[27]

In his early journalistic writings, Marx was often inconsistent with whom he considered working class or lumpen, sometimes using the term lumpen simply as an insult, and the distinction often served as cover for conceptual shortcomings in his broader system of thought.[28] In brief, during the revolutions of his time, if a group turned against the movement that Marx supported, he was more likely to call them lumpen. In his later and more mature writings, such as his famous treatise *Capital: A Critique of Political Economy*, lumpenproletarians are described as "people who succumb to their incapacity for adaptation."[29] The "vagabonds, criminals, prostitutes . . . orphans and pauper children . . . the mutilated, the sickly, the widows" were understood by Marx as "the dead weight of the industrial reserve army," the kind of people employers would never hire, even to suppress wages.[30] Marx explicitly defined lumpenproletarians as those most likely to die off, giving the concept a strong resemblance to later racialistic and Social Darwinist theories that misapplied evolutionary theory to human societies.[31]

Marx's limited capacity to empathize with the most oppressed groups of his time carried over into the socialist and communist organizations that took up his ideas in Europe. In Asia, Africa, and Latin America, by contrast, social movements were more willing to build upon Marx's insights and leave behind the less useful. Huey Newton and the Black Panther Party applied a similar filter, holding on to Marx's methods and discarding his biases. Later in the Party's history, Newton explained in detail:

> Now if you are a Marxist, then Marx's racism affects your own judgment because a Marxist is someone who worships Marx and the thought of Marx. Remember, though, that Marx himself said, "I am not a Marxist." . . . Marxists cherish the conclusions which Marx arrived at through his method, but they throw away the method itself – leaving themselves in a totally static posture. . . . In every discipline you find people who have distorted visions and are at a low state of consciousness who nonetheless have flashes of insight and produce ideas worth considering.[32]

Huey Newton, Bobby Seale, Eldridge Cleaver, and the Black Panther Party for Self-Defense reappropriated Marx's pejorative concept of the *lumpenproletariat* and used it to identify themselves, developing a political analysis of capitalism from the perspective of those who experience its most dehumanizing and lethal aspects. This obscure German term came to be used casually among the Panthers, as did other Marxist and socialist concepts. Indeed, it is to the Panthers that we likely owe the original coining of the Black vernacular term *bougie* – from Marx's critique of the *bourgeoisie* business class – used to refer to people with elitist sensibilities.[33] Overall, Newton and the Panthers were influenced by Marx's ideas but even more so by thinkers and revolutionaries who revised Marx's ideas and applied them to their own contexts.

In Cleaver's words, "Huey transformed the Black lumpenproletariat from the forgotten people at the bottom of society into the vanguard," and he did so "after studying Fanon."[34] For Newton, foremost among the revisers of Marx was the Black Caribbean political philosopher and psychiatrist Frantz Fanon. Seale marveled at Newton's grasp of Fanon's *The Wretched of the Earth*, and himself read the book six times.[35] Fanon's original title, *Les damnés de la terre*, is perhaps better translated as *The Condemned of the Earth*, emphasizing the same menacing prospect of death that Marx's original usage of the term lumpenproletariat carried, but now reclaimed by those very same people who insisted on living. Like Newton, Fanon also dictated his works, which were transcribed with input from his wife Josie Fanon.[36] In the late 1960s, US printings of Fanon's *The Wretched of the Earth* included subtitles like "The Handbook for the Black Revolution that is Changing the Shape of the World" and "The Handbook for Third-World Revolution."[37]

Although he primarily theorized about political conditions in Algeria, Fanon inspired Black readers in the West because he drew explicit parallels between "the village of the colonized, . . . the village of the native, the Negro village, the medina, [and] the reservation."[38] In Newton's analysis, building off of Fanon, "the Black lumpenproletariat – America's wretched of the earth" experience life much as the colonized people of the Third World do, all while living in the center of American empire:[39] "Penned up in the ghettos of America, surrounded by his factories and all the physical components of his economic system, we have been made into 'the wretched of the earth,' relegated to the position of spectators while the White racists run their international con game on the suffering peoples."[40] Fanon's use of the term lumpenproletariat was broader than Marx's: he used it to refer to anyone who had lost their access to a stable living due to colonial capitalism, so that it included especially peasants who had been removed from their land, migrant workers, and the working poor.[41] The term most of all referred to those who had just arrived in the cities to escape the lack of opportunity in the country, but who found urban opportunity to be an illusion and ended up living at the outskirts of the metropolis. Fanon considered these precarious people the most likely to lead revolt: "It is within this mass of humanity, this people of the shanty towns, at the core of the lumpenproletariat, that the rebellion will find its urban spearhead."[42] He viewed this sector of the population as radical because of their daily closeness to death and their profound existential inspiration and motivation to live despite it all. As he put it, here "life is lived at an impossibly high temperature."[43]

Newton and Seale were both children of recent migrants to the urban north from the rural south – Newton from Louisiana and Seale from Texas – and so Fanon's analysis was especially resonant. They had found few jobs available to them that were not demeaning, and many of their friends struggled to find any employment at all. In "On the Ideology," Cleaver explained that, for Black people, working-class and lumpen status were not very different and that the "the hard and fast distinctions melt away. . . . This is because of the leveling effect of the colonial process and the fact that all Black people are colonized, even if some of them occupy favored positions."[44] In 1969, a mere 2 percent of businesses in the US were owned by Black people.[45] Newton later would refer to Black people as a caste, given their severely limited class mobility.[46] In Panther leader Elaine Brown's autobiography, she identified the mixed population that made up the Black lumpen:

> They were the millions of black domestics and porters, nurses' aides and maintenance men, laundresses and cooks, sharecroppers, unpropertied ghetto dwellers, welfare mothers, and street hustlers. At their lowest level, at the core, they were the gang members and the gangsters, the pimps and the prostitutes, the drug users and dealers, the common thieves and murderers.[47]

Relying upon Marx's original, more limited definition of the lumpenproletariat, some scholars have pointed out that the Black Panther Party's early membership was not composed exclusively of unemployed, criminalized populations.[48] Indeed, Newton had been a burglar and was at one point virtually homeless, but he was also a college student and worked part-time. In an era when tuition at public universities was often very cheap or even free, it was more common for people to be both educated and unemployed, and people of different economic status often intermingled and shared political ideas, especially within the Black community. Merritt College, where Newton and Seale studied, was a major site of exchange in Oakland. As historian Donna Murch has explained: "The boundary between Merritt and North Oakland was completely porous. People passed on and off the campus, and many residents from the surrounding area hung out in the cafeteria, a major hub for debate."[49]

Through their expansion of the category of the lumpenproletariat, the Black Panther Party also highlighted the vulnerability of Black youth to criminalization and premature death, regardless of class. The average age in the BPP was nineteen, and care for the lives and well-being of the youth was a central focus. In James Baldwin's novel, *No Name in the Street*, he wrote about the Party:

> They announced themselves especially as a force for rehabilitation of the young – the young who were simply perishing, in and out of schools, on the needle, in the Army, or in prison. The black community recognized this energy almost at once and flowed toward it and supported it; a people's most valuable asset is the well-being of their young.[50]

Writing especially about the special vulnerability to addictive drugs that the youth are exposed to, New York Panther Cetewayo Tabor later affirmed in his popular essay "Capitalism Plus Dope Equals Genocide" that "it is the youth who make the revolution."[51] In 1970, 43 percent of Black youth under age twenty-one felt that the Black Panther Party accurately represented their personal views.[52] And 76 percent of Black adults, according to a May 1969 poll, either approved of or felt neutrally towards the Party.[53] Whereas mainstream media often branded the BPP as criminals, much of the Black community in the 1960s in fact regarded the Panthers as a *solution* to the problem of anti-social crime, not a cause of it. Black sociologist Stuart Hall described crime as "proto-political," for example, but praised the Panthers' ability to "command . . . blacks from the ghetto working class" as "troops" for their range of programs.[54] That the Party was at its founding associated with criminality was in part a side effect of the organization's insistence on working closely and identifying with the poorest and most oppressed populations. A focus on the lives of the criminalized – and their will to resist – was a cornerstone. It all began with empathy and an unwillingness to treat the people at the bottom of society as disposable.

Fanon did not identify part-time college students as part of the revolutionary class, nor did he emphasize drug-use as a particular vulnerability of the lumpenproletariat, but Newton and the Black Panther Party were conscious of moving beyond Fanon's writings, too. As "On the Ideology" explained:

> But even though we are able to relate heavily to Fanon, he has not given us the last word on applying the Marxist-Leninist

> analysis to our problems inside the United States. No one is going to do this for us because no one can. We have to do it ourselves . . . Huey P. Newton and Bobby Seale . . . adopted the Fanonian perspective, but they gave it a uniquely Afro-American content.[55]

Once, during a speech in New York, Newton used the term "Marxism-Leninism-Pantherism" to refer to their project.[56] Imprisoned Panther theorist George Jackson referred to himself as a "Marxist-Leninist-Maoist-Fanonist."[57] The Black Panther Party drew from Third World Marxism broadly, including figures like Mao Zedong, Che Guevara, Carlos Marighella, and Amilcar Cabral. The point was to develop an approach that would actually win freedom for Black people and the rest of humanity. James Baldwin described Newton's ongoing effort to strategize in an innovative manner:

> Huey believes, and I do, too, in the necessity of establishing a form of socialism in this country – what Bobby Seale would probably call a "Yankee doodle type" socialism. This means an indigenous socialism, formed by, and responding to, the real needs of the American people. This is not a doctrinaire position, no matter how the Panthers may seem to glorify Mao or Che or Fanon. (It may perhaps be noted that these men have something to say to the century after all, and may be read with profit, and are not, as public opinion would have it, merely more subtle, or more dangerous, heroin peddlers.)[58]

As early core Party member Elbert "Big Man" Howard put it, "we started to cherry-pick some of their philosophies and ways of thinking and apply it to what we wanted to do, 'cause we fully realized we were not in China, we were not in Cuba; . . . we had to come up with our own approach."[59] The Panthers' "Yankee doodle socialism," as Seale and Cleaver first phrased it, would not look like the socialisms of other regions of the world, but it would draw ideas from all of them.

In Defense of Life

It was from this perspective focused on the lumpen that Huey Newton pioneered a politics of care in defense of life, theorized, developed, and politicized by those most exposed to death themselves. The Black Panther Party's very first program was the creation of a traffic stop to protect the lives of school children.[60] Right by Newton's old elementary school ran a major street used by motorist commuters exiting downtown Oakland for suburbia. Decades later, he recounted the story in detail:

> I went to Santa Fe elementary school, and while I was there, many children were hit by cars. There was no traffic light in front of the school. It was a very busy street ... So, the first action of the Black Panther Party was to go down with our arms and be traffic police. At 3 o'clock when the school was let out, we would stop the traffic and allow the children to pass. Of course this would bring an army of police. They would take over the traffic jam that would occur ... We went to the planning commission of the city council and ... the Oakland City Council said that they had already passed some policy to put up a traffic light but it would be about five years ... So we went to the community and gathered a few hundred or maybe even thousands of signatures and took those to the City Council. We also would still police – when the police were not there, we would police the area. And every time we would try, the police would take over. So, the purpose was served anyway. The traffic light quickly went up in about, oh, three or four months after that event.[61]

By acting to defend the lives of the vulnerable, the Panthers took over government functions – displacing police and traffic infrastructure – and put pressure on the city government to do a better job of serving the people of the community. Most importantly, they demonstrated that anyone could do this work themselves. In grandiose visions of radical politics, it is easy to dismiss the BPP's first direct action. In Seale's account, he was straightforward: "Huey P. Newton wanted that light there on the corner, and worked to see that the light was there. If the power structure didn't put it there, the Panther Party was going to come out, block traffic, and direct traffic so that our young kids wouldn't die; so they would *survive*. It's that simple and it's that basic."[62]

Rarely publicized in accounts of the Party, the BPP's first social program marked the beginning of their consistent commitment to defending Black lives from racist and capitalist state neglect, while also modeling community control. This action *challenged state law* both by carefully breaking it and by enacting a superior social law that would be immediately embraced by the community. In one of Newton's first essays, "In Defense of Self-Defense," produced for a column of the same name in *The Black Panther* newspaper, he wrote:

> In order to promote the general welfare of society, rules and laws are established by men. Rules should serve men and not men serve rules. The man is greater than the rules or laws that he constructs. Much of the time the laws and rules which officials attempt to inflict upon poor people are non-functional in relation to the status of the poor in society. . . . It is the duty of the poor to write and construct rules and laws that are in their better interest.[63]

Despite popular depictions of the Black Panther Party as lawless, Newton navigated the relationship of the Party to law with considerable care and precision. The passage quoted above is itself an echo of a passage in the Bible, in which the figure of Jesus states: "The sabbath was made for man, and not man for the sabbath. Therefore, the Son of Man is Lord also of the Sabbath."[64] In the biblical account, Jesus challenges religious law by invoking the story of David stealing sacred bread from the Temple when David and his companions were in need of food. Newton's biblical reference made clear that he conceived of law as having a source other than the state, and that its workings should always be in the interest of people.

The second social program the BPP enacted, more famously, entailed *policing the police*. In 1966, armed with rifles and handguns as explicitly allowed by California law, Newton and Seale followed police officers and observed them in their harassment of the people of Oakland, maintaining a legal distance at all times. Newton would then read the law out loud from a textbook he carried with him. Among the passages he cited were those affirming civilians' right to remain silent when engaged by police, as established by the Supreme Court ruling in *Miranda v. Arizona* earlier that year. When people in the community were arrested, the Panthers followed the police and posted bail for them.[65] Less well known, before engaging in these "police patrols," Newton and Seale had intentionally exhausted all other legal means; these included delivering a petition with 5,000 signatures to the Police Review Board urging it to address civilian complaints about police brutality.[66] Later, Newton would promote the creation of a community board to hire, supervise, and fire police.[67]

Police officers and community members alike reacted to Newton and Seale's armed patrols with awe and wonder at what was a socially incomprehensible act. As Newton's transcriber J. Herman Blake later explained: "standing with a shotgun in the presence of police, in support of the African-American community was a revolutionary, death-defying act. I couldn't help but admire him, as did many of us."[68] It was simultaneously street theater, a crash course in the law, a militant expression of political freedom, and a radical act of care and communal defense. Police responded with confusion, but most important of all, they responded by giving in – until later, when they began a series of targeted false arrests of the Panthers. The unbelievable spectacle of what Newton and Seale did, however, obscured its *practical* dimension: this was a social program focused on the physical defense of the lives and well-being of the vulnerable, just like the traffic stop was. As New York Panther Kit Kim Holder later explained: "The police patrols were caretaking and resisting at the same time."[69] Even more than a decade later, Newton was still striving to have this point understood by others, writing in his doctoral dissertation:

> What never became clear to the public, largely because it was always de-emphasized in the media, was that the armed self-defense program of the Party was just one form of what Party leaders viewed as self-defense against oppression. The Party had always urged self-defense against poor medical

care, unemployment, slum housing, under-representation in the political process, and other social ills that poor and oppressed people suffer.[70]

From the perspective of police, the broader public, social commentators, and even educated allies, Newton's and Seale's guns represented violence. In an interview in 1970, Newton lamented: "Most of the intellectuals or so-called intellectuals didn't understand, but the people understood all the time because they know they need self-defense in order to survive. Self-defense falls under all the ten categories that are exemplified in our program."[71] All the social programs derived from a single sensibility: the need to care for and defend life. The fact that it was so often young Black men whose lives were being saved and protected essentially rendered the police patrols uninterpretable as acts of care. Ultimately, the aim for this program, as for all the social programs, was for people to see the opportunity to act for themselves and control their community. "We knew that no particular area could be totally defended; only the community could effectively defend and eventually liberate itself. Our aim was simply to teach them how to go about it."[72]

Denzil Dowell was a local, twenty-two-year-old Black youth who was murdered by police under questionable circumstances. Despite being disabled and unable to run, police claimed he had fled and jumped a fence. The police also claimed he had bled to death, but there was no pool of blood to be found at the scene. Newton applied the knowledge of police methods he had gained from his college courses to identify these and other inconsistencies in the police's account of Dowell's death. "The police murder us outright and call it justifiable homicide. They always cook up a story, but simple investigation will expose their lies. That is why we must disarm and control the police in our communities if we want to survive."[73] Mark Comfort, a local activist with roots in the Student Nonviolent Coordinating Committee (SNCC), was the first to bring Dowell's death to the attention of the Panthers.[74] Acting out of regard for Dowell's lost life and in observance of his family's grief, together they exhausted all available formal channels, speaking with multiple attorneys, filing petitions, and meeting with the County Sheriff, but to no avail.

> Like most Black families, the Dowells realized the treachery of the police and they were aware that there was little they could do about Denzil's death so far as the established institutions were concerned. They displayed the deep sorrow and sense of helplessness which was a very common thing among Blacks. I had seen it many times in my work in the communities and we were to see it again and again as we became more deeply involved in the life of the people.[75]

Newton and Seale made the case of Denzil's death the front-page story of the very first issue of *The Black Panther* newspaper.

While the newspaper could not bring back Denzil to his family, it was nonetheless launched as an act of care for his family and in defense of the memory of his life. In this regard, the paper was a social program designed to address the abandonment and disinformation that characterizes the death of Black and poor people in American society. In the introduction to a compilation of Newton's essays released in 1970, Eldridge Cleaver recalled: "When he first decided that we had to start a newspaper of our own we all tried to wiggle out of sitting down and doing what seemed to us to be such boring work, but Huey would always make us feel ashamed for not working hard enough."[76] The paper was also a principal source of funding for the Party throughout its history. Seale, Cleaver, Raymond Lewis, Frank Jones, and Elbert "Big Man" Howard were part of the editorial team early in the paper's history.[77] Throughout its existence, law enforcement responded by harassing Panthers and civilians possessing copies in public, raiding offices and destroying printing equipment, and, later, targeting and harassing airlines that transported the paper.[78]

Despite the importance he placed upon it, Newton did not feel capable of helping much with the newspaper itself beyond his dictated column. Another early social program he did spearhead, however, was a middle school tutoring program. Supporting children ages eight to fourteen, Newton assisted them with their schoolwork and taught them Black history through the works of W. E. B. Du Bois, Basil Davidson (author of *Black Mother*), and Melvin J. Herskovits (author of *The Myth of the Negro Past*).[79] He also specifically made sure not to let the children into the Party office, where arms were present. However, he was soon forced to cancel the program after teachers at the students' schools made reports to police, in hostile reaction to the fact that students were now bringing a knowledge of African civilization and Black history into the classroom. Newton was known for his care for children in particular – an outgrowth, likely, of his own traumas in school. It should come as no surprise then that all of the Party's early programs were oriented to preserving and defending the lives of children and youth.

Newton would also take charge on the day that the Black Panther Party for Self-Defense was tasked, along with another group, with providing security for Betty Shabazz's participation at a memorial for her late husband Malcolm X.[80] This second group called themselves the Northern California Black Panther Party, but having roots in SNCC and RAM, could claim an original lineage. The black panther symbol, which was widely popularized in the mid-1960s, was originally developed by the SNCC-based Lowndes County Freedom Party of Alabama. The two California Panther groups differed however; Newton stated frankly, "The Black Panther Party had been formed in the spirit of Malcolm; we strove for the goals he had set for himself."[81] Given the violent assassination of Malcolm X in 1965, Newton's Panthers carried arms in order to guarantee Betty Shabazz safe passage from the airport, while the other Panthers did not. She recounted:

> As I walked to the end of the walkway and made a slight right and saw the brothers standing out there dressed militaristically, I went, "Okay, I understand." And there was a young man, reciting part of the Constitution about carrying firearms. And it really did something to me. I just said, "Oh, wow. That's just really fantastic." And so then I got in a car and was swept away. I certainly didn't have any fear.[82]

Newton described the feeling of freedom he felt when defending women in particular from harassment by police.[83] His vocal confrontation of the police that day gained him and the BPP further respect within the Black community, but also more negative attention from law enforcement, the media, and conservative politicians.

The culture of racism they dealt with meant that almost all of the Party's social programs were villainized, targeted, and criminalized. As Newton later put it: "Being black in America is a violation and it always has been."[84] To stop the Panthers' police patrols, Republican congressman Don Mulford acquired the support of the National Rifle Association and introduced legislation banning open carry of arms altogether in California; the media even dubbed it "the Panther bill." The regularity with which the BPP's programs were *criminalized* obscures the reality of the early organization's careful public *legalism*. Seale would later describe this paradox optimistically:

> Huey was able to take the Panther Party and take the very concept of civil disobedience and put it on the cutting edge, while at the same time holding a legal posture. In other words, you distinguish civil disobedience from criminality. Now the power structure will just say you are all criminals, but we know that a civil disobedient stands out loud on the corner and states what he or she is opposed to, while the criminal is covert.[85]

The mischaracterization of the BPP's actions as criminal was clearest in the mainstream reaction to the Party's armed protest of Mulford's bill at the California state capitol.

On May 2, 1967, twenty male and female BPP members, Mark Comfort and his group the Oakland Direct Action Committee, and the family of Denzil Dowell together formed a "community delegation" to conduct a disciplined, armed but peaceful and legal protest at the state Capitol in Sacramento.[86] They began outside of the building but ended up in the legislative chambers after members of the media forced open its doors. The protest at Sacramento was portrayed as an "invasion" of the Capitol in the newspapers, although no member of the delegation used force at any point.[87] Newton later explained that their action was indeed in no sense an "invasion," but a public, political protest.[88] Quoting from Vietnamese communist Ho Chi Minh, he said: "military tactics made public for military reasons are unsound, while military tactics made public for political reasons are perfectly correct."[89] In other words, they were engaged not in a military action, but in a political action of protest, using arms as a legal, visual display to draw attention to a message.

The intention, as Newton made clear, was to convey a message about the racism behind the bill, not to attempt to stop its passage. "If the legislators got the message, too, well and good. But our primary purpose was to deliver it to the people. . . . The main thing was to deliver the message."[90] Indeed, it is not often remarked that Party chairman Bobby Seale was filmed several times reading out a statement Newton had composed (with the aid of Seale and Cleaver).[91] It opened by criticizing the US government's historical campaigns of genocide against Indigenous Americans, Black Americans, Japanese Americans, and the Vietnamese, and ended by calling the Black community to attention:

> At the same time that the American Government is waging a racist war of genocide in Vietnam the concentration camps in which Japanese-Americans were interned during World War II are being renovated and expanded. Since America has historically reserved its most barbaric treatment for non-White people, we are forced to conclude that these concentration camps are being prepared for Black people who are determined to gain their freedom by any means necessary. . . . The Black Panther Party for Self-Defense believes that the time has come for Black people to arm themselves against this terror before it is too late.[92]

Newton said of the media: "They were concentrating on the weapons. We had hoped that after the weapons gained their attention they would listen to the message."[93] That day, Newton had stayed behind because he was on parole; accordingly, it would be his job to do jail support. Although they did not believe themselves to be breaking a law, by this point the Panthers had been arrested on false charges so often that they had come to expect it. As the Party's Minister of Defense, Newton gave instructions to "take the arrest" if police attempted it.[94] They ended up detained under an obscure law that made it illegal to disrupt state assembly proceedings.

Under the now passed Mulford Act, it was clear that they would lose the ability to conduct armed patrols. However, as

Seale explained, Newton's intention all along was to "exhaust" the second amendment, revealing in an open fashion the contradiction between the explicit language of the Constitution and the practices of the government towards Black people.[95] The statement read at the Capitol drew attention to this point: "The Black Panther Party for Self-Defense calls upon the American people in general and Black people in particular to take careful note of the racist California legislature which is now considering legislation aimed at keeping the Black people disarmed and powerless."[96] Expecting the racist reaction of the police and the government, and drawing attention to their failure to live up to the ideals that police and government are said to represent, the Panthers made clear that it was *white America itself* that viewed arms as fundamental to the Black community's ability to determine its own destiny. And so, when the uniformed members of the Black Panther Party acted in precisely the manner that police or government should act, by enforcing the laws on the books and informing people of their rights, their ability to do so would predictably be taken away from them. Seale recalled:

> Huey's genius, as we used to call it, was his great ability, starting from a theoretical point of view, to show how we could move to heighten the contradiction as a means to educate the people or to capture their imagination. The very idea of patrolling the police was really grounded in a theory that Huey had, that if the idiot Ku Klux Klan could stand on the capitol steps and get publicity, then we could do the same thing, only our publicity would be about trying to raise the consciousness of black people to understand that we have to take a posture against this structured racism. Raising the contradictions to a higher level was key to how Huey thought and understood and analyzed a situation.[97]

At the same time, by following the laws to the letter, they also knew they were simultaneously exploding norms concerning what was even imaginable behavior for Black people. By the time the Mulford bill passed, the task had already been accomplished and the gap between what was legal and what was legitimate had been dramatically exposed in the view of so many in the Black community.

For so many others in American society, however, all they could see was the threat of Black violence. Newton would later write: "I did not know then how overshadowed my position paper would be by the 'colossal event' at the state capitol. We did not realize then that the media, even our own media, could be so dangerous a trap."[98] As Third World Feminist Chela Sandoval has argued, oppressed groups inevitably draw upon the resources available to them, including whatever is imposed upon them, and repurpose them.[99] As Black people, the Panthers leveraged the typical racist experience of being produced as objects into a spectacle of political symbolism deployed to draw attention, but in a manner that exceeded their expectations. In the eyes of many white people in the US and abroad, they were objectified into tropes of black masculinity that terrified some and appealed to others. But this does not mean that the Panthers' politics can be reduced primarily to spectacle or media savvy, as some have proposed.[100] Philosopher of Black Studies David Marriott has suggested: "Perhaps it is because black life is always on the outside of life that its death can only occur *in* politics as an enigmatic spectacle?"[101]

Perspectives that reduce Black politics to monstrosity, death, or spectacle reflect an inability or unwillingness to see Black humanity in general, and, in this instance, the Black Panther Party's extensive efforts to care for and defend life. For so many in the Black community, it was the latter that they saw, inspiring them to open new BPP chapters in cities that neither Newton nor Seale had ever traveled to. As they acquired this new attention, Newton and Seale also altered the ideological emphasis of their newspaper, which now became more explicitly decolonial and militant, since the government and police had "heightened the contradiction."

Political Consequences

Before forming the Black Panther Party for Self-Defense, Newton and Seale had been members of the Revolutionary Action

Movement and were thus influenced by that organization's combination of Black nationalism, Marxism, and internationalism. RAM's views had roots in debates from earlier in the twentieth century among Black members of the American Communist Party about the presence of an "internal black colony" spanning southern states where Black people were a majority or a plurality – the "black belt." Inspired by the decolonial revolutions then occurring in the Third World, RAM revitalized these earlier claims about an internal Black colony. In addition, inspired by Malcolm X and Fanon, RAM held that the "Black underclass" was "the vanguard of the world revolution."[102]

Like RAM, Newton also considered Black people colonized but placed an even greater emphasis on the perspective of the "Black Urban Lumpenproletariat."[103] Influenced by the increasing sight of militarized police, helicopters, and National Guard deployments in their communities in the late 1960s, Newton described the police as "an occupying army":[104] "In America, Black people are treated very much like the Vietnamese people, or any other colonized people. The police in our community occupy our area as foreign troops occupy territory."[105] And, like RAM, Newton also believed that the masses of Black people were in a unique position relative to other colonized peoples of the world because of their place at the center of capitalist empire. In the third issue of *The Black Panther*, he wrote:

> As long as the wheels of the imperialistic war machine are turning there is no country that can defeat this monster of the west. But black people can make a malfunction of this machine from within. Black people can destroy the machinery that's enslaving the world. America cannot stand to fight every black country in the world and fight a civil war at the same time.[106]

For Newton, the position of colonial subjugation at the center of Western capitalism was simultaneously "a strategic position" that empowered Black people to disable the "functioning of the remainder of the machinery."

Newton also combined the writings of Chinese communist Mao Zedong with his study of Black American history to analyze strategy. In the second issue of *The Black Panther*, released just after the protest at Sacramento, he offered "A Functional Definition of Politics." The essay opened with an invocation of Mao's version of the famous phrase, "war is the continuation of politics by other means," itself a play on the words of Prussian military theorist Carl von Clausewitz. As Newton phrased it:

> Politics is war without bloodshed. War is politics with bloodshed. Politics has its particular characteristics which differentiate it from war. When the peaceful means of politics are exhausted and the people do not get what they want, politics are continued. Usually it ends up in physical conflict which is called war, which is also political.[107]

With the Party's ability to put pressure on the police now severely limited by the Mulford Act, Newton's statement correctly predicted that the Panthers would soon be facing physical harassment from the police.

At this point in the development of his thought, Newton grappled continuously with a major tension. He understood clearly that political power may take many forms, but he believed that, at the time, the only power Black people had available to them was in a *negative* form, as a potentially destructive force. This was because of the disempowering effects of slavery. In an interview conducted during his time in jail in early 1968, he conveyed the main argument from "A Functional Definition of Politics":

> For instance, when any candidate is going up for political office, he always – in the white power structure – always has political power behind him. And political power is, uh, you can find it in a number of areas. You have feudal power, the farmers who own much land . . . for instance, if the farmers don't get what they want, they'll let the crops rot in the field . . . Then, you have big business power, or economic power, where the people who own big businesses will get behind a candidate . . . And we see that Black people don't have this economic power, they don't have land power, we've been robbed. . . .

> Our Black politicians have been ineffective. Much of the time it's not their fault. . . . Even if they get votes from Black people, simply to have a vote doesn't mean political power. In the political arena, a thing is not political unless there is a political consequence if the people don't get what they want. . . . And Black people in the past have not been able to offer this consequence. For instance, according to [Black historian] John Hope Franklin, the reason that Black Reconstruction failed, where you had many Black candidates holding office in the South, wasn't because these Black candidates were ignorant or inefficient. Many of the Black candidates had been educated in France and Canada, in England, and they were very efficient. But the reason it failed was because Blacks did not have economical or military power. After they put their man in office, he was still subject to these people who owned the land, he was still subject to these people who owned the military. . . .
>
> And, we say now we can develop a political consequence, we can develop political power by being a potentially destructive force – that Black people arm themselves in a political fashion, and then, if the aggression is continued against us, we'll be able to offer a political consequence.[108]

Newton states frankly that "the only strength" the Black community had was as "a potentially destructive force if we don't get freedom."[109] "To be political, you must have a political consequence when you do not receive your desires – otherwise you are non-political."[110] In "In Defense of Self-Defense," he added: "The power structure depends upon the use of force without retaliation."[111] This view, deeply informed by the experience of colonization, which assumes that beneath all politics exists a terrain of violence, is summed up in Newton's famous phrase: "An unarmed people are slaves or are subject to slavery at any given moment."[112]

This basic argument would be echoed by other scholars of the era who examined the unique power of disruption for disempowered groups. In the classic text of political science *Poor People's Movements* (1977), scholars Frances Fox Piven and Richard A. Cloward conducted long-term empirical analyses of the tactics employed by members of the Unemployed Workers' Movement, the Industrial Workers' Movement, the Civil Rights Movement, and the Welfare Rights Movement, and arrived at similar conclusions: "By our definition, disruption is simply the application of a negative sanction, the withdrawal of a crucial contribution on which others depend, and it is therefore a natural resource for exerting power over others."[113] Furthermore, they argued, because what is disruptive is defined by contextual dynamics and easily accounted for by those in power, "strategies must be pursued that escalate the momentum and impact of disruptive protest at each stage in its emergence and evolution."[114] Often, mainstream interpretations of riots tend to be exceedingly emotionally charged, disallowing a clear understanding of their strengths and weaknesses. However, empirical analyses of the long-term effects of the uprisings of the 1960s show that they did on the whole lead to increases in funding for social programs provided to Black and urban populations, improving life-outcomes and standards of living.[115]

Accordingly, when the riotous uprisings of the "long, hot summer" of 1967 began in response to police brutality, one might think that Newton would have been supportive, seeing them as a sign of political escalation and an exercise of the Black community's power.[116] However, Newton was opposed. This is because riots against racist conditions of life also tend to result in heavy death tolls for Black people, in precise contradiction with Newton's founding principles of caring for and defending Black life.[117] That summer, in "A Correct Handling of a Revolution," Newton wrote: "At this time the black masses are handling the resistance incorrectly. . . . The brothers and sisters were herded into a small area by the gestapo police and immediately contained by the brutal violence of the oppressor's storm troops. This manner of resistance is sporadic, short-lived, and costly in violence against the people."[118] Instead, he advocated silent, armed guerrilla actions, executed in "groups of two's and three's" as an ideal way to "exact a political consequence" on police. "When the masses hear that the gestapo policeman has been executed while sipping coffee at a counter, and the revolutionary executioners fled without being traced, the masses will see the validity of this type of approach to resistance." While Newton's position may seem counterintuitive and also provoke emotionally charged reactions, it is crucial to understand that the tactic was not inspired by "rage" (as so many depictions of the Panthers have claimed), but by a stern rationalism. Newton's rationale was that targeted guerrilla shootings reduced the cost to Black lives (and even police lives, for that matter), in contrast to the mass death and suffering caused by riotous rebellions. In this regard, the strategy followed the same basic principles as the rest of the BPP's programs: defend the lives of the oppressed and model community control. The aim in this instance was to disturb the police's casual devaluation of Black life and remind them of its sanctity. If Black people desired to respond to the injustice of Black death at the hands of police, Newton's approach, he reasoned, was a less lethal way to do it.

The aim, in short, was always to stop violence against Black people. As Newton wrote in "In Defense of Self-Defense" and would repeat during the Party's early years: "We are advocates of the abolition of war. We do not want war, but war can only be abolished through war, and in order to get rid of the gun, sometimes it becomes necessary to pick up the gun."[119] In the bigger picture, exercises of military power were merely a means towards the other forms of political power that would ensure life for the Black community:

> When the people move for liberation they must have the basic tool of liberation: the gun. Only with the power of the gun can the Black masses halt the terror and brutality directed against them by the armed racist power structure; and in one sense only by the power of the gun can the whole world be transformed into the earthly paradise dreamed of by the people from time immemorial.[120]

Nonetheless, the conception of violence as a necessary means to an end revealed a fundamental tension in Newton's ideology between, on the one hand, the desire to save and defend Black lives, and, on the other, the expectation that one may live a short life in the pursuit of that desire. Newton often quoted a line attributed to Russian anarchist Mikhail Bakunin: "The first lesson a revolutionary must learn is that he is a doomed man.

Unless he understands this, he does not grasp the essential meaning of his life."[121]

This existential contradiction would intensify for Newton and the Black Panther Party after the protest at Sacramento. Membership in the group increased, but Newton's aim was the creation of *popular* revolution, not one accomplished by a group of radicals. In his conception, the BPP would act as a vanguard, meaning that they would model revolutionary action, but not lead it. "The vanguard of the revolution doesn't have strength other than the strength of the people."[122] After all, the problem of the disconnect between radicals and the masses was why he and Seale left RAM in the first place. However, as police harassment increased, the Panthers often had to deal with it by themselves. Years later, Newton would reflect:

> The people misunderstood us and did not follow our lead in picking up the gun. At the time, there was no clear solution to this dilemma. We were a young revolutionary group seeking answers and ways to alleviate racism. We had chosen to confront an evil head on and within the limits of the law. But perhaps our military strategy was too much of "a great leap forward." Nonetheless, I believe that the Black Panther Approach in 1966 and 1967 was basically a good and necessary phase. Our military actions called attention to our program and our plans for the people.[123]

Although Newton's later reflections underestimated the active participation of the community, the Party did nonetheless struggle to figure out how to respond to repression. In "Correct Handling," Newton suggested that the Party would eventually have to go underground altogether, but they were still not connected enough to a mass movement for such a move to accomplish much. Between the summer of 1967 and late 1969, they would eventually shift course, but not before facing considerable harassment and suffering loss of life.

> Looking back, I think our tactic at Sacramento was correct at that time, but it was also a mistake in a way. . . . Our purpose was not to kill; it was to inform, to let the nation

> know where the Party stood. The police, however, took it to mean that the Party was only a front with weapons, that we would not defend ourselves. This attitude caused a number of problems for us, and it took some time to restore caution to the police after Sacramento.[124]

In order to stop the harassment and the new death threats they were now being subjected to, they had to face the necessity of defending themselves.

A Political Symbol

Late at night on October 28, 1967, Huey Newton and Gene McKinney, a friend and fundraiser for the Party, were pulled over by police officer John Frey. Officer Frey was infamous in Oakland for his racism, even among police, and he openly referred to himself as the *gestapo* – the Nazi secret police.[125] The interaction ended with Newton shot four times in the abdomen but surviving, another officer named Heanes wounded, and Officer Frey dead.[126] Newton maintained in court that he lost consciousness at several points that night and, while at the hospital, he was beaten by police.[127] He spent the next year jailed in solitary confinement at the Alameda County Courthouse as he stood trial. In late 1968, Newton stated:

> I was asked how did I feel about Officer Frey, and I explained that whenever anyone is killed or hurt, that I feel sympathy and great compassion for them. And I went on to explain that I had no responsibility for them, that I was innocent, but still that the Panthers are against killing and against all war. I explained our motto, that we are advocates of the abolition of war.[128]

With Newton off the streets, harassment of the rest of the Panthers escalated. That winter, both the Cleavers' and Seales' homes were raided by police. As a result, in March 1968, Newton passed "Executive Mandate No. 3," requiring that all members keep legally registered arms in their homes to defend against "outlaws." Invoking the St. Valentine's Day Massacre of 1929, when members of Al Capone's gang disguised themselves as police officers and murdered members of a rival gang, the jailed Newton stated: "History teaches us that . . . We have no way of determining that a man in a uniform involved in a forced outlaw entry into our home is in fact a guardian of the Law. He is acting like a law-breaker and we must make an appropriate response."[129] Newton was striving to maintain the publicly *legalist* stance that had characterized the Party's original strategies, including the depiction of the police as the true criminals.

In the same issue of *The Black Panther*, the Party also announced an official change to its name, dropping the words "for Self-Defense." They wanted to address misconceptions that they were a paramilitary group or armed security force, rather than a true political party.[130] Consistent with this, they began running BPP leaders as candidates for office with the Peace and Freedom Party (PFP), which included Newton running for Congress. The intention was to use "the electoral process" as a "means of educating people on issues . . . a means of talking to white people about racism, imperialism, and oppression, and as a means of building support, through the PFP, for the BPP and for black liberation."[131] Functioning "strictly from an educational level," the campaigns served also to draw attention to the movement to free Newton from jail.[132]

On the front page of the newspaper, alongside Newton's Executive Mandate, ran also an anonymously authored article titled "Speeding Up Time."[133] It reflected the organization's search for direction and inspiration in Newton's physical absence. Most likely written by Cleaver, it asked: "How do we move from where we are at this moment? In which direction, against which enemy, and with which weapon?"[134] It also marked a developing tendency already cultivated by Cleaver's "Free Huey!" campaign, which at times assumed Newton's inevitable martyrdom: "The Black Liberation forces have Malcolm X who is like unto John the Baptist, who prophesied the coming of another. Malcolm prophesied that his people were going to pick up the Gun and that it would be the ballot or the bullet. Huey P. Newton is like unto Jesus, in that he fulfilled the prophesy by picking up the Gun."[135]

The writer of the article sought to both deify Newton and treat his ideas as religious scripture. With Newton gone, it was easier to turn him into a symbol and even suggest his inevitable death, an approach at odds with the valuing of life that had inspired Newton's original strategies. In "Correct Handling of the Revolution," Newton had in fact argued that the era of social upheaval meant that Black people were inclined and motivated to seek out a "messiah" or leader figure, but he never made any claim to be that figure. On the other hand, he did seek to have the BPP claim the role of "the vanguard," and his writings about the existential fate of the revolutionary easily fed into others' ideas about martyrdom. As if expecting Newton's conviction, Cleaver distributed a leaflet, without consulting Newton's legal team, clearly implying that Newton had killed Frey.[136] Cleaver later admitted: "Huey P. Newton overnight became a symbol containing the potential of epic proportions that would lead us in war. . . . I took for myself the task of building this symbol."[137] As more people joined or allied with the organization, the BPP's membership and base of allies came to be populated more and more by people who praised Newton but either had little contact with him or treated him as an object.

Contrary to Newton's concerns, some people in the community did take up his ideas as published in the newspaper. For example, one group in San Francisco quietly undertook guerrilla action, just as prescribed in "Correct Handling of a Revolution."[138] There was also the task of accumulating weapons, which was sometimes done legally and other times not. The organization tried early on to establish a separation between aboveground and underground activity. In 1968, when San Francisco-based Panther Don Cox asked Seale what his responsibilities as Field Marshal were to be, Seale reportedly said, "Whenever you see something that needs to be done, do it."[139] Such kinds of ambiguous direction from leadership meant, however, that far too many members were increasingly engaged in undisciplined illegal activities. In one infamous instance, a new member who was armed with a gun while heavily drugged stopped at a gas station in a truck with the Black Panther Party logo emblazoned on the side.[140] Confused by the inebriated Panther's actions, the gas station attendant assumed he was being robbed, called the police, and a shoot-out resulted. The Panther, Bill Brent, would soon be removed from the Party, but there was little systematic effort to prevent such irresponsible activities until the start of 1969.[141]

In 1968, undisciplined shoot-outs undertaken by new members proliferated. In *This Side of Glory*, a semi-autobiographical book by BPP Chief of Staff David Hilliard and author Lewis Cole, which collected the accounts of dozens of former Panthers and allies, Hilliard criticized his own past participation in spontaneous violence. He paraphrased a reprimand from Seale: "'David, you really shot at those guys,' Bobby says. . . . 'We gotta talk about this. That ain't right. That's jackanape stuff. We believe in discipline. You gotta read and talk about Fanon, man, on spontaneity and its strengths and weaknesses. That's not what Huey would want at all."[142] In the book, Hilliard admitted that he was both intimidated and inspired by Eldridge's intellect and the more general environment of masculine posturing predominating in the Party at the time. Hilliard also presented evidence of Newton's increasing discontent with the direction of the Party, captured on recorded tapes and messages delivered from Newton's cell to the Central Committee: "You do not go in large groups like you would need to seize Merritt College, and you don't employ a whole *brigade* of Panthers and run around and talk about unleashing war against the system. This stuff is totally insane, and if you continue all we're going to have is a bunch of dead Panthers."[143] After Martin Luther King, Jr. was assassinated on April 4 of that year, more Black people across the country were inspired to take to the streets, join radical organizations, or otherwise take up political activity. As Bill Brent later recounted, Cleaver grew "impatient" with "Huey's refusal to endorse reckless attacks on the police in response to the assassination of Martin Luther King, Jr., and planned one anyways."[144]

On April 6, in a concealed decision-making process, Cleaver organized a group car ride with about a dozen key Party members that ended up in a major shoot-out with police. "It was an aborted ambush because the cops showed up too soon."[145] Founding Panther Lil' Bobby Hutton was tragically murdered by police as he attempted to surrender.[146] Don Cox summed up the outcome: "The only members of the Central Committee left on the streets that had been close to the day-to-day decision-making were Bobby Seale and Eldridge's wife Kathleen. Everyone else was in jail, in the hospital, or dead."[147] After being bailed out, Cleaver soon fled the country, ending up in Cuba and eventually Algeria. The death of Hutton, who was only seventeen at the time and had been recruited as the Party's third member, hit Newton particularly hard.[148] Party ally Alex Hoffman recalled: "Huey thought April 6 was absolutely crazy. . . . Afterwards he was very depressed. Terribly depressed. He was upset because Bobby Hutton was killed. And he was upset that you [David Hilliard] hadn't kept Eldridge in check. Though I think he knew Eldridge was an overpowering personality."[149]

Newton was increasingly critical of how political violence was being taken up by the Party, but his view was in the minority. Some years later, Newton reflected on his shift in strategy:

> I thought that the arms had served their purpose as far as being a catalyst to gain the enthusiasm of the community. I felt that we should turn away from the arms because too much had been made of them.[150]
>
> As a matter of fact, when I was in high school, I wanted to leave high school in 1958 and join the Cuban revolution. . . . So what I'm really trying to say is that I believed an armed insurrection could work. After I was shot and went to prison, that ended that illusion. I had time to think. I spent three years in solitary. So I had a lot of time and the first year I was in prison, I tried to get the party to stop the shooting, to stop the talk about the gun thing. They voted me down. We always had a Central Committee. They were mesmerized by Eldridge Cleaver.[151]

In June of 1968, following the assassination of Senator Robert Kennedy, Newton explained:

> First of all, our position on guns and violence in general, on war in general, is one of being against war and being against violence. And this is not a changed position. If it seems in contradiction to some of my earlier statements, it's simply because people have not understood what I was saying in the first place. . . . We absolutely are against people killing

> each other and committing violence on each other, but also we recognize that we don't advocate that the oppressed people, the victims, leave themselves subject to the aggression of the criminal. . . . In the final analysis, we stand for total disarmament.[152]

Between Newton's founding of the Party and the period when he was in jail at the Alameda County Courthouse – before he was convicted, processed, and taken to prison at Vacaville – his overall position remained basically consistent, even as it exhibited a strategic shift in emphasis regarding the precise application of political violence. Ironically, however, despite the elevation of Newton as a symbol, his actual views became increasingly unpopular within the Party. In later unpublished recordings, Newton maintained: "The Party was started as a vehicle for the people and I saw Eldridge destroying this dream by alienating the people. This contradiction between me and the Central Committee went on for a long time."[153]

Cleaver would later celebrate the shoot-outs with police as "secret" battles in a "war," though his use of the word "war" belied that these actions were often pursued with little planning, did not mobilize much of the Black community, and ultimately drew negative attention to the Party.[154] In Hilliard's assessment: "we're not very effective as fighters: we're the victims in most street encounters with police."[155] Decades later, Seale counted twenty-eight Panthers and fourteen police officers killed by the end of 1969.[156] Party armorer Flores Forbes tallied over thirty Panthers dead across two years.[157] By 1972, Newton counted forty total.[158] Some have suggested that such figures may be interpreted as a passable rate of loss for a group in active combat with the power of late twentieth-century US police forces.[159] Nonetheless, even in 1967 when Newton argued for the necessity of political violence, he never suggested that the Black Panther Party could *by itself* accomplish much of anything that way.

In the meanwhile, with Newton facing the gas chamber, his trial and the Free Huey! movement Cleaver created were drawing international attention. Newton's legal team was led by Charles Garry and included Alex Hoffman, Fay Stender, John Escobedo, Carlton Innis, and *Ramparts*' editor Edward Keating. Newton deliberately used the trial as a political tool to demonstrate that "having to fight for my life was the logical and inevitable outcome of our efforts to lift the oppressor's burden."[160] Reasoning that the state seeks to demonstrate its power to completely degrade the individual through capital punishment, Newton – always the existentialist – personally considered the act of "fac[ing] execution . . . with grace and dignity" as "the ultimate form of truth."[161] Despite being the defendant, he seized the opportunity to take the witness stand and explain the historical, political, and philosophical origins of the Black Panther Party, addressing himself to the jury rather than the prosecutor.[162] It was said that Newton had the jury "rapt" and "mesmerized."[163]

Charles Garry innovated the strategy of critiquing the racial composition of the jury, part of a process Newton called a "revolutionizing of the court system."[164] "'Not one single juror resides in the West Oakland ghetto, my client's community,' charged Garry. 'None are his peers – of his economic standing.'"[165] Newton's primary line of defense was that, after being shot by Officer Frey, he could not clearly remember events as he went in and out of consciousness, a point supported by the testimony of psychiatrist Dr. Bernard Diamond.[166] In addition, Garry focused on raising reasonable doubt about several other dynamics: inconsistencies in the stories of the witnesses called by the prosecution, foul play on the part of the prosecutor's office, and the possibility that Officers Frey and Heanes may have shot each other.[167] He even raised the possibility that Newton's friend Gene McKinney, who had ridden in the passenger seat – and pled the fifth – might have fired the gun that slayed Frey.

Between September 8 and 12, 1968, Newton was found guilty of manslaughter and not guilty of assault with a deadly weapon on a police officer. The jury had essentially concluded that Newton had killed Officer Frey, "but only after severe provocation, and in a state of passion."[168] Newton received a sentence of two to fifteen years, but because he avoided the death penalty, it was seen as a victory by the Party. The Oakland police department responded that night by sending on-duty officers to shoot up the windows of the Oakland Party offices at 1:30 a.m.[169] Newton was moved to the California Medical Facility at Vacaville prison, where he spent twenty-five days. Two months later, Richard Nixon was elected President of the United States and, as sociologist Joshua Bloom and historian Waldo E. Martin have noted, government treatment of the Black Panther Party suddenly changed dramatically. In *Black Against Empire*, they detail:

> Before Nixon's election as president, there had not been a single police raid of a Black Panther office. Police had stopped and arrested small groups of Panthers selling the *Black Panther* newspaper. They had also confronted Panthers in spontaneous conflicts outside Panther offices in New York and Denver, and in the Bay Area, they had raided the homes of Bobby Seale and the Cleavers, encountering minimal resistance. But state repression of the Panthers intensified after Nixon's election. Even before Nixon took office in January 1969, police and federal agents began staging raids on Panther offices. It is not clear whether the wave of raids of Panther offices that followed was the independent response of local police to the victory of Nixon's Law and Order campaign in the polls or whether the FBI systematically encouraged the change in policy nationwide. In either case, no form of repression was more direct, more provocative, or more violent.[170]

In December 1968, the offices in Indianapolis, Denver, and Des Moines were raided and ransacked, and the office in Newark was bombed. In April 1969, twenty-one members in New York City were raided in their homes and arrested, a bomb exploded at the office in Des Moines, and police raided the San Francisco office using submachine guns, rifles, and tear gas. In June, Milwaukee members were surrounded and arrested en masse, and the office in Sacramento was raided. In July, San Diego was raided. In August, the Richmond office was surrounded. In September, Panthers in San Diego were raided in their homes, and members at the Philadelphia office were raided and arrested. In December 1969, the first major deployment of SWAT (Special Weapons and Tactics) was launched against the Southern California chapter headquarters in Los Angeles; a five-hour shoot-out ensued, involving 350 police officers, a tank, and a helicopter that dropped dynamite on the roof, all of which the Panthers inside managed to endure without incurring any loss of life. Notably, in some of these incidents, well-prepared Party or community members managed to fend off police, collectively repair office infrastructure, and provide effective jail support for those arrested. Overall, the repression generated community support for the Panthers. At the same time, however, the costs incurred in terms of mental and physical health, infrastructure, legal fees, and time spent were enormous, but none so high as for those members targeted for assassination that year.

In January 1969, lead organizers Bunchy Carter and John Huggins were murdered at the University of California, Los Angeles by members of Us, a Black nationalist organization whose leader Ron Karenga had known ties to local police.[171] It was later revealed that the Us members involved were also FBI informants.[172] The Panthers suspected conspiracy and sought to respond. However, "lacking the ability to 'sense' the conditions, [Newton] said he could not instruct the Party how to handle the crisis."[173] At this point imprisoned at the California Men's Colony in San Luis Obispo, far from both the Bay Area and Los Angeles, Newton's problem was that the political climate in the outside world was intensifying all the time, but he had no well-informed strategy to offer the Party. That said, since the conflict at UCLA was in fact being actively fostered by the FBI, Newton was likely wise to refuse to retaliate.[174]

> Some of the comrades in the Party sent messages asking me to let them go after Karenga, but I refused to do this. Open warfare between us would only harm the community, whose needs came before our desire for revenge. In time I knew the community would deal with Karenga, and eventually it did: a community tribunal was held in Los Angeles, and it found him guilty of deceiving the people.[175]

Months later, facing continuing violence from Us, the Panthers eventually took defensive action, but in a discreet manner.[176] Afterwards, with losses to beloved Party leaders affecting morale, in early 1969 new leaders and the rank-and-file membership started giving shape to a new strategy.

New Approaches to Survival

With Cleaver in exile, Seale and Newton sought to return to the community-oriented work with which they began the Party. In September 1968, the Central Committee started publishing calls in the newspaper for volunteers for a breakfast program.[177] With Bobby Seale's approval, Ruth Beckford-Smith, a dance teacher to Newton's former girlfriend LaVerne Williams, started the Party's first free breakfast program to feed schoolchildren.[178] A member of St. Augustine's Episcopal Church in West Oakland, she consulted a nutritionist, collected donated food from local businesses, and began serving meals at the church in January of 1969.[179] This second wave of Party programs was also inspired by the community programs that Mao Zedong developed during his efforts to organize the people of the countryside, and Newton had read all four volumes of Mao's writings.[180] Simultaneously, the breakfast program fit clearly into the kinds of work the Party had engaged in during its first year, modeling how to defend Black life. In March, Newton published a statement in support of the program:

> This program was created because the Black Panther Party understands that our children need a nourishing breakfast every morning so that they can learn. . . . It is a beautiful sight to see our children eat in the mornings after remembering the times when our stomachs were not full, and even the teachers in the schools say that there is a great improvement in the academic skills of the children that do get the breakfast. At one time there were children that passed out in class from hunger, or had to be sent home for something to eat. But our children shall be fed, and the Black Panther Party will not let the malady of hunger keep our children down any longer.[181]

Newton's language demonstrated a sincere empathy with the experiences of the children. He also provided a politicized analysis of the program's purpose, emphasizing survival and the establishment of new institutions to replace the current ones:

"We must survive this evil government and build a new one fit for the service of all the people."

Importantly, while making an appeal to the community at large, Newton was also clear that the point was for such programs to be run by the community itself and not by the Party: "The Breakfast Program has already been initiated in several chapters, and our love for the masses makes us realize that it must continue permanently and be a national program. But we need your help and that means money, food, and time. We want to turn the programs over to the community, but without your efforts and support we cannot." In a later interview, Newton described the breakfast program in terms of cognitive health, an insight whose importance endures today: "we know that you can't fight a revolution if your children are growing up – who are your future – are dying, suffering brain damage from malnutrition, poor medical care, lack of certain fundamentals of education."[182] In April 1969, Seale made the breakfast program mandatory for all national chapters. At its peak, the Party fed 250,000 children a day, leading J. Edgar Hoover to declare the free breakfast program "potentially the greatest threat" to the FBI's efforts to "neutralize the Black Panther Party and destroy what it stands for."[183]

Increasingly, with Newton now moved to a prison far away from Oakland headquarters, it would be the rapidly expanding rank-and-file membership and leaders in other chapters who would, through their own experiences, identify the needs of the community and move the Party towards programming responsive to those needs. The most prominent among this new crop of leaders was Fred Hampton, deputy chairman of the Illinois BPP. In early 1969, Hampton's chapter in Chicago and the Black community it served were facing increasingly violent police repression. Hampton interpreted this as an effect of political actions recently taken by white allies. During the Democratic National Convention held in August 1968, members of the white, middle-class Students for a Democratic Society and its splinter group the Weather Underground Organization (WUO) had engaged in destruction of stores and other buildings in downtown Chicago. Police responded harshly, leading even the National Commission on the Causes and Prevention of Violence to characterize the events as a "police riot."[184]

In the weeks that followed, the Chicago Police Department began raiding apartments and making arbitrary arrests in the city's Black community under the excuse of searching for perpetrators. Because it was well known that the WUO had an alliance with the BPP, portions of the Black community began blaming the Party.[185] Hampton and the Chicago chapter, which had been in extensive debates with the WUO about strategy and tactics, responded by denouncing the WUO publicly.[186] In her autobiography, Elaine Brown, then a leader in the Southern California BPP, described how the debate escalated to the top of the Party national leadership, eventually turning into an argument between the new, twenty-one-year-old leader from Chicago and the thirty-four-year-old Party elder in exile, Eldridge Cleaver. According to Seale, Cleaver attempted to give direct orders to Hampton to embrace the WUO's tactics – which would later include bombings of government infrastructure – but Hampton would not budge:

> That conflict had so outraged Eldridge in exile that he had openly criticized Fred, in an essay he sent for publication in the Party newspaper. He charged Fred with failing to appreciate that any attack on the pig power structure was correct, and for failing to respect the Party's coalitions with white radical organizations. He demanded that Fred retract his statements. Fred refused.[187]

On October 9, 1969, two weeks into the start of the famous Chicago 8 trial which placed the blame for the rioting on several prominent radicals (including Bobby Seale), Hampton openly denounced the Weather Underground in the mainstream media:

> We think that it is anarchistic, opportunistic, individualistic; it's chauvinistic, it's custeristic, and *that's* the bad part about it. It's custeristic in that its leaders take people into situations where the people can be massacred, and they call it revolution. . . . We say that they're doing exactly what the pigs want them to do, when they take people down and play around, and the pigs are prepared for this, and they'll wipe all of those young people out. We think that these people

> may be sincere, but they're misguided . . . That's not a revolution, it's insanity . . . It's a potential massacre, that's what it is. . . . And we don't support that because we say all power to the people. All the power is manifested *in* the people. We don't have any people whose lives we believe should be thrown away.[188]

Hampton's principled rejection of indiscriminate rioting and property destruction echoed Newton's earlier critique of riots, but he took an even more stern position, absolutely refusing to treat human lives as objects within a radical's distorted political vision. To Hampton, doing so aligned with the desires of police in that it treated people's lives as disposable.

A couple of weeks later, the remaining Party leadership traveled to Chicago to meet with Hampton in person to try to work out the differences in strategy.[189] Decades later, Elaine Brown offered a glimpse into the results of that discussion:

> Hampton was taking a very hard line and David was going to find out what were the problems and try to resolve them. And [they] actually did an incredible job, which is a piece of the history some people don't like to discuss, but in any case, Fred had a very principled position and it was a difficult moment. . . . [Fred's wife] Debra and I slept in [Fred's] big bed while David and the men debated all night long about the principle of this and the rightness of this.
>
> And at 7 o'clock in the morning everybody got up . . . And Fred Hampton had all these people out in the school yard ready to start the breakfast program. And in Chicago this is a serious thing. It's one thing to have the breakfast program in L.A. . . . It's another to go to the breakfast program in Chicago when it's, you know, zero below zero, you know, and talk about cooking some breakfast, and getting some eggs and all that.[190]

To be clear, Fred Hampton did not undervalue the role of violence in bringing about political change. This is evident from his most famous speech "You Can Murder a Liberator, but You Can't Murder Liberation." Rather, Hampton would not sideline the suffering and deaths of Black people in a manner that contradicted the purpose of revolutionary struggle in the first place. The point was to raise people's revolutionary consciousness until they "are educated to the point that they can run things themselves."[191]

Hampton's principles reflected a sharply focused, almost insular concern with the well-being of oppressed people. In one sense, this level of focus was at odds even with certain aspects of Newton's argument for "exacting political consequences," given that approach's concern with obtaining the *recognition* of the oppressor group. Hampton was concerned with oppressed people's lives above all. The very survival of Black and oppressed people was a matter of political struggle in and of itself. While not rejecting armed struggle altogether, the new theoretical paradigm that Hampton contributed – critically revising Newton – reflected a new awareness that destructive power was not "the only strength" that the Black community had, after all. It was a realization that the ability to sustain life, to *make* people *live*, was an exercise of power, too. In line with this, the Chicago chapter's free breakfast program and free medical clinic were among the most successful in the Party. Esteem for Hampton in the organization grew quickly thereafter. Bobby Seale later stated that, had he himself been killed, the plan was for Hampton to take over as Chairman of the Party.[192] Newton stated that he saw Hampton becoming the national leader of international relations.[193] Within a couple of months, however, Fred Hampton would be murdered by Chicago police officers as he lay sleeping.[194]

The earlier rift in the Party would remain enough of an underlying tension for the FBI to eventually leverage it later. In a year, Cleaver would claim to be part of the "left wing of the party" and make out the difference in strategies to be a matter of courage and manhood.[195] Nonetheless, there would be peace at least for now: David Hilliard took a hardline position in defense of the new social programs, and the BPP Central Committee devoted more of its efforts to centering them. Innovative programs were being developed by the thousands of new members, the overwhelming majority of whom were now women responding to the local conditions in their communities.

For an organization that had for its first six or seven months been all-male, the shift it underwent by October 1969 to become

60 percent female was dramatic, and perhaps unsettling to some.[196] Early on, the BPP had been literally a boys' club, but in the spring of 1967 the second issue of the newspaper publicized the organization as a place where revolutionary Black women could meet revolutionary Black men.[197] One major exception to the narrative that the Party was originally all-male, however, is the early role played by Artie Seale, Bobby's wife. Party historian Billy X Jennings has provided context:

> She did so much, but is not given the credit. She edited the Ten Point Program, typed it up. Loaned Huey and Bobby money to get things going, she even cooked for Party members in the early days. She also went to Sacramento in 1967 to protest the Mulford Act. Worked on the early issues of the BPP newspaper. A strong and outspoken person. Supported Bobby while he was in jail and prison, she would bring messages from Bobby when she visited.[198]

After Artie Seale, Tarika Lewis was likely the first woman to join the Party. Despite her youth, she carried herself with bravado; according to historian Robyn C. Spencer-Antoine, Lewis was said to have declared to the all-male group, "Ya'll have a nice program and everything. It sounds like me. Can I join?"[199]

Huey Newton and Bobby Seale founded the Party in part in a spirit of defiance, and that was inevitably bound together with a sense of masculine courage. On the other hand, the image of patriarchal masculinity that the BPP came to be stereotyped with was primarily imposed by a white, mainstream media that fetishized the sexuality of Black men and women alike. The Black Panther Party was no more patriarchal than white organizations and institutions of the same period. When repression hit the organization hard in 1969, men were disproportionately targeted, a reflection of the government's own patriarchal bias and preconceptions about who they considered significant to Party operations. Bobby Seale's purge starting in January 1969 also resulted in the removal of undisciplined men.[200] Panther women rose to the occasion, and LA Panther Joan Kelley-Williams recalled: "In chapters where there was greater police harassment, more raids, more confrontations with the police, women had a fairly equal share of responsibility for what we call security."[201] Panther Frankye Malika Adams later remarked: "Women ran the [Party] pretty much. I don't know how it came to be a male's party or thought of as being a male's party."[202]

Some of the women who joined the Party were of lumpen-proletarian background – sex workers and pimps, drug addicts, and welfare recipients. Panther Regina Jennings developed a devotion to the Party because they helped her overcome her drug addiction. She described her "struggle from drug addict to soldier [as] a hard fought personal war."[203] Many other women who joined, however, were college-educated, and often at higher rates than the men were, increasing their likelihood of moving into positions of high rank and leadership within the Party at the same time that much of the male leadership was being imprisoned, exiled, and murdered. In a revolutionary organization with constant needs, if you possessed the skills to accomplish a specific task, the matter of your gender was soon disregarded.

Nonetheless, eliminating the presence of sexist norms brought into the Party from broader society required active struggle on the part of female members and their male allies. By 1969, an internal turn against male chauvinism in the Party had gained momentum, led by women like Roberta Alexander and Marsha Taylor in Northern California, with Los Angeles being another center, although the critique of sexism was uneven across chapters and multiple waves of struggle would be necessary over the years.[204] Panther veteran Norma Armour Mtume summed up her analysis:

> It wasn't the easiest thing. I mean, we – based on principles – we tried to make all things equal, that women could do what men could do. And the men cooked, the men cleaned, there were men assigned to the children's centers and what not. But, like I said, the people who were in the Party were people who . . . came into the Party, so they brought those same behaviors, and same chauvinism that – not just men in our community, but all over the world, the patriarchal societies [had]. So, that was something that you constantly had to deal with.[205]

At their worst, some men in the Party used their rank to pressure women into sex.[206] Such behavior forced some talented women out of the BPP.[207] Nonetheless, Party veteran Phyllis Jackson credited Newton's original list of Party rules, inspired by his reading of Mao, for establishing an early, organizational baseline against chauvinism.[208] Panther veteran Haven Henderson emphasized: "there was a structure there that said that we *should* wage that battle."[209] For thousands of Black women activists in the 1960s, forced to choose between working through the sexism internal to the Black Panther Party on the one hand, and putting up with the racism of the white feminist organizations on the other, the choice was an easy one. Overall, in the view of Panther Janet Cyril, "the Black Panther Party was one of the most explicitly feminist Black organizations that she participated in."[210]

Both as rank-and-file members and as leaders, women helped reorient the direction of the Party and its programs. Panther men like Reginald "Malik" Edwards, Steve McCutchen, and Mark Holder have attested to being challenged intellectually by the sophisticated analyses produced by women in the Party and to being influenced by how they applied that knowledge.[211] Women like Elaine Brown, Ericka Huggins, Judi Douglass, and later Jonina Abron played major roles in editing the newspaper, shaping its content and the Party's ideology during long stretches of time when male founding figures like Newton were absent.

Arguably the greatest effect of women's practical leadership over the BPP was in shaping the growth and flourishing of programming. Free programs developed by members in local chapters over the full history of the Party included: legal aid education; busing to prisons for families of incarcerated people; a senior escort; pest control and extermination; plumbing and home repair; cooperative housing; education for children and adults; and free food, clothing, and shoe distribution.[212] Panthers were also asked by community members to respond to mental health crises, domestic violence disputes, and community conflicts.[213] These efforts delegitimized federal, state, and local governments by demonstrating that regular people could produce with fewer resources what the government failed to do with more. They modeled self-determination and community control by swaths of the population that dominant discourses regarded as worthless.

In addition, these programs facilitated meaningful collaborations between the Black poor and Black professionals or business owners who agreed with the Party's platform and supported it materially with funding, free labor, connections, and other resources. Contrary to stereotypes, Newton and Seale had always advocated for the integration of middle-class Black people into the organization. One of their first attempts at doing so, the failed merger in 1967 with the Student Nonviolent Coordinating Committee, had been aimed at addressing the BPP's lack of administrators, advisers, writers, and educated organizers. In Newton's account, he, Seale, and Cleaver were all in agreement "to draft all of the [SNCC] leadership into administrative positions and let them run the Party . . . We did not intend to have a coalition with them, we saw ourselves as merging with them."[214] These plans included even moving operations to Atlanta.[215] However, according to Newton, SNCC members were paranoid and did not believe the Panthers would completely give up power in such a fashion.[216] The merger was also directly targeted by the FBI.[217] Newton's early concerns about the Party's lack of educated organizers explains why, given his writing abilities, Cleaver was appointed to a leadership position so quickly, despite his history of violence towards women. Ironically, this was also why so many college-educated women – some of whom came from more privileged backgrounds and racially mixed families – rose into positions of leadership so quickly as well. It all reflected the BPP's practical policy of assigning more responsibilities to those with greater skills.

Still in prison but observing the changes in the Party, in the summer of 1970 Newton expressed in simple terms the continuity between the first programs from 1966 and those from 1969: "Violence comes in many forms. To deprive children of food is a manifestation of violence. To deprive our people of necessary housing is another. To deprive us of full employment is a violent action. In short, we will defend ourselves against the violent system so that violence will end."[218] Arguably the most impressive program of self-defense came in the form of the People's Free Medical Clinics (PFMCs). Bringing in Black medical professionals and allies to provide services to the community for free, the PFMCs provided testing for blood pressure, lead levels, sexually transmitted infections, sickle cell anemia, and pap smears, plus referrals and accompaniment to other hospitals and doctors.[219] Vivian McMillan, a member in the Winston-Salem chapter, described being motivated as a medical student after seeing how capitalism renders people's lives as disposable:

> When I was in college for the EMT certificate, a woman in the community died because the ambulance service came to pick her up and she did not have money. They told her she would be okay. They left her there and she died. That was unheard of for me, that someone should be refused a ride to the hospital. That was what started the whole push for funding a People's Free Ambulance Program. I dedicated quite a bit of my life to that. . . . At one point I dropped out of college to devote myself full-time to the Party.[220]

Identifying the strategic importance of medical power, Minister of Education Raymond "Masai" Hewitt took the lead in calling for an expansion of the clinics in November of 1969; a few months later, the imprisoned Bobby Seale made the establishment of PFMCs a requirement for all chapters.[221] Black scholar of science and history Alondra Nelson opens her book *Body and Soul*, a pivotal examination of the BPP's health programs, by reframing Newton's maxim on war: "Health is politics by other means."[222] Panther Norma Armour has also pointed out that military veterans played a major role in establishing and staffing the medical infrastructure that sustained the Party.[223] In the words of Oakland Panther Osa Russell-White, "We were looked at as healers, rescuers, and soldiers: everything that the community needed."[224]

The Panthers' political aim to care for and defend life encountered one of its most emotionally difficult contradictions when it came to the matter of raising children. While the predominantly middle-class white women of the feminist movement of the era fought for access to abortion, women of color instead were often critical of the role that the modern medical establishment had played in forcing sterilizations on Black, Puerto Rican, Indigenous, incarcerated, immigrant, and poor women and men. This perspective was reflected in a wave of articles in *The Black Panther*, starting in 1969, equating "birth control" with "genocide," with one author, Evette Pearson, urging "the Black man" to "educate your woman to stop taking those pills."[225] An article from February 1970 critiqued mainstream panic about "overpopulation" as a short-sighted view reflective of a capitalist culture with skewed priorities: "The relevant question is not, 'If you have all those babies, how will you care for them?' But 'Why can't we all get enough to care for our children?'"[226] And an article from the spring of 1971, "Sterilization: Another Part of the Plan of Black Genocide," criticized laws in nine states that mandated the sterilization of women on welfare who had children while unmarried.[227]

Consistent with this, the Party celebrated the births of "Panther cubs." The August 2, 1969 issue of the paper, titled "The Youth Makes the Revolution," featured a cover piece on the Cleavers' newborn.[228] At the other end of the spectrum was the experience of Ericka Huggins, who, while nursing her baby in a jail cell after the assassination of her husband John, was taunted by a police officer who yelled, "You don't have any right to raise a baby!"[229] As historian Kiran Garcha has argued, these kinds of experiences reinforced to Party members that the mere existence of Black children was a political matter, and if "change" was synonymous with "revolution," then these children were to be "little changers."[230] And yet, the Panther political perspective that framed "making babies for the revolution" as an existential necessity exacerbated uneven relations between men and women, putting disproportionate pressure on Panther women to care for children while still fulfilling their other Party obligations.[231] Being a Panther was already a full-time job that led too often to poor diets and a dangerously unhealthy lack of sleep, to say nothing of the traumatizing stresses of state persecution. In their memoirs, Panther women often describe how rarely they were able to raise their own children while being full-time activists in the movement, especially as leaders.[232] In the final analysis, whether the means was a stop sign, a gun, a plate of food, or a white medical coat, the struggle to care for and defend Black life would remain a challenge with high costs given the conditions of colonization.

3

The Theory of Intercommunalism

This four-fifths of humankind will rise up in their ghettos, from East to West, to announce their humanity in the name of the wretched of the earth.

Huey P. Newton (1974)[1]

Liberated Territory

From exile in Algeria, Eldridge Cleaver wrote: "Will my child ever be able to sit down to a Black Panther breakfast, and will Kathleen and I, with our child – and I'm counting this Panther before he claws his way out of the womb – ever be able to visit the People's Park? What we need is some liberated territory in Babylon that we are willing and prepared to defend, so that all the exiles, fugitives, draft-dodgers, and runaway slaves can return to help finish the job." In perhaps Cleaver's most insightful piece of writing, "On Meeting the Needs of the People," he went on to critique "the cluster of beliefs that have been spawned by the soothsayers of greed to sanctify their possession of the earth under the guise of private property."

> If we can understand Breakfast for Children, can we not also understand Lunch for Children, and Dinner for Children, and Clothing for Children, and Education for Children, and Medical Care for Children? And if we can understand

> that, why can't we understand not only a People's Park, but People's Housing, and People's Transportation, and People's Industry, and People's Banks? And why can't we understand a People's Government? . . .
>
> We are trapped between our visions of what life could be like and what it really is: a people's Government in which a rational arrangement is made, and the present reality – helicopters dispatched over college campuses to spread clouds of noxious gasses in order to intimidate the people and to stifle their protests; troops marching in battle formation down our streets; taking aim, taking deadly aim, at citizens, actually aiming at vital spots of the body, actually pulling triggers, and actually killing people.[2]

As violent state repression escalated, Cleaver was inspired to connect the Panther's expanding assemblage of social programs with the recent occupation of University of California property by student activists in Berkeley, California. Inspired by an Indigenous history during which the land was "owned" by no one, but also by decolonial movements in the Third World that had taken the land back, the activists at the "People's Park" in Berkeley used different terms to describe the project: "the land question," "liberated zones," "liberated territories," and "the territorial imperative."[3] Building upon these ideas, Cleaver argued that the movement needed to connect a territorial emphasis to an international vision.

In other countries, local movements were imitating the model set by the Party and were calling themselves Panthers – in Nova Scotia (Canada), Bermuda, the Bahamas, the United Kingdom, Israel-Palestine, India, Australia, New Zealand, and Polynesia.[4] While in Algeria, Cleaver was joined by other members of the Central Committee – Communications Secretary Kathleen Cleaver, Minister of Culture Emory Douglas, and then others – who together participated in the first Pan-African Cultural Festival in July 1969.[5] In June 1970, they formally established the Black Panther Party's international embassy in a building in the city of Algiers provided by the Algerian government. Cleaver's International Section quickly established connections with the leaders of liberation movements and new governments in Africa and Asia: Zimbabwe, Guinea-Bissau and the Cape Verde Islands, South Vietnam, North Korea, Palestine, and the Congo. According to Bloom and Martin, "the Algerian government accredited the Black Panthers as one of twelve liberation movements that merited support" in their revolutionary efforts to displace the governments in their home countries.[6] Distance from the center of American empire granted the International Section greater creativity in thought and action, but, as "runaway slaves," their minds remained focused on organizing for the liberation of the Black and oppressed back home.

Meanwhile, back in the United States, the number of chapters was reaching a peak. Scholar of Black Studies Judson Jeffries has produced brilliant work across a trilogy of books piecing together the histories of the less-recognized chapters of the Black Panther Party.[7] These edited collections – *Comrades*, *On the Ground*, and *The Black Panther Party in a City Near You* – feature essays on the chapters and branches in Baltimore, Winston-Salem, Cleveland, Indianapolis, Milwaukee, Philadelphia, Los Angeles, Houston, Seattle, Kansas City, Detroit, Des Moines, New Orleans, Atlanta, Washington, DC, Boston, and Dallas. Extending that work with essays on New Bedford, Birmingham, Detroit, and Milwaukee, historians Yohuru Williams and Jama Lazerow have pointed out in *Liberated Territory* that so many organizations were inspired by the Panthers and copied their strategies without becoming formal chapters, that it is more appropriate to speak of a *Black Panther movement*.[8]

In her autobiography, *A Taste of Power*, Elaine Brown explained how the formal chapters of the BPP were organized:

> The party's chapters were organized by state, except in California, where there was a chapter for Northern California and, the one we were members of, the Southern California chapter. Within a chapter were branches, organized by city, and within the branches were sections. These were divided into subsections, which were divided into squads. Ideas and information flowed up and down the chain of command. Orders went from the top to the bottom. It was a paramilitary structure.[9]

Historian Donna Murch says there were branches in sixty-one cities and twenty-six states.[10] In late 1970, Huey Newton counted a total of "approximately 77 [sites], including the community centers, medical centers, and various programs around the country."[11] These included the National Committees to Combat Fascism – multiracial front organizations under the BPP umbrella that allowed white people to join and also served as a way to vet new members, started in 1969 as a way to intercept government informants.[12] The Panther leadership generally avoided stating in public how many members they had in total, but Seale later argued that there were 5,000 members at the end of 1968, before their first purge.[13]

With the Party undergoing simultaneous expansion and repression, domestically and abroad, on August 5, 1970 Newton was suddenly released from prison on appeal. During his trial, the jury had not been informed that Newton's claim that he lost consciousness after being shot could serve as a complete defense against all charges of criminal homicide. In fact, the trial court was found to have erred and committed prejudicial error on a total of three counts.[14] As a result, the verdict was overturned, and Newton was released on bail. There would be two subsequent mistrials during the 1970s, but eventually the prosecution would drop the charges. Deeply moved by the collective power of "the people" to bring about his release, upon encountering the crowd of 10,000 gathered outside to greet him, Newton exclaimed, "I am we!"[15]

After one year of jail and two years of prison, upon Newton's return, he introduced a new theory that sought to integrate the gains from the combined insights of the transformed Black Panther Party: Hampton's critique of political violence that disproportionately exposes the oppressed; the work of the rank-and-file women to expand the social programs; and Cleaver's proposal of territorial control. Newton's theory would creatively place these innovations within a new analysis of what it meant to exist and struggle for revolution within the United States in the late twentieth century. It needed to be a theory of what a social movement would have to look like to be *truly* successful while simultaneously existing at the center of the most militarily powerful civilization in world history. It would be necessary first to redefine that phenomenon.

In the autumn of 1970, while on a tour of the East coast, Newton presented his new theory. "First of all, the United States is not a nation. The power of the United States transcends its own geographical boundaries and those of other people."[16] Newton's unpublished papers include several essays dedicated to what he called the theory of *intercommunalism*. Central to this understanding of global politics was a rejection of the idea that the United States could any longer claim to be a nation, given that its economy was inextricably tied up with the economics and politics of other nations – and always by force. "American imperialism had done to the nations of the world what American racism and exploitation had done to the communities of the poor and oppressed inside its own borders: robbed them of their integrity and independence. This led to the understanding that the nation, as traditionally defined, no longer existed."[17] Instead, Newton argued, there exists only empire. "The United States, or what I like to call North America, was transformed at the hands of the ruling circle from a nation to an empire."[18]

Newton specified that it was not truly the US state that exercised imperial power as much as it was the capitalists in power who control even the decisions of the American government: "I'm blaming first and foremost the seventy-six companies who control Nixon. These are the monopolies or oligarchies that control not only the people in this country but also who run the empire."[19]

> Such a "ruling class" can, in fact, be readily shown to exist. Its locus of power and interest is in the giant corporations and financial institutions which dominate the American economy, and moreover, the economy of the entire Western world. . . . This does not mean, of course, that the business community as such must prefer a particular candidate or party for that candidate or party to be victorious. It means, much more fundamentally, that short of committing political suicide, no party or government can step outside the framework of the corporate system and its politics, and embark on a course which consistently threatens the power and privileges of the giant corporations.[20]

In Newton's view, these massive "American" businesses are better understood as transnational, imperial entities. In an essay titled "The Technology Question," he quoted the President of International Automotive Operations for Ford Motor Company, Robert Stevenson: "We look at a world without any boundary lines. We don't consider ourselves basically American. We are multi-national; and when we approach a government that doesn't like the United States, we always say, 'Who do you like; Britain, Germany? We carry a lot of flags.'"[21] Newton first believed that the empire's wars were motivated exclusively by the desire to extract resources, but by 1972 he revised this view and came to the conclusion that it is very often the forced creation of new markets – new consumer bases – that is a primary motivation to expansion.[22] In "Intercommunalism" (1974), he explained: "This is the core of America's messianic crusade: that the world must be made over in the American image (read: subjected to the American corporate system) if the American Way of Life (read: the corporate economy) is to survive at home."[23]

Although full data is not made public by the Pentagon, as of 2021, the US military operated at least 750 military bases in at least eighty countries.[24] In addition, since the Korean War in 1950, the power of the US Congress to officially declare war by majority vote has with increasing frequency been disregarded by the Executive branch, which has been able to unilaterally declare "police actions" through the Office of the President and then pressure Congress to fund them. In Newton's era, the Vietnam War was officially a "police action" rather than a declared war, and Newton specifically pointed to the prevalence of this kind of language, while US soldiers' lives were exploited in the process: "Even the vocabulary of the ruling clique reflects this new phenomenon . . .we can even refer to this army as the intercommunal police force. They control communities they do not live in and have no interest in, and they are controlled by the ruling clique for purposes of profit, personal advancement and military might."[25]

Beyond military power, Newton also argued that "mass media plus the development of transportation make it impossible for us to think of ourselves in terms of separate entities, as nations."[26] Newton said of Third World peoples: "They're going through a cultural transformation similar to that which Black African people did when brought here. They're looking more and more Western everyday . . . so the difference between us is only quantitative, not qualitative."[27] More than a decade before the term "globalization" was coined by Harvard economist Theodore Levitt, Newton in 1970 described this collective connectivity created by the capitalist world system as *reactionary intercommunalism*. He called it "reactionary" because it is a connectivity held together by oppression and social control. "This is a distorted form of collectivity. Everything's been collected but it's used exclusively in the interest of the ruling circle."[28] In 2009, Elaine Brown explained: "Though he did not live long enough to know of the Internet, Huey argued that as technology was bringing the world ever closer together, the world's people were poised to recognize their common oppressor and unite around their common oppression."[29]

Today, many of Newton's ideas are likely to strike readers as clearly applicable to our present, with some points even appearing obvious. In 1970, however, Newton struggled to have the theory of intercommunalism understood at all. In speeches delivered in front of thousands across the country in late 1970 and early 1971, his argument that "nations no longer exist" confused supporters who were expecting him to declare a military campaign for Black people's national independence.[30] And, despite often speaking at universities and colleges, his efforts to explain the philosophical methods underlying his ideas just further confused most of those in attendance.[31] "So far I haven't been able to do it well enough to keep from being booed off the stage, but we are learning."[32] Audiences were surprised, also, and even disoriented, by Newton's high-pitched voice, his "California-country" drawl, and his tendency to lay out chains of ideas in a long, continuous manner.[33] As J. Herman Blake described it: "Newton explained that in his mind, *everything* was connected."[34]

New York Panther Assata Shakur later recalled: "almost no one understood Huey's long speeches explaining intercommunalism," and his long elaborations on Hegelian philosophy were a "sheer disaster."[35] According to one report, "at Yale, half the audience walked out on him."[36] Newton later claimed that "the campus lecture tour was the worst experience I have had in my life."[37] Furthermore, Newton's warnings against open armed struggle were interpreted by many Party members as a sign of retreat and pacifism. After three years of elevating him as the human symbol of a revolution unfolding in the streets, people were disappointed to find that he was nothing like the figure in the wicker chair on the posters. When Newton was arrested in October 1967, the organization had consisted of only a few dozen members; now it consisted of thousands, and almost none of them had ever met him.

Newton worked to reword his explanations, presenting intercommunalism as just another strategic shift in the Party's history of continuous adaptations. "In 1966 we called our Party a *Black Nationalist* Party. We called ourselves Black Nationalists because we thought that nationhood was the answer. Shortly after that we decided that what was really needed was revolutionary nationalism, that is, nationalism plus socialism."[38] Back in 1966 and 1967, Newton and Seale had pointed to the dictatorship of "Papa Doc" François Duvalier in Haiti, which they criticized for claiming to "promote African culture" while nonetheless being capitalist. "He merely kicked out the racists and replaced them with himself as the oppressor."[39] Without socialism, they reasoned, most Black people were likely to remain in poverty due to capitalism's necessarily hierarchal structure.

After becoming Revolutionary Nationalists, they saw shortcomings in that as well. In 1969, Newton argued that even a Black socialist nation would not be sustainable: "If Blacks at this very minute were able to secede from the union, and say have five or six states, it would be almost impossible to function in freedom side by side with a capitalist imperialistic country. . . . In fact, by all logics, we would suffer imperialism and colonialism even more so than the Third World is suffering now."[40] The Panthers realized that they had to ally with all other oppressed nations and groups in order to stand a fighting chance against US power, so they became *internationalists* and established solidarities with decolonizing nations.

However, as Newton came to grasp, even the socialist nations they might ally with were not truly independent nations either, for their decisions were heavily affected, when not altogether controlled, by global capitalism. Newton's earlier observations about the similarities between the colonized people internal to the United States and the colonized of the Third World now had a different meaning. He was arguing that the forces of empire had essentially flattened the basic condition of all oppressed communities, eliminating prior national sovereignties:

> How do we define certain communities such as North Vietnam and the provisional government in the South? How do we explain these communities if in fact they too cannot claim nationhood? We say this: we say they represent the people's liberated territory. They represent a community liberated.[41]

> So their liberated territory is very similar to what happened in the riots and rebellions in Detroit where, for about 4 or 5 days the blacks there held about 8 blocks and they drove the local police and the national guard out and the peace was not restored . . . They only held their territory for 4 days; they could have had a revolutionary provisional government and we would have recognized it.[42]

Reactionary intercommunalism, Newton explained, had reduced the world to a collection of communities that lack control over their local conditions of life and can at most only become "liberated territories" within and despite that larger empire.

Given Newton's socialist views, he had already been of the perspective that the blurring of borders might be a desirable outcome, stating that "the long-term goal is to create a world where nations don't exist at all anyway."[43] However, he lamented, "the non-state has been accomplished but it is reactionary" rather than "revolutionary."[44] And yet, these same shared conditions of oppression are the possible grounds, Newton argued, for a shared sense of experience, a possible universal sense of identity, and potentially revolutionary collective action. In the process of being subject to reactionary intercommunalism, people would hopefully come to understand each other and themselves differently, as one global humanity:

> If we believe we are brother with the people of Mozambique, how can we help? They need arms and other material aid.

> We have no weapons to give. We have no money for materials. Then how do we help? . . . They cannot fight for us. We cannot fight in their place. We can each narrow the territory that our common oppressor occupies. We can liberate ourselves, learning from and teaching each other along the way. But the struggle is the same; the enemy is the same.[45]

> We believe that the developing countries, Asia, Africa, and Latin America are really the countryside of the world while the United States is the city of the world, and we believe as each country becomes free in the rural area, it will literally choke the city because the city needs the raw materials. . . . As each country becomes free, it increases our chances, one step forward, to our freedom.[46]

Revolutionary intercommunalism is a system consciously produced by people's efforts to "reinforce the positive aspects of their social experiences" in order to "establish cultural institutions [that] perpetuate what they feel is the good life."[47] At a speech delivered in New York in 1970, Newton explained that because reactionary intercommunalism is *already* a planned, global economy that hoards the world's resources for the benefit of a few, a revolutionary "redistribution of goods would have to be by definition a plan for a world economy" as well, but organized upon egalitarian principles from below by the people themselves, not by a centralized government or a corporate elite.[48] Such an economy, a "socialist economy," he argued, "will have to take into consideration Africa, Asia, Latin America, because these are the people it robbed in order to develop this technological empire that now exists."[49]

In 1970, when he presented this theory, perhaps its most confusing aspect was that it required reinterpreting a whole set of political terms – nation-states, colonies, citizenship, borders – as practically obsolete, and rendered so by capitalism itself. It is then perhaps unsurprising that, in the decades since, these very topics have become objects of cultural anxiety, tension, and uncertainty.

> When the people seize the means of production, when they seize the mass media and so forth, you will still have racism, you will still have ethnocentrism, you will still have

> contradictions. But the fact that *the people* will be in control of all the productive and institutional units of society – not only factories, but the media too – will enable them to start solving these contradictions. It will produce new values, new identities; it will mold a new and essentially human culture as the people resolve old conflicts based on cultural and economic conditions.[50]
>
> We believe that there are no more colonies or neo-colonies. If a people is colonized it must be possible for them to decolonize and become what they formerly were. . . .The people and the economy are so integrated into the imperialist empire that it's impossible to "decolonize," to return to the former conditions of existence. If colonies cannot "decolonize" and return to their original existence as nations, then nations no longer exist. Nor, we believe, will they ever exist again.[51]

In using the term "neo-colonies," Newton was building upon the analysis put forth by Ghanaian president Kwame Nkrumah in his classic *Neo-Colonialism: The Last Stage of Imperialism.*[52] Nkrumah argued that the decolonial movements for national independence had been rendered obsolete by new forms of economic control exerted by former colonial powers. This included – as it still does today – the forcing of Third World states to sell or buy goods at particular prices, the external manipulation of monetary policies, and sometimes direct control of natural resources. Newton's idea of revolutionary intercommunalism also bears a resemblance to Nkrumah's bold vision of a socialist Africa united to defend itself against exploitation by global capitalist forces. Newton conveyed support for Nkrumah's original vision, while remaining critical of any version of Pan-Africanism that was not socialist:

> The unity that Dr. Nkrumah called for carried the demand of solidarity based upon certain principles: specifically, pooling resources from all separate countries of Africa into an all-African treasury to produce the industrial and technological development that could ensure Africa true economic and political independence. This in turn would allow for a

> fair distribution of wealth to every African along socialist lines.[53]

As writer Nayla Tozin has pointed out, however, a vital difference between the two ideologies lies in the fact that Nkrumah's African Union was to be organized from the top down, while Newton's revolutionary intercommunalism was conceptualized as bottom-up, built by grassroots communities, from the local, outwards, towards the global.[54]

The Colonization of America

Because Newton's theory of intercommunalism was so poorly received in its day, there has been little analysis of it until very recently. Even Newton's strongest supporters in Oakland generally did not really understand the idea, with few exceptions. One extremely important but rarely understood part of intercommunalism consisted in how it related to the Black Panther Party's original position that Black people in the US are colonized.[55] In the New York City chapter especially, many Party members who had been strongly influenced by the Black nationalism of Marcus Garvey and Malcolm X believed strongly in both the "internal colony" thesis and the need for an independent Black nation-state. For these members in particular, Newton's theory of intercommunalism appeared at first glance to be a complete abandonment of their core beliefs as Panthers. Newton had, after all, discarded the concept of *colonies* altogether.

> And people argued with me all day and all night, asking, "How can you possibly be a colony? In order to be a colony you have to have a nation, and you're not a nation, you're a community. You're a dispersed collection of communities." Because the Black Panther Party is not embarrassed to change or admit error, tonight I would like to accept the criticism and say that those critics were absolutely right. We are a collection of communities just as the Korean people, the Vietnamese people, and the Chinese people are a collection of communities – a dispersed collection of communities

> because we have no superstructure of our own. The superstructure we have is the superstructure of Wall Street, which all of our labor produced.[56]

However, overlooked in this shift was the fact that Newton still believed that Black people were historically colonized and furthermore *had remained colonized*. In fact, counterintuitively, he would ultimately argue that *all American people are colonized*.

Around the time he left prison, he began to clarify his thinking on the colonial status of Black people: "We say in the first place that we're a colonized people, and even though we are colonized not in a classical sense, because we are a colony brought home to the mother country, but we are colonized nevertheless."[57] In Newton's later unpublished essay, "Intercommunalism: A Higher Level of Consciousness," he makes the point most clearly:

> For some time we have claimed that black communities and other oppressed communities in the United States are colonies. However, critics have objected to this on the grounds that these are not examples of classical colonialism, where the colonized always outnumber the colonizers. However, to assume that blacks are not colonized is a limited view which comes from poor thinking – that is viewing the United States as a nation. When we recognize the situation for what it is, that the United States is an empire, and when we think in terms of intercommunalism, it becomes clear that black communities are dispersed communities, colonized in the same manner as those dispersed communities in other parts of the world.[58]

In *Revolutionary Suicide*, published years later, Newton continued to describe the modern United States as *colonial*, referring to "Black revolutionaries in America, whose lives are in constant danger from the evils of a colonial society."[59]

The view that Black people are colonized was a much more widespread and popular view in the 1960s than is today acknowledged or remembered. Even Dr. Martin Luther King, Jr., who never advocated for an independent Black nation-state, believed that Black people living in the slums of Chicago were subject to "domestic colonialism." And, like Newton, King understood colonialism not in simplistically racial terms, but rather in terms of economic, political, and military control:

> The Northern ghetto had become a type of colonial area. The colony was powerless because all important decisions affecting the community were made from the outside. Many of its inhabitants even had their daily lives dominated by the welfare worker and the policeman. . . .
>
> We viewed slums and slumism as more than a problem of dilapidated, inadequate housing. We understood them as the end product of domestic colonialism: slum housing and slum schools, unemployment and underemployment, segregated and inadequate education, welfare dependency and political servitude.[60]
>
> The Rev. James Bevel and our Chicago Staff have come to see this as a system of internal colonialism, not unlike the exploitation of the Congo by Belgium.[61]

W. E. B. Du Bois also wrote of the "colonial status" of Black people in the US, as did the influential Black socialist Harold Cruse. Social psychologist Kenneth Clark's *Dark Ghetto: Dilemmas of Social Power* argued for the idea in 1965, and so did sociologist Robert Blauner in his 1969 article "Internal Colonialism and Ghetto Revolt," highlighting the lack of locally controlled institutions in poor, Black communities.[62] However, it was likely the work of Black journalist and editor Robert L. Allen that gave the idea its greatest scholarly legitimacy through his influential 1969 book *Black Awakening in Capitalist America*.

Some of these accounts did rely in part on racial dominance as a way to understand colonization, but the most well-known theorist of colonization, Frantz Fanon, did not define colonization this way. For Fanon, the creation and construction of racial categories and racial difference is an *effect* of colonization, not its cause. According to his definition, "the colonial situation is, first of all, a military conquest continued and reinforced by a civil and police administration."[63] This idea that what appears to be governance is rather just formalized, lower-intensity war matches up with Newton's view that "[p]olitics is war without bloodshed [and] war is politics with bloodshed." For the colonized, much of the reality that they experience daily clearly reflects conditions of war. However, Newton also believed that a community's past or even present experience of being colonized can become obscured from their awareness, given a long-ago enough history and/or a powerful enough process of colonization.

In 1968, the Black nationalist organization Republic of New Afrika (RNA) formed out of the Detroit Riots of 1967. Advocating for reparations and declaring a provisional government, their identification as New Afrikan citizens signaled their effort to combine an awareness of African cultural history with a political strategy that took into account the condition of being colonized in the New World. During Newton's imprisonment in 1969, he responded to a letter from the RNA, addressing several topics in a tone of friendship and solidarity. Central among them was the matter of the BPP's original Ten-Point Program and its inclusion of a call for Black people to participate in an official vote, overseen by the United Nations, for the establishment of an independent nation-state. While validating the "psychological value of fighting for a territory," in his letter Newton was critical of both the prospects and strategic advantages of a Black nation-state, given the power of American empire. His remarks also offer an insight into his thinking already in 1969 about the colonial condition:

> The Black Panther Party's position is that the Black people in this country are definitely colonized, and suffer from the colonial plight more than any ethnic group in the country. Perhaps there is the exception of the Indian, but surely as much even as the Indian population. We, too, realize that the American people in general are colonized. And they are colonized simply because they are under a capitalist society which has a small clique of rulers who own the means of production and control all decision making.[64]

Newton's unique view that *Americans in general* are colonized goes back in fact to the earliest days of the Party, though it is rarely remarked upon.

In "In Defense of Self-Defense," while describing the historical contradictions at play during the time of the American Revolution, Newton argued:

> Now these same colonized white people, these ex-slaves, robbers, and thieves, have denied the colonized black man the right to even speak of abolishing this oppressive system which the white colonized American created. They have carried their madness to the four corners of the earth, and now there is a universal rebellion against their continued rule and power.[65]

Newton lays out an analysis of American history that highlights the fact that the overwhelming majority of Europeans brought to the British colonies in North America came from the poorest classes and included enslaved convicts, trafficked orphans, and indentured servants. This emphasis in his early column in *The Black Panther* would be later edited out when his essays were published in the 1972 collection *To Die for the People*. While streamlining Newton's language considerably, main editor Toni Morrison (plus J. Herman Blake and Jim Silberman) also changed some of his argument, removing most of his references to "colonized Americans" and "colonized white people" and rewriting "ex-slaves, robbers, and thieves" as "bondsmen, paupers, and thieves."[66] Indeed, there are considerable differences between Newton's original essays in the newspaper and the versions in the edited collections, with the originals more often including philosophical justifications for his political arguments. The originals also include more self-critical remarks on Newton's part and are in general less *declarative*, unsettling the image of self-assured authority that his supporters expected and no doubt desired.

Also likely confusing was the content of Newton's argument. What could it possibly mean to argue that white people were colonized too? The analysis was not a mere passing remark that could be revised away, but was in fact fundamental to Newton's political views and informed why the BPP was ever willing to ally with the white working class at all. A decade later, in 1978, while he was completing his doctoral degree, Newton produced a full-length scholarly essay arguing that the British common people first experienced a thorough "internal colonization" before they were drafted to colonize the peoples beyond Europe. In the unpublished "Eclipse of Community: The Making of the English Working Class," Newton stated, "The English capitalist's first and most complete success at colonization was practiced upon his own countrymen."[67] Drawing on the work of Marxist British historian E. P. Thompson, Newton laid out the evidence that the enclosure of common lands by capitalists and its violent enforcement resulted in mass displacements of English peasants and made possible their forced move to industrial labor. This displacement was a process of colonization, argued Newton: "Once the English populace was 'freed' from its roots in the traditional village, generating a new surplus labor force ripe for exploitation by industrial entrepreneurs, the colonization of England was complete."[68] "That the colonizers were native-born does not change the character of the conquest."[69]

In this essay, Newton then built upon the scholarship of German sociologist Ferdinand Tönnies to explain the *cultural* colonization that followed, identifying the British peasantry's shift from a traditional culture of communalism (*Gemeinschaft*) to an individualistic society structured by contractual relations (*Gesellschaft*).[70] "Obligations of mutuality, which had once governed human relationship, became outmoded by the sweep of capitalist modernization."[71] Describing how capitalist culture affects colonized peoples *in general*, Newton emphasized: "Where once capitalist social relations had to be enforced by naked power, the disease of self-interest has now infected native populations."[72] He ends the essay with a provocative suggestion about why decolonial revolutions were able to develop during the twentieth century in the Third World: "Only where the dissolution of communalism had not proceeded as far – in Eastern Europe, Asia and Africa – did the resistance to capitalism grow to revolutionary proportions. Ironically, it was in the 'colonies' where the populations were not so thoroughly or successfully colonized as in England."[73] Newton argued that the Third World and Eastern Europe were *less thoroughly colonized* than capitalist Western Europe was, not just economically and politically, but most of all culturally.

Crucially, where cultural domination is *less* thorough, the use of physical violence is *more* common. For this view, Newton was building directly upon Fanon's opening remarks in *The Wretched of the Earth*, where he states:

> The colonized world is a world cut in two. . . . Within the capitalist countries, between the exploited and the powerful there intervene a multitude of moral teachers, counselors, and "disorientators." Within the colonial regions, on the contrary, the policeman and the soldier, by their immediate presence and their frequent and direct action maintain contact with the native and advise him, by means of rifle butts and napalm, not to budge. One can see, power's intermediary uses a language of pure force. The intermediary does not lighten the oppression, does not veil the domination.[74]

According to Newton's line of reasoning in his correspondence with the RNA, Black people "suffer from the colonial plight more than any ethnic group in the country" while nonetheless maintaining some level of native cultural autonomy. By contrast, the modern and capitalist identity of "whiteness" has essentially obliterated the communal culture of European Americans, who have been colonized for longer. This fits with the Black Panther Party's regular observation that the police are *physically* violent towards the Black community on a more regular basis, while the white college students of their time were just beginning to be exposed to this violence and the reality of the brutality of the empire. The white students are usually sufficiently controlled through what political scientists term "soft power," but occasionally the naked force of violence is deployed. As Seale explained at a speech at the University of California, Berkeley: "We are saying now that you can draw a direct relationship that is for real and that is not abstract anymore: you don't have to abstract what police brutality is like when a club is there to crush your skull; . . . you can see in fact that the real power of the power structure maintaining its racist regime is manifested in its occupying troops, and is manifested in its police department – with guns and force."[75]

The argument that medieval Europeans experienced something like an internal colonization has sometimes been used by white supremacist conservatives to argue for a return to a constructed past version of European nationality – a white nationalism. Newton's conception differs greatly from these views for several reasons. He was always critical of the mythicizing elevation of traditional cultures as a means to liberation. This was consistent with his and Seale's early critiques of efforts by some Black nationalists to claim to return to African cultural values as a path to political liberation. Instead, in Newton's view, moving *forward* from one's position in the present through a new "revolutionary culture" is the only progressive possibility. This was precisely Fanon's argument in *The Wretched of the Earth*, in which he described revolutionary culture as growing out of the creative recombinations and inventions of the colonized during their process of resisting the colonial system. As Party artist and Minister of Culture Emory Douglas explained: "Out of this struggle comes a new way of life based on the politics of the people's struggle."[76] Furthermore, Newton was critical of nationalisms because he believed that nations are obsolete altogether. As discussed earlier, he argued that it is impossible for people to "'decolonize' and return to their original existence as nations." Therefore, according to Newton – and contrary to conservative projects that aspire to make the country "great again" – even the US has ceased to be a nation-state and never will be again.

Consistent then with the theory of intercommunalism, Newton came to conclude that Americans, living at the center of the empire, are the most colonized of all: "At one time I thought that only Blacks were colonized. But I think we have to change our rhetoric to an extent because the whole American people have been colonized, if you view exploitation as a colonized effect."[77] To be precise and clear, "exploitation" is the accumulation of profit from the labor of another, and Newton is pointing out that exploitation of a person is only possible after they have been colonized – removed from their natural relationship to the land and then forced to work for a business owner and a wage. Newton was making clear that capitalism *always* requires a prior colonization:

> So, therefore, the whole American people are colonized people and even more so than the people in these developing

> countries where the militaries operate. And these are the points that we have to get across to the people to show them that we are a colonized people and lift their consciousness to a point to have a successful revolution.[78]

In his original remarks in the newspaper, he added: "Well, anyway, I won't go on with that. But I hope you get the point, and I hope I'm clear enough. But that is why the [white] Peace Movement is so important." Newton was likely aware that his line of argument remained misunderstood, evidenced in the fact that these ideas were never referenced in writing at any point by anyone else in the Party.

Newton had a unique theory of the American colonial condition that merged Third World decolonial thought with the revolutionary American liberal tradition.[79] This unique synthesis took into account the US's unique history as both a former colony and an empire. Despite the changes made to the Ten-Point Program between 1966 and 1972, one part that remained untouched was the direct quotation from the Declaration of Independence, which expressed the right of "the People" to fundamentally replace their government:[80]

> governments are instituted among men, deriving their just powers from the consent of the governed; [and] whenever any form of government becomes destructive of these ends, it is the right of the people to alter or abolish it, and to institute a new government, laying its foundation on such principles, and organizing its powers in such form, as to them shall seem most likely to effect their safety and happiness.

Two months after Newton was released from prison, he delivered a speech at the People's Constitutional Convention, an event organized by Eldridge Cleaver as a fulfillment of this part of the Ten-Point Program.[81] Philadelphia Panther Mumia Abu-Jamal later described the event as "a very real, conscious attempt to subvert the history of the colonials, by creating a historical icon: a constitution in which all ignored segments of the American polity could be heard and be represented."[82] The Convention failed to live up to its aims, in part due to Newton's skepticism about the practical sense in calling for a constitution without a working government. Nonetheless, Newton's effort to synthesize decolonial thought with modern liberalism remained consistent throughout his life.

In a 1974 political pamphlet titled "Eliminate the Presidency," Newton used Fanon's language in order to refer to all Americans: "We, wretched of the earth collected on these shores, could iron out the rough points if we clung to the idea of democracy: government by the people, of the people, for the people – all the people!"[83] And yet, in his later dissertation of 1980, Newton argued that "the two most crucial problems which have hindered the development of truly democratic government in America" are 1) "class and racial cleavages" and 2) a distrust by the ruling class of "any institutionalized democracy involving the mass population."[84] "There has been, in other words, from the very beginning of the American republic as we know it, a systematically cultivated polarization" by groups in power that has relied upon that "deeply ingrained belief that society by nature [is] divided into superior and inferior classes of people."[85]

The Lumpenization of the People

> In this country the Black Panther Party, taking careful note of the dialectical method, taking careful note of the social trends and the ever-changing nature of things, sees that while the lumpenproletarians are the minority and the proletarians are the majority, technology is developing at such a rapid rate that automation will progress to cybernation, and cybernation probably to technocracy. . . . If revolution does not occur almost immediately, and I say almost immediately because technology is making leaps (it made a leap all the way to the moon), and if the ruling circle remains in power the proletarian working class will definitely be on the decline because they will be unemployables and therefore swell the ranks of the lumpens, who are the present unemployables. Every worker is in jeopardy because of the ruling circle.[86]

On November 18, 1970, Newton presented his theory of intercommunalism to an audience at Boston College. Central to this speech was the argument that the American industrial working class would soon begin to shrink dramatically, displaced by innovations in technology. Human labor, Newton argued, would be replaced by automated machines and eventually computers. He saw *lumpenization* as increasingly common, an effect of the capitalist class's perpetual drive "to make as much money as possible, and pay the people as little as possible."[87] He was concerned about what this would mean for most Americans, but he recognized also that Black people already had known unemployment and the lumpenproletarian condition all too well.

The next February, Newton continued to present his ideas during a three-day seminar held at Yale University. In those discussions, he argued that the declining working-class proletariat would have a choice to make between striving for solidarity with the rest of the lumpenproletariat or instead choosing the "reactionary" path:

> And as these people become unemployables, they will become more and more alienated; even socialist compromises will not be enough. You will then find an integration between the black unemployable and the white racist hard hat who is not regularly employed and mad at the blacks who he thinks threaten his job. We hope that he will join forces with those people who are already unemployable, but whether he does or not, his material existence will have changed. The proletarian will become the lumpen proletarian. It is this future change – the increase of the lumpen proletariat and the decrease of the proletariat – which makes us say that the lumpen proletariat is the majority and carries the revolutionary banner.[88]

Much can be said today about the applicability of Newton's projections globally, where in so many countries millions struggle to lay claim to or maintain a grasp of fading visions of modern lived comfort, standards that billions across the century never glimpsed in the first place. His predictions resonate most loudly, however, for the United States. Sociologist John Narayan has written extensively about the applicability of Newton's ideas, explaining that "as the impact of reactionary intercommunalism took effect, and the wages of whiteness became ever absent, Newton believed that communities in the US would often 'feel more and more that it's a race contradiction rather than a class contradiction.'"[89] In Newton's view, race would continue to be leveraged to divide the population, even as humanity increasingly shared conditions of vulnerability. In his 1974 essay "Dialectics of Nature," he surmised that "even the populations of the Anglo-American Empire itself are in the process of being 'nativized' and pauperized in the name of the 'energy crisis.' This crisis is, however, one of capital, not one of energy."[90]

While contemporary economists debate over whether automation is best understood as a cause or a symptom of global capitalists' financial restructuring of infrastructure and assets, Newton's ideas nonetheless reflect considerable foresight. In part, he was directly inspired by the writings of Detroit socialist James Boggs, of whom Newton was a close reader.[91] In his 1963 *The American Revolution: Pages From a Negro Worker's Notebook*, Boggs was most concerned with the problem of whether humanity would recognize quickly enough the need to fully reorganize our economies in light of the transformative impacts of technology. To Boggs, the challenge was to exercise agency over this shift, which was redefining the human being's relationship to labor itself:

> Today when automation and cybernation are shrinking rather than expanding the work force, many people still think in the same terms. . . . They have not been able to face this fact because they have no clear idea of what people would do with themselves, what would be their human role, or how society would be organized when work is no longer at the heart of society.[92]

To Boggs' analysis Newton added a forecast about the falling value of the workers to the class of people who oversee and govern them:

> Today's capitalist has developed machinery to such a point that he can hire a group of specialized people called

> technocrats. In the near future he will certainly do more of this, and the technocrat will be too specialized to be identified as a proletarian. In fact that group of technocrats will be so vital we will have to do something to explain the presence of other people; we will have to come up with another definition and reason for existing.[93]

Technocracy is a form of government that is run by a class of technical experts whose job it is to regard all social phenomena, including the population itself, as data to analyze.

In predicting mass lumpenization, Newton saw much of humanity being regarded by elites as politically undesirable, socially inferior, and, thus, a danger to the overall health of the social body. In terming this broad sector of the population as *lumpenproletarian*, Newton was also signaling that he expected more and more of the population to be dehumanized as *criminals*. In other words, more of humanity would be thrown into something akin to the condition of Blackness, the condition of the youth, and the condition of the disabled. To be produced as part of the surplus population under capitalism is to be allowed or even actively made to perish.

However, this also meant, in turn, that more of the population might be in a position to take control over their own self-definition and purpose, motivated to transform society as a whole. "This is why reactionary intercommunalism, while it causes its own destruction, also lays the foundation for its own transformation; because without modern communication and all the rest of it, how would the youth of the world develop a common identity? A sense of themselves as oppressed?"[94] Newton saw cause for optimism in the very technologies used to devalue people, as human beings naturally use the tools at their disposal to make new meaning of their lives and strive for something better:

> At the same time, we say that this technology can solve most of the material contradictions people face, that the material conditions exist that would allow the people of the world to develop a culture that is essentially human and would nurture those things that would allow the people to resolve contradictions in a way that would not cause the mutual

> slaughter of all of us. The development of such a culture would be revolutionary intercommunalism.[95]

For Newton, at every juncture, there exists the possibility of choosing the path of freedom and the defense of life. "We can set the best example for our children by showing them how to love and how to fight against things that jeopardize the freedom of the people."[96]

In the broader scope of history, the era of the comfortably waged worker was relatively short-lived and exceptional. In the United States, the buying power of the working class was at its highest in 1970 and has declined more or less consistently since then.[97] On the world scale, more than 60 percent of workers worldwide are in temporary, part-time or short-term jobs and facing falling wages.[98] In 2022, feminist theorist Kathi Weeks affirmed, "The itinerant, informal, and occasional workers most clearly associated with Marx and Engels' original definition [of the lumpenproletariat] are becoming increasingly standard."[99] The standardization of the lumpen condition is not only about exposure to unemployment, however, but also about what kinds of things people do to compensate for their limited income. The US has increasingly seen the legalization, growth, and cultural normalization of formerly criminalized activities: gambling, online sex work, the sale of drugs, addiction, a "hustle culture" of self-commodification ("entrepreneurialism"), part-time work epitomized in the gig economy, and regional migration for seasonal work contracts.

At the same time, the conditions of criminalization and social control that used to exclusively target the poor have become generalized, too: the rate of incarceration has increased by 500 percent since 1970, electronic camera surveillance that used to be present only in urban spaces has proliferated, and digitized social credit systems once used for welfare recipients now take modern forms in the online availability of criminal and personal records. As sociologist Robert L. Allen pointed out in the 1960s: "African-Americans were fearful that concentration camps were being set up for rebellious black youth. Of course, these fears were dismissed by the media as unfounded, but today we have witnessed the growth of an enormous prison industrial complex that thrives on the incarceration of black males and other youth of color."[100] Since then, what other early warning calls from the Black community have been ignored? In 2024, Black philosopher of science Ruha Benjamin urged that we "consider the ongoing threats to our shared social imagination from the imposition of a techno-utopian, eugenic imagination that seeks to colonize all ways of thinking and being in the world."[101]

As lumpen conditions become generalized, they also become profoundly normalized and accepted. Americans continue to culturally identify as "middle class," even as their standards of life approach conditions of poverty. Cultural colonization means that people are more inclined to identify with the lifestyles of the super-wealthy, even as those very people look down upon the rest of us. Because the lived conditions of Black people, the poor, and the most oppressed are associated with the subhuman and the inferior, many struggle to psychologically relate to these realities, even as more of our lives increasingly resemble them.

And yet, Newton also believed that lives lived under greater oppressions also contain within them unique insights and clarity about the value of human dignity. It was his deep belief in the generosity and spirit of openness typical among the poorest that J. Herman Blake once called "the genius of Huey Newton, in my opinion."[102] Blake spoke with inspiration of the "brilliance of bringing that perspective to bear in a mass, organized way."[103] The spirit of communal care that develops out of sheer necessity among the poorest might be precisely what is needed to invigorate a movement for collective well-being.[104] Otherwise, as Newton argued, the normalization of impoverishment, the caging of human beings, and the expansion of newer technologies of colonization pose a threat to us all, likely to worsen unless we act collectively.

4

The Soul Breaker

It is impossible to summarize the biological response to an act of will in a life of submission.

Elaine Brown (1992)[1]

Solitary Confinement

The year is 1964. Two years before co-founding the Black Panther Party, a twenty-two-year old Huey P. Newton is confined to solitary confinement, in a sensory deprivation cell known as "the soul breaker." In a space "four and a half feet wide, six feet long, ten feet high," he is kept in complete isolation, with no possessions, naked, in perpetual darkness:

> The floor was dark red rubber tile, and the walls were black. . . . There was no bunk, no washbasin, no toilet, nothing but bare floors, bare walls, a solid steel door, and a round hole four inches in diameter and six inches deep in the middle of the floor. The prisoner was supposed to urinate and defecate in this hole. . . . After a few days the hole filled up and overflowed, so that I could not lie down without wallowing in my own waste. . . . After two or three days most men would begin to scream and beg for someone to come and take them out.[2]

Recounting his experiences in solitary, Newton described what later psychiatrists would term "SHU syndrome." Such "security housing units" produce depression, suicidal behavior, and a disintegration of one's felt sense of self and the external world.[3] Newton explained:

> Outside jail, the brain is always being bombarded by external stimuli. These ordinary sights and sounds of life help keep our mental processes in order, rational. In deprivation, you have to somehow replace the stimuli, provide an interior environment for yourself. . . . I began to reflect on the most soothing parts of my past . . . to reinforce myself in some kind of rewarding experience . . . but if you are not disciplined a strange thing happens. A pleasant thought comes, and then another and another, like quick cuts flashing vividly across a movie screen . . . Then they start to pick up speed, pushing in on top of one another, going faster, faster, faster, faster. The pleasant thoughts are not so pleasant; they are horrible and grotesque caricatures, whirling around in your head. Stop! I heard myself say, stop stop stop![4]

The young Newton was able to overcome this mental disorientation through a combination of physical exercises, held postures, and a conscious exertion of his will.

> Over a span of time – I do not know how long it took – I mastered my thoughts. I could start them and stop them; I could slow them down and speed them up. It was a very conscious exercise. For a while, I feared I would lose control. I could not think; I could not stop thinking. Only later did I learn through practice to go at the speed I wanted. . . . Soon, I could lie with my back arched for hours on end, and I placed no importance on the passage of time. Control. I learned to control my food, my body, and my mind through a deliberate act of will. . . . No longer dependent on the things of the world, I felt really free for the first time in my life.[5]

This feat allowed him to reorganize his own thoughts and his affects – those most basic emotions based in the evolutionarily older parts of our brains and physical bodies – through exercise and willful intentionality over his body and mind. Surrounded by darkness and confusion, experiencing profound epistemological disorientation, Newton found freedom in self-control. This is how he described his experience of overcoming in his autobiography *Revolutionary Suicide*. And yet, his unpublished writings offer a somewhat different picture of how he found freedom.

As a whole, the published *Revolutionary Suicide* is a counterintuitively tranquil book, despite the personal and social sufferings Newton describes in it, the wide-ranging learnedness and intellectualism, and his effort to inspire both his politically moderate and militant readers. It is nuanced and careful when it describes lumpen life so that those realities may be empathized with. Yet, perhaps because of the care put into it, *Revolutionary Suicide* was dismissed by mainstream critics in its era for not being antagonistic enough, a disappointment for those expecting rage, bigotry, or violence.[6]

The archive containing Newton's unpublished writings and personal papers is massive. Among the more than 200 boxes are about 300 pages of an alternative version of his autobiography, transcribed by J. Herman Blake. Its front page features the title *These Graves Are All Too Young*, as well as an excerpt from the poem that inspires it: Percy Bysshe Shelley's *Adonais: An Elegy on the Death of John Keats*.[7] The quoted fifty-first stanza begins: "these graves are all too young as yet / to have outgrown the sorrow which consigned / its charge to each." Shelley's lines are a reference to the death of his young son, which he was still striving to recover from.[8] By comparison with *Revolutionary Suicide*, *These Graves Are All Too Young* is even more humane and cerebral. Thematically it is more focused on detachment and notions of freedom rooted in independence from socially constructed desires. It is more philosophical in general, explicitly discussing epistemology (the study of how we know) and ontology (the study of what being is), and it consistently emphasizes the importance of honesty in social and political matters.

In both texts, Newton identified his experiences in solitary as the source of his first experience of true freedom. In contrast with *Revolutionary Suicide*, however, *All Too Young* described this freedom as following from *detachment* rather than *control*:

> I realized that in order to survive through this experience it would be necessary for me to detach myself from the things I had previously thought were necessary for bare existence . . . When I had done this in my mind, I saw that I could live through the experience and not decay physically or become mentally disturbed. . . . And when I saw that they were not going to conquer my will I recognized that I had a strength which they did not possess: I was in their control but I actually felt stronger than them. I understood them much better than they understood me, and I also found myself no longer dependent on the things they had taught me were necessary to survive. When I realized that I no longer needed these things, then I really felt free.[9]

Panther Elaine Brown, who had an intimate relationship with Newton in the 1970s and also chaired the BPP during his exile in Cuba between 1974 and 1977, offered in her autobiography her recollection of how Newton described the experience to her. Remarkably, her description reads like a synthesis of both of Newton's written narratives, but with a greater emphasis on the themes that appear in *All Too Young*. She described how he exerted a measure of psychological self-control but what ultimately allowed him success was the act of release. In her words:

> He fell on his back and tried to find a position that would ward off madness. He began to hear the sound of his own breathing. He clung to it. He heard his heartbeat start to regulate. That was when he "let go," reached out with his mind to the expanse of infinity. He began to feel at peace, he said. He stopped throwing up, and he stopped trying to mark time.[10]

If we take all three narratives into account, we can infer that Newton managed to figure out a particular balance between willful self-control on the one hand and detached release on the other, with self-control as the principal element and release as the secondary, in order to not completely lose his mind and instead find freedom. His jailers had attempted to exert complete control over him, seizing his body and violating his mind in order to "break his soul." He refused to be a victim, instead insisting on survival and defense of his body and self. This refusal to have his experiences determined by others was grounded, first, in control of the flows of his body and a conscious management of his inner experiences, and then, ultimately, in physical exercise, discipline, and relaxation. After his release from prison, Newton learned that he had independently discovered a traditional "Zen Buddhist posture."[11]

Newton's experiences in solitary were foundational for him in several ways.[12] They shaped not just how he understood freedom but how he viewed the nature of reality as a whole. Years later, when explaining the philosophical ideas behind the strategy of how the Black Panther Party should move forward, he would begin from the position of *radical doubt*, much as he had been forced to do within the soul breaker. Absolutely everything about reality would be questioned, and it was from that stance that he would build a method for practical action. We can also see in Newton's prison experiences an early example of the principal method that he applied throughout the rest of his life: *dialectical materialism*. That is, he sought to leverage the negative against the positive to arrive at a position of progress. And, finally, Newton's later theory of how to politically organize the experiences of the people, through what he termed the *structured vehicle*, was essentially an extension of the same approach he took in the cell to channel his own experiences towards freedom.

Radical Doubt

Most of the first philosophers that Newton read were skeptics – thinkers whose approaches were shaped by doubt about how we can claim to know what we know about the world. After "struggling through . . . Socrates, as well as . . . Aristotle, Hume, and Descartes, I began to question what I had always taken for granted. . . . In a way, the turmoil and conflict I was experiencing were a kind of madness, with no way out."[13] As he learned philosophy, he took the ideas to heart, and questioned everything about his life. He considered joining a monastery, "not so much out of religious conviction as for the isolation and time to examine these questions in peace."[14] He began to doubt his very senses and even the meaning of pain and suffering, walking barefoot in the rain, embracing asceticisms and existentialisms: "From then on, I began to engage friends in existentialist discussions. If a brother was hungry, I would say that it is all the same whether you are hungry or full, whether you are cold or warm. It is all the same. They *really* thought I was crazy."[15] Even before his experience in solitary, Newton had concluded that, to a larger degree than we usually acknowledge, how we relate to our experiences is up to us.

The first full essay that Newton dictated for *The Black Panther*, "Fear and Doubt," was also inspired by existentialism and a close examination of lived experience.[16] Themes in this essay included utter confusion, self-blame, forms of compensation, and impostor syndrome. Despite many similarities to Frantz Fanon's treatise *Black Skin, White Masks*, the relationship between Newton's essay and Fanon's work has not been discussed by scholars. And yet, Newton read Fanon's books with devotion.[17] In the spring of 1970, while still imprisoned, he invoked Fanon in his debates with the psychiatrists assigned to produce a psychological profile of him:

> The psychiatrist insisted that I had a bias against psychological testing. He was correct. In response to this I showed him flaws in the psychological systems of Freud, Jung, Skinner, and others that made these systems inapplicable to Black people. When he asked whether there was any psychological system that I could trust, I told him I accepted the theories of Frantz Fanon. He had never heard of him, so I suggested some books by Fanon that he could read, and left.[18]

Like in Fanon's *Black Skin, White Masks*, the subject of Newton's "Fear and Doubt" is the specifically male Black subject whose experience of racial oppression throws him into a profound feeling of non-being and ontological nihilism relative to the world. Both Fanon and Newton viewed subjective experience as inseparable from how we are treated socially, and thus described Blackness as akin to being turned into a "non-entity." Yet, whereas Fanon's analysis of the Black male figure was largely concerned with how he is rendered "an object in the midst other objects" and an evil fantasy in the minds of the whites who encounter him, Newton's concern was with how this Black male figure relates to both other Black people in his community and to the broader white society.[19] According to Newton, "Society responds to him as a thing, a beast, a nonentity, something to be ignored or stepped on," but also, "as a man, he finds himself void of those things that bring respect and a feeling of worthiness. He looks around for something to blame for his situation, but because he is not sophisticated regarding the socio-economic milieu and because of negativistic parental and institutional teachings, he ultimately blames himself."[20]

As a philosopher, Fanon's approach to understanding the human condition in general and Blackness in particular was based in the philosophy of phenomenology, an approach to knowledge that centers lived experience as the basis of knowledge of self and world. Fanon incorporated phenomenology into his writing after attending the influential lectures of French philosopher Maurice Merleau-Ponty at the University of Lyon in the late 1940s.[21] And Merleau-Ponty was himself inspired to study phenomenology after attending the first lectures on the topic at Sorbonne University delivered by Edmund Husserl, who is considered a founding philosopher of phenomenology.[22] Phenomenology, especially as formulated by Husserl, "is a philosophical reflection on the way in which objects show themselves – how objects appear or manifest themselves – and on the conditions of possibility for this appearance."[23]

Fanon also built upon the work of philosopher G. W. F. Hegel, who preceded and influenced Husserl and covertly included a critique of racial slavery in his classic *Phenomenology of Spirit* (1807). According to Hegel, the master ("lord") depends upon the slave ("bondsman") existentially for their sense of being (as master), whereas the slave has the independence of their labor through which they can be confident that they exist independently.[24] Newton read Hegel and made use of some of his ideas, but was also critical because Hegel believed that ideas have independent existence in the world (since we can be said, after all, to "experience" them), a philosophical view known as *idealism*. Although Newton did not read Husserl until the late 1970s, his approach to phenomenology was rather closer to Husserl's than to Hegel's.

All three of Newton, Fanon, and Husserl relied upon a deeply *skeptical* foundation to their thought, and they doubted the independent existence of not just ideas but even matter.[25] For these three thinkers, the earlier philosophical skeptic René Descartes was a key influence. In Descartes' *Meditations* (1641), the philosopher began with an account of sitting in his library engaged in a profound questioning of virtually all of his felt reality. Through three major steps, Descartes questioned 1) whether his five senses might be faulty, 2) whether all his senses might in fact be useless because he might be dreaming, and 3) whether even how he experiences might be in fact controlled by a *génie* – a "demon" or evil "genius." A contemporary analogy for the evil *génie* example is the idea that one's brain might be being controlled by a deceptive machine, directly or remotely.

In his approach to philosophical questions, Newton's starting point was, like Descartes', profoundly grounded in skepticism. At the peak of the Party's existence, during a week-long seminar held at Yale in 1971 with psychologist Erik Erikson, Newton's introductory speech began exactly this way, admitting to the arbitrariness of knowledge, considering both idealism and nihilism, and invoking Descartes' three doubts, though without naming him:

> The Black Panther Party has chosen materialist assumptions on which to ground its ideology. This is a purely arbitrary choice. Idealism might be the real happening. We might not be here at all. We don't really know whether we are in Connecticut or in San Francisco, whether we are dreaming and in a dream state, or whether we are awake and in a dream state. Perhaps we are just somewhere in a void; we simply can't be sure.[26]

> There are many different ideologies or schools of thought, and all of them start with an *a priori* set of assumptions. This is because mankind is still limited in its knowledge and finds it hard, at this historical stage, to talk about the very beginning of things and the very end of things without starting from premises that cannot yet be proved.[27]

Husserl used the ancient term *epoché* to refer to this radical suspension of belief that puts everything, including the self, into question.[28] According to ancient philosopher Sextus Empiricus, *epoché* is a mental state according to which one neither denies nor affirms anything. In Newton's view, radical doubt of everything was not just necessary as a starting point in order to produce political thought, but was in fact unavoidable. Newton had already experienced this profound *epoché* through existential philosophical questioning, through the lived experience of Blackness, and, most of all, in the solitary confinement of the soul breaker. From there, by overcoming the abyss of doubt, he developed a strong basis for a sense of self, freedom, power, and eventually, political organization.

Experience and Reason

Newton's approach to philosophy was grounded in the skeptical tradition as a starting point, but he worked his way to greater knowledge through the scientific method. By definition, science combines on the one hand *observations*, which are strictly speaking a limited set of subjective experiences, with on the other hand *generalizations*, which are based upon those observations and produced through the application of *rationality*. In short, Newton saw the process of developing knowledge for political change as best grounded in the pursuit of a scientific striving towards objectivity:

> I would like to explain to you the method that the Black Panther Party used to arrive at our ideological position, and more than that, I would like to give to you a framework or a process of thinking that might help us solve the problems and the contradictions that exist today. Before we approach the problem we must get a clear picture of what is really going on; a clear image divorced from the attitudes and emotions that we usually project into a situation. We must be as objective as possible without accepting dogma, letting the facts speak for themselves. But we will not remain totally objective; we will become subjective in the application of the knowledge received from the external world. We will use

> the scientific method to acquire this knowledge, but we will openly acknowledge our ultimate subjectivity.[29]

> The only constant we have is the goal of freedom for black people. And that's actually a *subjective* goal. . . . But in order to attain our subjective goal, we have to become as objective as possible.[30]

Observation was the cornerstone of the Black Panther Party's practice as "scientific socialists," exemplified in the surveys that Newton and Seale conducted in the earliest days of the Party, as well as their reflections on their own life experiences.[31] Even the original version of "Correct Handling of a Revolution" began with an analysis of how humans learn and develop an "indirect relationship to the object."[32]

To understand how Newton was able to see a clear line connecting lived experience and science requires a clear understanding of the tradition of *empiricism*. Strictly speaking, empiricism is based on the application of a disciplined approach to subjective experience – contrary to some popular beliefs that associate empiricism with abstract data. Newton stated that "empiricism means observation and experience," and the word empiricism itself comes from the Latin root *empeiria*, which translates literally as "experience."[33] The English word was first used in the seventeenth century to describe an approach in medicine, as in "a physician guided by experience."[34]

In *Revolutionary Suicide*, when Newton names a second set of philosophers that were foundational for him in college, all of them are identifiable as part of the Western tradition of empiricism:

> I talked to the brothers about things that Hume, Peirce, Locke, or William James had said, and in that way I retained ideas and sometimes resolved problems in my own mind. These thinkers had used the scientific method by applying their ideas to particular formulas. They excluded those things that did not fit into the formulas.[35]

On the whole, these philosophers held the view that knowledge comes from experience primarily. For some of them, experience is the only source of knowledge, while for others experience is the best approach to knowledge, but all in some manner affirm its centrality. All in all, *everything* is said to be just another type of experience. The dominant term in philosophy for describing the points of "sense data" that make up experiential knowledge is *phenomenon* (when singular) or *phenomena* (when plural). These words come from the Greek *phainomenon*, meaning "that which appears." And, as we discuss further on, Newton explicitly defined *power* as the ability to define a phenomenon and make it act in a desired manner.[36]

In a 1970 interview, Newton affirmed his deep interest in pragmatism, an American philosophical school with roots in empiricism: "I was very interested by pragmatism, and after we did a unit on it of two weeks, I went back to pragmatism – Peirce, [and] I studied William James in depth. Then on the [19]20s when logical positivism took over with A. J. Ayer, I went over that and I could understand it because I studied everything about it."[37] Yet, unlike the pragmatists, who have been characterized – by philosopher Cornel West – as "evading" the implications of radical doubt in order to focus on matters of practice, Newton's practical philosophy actively and creatively integrated the question of how we can truly know into his concept of politics.[38] His approach was thereby a unique intervention into the American philosophical tradition.

Newton managed to accomplish this because he understood that the "analytical tradition" of the Anglo-American philosophers (some of whom focused on experience, empiricism, and pragmatism) and the "continental tradition" of the European philosophers (some of whom focused on experience, radical doubt, and phenomenology) shared a foundational influence in the ideas of German philosopher Immanuel Kant. Kant's ideas were the focus of a series of lectures Newton delivered in 1971 at Merritt College titled "A Primary Introduction to Phenomena" as well as a set of political education classes he taught in Oakland.[39] Kant's writings are considered among the most dense in the canon of Western philosophy. Kant brought attention to and grappled with the limits of the concept of *phenomena* after reading the work of his greatest influence, Scottish philosopher David Hume, who instead used the word "impressions" to talk about this basic element of experience.[40] Kant and Hume agreed that our experiences are basically all we can ever know, but Kant further argued that pure reason allows us access to truth as well (see below).

Hume is twice mentioned in *Revolutionary Suicide*, in the context of Newton's studies at Merritt College.[41] Hume was both a skeptic and an empiricist, which means that he accepted that all we can know is that we experience, even if we cannot truly know what causes it. For Hume, the self is "nothing but a bundle or collection of different perceptions, which succeed each other with an inconceivable rapidity, and are in a perpetual flux and movement."[42] "What we call a mind, is nothing but a heap or collection of different perceptions, united together by certain relations, and supposed, though falsely, to be endowed with a perfect simplicity and identity."[43] Besides being known as a founding empiricist, Hume also directly influenced phenomenology, because Husserl developed his philosophy of phenomenology through his reading of Hume, crediting him with producing "the first phenomenology."[44] The real historical relationship between these schools of thought helps explain why Newton's thinking was able to connect so many seemingly different thinkers.[45] He understood clearly that they are all simply analyzing the phenomena of experience and observation in some manner or another.

When it comes to analyzing experience and appearances, sometimes empiricism is understood to focus excessively on the sense of sight; this is an appropriate characterization of the empiricism of John Locke. However, most philosophical empiricisms – like David Hume's skeptical empiricism or William James's radical empiricism – strive to take *all the senses* into account in a way similar to phenomenology, just as a rigorous scientist uses all their senses when noting differences in the phenomena they observe. Being practical, however, Newton also sought to avoid the excessive *subjectivity* associated with some philosophies of experience. For him, empiricism's focus on observation should be a route to grasping the "objective" external world as much "as possible." And so, though he conceded that we cannot know "the objective" for certain, he identified himself as a materialist grounded in scientific observation:

> But because the members of the Black Panther Party are materialists we believe that some day scientists will be able

> to deliver the information that will give us not only the evidence but the proof that there is a material world and that its genesis was material – motion and matter – not spiritual. Until that time, however, and for the purposes of this discussion, I merely ask that we agree on the stipulation that a material world exists and develops externally and independently of us; and we assume that the human organism, through its sensory system, has the ability to observe and analyze that material world.[46]

Newton clearly identified limits to empiricism, and in his first speeches after leaving prison he spoke of the need to grapple with and overcome those limits.

At Boston College, Newton explained how he navigated the limits of empiricism, as well as those of rationalism, in order to develop a dialectical materialism:

> The scientific method relies heavily on empiricism. But the problem with empiricism is that it tells you very little about the future; it tells you only about the past, about information which you have already discovered through observation and experience. It always refers to past experience.
>
> Long after the rules of empirical knowledge had been ascertained, a man by the name of Karl Marx integrated these rules with a theory developed by Immanuel Kant called rationale. Kant called his process of reasoning pure reason because it did not depend on the external world. Instead it only depended on consistency in manipulating symbols in order to come up with a conclusion based upon reason. For example, in this sentence "If the sky is above my head, when I turn my head upwards, I will see the sky" there is nothing wrong with the conclusion. As a matter of fact, it is accurate. But I haven't said anything about the existence of the sky. I said "if." With rationale we are not dependent upon the external world. With empiricism we can tell very little about the future. So what will we do? What Marx did. In order to understand what was happening in the world Marx found it necessary to integrate rationale with empiricism. He called his concept dialectical materialism. If, like

> Marx, we integrate these two concepts or these two ways of thinking, not only are we in touch with the world outside us but we can also explain the constant state of transformation. Therefore, we can also make some predictions about the outcome of certain social phenomena that is not only in constant change but also in conflict.[47]

Newton used the word "rationale" to refer to rationalism, the application of formal logic to ideas to attain knowledge. Kant believed that we cannot truly know the objective world in itself, but he also believed that our capacity for rationality can nonetheless provide some access to truth and thereby validate some of our experiences. In just a few sentences, drawing from these traditions, Newton offered a critique of empiricism based on its *temporal* limits and a critique of rationalism based on the importance of *context*. Once again, Newton strives to strike a balance between two elements in order to reach a synthesis from which he can move forward, as he did in the soul breaker.

For Newton, these questions were connected to an ongoing global debate in the twentieth century among philosophers of the political left over the philosophical and practical meaning of *materialism*.[48] How does one obtain a good enough understanding of the material world so that the practical and strategic moves that one makes are successful politically? After all, in the often-quoted words of Karl Marx: "The philosophers have only variously interpreted the world; the point, however, is to change it."[49]

In interviews many years later, Newton identified Vladimir Lenin's *Materialism and Empirio-Criticism* as important for helping him in college think through precisely how he would relate to the question of knowledge and politics.[50] Specifically, he found the Russian communist leader's analysis inadequate, and during the "Primary Introduction to Phenomena" lectures he critiqued Lenin for his "mechanistic materialism" and "dogma."[51] This critique of mechanistic materialism targeted oversimplified accounts of the physical world according to which "change is based on permanent and stable things with definite fixed properties [and] change takes place only as the result of some external cause."[52] This is essentially the version of physics established by Isaac Newton, according to which 1) the world consists only of physical matter, and 2) every effect follows from a prior cause. Huey Newton considered this theory inadequate because it failed to explain the beginning of the universe.

Notes from J. Herman Blake's notebook state: "The mechanistic materialist cannot explain development. For him things operate in a static manner. He cannot explain the beginning of things except in an idealistic way."[53] Newton explained to his audience: "At this point I can't prove that motion is put into matter by a material force itself, because Lenin couldn't prove it. He didn't, he hedged in *Empirio-Criticism* and I'm not going to do that so I criticize Lenin for his *Empirio-Criticism*, just as [I do] Cornforth. They're not good books because they try to indoctrinate you."[54] Lenin's defense of "mechanistic materialism" included a rejection of the "scientific phenomenalism" of Ernest Mach. Mach's writings, which were gaining popularity in Russia in the years leading up to the Soviet revolution in 1917, criticized the ideas of Isaac Newton and argued that science was most precise when it acknowledged observation and sensory experiences as *relative*. Mach's ideas ended up influencing Albert Einstein's theory of relativity, as well as phenomenology, American pragmatism, and logical positivism – all schools of thought that appealed to Huey Newton.[55] Albert Einstein famously established that measurements of motion are in fact physically affected by the observer's frame of reference – that time, space, and motion are relative to the speed and gravity of the observer.

Opposed to Mach's new ideas, Lenin called him a "sophist" (a philosopher who uses words to deceive) and accused him of "Kantian and Humean agnosticism."[56] Lenin dismissed these kinds of nuanced approaches to experience and reason, asserting instead that if an action is successful it proves that the philosophy behind it was correct.[57] In Newton's view, however, this was an example of refusing to deal with the limits of human knowledge and simply asserting that we know. Like Lenin, Newton was deeply devoted to revolutionary practice, but he was also genuinely invested in finding honest answers to philosophical questions. More importantly, a false philosophy would inevitably lead to flawed politics. In sum, Newton valued creative syntheses of empiricism (experience) and rationalism (reason) and he was critical of overly mechanistic interpretations of reality.[58]

There has also been little attention paid to the fact that Newton explicitly identified logical positivism, another synthesis of empiricism and rationalism, as influential not just for his own philosophical development but, by extension, for the practice of the Black Panther Party.[59] Newton made strategic use of the philosophy when coining new language to be used by the Party:

> I was impressed with A. J. Ayer's logical positivism, particularly his distinction between three kinds of statements – the analytical statement, the synthetic statement, and statements of assumption. These ideas have helped me to develop my own thinking and ideology. Ayer once stated, "Nothing can be real if it cannot be conceptualized, articulated, and shared." That notion stuck with me and became very important when I began to use the ideological method of dialectical materialism as a world view. The ideology of the Black Panthers stands on that premise and proceeds on that basis, to conceptualize, articulate, and share. Some key aspects of Black Panther ideology and rhetoric, like "All Power to the People" and the concept "pig," developed out of that. They were not haphazardly introduced into our thinking or vocabulary.[60]

Analytical statements are those whose truth-value (the matter of whether they are true or false) is due to the very definitions of the words themselves (e.g. *All panthers are mammals*). By contrast, synthetic statements are those whose truth-value depends on an interpretation of dynamics in the world (e.g. *Some panthers are black*).[61] In *All Too Young*, Newton implicitly defined "facts" as essentially analytic and "truth" as essentially synthetic: "Facts are those phenomena which exist in the external world, and which are independent of the existence of man. Truth is the understanding which man develops based upon the facts of the external world, so there can be no truth without man."[62] In his lectures at Merritt College, he explained: "You could have facts without your individual existence, objective facts, but you cannot have truth without the existence of someone to articulate or say the word."[63]

In *Revolutionary Suicide*, Newton also attributed how he thought about language to the influence of philosopher Friedrich

Nietzsche. This influence is perhaps counterintuitive, because Nietzsche's approach to philosophy was profoundly anti-rationalist. But Nietzsche was also an early existentialist, and his writings appealed to Newton in varied ways. One way was through the belief that language directly shapes how we experience reality. Accordingly, one can identify a strong correlation between Newton's definition of "truths" as inseparable from human understanding and Nietzsche's famous "transvaluation of values," the idea that truths and values are socially constructed by humanity and thus inseparable from struggles over power.[64]

> Words are another way of defining phenomena, and the definition of any phenomenon is the first step to controlling it or being controlled by it.
>
> When I read Nietzsche's *The Will to Power*, I learned much from a number of his philosophical insights. This is not to say that I endorse all of Nietzsche, only that many of his ideas have influenced my thinking. Because Nietzsche was writing about concepts fundamental to all men, and particularly about the meaning of power, some of his ideas are pertinent to the way Black people live in the United States; they have had a great impact on the development of the Black Panther philosophy.
>
> Nietzsche believed that beyond good and evil is the will to power. In other words, good and evil are labels for phenomena, or value judgments. . . . Man attempts to define phenomena in such a way that they reflect the interests of his own class or group. He gives titles or values to phenomena according to what he sees as beneficial: if it is to his advantage, something is called good, and if it is not beneficial, then it is defined as evil.[65]

Newton goes on to describe how the word *villain* was first used in Europe to criminalize poor people who lived in *villages*, how the word *black* was first imposed onto Afrodiasporic people to dehumanize them (though later reappropriated as a term of empowerment), and how the Black Panther Party employed the term *pig* against police officers to allow members to verbally and psychologically challenge police without being arrested for vulgarity.[66] "The Panthers are always coining words because we have to keep defining the new reality, the new phenomena."[67]

> Another expression that helped to raise Black people's consciousness is "All Power to the People." An expression that has meaning on several levels – political, economic, and metaphysical – it was coined by the Black Panther Party around the same time as "pig," and has also gained wide acceptance. When we created it, I had in mind some distinct philosophical goals for the community that many people did not understand.[68]

Power: Defining Phenomena

Because Newton was an expansive thinker, he built upon overlaps and connections between the ideas of different philosophers. Despite profound differences between, say, the scientific empiricists and the anti-rationalism of Nietzsche, Newton drew from both and built upon their shared influences, adding depth to his own concepts in a way that is easily overlooked.

Radical empiricist William James described "pure experience" as "the immediate flux of life which furnishes the material to our later reflection with its conceptual categories . . . a *that* which is not yet any definite *what*."[69] In a different context, inspired by the ancient Greek aphorism that "one never steps in the same river twice," Nietzsche wrote: "Yes my brothers, is everything not *now in flux*? Have all railings and footbridges not fallen into the water? Who could still *hang on* to 'good' and 'evil?'"[70] In the original version of his speech at Boston College, we see that Newton used the same concept of "flux," likely inspired by both philosophers: "So tonight I would ask you to stipulate that an external world exists. . . . The second thing that I would like for you to stipulate is that things are in a constant state of change, or transformation, rather. In other words, flux, flux, all is flux. After we agree to that, we can go on with our discussion."[71] For Newton, the basic ground of reality is indeterminable and subject to constant change. In fact, the basis of reality is *change* itself.

While Newton drew from a wide range of philosophical influences, he remained throughout the course of his life most consistently an existentialist. That is, he believed deeply in the importance of human choice and self-determination in the face of flux, uncertainty, and human limits. "Indeed we are all – Black and white alike – ill in the same way, mortally ill. But before we die, how shall we live? I say with hope and dignity; and if premature death is the result, that death has a meaning that reactionary suicide can never have. It is the price of self-respect."[72] Newton considered the character of the "Preacher" in the Bible's book of Ecclesiastes "the first existentialist."[73] In his early twenties, he internalized the ideas of existentialists Albert Camus and Jean-Paul Sartre.[74] In his late thirties, he read Søren Kierkegaard extensively.[75] At the height of the Party's influence, however, his ideas were profoundly Nietzschean.[76] Against a ground of flux, against existential uncertainty especially for the most oppressed, Newton affirmed the "will to power":

> Once we apply knowledge in order to *will* a certain outcome[,] our objectivity ends and our subjectivity begins. We call this integrating theory with practice, and this is what the Black Panther Party is all about.[77]
>
> When we coined the expression "All Power to the People," we had in mind emphasizing the word "Power," for we recognize that the *will to power is the basic drive of man*. But it is incorrect to seek power over people. We have been subjected to the dehumanizing power of exploitation and racism for hundreds of years; and the Black community has its own will to power also. What we seek, however, is not power over people, but the power to control our own destiny. For us the true definition of power is not in terms of how many people you can control. To us power is, first of all, the ability to define phenomena, and secondly the ability to make these phenomena act in a desired manner.[78]

So many of the Black Panther Party's terms, concepts, and images have become so integrated into popular and mainstream culture that their philosophical and politically charged origins have been completely forgotten. This is perhaps truest for Newton's concept of *power*, central to the Party motto "all power to the people" and later popularized through the derivative term *empowerment* (coined in the 1990s). Newton's concept of power is about redefining reality through how we define and relate to our experiences and changes occurring in our communities. Newton's definition departs from the original meaning of power, which has Latin roots referring exclusively to authority and military force. Newton's notion of *power* is instead expansive enough that *anyone* can exercise it in *any dimension* of their lives, insofar as they are *defining phenomena* – the flux of experiences – in a manner that aligns with their desires.

The term "Black power" was perhaps first used in 1954 by socialist author Richard Wright for the title of his novel, *Black Power: A Record of Reactions in a Land of Pathos*. It was echoed by Harlem congressman Adam Clayton Powell, but ultimately popularized during a rally in 1966 by SNCC activists Stokely Carmichael and Willie Ricks. Although the phrase had socialist roots, its most mainstream uses tended to align it with Black capitalism.[79] Accordingly, Newton and the Black Panther Party in fact rarely used the phrase "Black power."[80] Instead, building upon their more inclusive motto "all power to the people," Newton put forth the most philosophically rigorous definition of *power* in the era, beginning in 1968.[81] Although French philosopher Michel Foucault's writings on *power* are better known among some, it is most likely that Foucault himself was inspired to formulate his distinct concept of *power-knowledge* – a Nietzsche-influenced idea of power as inseparable from "truth" – as a result of his encounter with *The Black Panther* newspaper and Newton's writings in 1968.[82]

Notably, Newton's definition might be said to carry a central tension or ambiguity. On the one hand, because *phenomena* include literally everything that appears to any of our senses, from aspects of the self to everything external to us, the exercise of *power* can at its extremes extend over anything and everything. On the other hand, in the above quotation, Newton is explicit that the power to dominate is not the type of power that the Black community (he argues) is interested in, because the experience of Blackness has consisted of precisely this sort of dehumanizing treatment. Newton's use of Nietzsche's will to power did not veer towards the ruthless abandonment of ethics that predominates in so many interpretations of the German philosopher's ideas.[83] For Newton and the BPP, Black power was always principally about *self-determination* and the recognition that true self-determination includes power over key aspects of one's phenomenal environment as well: "we have to acknowledge that and say that in order for the people to be free, they will have to control the institutions of their community, and have some form of representations in the technological center that they have produced."[84] In addition, it is clear that Newton saw conscious awareness as a necessary step for people to be able to *define* and *will* power over the flux of experience that control them, whether those controls be "internal" (he cites Freud) or "external" (he cites Marx):[85]

> The primary concern of the Black Panther Party is to lift the level of consciousness of the people through theory and practice to the point where they will see exactly what is controlling them and what is oppressing them, and therefore see exactly what has to be done – or at least what the first step is.[86]
>
> We call it "communism" because at this point in history people will not only control the productive and institutional units of society, but they will also have seized possession of their own subconscious attitudes toward these things; and for the first time in history they will have a more rather than less conscious relationship to the material world – people, plants, books, machines, media, everything – in which they live. They will have power, that is, they will control the phenomena around them and make it act in some desired manner, and they will know their own real desires. The first step in this process is the seizure by the people of their own communities.[87]

Dialectical Materialism

For the most part, Newton also avoided what Nietzsche critically referred to as "slave morality."[88] This is when the oppressed, simply by inverting the values of the oppressor, take the view that everything having to do with the oppressor is evil and everything associated with the oppressed is good. Instead, because he was invested in the method of *dialectical materialism* above all, Newton was always inclined to interpret phenomena in their complexity, holding the view that everything has both good and evil within it:

> The dialectical materialist believes that everything in existence has fundamental internal contradictions. For example, the African gods south of the Sahara always had at least two heads, one for evil and one for good. Now people create God in their own image, what they think he – for God is always a "He" in patriarchal societies – is like or should be. So the African said, in effect: I am both good and evil; good and evil are the two parts of the thing that is me. This is an example of an internal contradiction.
>
> Western societies, though, split up good and evil, placing God up in heaven and the Devil down in hell. Good and evil fight for control over people in Western religions, but they are two entirely different entities. This is an example of an external contradiction.[89]

During the existence of the Black Panther Party, Newton applied the method of dialectical materialism constantly.

Describing his experiences as a prisoner after the Frey case, he avoided villainizing the guards, instead striving to understand their existential condition. Caught up in their own "resentment" towards the prisoners, by contrast, the guards responded with disbelief at Newton's willingness to undergo the torture of solitary confinement which they imposed upon him.[90] When Newton was finally released, one guard responded by conversing with Newton about his personal life in an attempt to connect and affirm their mutual humanity.

> Why he attempted this conversation is hard to figure out, but I guess he was trying to let me know that he realized he could no longer consider me his inferior. Since our convict-guard relationship had changed, he wanted me to know that he was a human being with certain thoughts and

> feelings. He even offered me a cigarette, but I told him I did not smoke. Then he went into a long monologue about how he almost got cancer from smoking, that he had had pleurisy and had caught it just in time. He went on and on, mostly talking to himself. Guards are odd people. It is incomprehensible to me how a person can endure such a meaningless life day after day, year after year, and seem to be satisfied with it. . . . People like him are really lost, as so many people are, without a purpose in life or the ability to relate to others.[91]

Newton wrote also about the people who composed his parole board, reflecting on their inability to grasp his willingness to assert his humanity. The way he responded to their disparagement of his choices was to attempt to grasp the logic underlying theirs:

> I told them I was willing to obey rules I disagreed with, but I would never obey rules that denied my dignity as a human being. Furthermore, I urged them to disobey those rules that violated *their* integrity and dignity. One of the board members, a Negro, was so shocked that he expressed doubt about my sanity. This is a good example of the mentality controlling prisons across the land, one so narrow that it regards human dignity and strength of character as abnormal.[92]

Of all the philosophical systems that Newton engaged with, the most important for his leadership of the BPP was without a doubt dialectical materialism. And, despite the later frictions and fracturing that would occur in the organization, the concept remained highly regarded by Panthers for decades after.

Inspired by his reading of Marx, Engels, Mao, and Fanon, Newton embraced this modified materialism informed by Friedrich Engels' idea that all material change is driven by the "motion internal to all matter." That is, everything carries within it forces of change. Because it does not involve a simplistic conception of matter that reduces everything in the world to just physical things ("mechanistic materialism"), Newton considered dialectical materialism compatible with his belief that all we can really say for certain is that we have experiences. During his speech at Boston College, Newton critiqued Marxism in a few ways, but he affirmed dialectical materialism above all, claiming even that Marx subscribed to dialectical materialism rather than Marxism.[93]

A helpful and standard way to understand dialectical materialism is through the image of two opposed elements that produce a third element following their interaction. However, strictly speaking, the idea that one must start with a binary follows from a misinterpretation of the linguistic roots of the word *dialectic*. Like in the words *dialect* and *dialogue*, the root "*dia*" does not mean "two" – that would be the Greek "di" – but instead means "through." The second root in the word *dia-lectic* comes from the Proto-Indo-European word *legein*, which means "to speak" and is the origin of many words (e.g. *logic*, *lexicon*, *legal*, and *logarithm*). Altogether, *dialectic* may be best understood as meaning "through reason or discussion." While describing dialectical materialism in terms of two opposed elements producing a third element can help to simplify the concept, it can also mislead. Dialectical materialism in fact describes the interrelation of *many* elements simultaneously, because the world is of course so complex and cannot be reduced to binaries.

One motto of the Black Panther Party that Newton developed was the idea that "every determination brings about a limitation and every limitation brings about a determination."[94] This means that everything that comes into existence has outer limits, and every outer limit is simultaneously the start of a new thing, which in turn has its own limits. "In other words, while one force may give rise to one thing it might crush other things, including itself."[95] During his seminar at Yale in 1971, Newton described dialectical materialism through the example of the historical struggle between economic classes – "the haves and the have nots":

> This struggle between mutually exclusive opposing tendencies within everything that exists explains the observable fact that all things have motion and are in a constant state of transformation. Things transform themselves because while one tendency or force is more dominating than another,

> change is nonetheless a constant, and at some point the balance will alter and there will be a new qualitative development. New properties will come into existence, qualities that did not altogether exist before. Such qualities cannot be analyzed without understanding the forces struggling within the object in the first place, yet the limitations and determinations of these new qualities are not defined by the forces that created them. . . .
>
> Now, because things do not stay the same we can be sure of one thing: the owner will not stay the owner, and the people who are dominated will not stay dominated. We don't know exactly how this will happen, but after we analyze all the other elements of the situation, we can make a few predictions. We can be sure that if we increase the intensity of the struggle, we will reach a point where the equilibrium of forces will change and there will be a qualitative leap into a new situation with a new social equilibrium. I say "leap," because we know from our experience of the physical world that when transformations of this kind occur they do so with great force.[96]

It is clear from this description that dialectical materialism inherently has something to say about the future, about the conditions that unfold as a necessary effect of the "motion in all matter." This is, according to Newton, because it synthesizes empiricism with rationalism. Furthermore, the practical application of dialectical materialism entails actively identifying the internal tensions in a phenomenon and maybe even taking a role in pushing those tensions towards their limits. Only some of these tensions, called *contradictions*, are truly *antagonistic contradictions*, meaning that they are sensitive enough to transform the whole situation.

If we consider our earlier discussion (in Chapter 2) of the BPP's earliest programs, we can identify that certain programs pushed at the "contradictions" in American society more than others, thereby powerfully disturbing the status quo. The police patrols resulted in harassment by the police because they threatened the Oakland Police Department's white supremacist monopoly over the use of arms in a territory. The breakfast program, however, drew even the attention of the Director of the FBI because it challenged the federal government's claim over the power to reproduce life itself.

Any one particular action contains in itself its own range of possibilities and problems, or *determinations* and *limitations*. We see then that dialectical materialism, when applied practically, is a methodology of trial and error – a scientific method. As a result, one may sometimes produce effects that go beyond what one intended, and Newton reflected later that perhaps some of the Panthers' actions produced "too much of 'a great leap forward.'"[97]

Historians Robin Kelley and Betty Esch have written about Newton's efforts to convey some of these ideas to other members in the Party: "Shortly after his release from prison in August 1970, Newton proposed the creation of an 'Ideological Institute' where participants actually read and taught what he regarded as the 'classics.'"[98] For use at the institute, Newton produced a visual representation of dialectical materialism "in equation form" (see diagram below), illustrating how dialectical materialism combines the idealism of abstraction (pure reason) with the materialism of experience (empiricism) to create a practical method for political practice.[99]

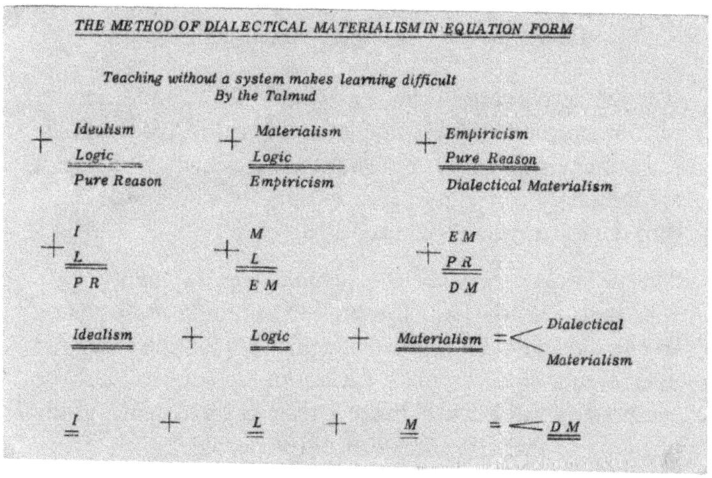

Teaching materials from the Black Panther Party Ideological Institute, 1970–1971.
Used with permission by Dr. Huey P. Newton Foundation.

Process and the Structured Vehicle

As discussed above, Newton was critical of "mechanistic materialism," the view that one can describe the world completely and adequately in terms of physical matter. This necessarily meant that he was also critical of traditional Marxist understandings of the political party. For Newton, you cannot understand a political organization by merely identifying its members (as bodies), or where they meet (in space), or other physical aspects of their existence. By that logic, if an organization's members are destroyed, then the organization ceases to exist. Instead, the Black Panther Party believed, as Fred Hampton put it, "You can kill a revolutionary, but you can't kill revolution."[100] Newton understood revolution not as a set of actions that people take, but as an aspect and "process" of reality itself.

To play a role in this process of reality, Newton argued, what is required is a "structured vehicle." Essentially, this represented a more phenomenalistic approach to how political organizations should be understood and described. For Newton, a structured vehicle is a more accurate way to understand reality and then organize human experiences towards political goals. As he explained in his important "May 1st Statement" of 1971:

> It is the revolutionary concepts which define and interpret phenomena and establish the goals toward which the political vehicle will work. A revolutionary vehicle is in fact a revolutionary concept set into motion by a dedicated cadre through a particular organized structure.[101]
>
> The political vehicle of the people must be guided by a consistent ideology which represents nothing more than a systematic and organized set of principles for analyzing and interpreting objective phenomena. An ideology can only be accepted as valid if it delivers a true understanding of the phenomena that affect the lives of the people.[102]

For Newton, a "revolutionary structured vehicle" is an epistemological apparatus – a method or habit – that channels and organizes lumpen phenomenal existence (the lived experience of the most oppressed) dialectically in the direction of "revolutionary process." Of course, there can also exist "reactionary structured vehicles" that channel experiences in harmful and regressive ways. Colonial society already does this insofar as it channels people's suffering back onto themselves and their communities. In the rest of this chapter and the next, I explain the "structured vehicle" as a specific strategy that Newton and the Black Panther Party came up with but that was never fully put into practice.

In the 1960s, many theories of political organization were produced by activists thinking through how to bring about "social transformation" or revolution. By the 1970s it had become increasingly common to criticize the traditional political party form or even abandon it altogether. The BPP's shift in theory reflected this broader tendency, even as some of their practices lagged behind their theory.[103] Perhaps the easiest way to grasp Newton's concept of the structured vehicle is to compare it with some concepts and dynamics from today. In brief, the idea was not simply to categorize or count members as objects, but to channel the flow of their experiences – such as thoughts, emotions, and *affects* (the most basic feelings rooted in our bodies, such as hunger, fear, and excitement). Importantly, because *phenomena* is so expansive a term, a structured vehicle by definition is letting in the unknown, uncertain, and variable, not just predetermined kinds of objects. And yet, by applying "as objective as possible" an understanding of society, one can make educated guesses about the kinds of experiences that occur for people and are thus available for channeling. As Newton put it: "One cannot always predict the outcome, but one can for the most part gain enough insight to manage the process."[104] This process of letting in experiential inputs to produce a particular kind of experiential output is perhaps most easily observed today in areas of cultural and arts production, social media, marketing, and political campaigns.

One can also use this frame to understand the largest political mass mobilization in recent years: the uprisings in support of the movement for Black Lives in the United States and abroad, first in 2014–16 and then again in 2020. Tens of millions of people were brought to the streets, in part because of the efforts of pre-existing organizations with long histories of dedicated work, but perhaps most powerfully through the decentralized amplification of digital social media campaigns, hashtags, and algorithms. The algorithms channeled and organized all kinds of thoughts, feelings, and affects – phenomenal experience – in political directions, producing powerful political effects. These effects included the looting and redistribution of goods, the destruction of police precincts and monuments, mass resignations of police officers, major changes in how people thought and felt about police conduct, and eventually the introduction of laws that regulated police behavior. Some of the most useful and insightful analyses written about the dynamic movements of crowds during these uprisings are similar to Newton's idea of the structured vehicle, shifting away from analyzing persons and instead towards a more phenomenalistic analysis of crowd flows, networks, rhythmanalysis, and pragmatics (also using William James' concept of flux).[105] Indeed, unique forms of crowd intelligence arise in mass movements that sometimes cause crowds to direct themselves, and other times lead the crowds to be responsive to structures and forms they encounter.

As we saw in the Black Panther Party's critique of riots, only some of the directions that mass movements take can be said to be "revolutionary," and in fact the choices people make are perhaps more likely to be "reactionary" or "counterrevolutionary" by default, both because those routes are more accessible and, most of all, because they are set up by existing colonial structures. Importantly, in using the term "revolutionary," Newton and the BPP meant something very specific, despite the connotations and baggage that this term carried back then and still carries today:

> We realized at a very early point in our development that *revolution is a process*. It is not a particular action, nor is it a conclusion.[106]

> Any action which does not mobilize the community towards the goal is not a revolutionary action. The action might be a marvelous statement of courage, but if it does not mobilize the people towards the goal of a higher manifestation of freedom it is not making a political statement and could even be counterrevolutionary.[107]

For Newton, one of the biggest problems with Marxism was the idea that one can predict or predetermine a historical end-point based on an understanding of struggles past or present.[108] Instead of a straight line, Newton described the movement of time and struggle as a "spiral."[109] Given his dialectical materialist approach, he believed that the future is constantly being constructed and shaped by the choices available in the present, from which position one has the option to choose "revolutionary" paths. For this reason, Newton insisted that political practice has to be understood as a method above all and not a set of principles that are pre-established:

> Young people generally feel that the role of the revolutionary is to define a set of actions and a set of principles that are easy to identify and are absolute. But what I was trying to explain to them was the process: revolution, basically, is a contradiction between the old and the new in the process of development. Anything can be revolutionary at a particular point in time, but most of the students don't understand that. And most other people don't understand it either.[110]

Against the dominant stereotype that the Black Panther Party single-mindedly understood armed struggle as revolutionary and other approaches as counterrevolutionary, Newton insisted that the meaning of any particular action was always contextual.[111] As explained earlier, arms could only ever be a tool, useful at some points but not at others. "At one point one thing might be proper, but the same action could be improper at another time."[112] Newton's use of the term *revolution* is thus not just much more complex and nuanced than what the dominant usage evokes, but it is also virtually completely neutral about what it may refer to. Ultimately, the only context-independent characteristic that Newton identified as absolutely necessary for revolution is that it be popular by definition – a mass activity.[113] "We recognized that no party or organization can make the revolution, only the people can. All we could do was act as a guide to the people because revolution is a process that moves in a dialectical manner."[114]

5

The Structured Vehicle and the Revolutionary Defense of Community

As we socialists say, our survival programs will bring the people to a higher level of consciousness and when they reach that point they will make the necessary changes for freedom, not only in the jails but also in the society. You cannot really free a political prisoner if the society itself is enslaved.

Huey P. Newton (1972)[1]

Between Spontaneity and Organization

In his conceptualization of the "structured vehicle," Newton understood the Black Panther Party as fundamentally connected to but nonetheless distinct from the mass of the population. "We lead the people by following their interests, with a view toward raising their consciousness to see beyond limited goals."[2] In an interview soon after his prison release in 1970, he stated that "the Party would like to educate and eventually be the spearhead of change. But as far as being a mass organization, we've never claimed or want to be a mass organization. We're a vanguard or a cadre group of organizers."[3] Accordingly, the Party's character as an organization composed of people with the same types of experiences as those they wished to teach and help direct was fundamental. According to Newton, what allowed for this continuum of experience between the people and the organization was the fact that the Party was a natural outgrowth of the community itself. "Oppressed Black people – *the lumpenproletariat* – did not have a structured organization to represent their true interests until the Black Panther Party arose *from within the community*, motivated by the needs and conditions of the people."[4] "We are revolutionists and we represent and we are the people in poverty."[5] As New York Panther Jalil Muntaqim would later put it, "we are our own liberators."[6]

As explained earlier, Frantz Fanon's *The Wretched of the Earth* was a key to how the Panthers understood both themselves and the population they came from. According to Fanon, the lumpenproletariat's everyday efforts towards survival by definition exceed colonial law.[7] "The constitution of a lumpenproletariat is a phenomenon which obeys its own logic."[8] That is, through their persistent struggle to survive, the lumpen embody an irrepressible vitality that is the side effect of the fact of their oppression. This persistence towards living is also profoundly variable; it may produce self-destruction at some times but may also produce its own self-emancipation. However, explained Fanon, in order to control this immanent life-force, the colonial authorities actively seek to create and cultivate more variability, erratic behavior, and "instability" among the oppressed through the creation of more landlessness, misery, and "physiological wretchedness." "He will create spontaneity with bayonets and exemplary floggings."[9] Elites intentionally foster this spontaneity in order to channel it into anti-social criminality, gangs, and police forces – and Fanon specifically describes how the poor were recruited into armed forces against each other in colonial Algeria, Angola, and the Congo.[10] Political theorist María José Méndez uses the concept of "violence work" to describe the *labor* of violence done by these groups, recruited and channeled by those in power.[11]

Accordingly, as Bobby Seale explained, "Fanon explicitly pointed out that if you didn't organize the lumpen proletariat . . . the power structure would organize these cats against you."[12] Ultimately, Fanon held the view that the "lumpen" are able to push historical change forward precisely *because* they are desperate, unmanageable, and exist *beyond* the frames of standard politics. In the words of Los Angeles Panther and former gang leader Bunchy Carter: "We're dealing with volatile elements – pigs, niggers, and fools. We're trying to create a revolutionary force out of insanity, an insanity the Man created."[13] This flux of experiences of daily suffering, traumatic proximity to death, and striving for survival and life despite it all are what Newton and the Black Panther Party sought to channel through a "structured vehicle." They understood themselves as both the lumpen-proletariat *and* the revolutionary party channeling the flow of their own life experiences dialectically towards their own liberation.

Despite dominant interpretations of Fanon's *Wretched* that reduce its argument about decolonial violence to a "mechanistic materialist" account of clashes between bodies, the book is best understood through the concept of phenomena. Fanon's methodology remained grounded in the same philosophical approach (phenomenology) that framed *Black Skin, White Masks*, and *Wretched* opens in explicitly phenomenological terms: "decolonization is a violent *phenomenon*."[14] That is, decolonization is a mass experience of the re-ordering of experience itself.[15] Problems of translation have obscured this fact about the book, but, overall, Fanon's arguments about the transformative and traumatic effects of violence, and the wide range of phenomena that should be understood as violent, can be understood more clearly if the book is read phenomenologically.[16]

What did this all mean in practice? For Newton, the intention was to channel both individual and collective lived experience in a revolutionary direction. Field Marshal George Jackson stated it simply: "We attempted to change the black criminal mentality into the black revolutionary mentality."[17] Both the model of Malcolm X's life and the BPP's decolonial analysis helped Panthers grasp their past lives in more political terms. New York Panther leader Dhoruba Bin Wahad wrote: "The first time that I became a political prisoner, of course, I didn't call myself that, when I was 14 or 15. I went to youth house for what was, I believe, a burglary."[18] Another New York Panther and former gang member, Afeni Shakur, described what she changed and what she kept: "All the things I used to do against my people or against people or against humanity, all of those traits that I had that I know are incorrect, they've been turned around and I just don't use them against the people anymore. I could use them against the enemy."[19] Conversion to the "revolutionary mentality" was not about repressing one's energies, but about redirecting them. BPP members recognized an explicit continuity between the inevitability of transgressing colonial laws as a poor person, the criminalization of Black life itself, and the willingness to actively break the law as an activist.

Newton understood his own conversion as a shift away from the uncontrolled frustration he used to let out against his friends in the streets, towards a targeted deployment of his intelligence that allowed him to sustain himself. "Once into petty crime, I stopped fighting. I transferred the conflict, aggression, and hostility from the brothers in the community to the Establishment."[20] Later, he invoked Marxist and anarchist philosophy to articulate his developing views in critique of the accumulation of private property by the wealthy: "What is property? Property is theft."[21] Once Newton and Seale had recruited a few early members, they worked on converting their friends from the streets. Newton described how these comrades learned to make radical use of their criminal activities or altogether refocus their energies into protecting the community:

> This recruiting had an interesting ramification in that I tried to transform many of the so-called criminal activities going on in the street into something political, although this had to be done gradually. Instead of trying to eliminate these activities – numbers, hot goods, drugs – I attempted to channel them into significant community actions. Black consciousness had generally reached a point where a man felt guilty about exploiting the Black community. However, if his daily activities for survival could be integrated with actions that undermined the established order, he felt good about it. It gave him a feeling of justification and strengthened his own sense of personal worth. Many of the brothers who were burglarizing and participating in similar pursuits began to contribute weapons and material to community defense. In order to survive they still had to sell their hot goods, but at the same time they would pass some of the cash on to us. That way, ripping off became more than just an individual thing. Gradually the Black Panthers came to be accepted in the Bay Area community. We had provided a

> needed example of strength and dignity by showing people how to defend themselves. More important, we lived among them. They could see every day that with us the people came first.[22]

This inseparability of the Party from the means to survival that poor people pursued would remain a cornerstone for the organization, although what this looked like would vary at different points in Party history. Most of this activity was kept underground. Elaine Brown later wrote: "we were indeed as newspaper headlines frequently suggested, outlaws."[23] Importantly, however, political law-breaking was not to be romanticized but rather grasped as one tool – whose usefulness might change – in the process of revolutionizing society, so that one day poor people would not have to live their lives at the edge of legality.

In early 1971, at the height of the Party's success, prominent Party ally Angela Davis wrote her influential essay "Political Prisoners, Prisons and Black Liberation" while held in a jail cell for allegedly assisting a prison break. Clearly written in close collaboration with the Party, the essay grappled extensively with "the lumpen question." It historicized the origins of our modern idea of crime, offered a defense of political law-breaking, and gestured towards an analysis of the relationship between lumpenproletarian life and revolutionary politics. Perhaps most resonant, however, was how Davis captured in words the impossible position Black people have historically been placed in, given both the long history of colonialism and slavery and the continued effects of racist laws and practices: "In resisting, we have sometimes been compelled to openly violate those laws which directly or indirectly buttress our oppression. But even when containing our resistance within the orbit of legality, we have been labeled criminals by a racist legal apparatus."[24]

In many ways, Davis expressed with clarity, balance, and eloquence what few BPP leaders at the time were in a position to articulate, due either to their experiences of repression, conditions of imprisonment or exile, or their more limited literacy and education. Moreover, Davis managed to discuss topics that even Newton was restrained from verbalizing, given his intention at the time to reduce the violent state repression targeting Party members. She summarized Fanon's argument within a more Marxian framing:

> The occurrence of crime is inevitable in a society in which wealth is unequally distributed, as one of the constant reminders that society's productive forces are being channeled in the wrong direction. The majority of criminal offenses bear a direct relationship to property. Contained in the very concept of property, crimes are profound but suppressed social needs which express themselves in anti-social modes of action. Spontaneously produced by a capitalist organization of society, this type of crime is at once a protest against society and a desire to partake of its exploitative content. It challenges the symptoms of capitalism, but not its essence.[25]

Davis emphasized the "urgent need to organize the unemployed and lumpenproletariat, as indeed the Black Panther Party as well as activists in prison have already begun to do."[26] This need was and remains urgent because the colonizer's co-optation of the lumpenproletariat into "wretchedness" against itself and society as a whole *will never end* as long as colonization exists. Finally, and crucially for our discussion here, Davis addressed the matter of self-defense and its criminalization: "Whenever Blacks in struggle have recourse to self-defense, particularly armed self-defense, it is twisted and distorted on official levels and ultimately rendered synonymous with criminal aggression."[27]

Self-Defense

The Black Panther Party's notion of self-defense was inspired by and drew from many sources, but foremost among these was Malcolm X. Malcolm framed self-defense as a natural response to the experience of violence. In fact, he considered the labeling of self-defense as "violence" as yet another way in which Black people's lives are devalued: "I am not against using violence in self-defense. I don't call it violence when it's self-defense, I call it intelligence."[28] In 1963, Malcolm called out the cognitive dissonance among Black communities of the time, pointing out that violence was readily deployed by Black soldiers and Black police, but rarely in defense of their own communities:

> You'll bleed for white people, but when it comes time to seeing your own churches being bombed and little Black girls murdered, you haven't got no blood. You bleed when the white man says bleed. . . . I hate to say this about us, but it's true. How can you be non-violent in Mississippi as violent as you were in Korea? . . . If violence is wrong in America, violence is wrong abroad. If it's wrong to be violent defending Black women and Black children and Black babies and Black men, then it's wrong for America to draft us and make us violent abroad in defense of her.[29]

Malcolm identified how most violence under American empire is made invisible, while acts of self-defense by Black and oppressed communities are rendered hyper-visible through criminalization. In addition, and importantly, his argument suggests that, for Black people, a lack of self-love perpetuates this dynamic. Black people and oppressed communities are often encouraged to feel *shame* for their reflexive desire to defend themselves. Instead, Malcolm insisted: "*Preserve* your life; it's the best thing you've got."[30] Newton echoed this: "Each person has an obligation to preserve himself."[31] "If a man has no right to self-defense, then he has no right to live."[32]

Regarding the principle of self-defense, Newton and Seale were also specifically inspired by Robert F. Williams, president of the Monroe, North Carolina chapter of the National Association for the Advancement of Colored People (NAACP), and later President of the Republic of New Afrika.[33] Williams' 1962 book *Negroes with Guns* detailed how his organization carefully considered when to use non-violent protest and when to carry arms in order to achieve particular goals, including instances when the open carrying of arms helped prevent assaults by police.[34] Their approach was contextual and strategic. In *Revolutionary Suicide*, Newton also mentioned the writings of the Louisiana-based organization Deacons for Defense as another inspiration.[35] Newton's and Seale's southern roots were formative, given the cultural use of arms for hunting and self-defense. Even the symbol of the black panther had southern origins, having first been used by the SNCC-led Lowndes County Freedom Party of Alabama. Newton and Seale had read that they had armed themselves to protect people during a voter registration drive.[36] In describing their replication of the symbol, Newton explained that "The panther is a fierce animal, but he will not attack until he is backed into a corner."[37]

As Malcolm suggested, self-defense is best grasped not as an abstract law or political position, but as an act of life. Self-defense is indeed natural. Like a plant bud whose very form helps it shield itself in the process of its growth, as it slowly inches outwards through space-time like a spearhead, forms of life defend themselves in order not to be destroyed by other forms of life. All beings that do not defend themselves inevitably become matter for consumption, extraction, exploitation, or destruction by competing life forms. This particular aspect of exposure to consumption is summed up in Black feminist philosopher Joy James' concept of the "captive maternal." James defines captive maternals as those who sustain the vulnerable but whose very existence also sustains and "enables the possessive empire that claims and dispossesses them."[38] Though James' concept is inspired by the particular forms of social control that African mothers were subject to under enslavement, the concept is meant to be inclusive – "a function, not an identity" – and applicable today.[39] The figure of the captive maternal embodies "service, caretaking, sacrifice, and resistance to dishonor and disposability," at the same time that their range of movement may be limited. "We move or fall, breathe or suffocate, while living and caretaking amid hostilities towards Black life."[40] Similar in some ways to the plant bud, the captive maternal grows but only through a constant adaptive struggle. Importantly, however, the bud takes shape in a *defensive* form as it grows.

"We feel that our revolutionary program must be guided by a feeling of love – armed love we sometimes call it," Newton stated in 1971.[41] He described "love" as "the whole thing that life is based on."[42] "Love is more constant than light."[43] And so, just as the preservation of *life* was the basis of the Newton's conception of *defense*, so was *love* the basis of the concept of *life*. Love and defense might appear to some as contradictory when considered together, but that limited view should be overcome, Newton maintained: "In spite of the racism in this country, in spite of the history of oppression against us, we have to show our children how to love and how to defend ourselves. The only way the people of the world can resolve the contradiction between love and defense is to reverse the dominance, at which point we can keep the love and get rid of the gun."[44] In other words, once love becomes more dominant in society than violence is, then one can abandon the need to use violence to defend it.

New York Panther Safiya Bukhari's writings highlighted that members of the BPP commonly quoted Argentinian revolutionary Che Guevara's remark "that a true revolutionary is motivated by great feelings of love."[45] Accordingly, a true understanding of the Party's attitude towards the use of arms must land upon the centrality of their love for the lives of the oppressed. In the words of Malcolm X, this meant embracing the will to defend the oppressed – themselves and others – "by any means necessary." The exercise of defense may be neurological, psychological, cultural, legal, economic, physical, or military. What remains consistent is that it must be effective in order to qualify as defense and adequately preserve the form of life at hand.

For several months after his release from prison in 1970, Newton and the Central Committee struggled to balance the need for strategic defense with the more assertive desire for military offense that some members had encouraged over the three years that Newton was incarcerated. Ultimately, Newton landed upon a particular phrasing that sought to walk a fine line between the language of revolution and the language of survival. In his speeches on intercommunalism in late 1970 and 1971 he became increasingly consistent:

> A Ten-Point Program is not revolutionary in itself, nor is it reformist. It is a survival program. We, the people, are threatened with genocide because racism and fascism are rampant in this country and throughout the world. And the ruling circle in North America is responsible. We intend to change all of that, and in order to change it, there must be a total transformation. But until we can achieve that total

> transformation, we must exist. In order to exist, we must survive; therefore, we need a survival kit: the Ten-Point Program.[46]

The Party's increasing emphasis on survival programs, Newton stated, was not revolutionary in itself. That said, to merely exist when one is subject to genocide *is* a victory. Fanon wrote: "To live is to not die. To exist is to keep living. Every date fruit is a victory. Not the result of work, but a victory felt as a triumph of life."[47] However, through a careful arrangement of their life-preserving programs, the BPP intended to make them revolutionary. The institutions that sustained their populations through free food, medical care, housing, and education were radical because they held off the genocidal effects of colonialism and capitalism, but to become revolutionary they would need to be guided and channeled by a structured vehicle.

Communal Defense

Newton argued that the Black Panther Party's communal living arrangements were natural outgrowths of the typical conditions of life for the Black and poor.[48] The Panther pads, as they were called, were intentional communities where many full-time members lived together and shared resources, explicitly inspired by Maoist experiments in communal living in China. At the same time, for many, such living arrangements were not so different from the ways that Black and poor people had traditionally sustained themselves, given the difficulty of finding housing in discriminatory urban markets. For similar reasons, the pads of some chapters struggled with internal patriarchal dynamics, a reflection of the colonial conditions the Panthers struggled against more broadly. Nonetheless, the hope and plan was that these spaces would become the core for the *local* strongholds of the *global* network making up a revolutionary intercommunalism.[49] George Jackson used the phrase "the black commune" to refer to them, and they were intended to connect to the broader public through the survival programs, serving as the scaffolding for an "autonomous infrastructure."[50] As part of this process,

Newton urged that the BPP's central headquarters, which had been moved to the whiter city of Berkeley during his imprisonment, be moved back into the Black community in Oakland, at the site of a breakfast program.[51]

By connecting housing to medical care, food, education, and self-defense, the Panthers hoped to establish independent institutions that could compete with and displace the inadequate institutions of American capitalist society. Some socialists refer to this strategy as "dual power."[52] Newton explained:

> All these programs were aimed at one goal: complete control of the institutions in the community. Every ethnic group has particular needs that they know and understand better than anybody else; each group is the best judge of how its institutions ought to affect the lives of its members. . . . The most important element in controlling our own institutions would be to organize them into co-operatives, which would end all forms of exploitation. Then the profits, or surplus, from the co-operatives would be returned to the community, expanding opportunities on all levels, and enriching life. Beyond this, our ultimate aim is to have various ethnic communities cooperating in a spirit of mutual aid, rather than competing. In this way, all communities would be allied in a common purpose.[53]

Cooperatives are socialist inwardly while competing with capitalists outwardly. Newton eventually used the term "stronghold" to refer to the social programs, property ownership, business apparatuses, and black-market projects developing around the BPP's Oakland center, as well as at other locations.[54] Elaine Brown said that "stronghold" was "a one-word idea that captured what the Party intended to erect inside the walls of the citadel of capitalism."[55]

Importantly, the theory of intercommunalism affirmed that there could be no true "outside" to American capitalist empire – no "maroon community" to which one could run away and be fully free. While some "liberated territories" at the edge of empire might be somewhat freer than others, in the final analysis, "the people and the economy are so integrated into the imperialist empire" that there could be no escape from it, only a struggle against it.[56] In later writings, Newton emphasized that the matter of land was even more vital to life for the poor than it would be for elites: "The people of the oppressed territories might fight on the land question and die over the land question. But for the United States, it is the technology question, and the consumption of the goods that the technology produces."[57] Fanon made the point even more simply: in contrast to "the intellectuals," "the people . . . take their stand from the start on broad and inclusive positions. *Land and bread*: how to get the land and the bread? And this stubborn aspect – seemingly limited and shrunken – of the people, is definitively the most valuable and the most efficient operating model."[58]

The "Black commune" was conceptualized as a natural extension of Black life, but the Panthers also emphasized that such structures would eventually be able to leave racial separation behind. Jackson stated that "Black, brown and white are all victims together. At the end of this massive collective struggle, we will uncover our new man, the unpredictable culmination of the revolutionary process."[59] Nonetheless, recognizing that racism would likely take a very long time to overcome – as a psychological obstacle stronger even than capitalism – Newton proposed ethnic communal control as a necessary step for the Black community to defend itself against racism during struggle:[60] "In our communities we would not be affected by the cultural lag as much because we would be together[,] and we would be controlling our destiny in a semi-autonomous way but yet together in a national sense[,] because we would be represented in all those forces that will make the change that is necessary to wipe out racism."[61] However, a glance at the history of Black independence, Indigenous autonomy, and most efforts to control territory by colonized and oppressed peoples reveals the near inevitability of repressive violence. Decolonial autonomy is always a threat to both state and capital. It is a threat to the state because independent governance is an implicit challenge to its authority. And it is a threat to capital because free resources threaten profit margins by challenging the commodification of goods. Accordingly, the Black Panther Party's greatest insight in their strategy for the communes was to incorporate the expectation of state repression into their plans. "We expected repression," Newton said.[62] In fact, it was precisely this expectation that would make the difference between their program being one of mere *survival* versus one of *social transformation* and *revolution*.

After George Jackson was assassinated in 1971, the French prison-abolitionist Groupe d'information sur les prisons (Prison Information Group), led by philosophers Michel Foucault, Gilles Deleuze, and others, released an anonymous pamphlet describing precisely this BPP strategy:

> In the Black revolutionary movement, Jackson wanted to be perceived as a military figure. However, the most crucial aspect of his reflections resides in the theorization of the relationship between military and political actions. . . . Jackson, the militant, condemned the military activism of the Weathermen and their actions, organized without strategic preparation and the political support of the masses. He gave his support to Newton and his popular action programs, such as the free distribution of meals to black children in the ghettos. Because these programs enabled the black community to organize itself, they would find themselves increasingly threatened by fascist repression. Soon, Jackson said, these programs could no longer even be conceived without a military cadre.[63]

As close readers of *The Black Panther* newspaper and Jackson's interviews, the French radicals came to realize that Newton's allegedly "pacifist" and "reformist" shift away from political violence in fact concealed a more nuanced strategy that built upon the dialectical interplay between the oppressor and the oppressed. In short, as the lumpenized majority joined these institutions, the state would be expected to attack them, ensuring that these populations would respond in turn by defending the very institutions that sustained them.

In 1970, George Jackson was in charge of organizing the August 7 movement within the prison, as a trained cadre that would defend these "liberated territories." Jackson's organization, the Black Guerrilla Family (a subset of his broader Black Militant Front), consisted of some of the most discarded members of society, prisoners who trained specifically for the chance "to help our people" upon release.[64] During the two years Newton was imprisoned in San Luis Obispo and Jackson remained at San Quentin, they were in constant communication through notes passed via the prison grapevine and messages delivered by people who visited them both.[65] In a letter to Newton dated February 28, 1971, Jackson wrote: "Thanks for helping us beautiful, hard, disciplined brothers in here. I'd like to deliver them to you some day."[66] In a strategy that combined radical care for the most abandoned with the defense of social programs, former gang members and imprisoned Panthers played a special role that allowed them to reinvent themselves in service to the community: "Our present problem as soldiers is to protect our political people at their work and enforce the increasing demands that the people, as a political result, will make upon power."[67]

One can imagine this strategy being combined with a simultaneous effort to heal and resocialize all those who have experienced incarceration so that they do not also harm their communities – a merger with the contemporary strategies of *abolition feminism*.[68] Abolition feminism, which calls for the replacement of carceral institutions with community-based alternatives to dealing with social harm, has direct historical roots in the Black Panther Party's focus on the prison as a site of struggle and transformation. As Angela Davis has explained, abolition "is a mandate for revolution."[69]

In Newton's more philosophical framing, the phenomenal flux of experience would be redefined, channeled into a revolutionary process of communal care and defense of autonomous institutions. Through an exercise of will, the structured vehicle would thus directly channel the suffering and lived experience of the masses into physical and existential self-defense, in light of their needs and desires. In George Jackson's *Blood in My Eye*, one can find traces of the same focus on process: "The materialist approach is to examine things in their total sequence, see them in process, not to merely establish their being in fixed sequential images, but to take in the state of being in process."[70] Letters between George Jackson and his younger brother Jonathan convey in more practical terms what Newton had described in a more abstract and concealed way:

> [Jonathan Jackson:] I think you were on the right track with the idea concerning repression. It is, it has to be part of the revolutionary process, a necessary stage in the development of revolutionary consciousness. The situation being as it was and is, the Black experience is what I'm referring to here.[71]
>
> [George Jackson:] Building consciousness and revolutionary culture against the repressive, natural defense reflexes of the system means taking realistic day-to-day issues like hunger, the need for clothing and housing, joblessness. It involves provoking repression – feeding on it. ... Improvising on reality is the key principle underlying the building of a united left and raising the consciousness of the people.[72]
>
> We feed consciousness by feeding people, addressing ourselves to their needs, the basic and social needs, working, organizing toward a united national left. After the people have created something that they are willing to defend, a wealth of new ideals and an autonomous subsistence infrastructure, then they are ready to be brought into "open" conflict with the ruling class and its supporters.[73]

Across scattered interviews and texts, in coded language, one can find more traces of this strategy in the words of the rest of the BPP leadership:

> [Bobby Seale:] They're going to have to come down and arrest the bags of free food, they're going to have to arrest the factory that makes the free shoes, they're going to have to arrest our free medical clinics, they're going to have to arrest our free busing program, etc. And that's a contradiction between the people in the community and the police department. At some point or another, the people can actually choose to defend that food and those clinics that they know they have a right to as decent human beings.[74]
>
> [Huey Newton:] Then when the police or any other agency of repression tries to destroy the program, the people will move to a higher level of consciousness and action.[75]

> While the defense might take on offensive characteristics, in the final analysis it would be self-defense because the people never initiate anything, they only respond to what has been initiated against them.[76]

> A lot of so-called revolutionaries simply do not understand the statement by Chairman Mao that "Political power grows out of the barrel of a gun." They thought Chairman Mao said political power is the gun, but the emphasis is on "grows." The culmination of political power is the ownership and control of the land and the institutions thereon so that we can then get rid of the gun.[77]

These institutions would be revolutionary because, in the process of defending life, care, and autonomy, they would be building a new society.

A student newspaper at Harvard described how this fit in with Newton's project of revolutionary intercommunalism: "Newton said that the Panthers seek a world revolution which will establish a global group of interdependent socialist communities, or 'intercommunalism within a cooperative framework.'"[78] In a different interview, Newton advocated "proportional representation of all ethnic groups" "in a socialist framework" signified by "the black and red banner."[79] In *Blood in My Eye*, George Jackson elaborated in detail on the ideas they came up with in 1971:

> These communes will be tied to one another by a national and international vanguard party and joined with the world's other revolutionary societies. . . . Carrying out a commune in the central city will involve claiming certain rights as our own – out front. Rights that have not been respected to now. Property rights. It will involve building a political, social and economic infrastructure, capable of filling the vacuum that has been left by the establishment ruling class and pushing the occupying forces of the enemy culture from our midst. The implementation of this new social, political and economic program will feed and comfort all the people on at least a subsistence level, and force the "owners" of the enemy bourgeois culture either to tie their whole fortunes

> to the communes and the people, or to leave the land, the tools and the market behind.[80]

Presumably, a democratic and decentralized form of coordination would be preferred to any kind of centralized structure, as former Panther Lorenzo Kom'boa Ervin and others have proposed in their elaborations on intercommunalism.[81]

In 2003, writing about the abolition of the prison and other institutions of unfreedom that exert colonial control over our bodies and minds, Angela Davis wrote: "The creation of new institutions that lay claim to the space now occupied by the prison can eventually start to crowd out the prison so that it would inhabit increasingly smaller areas of our social and psychic landscape. Schools can therefore be seen as the most powerful alternative to jails and prisons."[82] Newton agreed that education "that exposes the true nature of this decadent American society" is indispensable, but also affirmed that these institutions would have to be defended. Only then could communities committed to liberation effectively consolidate their gains against waves of perpetual colonial sabotage.

For Newton and the other theoreticians of the Black Panther Party, it was the very vulnerability of the "most oppressed" – *everyone* colonized and lumpenized by American empire, subject to dehumanization, genocide, and fascism – that would serve as the experiential source for the will to bring about a complete social transformation. By definition, this would be based in the will to live, to love, and to defend each other as a community. Efforts to abolish violence that do not combat its underlying cause – the colonial condition – are bound to fail to revolutionize society, as long as colonial technologies of control exist and continue to reproduce violence. In order to defend oneself successfully, however, it is of utmost importance that one have a *true understanding* of what one is up against. What is the true nature of this declining American empire and its technologies of surveillance, social control, and repression? Without such an understanding, even in defending oneself, one is *almost certain* to struggle in a manner that will worsen and tighten the chains of oppression. This would then not be at all revolutionary, in Newton's sense of the word, but just the opposite, counterrevolutionary.

A Split in the Party

For Newton and his allies in the Party, the strategy for communal defense was based on a deep-seated belief that the BPP could not "make revolution" by itself; it could only at best "guide the process." Accordingly, he was emphatic that the desire among a minority of members to engage in open armed struggle was doomed to failure. Throughout 1971, as the Party fractured, Newton tried to clarify his position: "Of course people do courageous things and call themselves the vanguard, but the people who do things like that are either heroes or criminals. They are not the vanguard because the vanguard means spearhead, and the spearhead has to spearhead something. If nothing is behind it, then it is divorced from the masses and is not the vanguard."[83] Since 1967, Newton and Seale had used the term "vanguard" to lay claim to a leading role as models in relation to the broader left.[84] And, between 1967 and 1970, many groups, from the white Students for Democratic Society to the American Indian Movement, actively affirmed the Black Panther Party as *the vanguard*.[85] The term itself had roots in the Russian Revolution and Lenin's organization, which used the label to identify themselves as leaders and catalysts. Lenin was critical of Marx's idea that the working class would naturally by itself lead a revolution, especially given economic conditions in Russia at the time. Lenin argued that the role of a vanguard party was to elevate the consciousness of the masses.

In retrospect, Newton and the BPP seem to have used the word in two different ways that were sometimes conflated. One sense was clearly inspired by the socialist and communist revolutions and included the claim that the BPP had a stronger understanding of reality, which they sought to apply in the act of modeling political actions for the people and organizing them. In 1968, during a major meeting of Black activist groups in Los Angeles, Bunchy Carter openly stated: "I also came here to let you know that it is the position of the Black Panther Party for Self Defense that we are the vanguard of revolution in the United States. We are the vanguard party."[86] From this standpoint, Newton felt justified in critiquing sections of the Party and of the left as "adventurist" or "non-revolutionary" if he thought they were advocating political activity that was harmful to the people or that they could not relate to. In his important essay, "The Defection of Eldridge Cleaver from the Black Panther Party and the Defection of the Black Panther Party from the Black Community," Newton explained:

> In their quest for freedom and in their attempts to prevent the oppressor from stripping them of all the things they need to exist, the people see things as moving from A to B to C; they do not see things as moving from A to Z. . . . Therefore, when the revolutionary begins to indulge in Z, or final conclusions, the people do not relate to him [*sic*]. Therefore he is no longer a revolutionary if revolution is a process.[87]

There was also a second use of the word *vanguard*, however, describing not the Party itself, but that section of the population that they saw as most likely to engage in resistant activity. This usage, which was primarily descriptive and basically sociological, was directly derived from Fanon's description of the "wretched of the earth" as the "spearhead" of revolution.[88]

> We say that black people are the vanguard of the revolution in this country, and, since no one will be free until the people of America are free, that black people are the vanguard of world revolution. We don't say this in a boasting way. We inherit this legacy primarily because we are the last, you see, and as the saying goes, "The last will be the first."[89]

Strictly speaking, this usage of vanguard does not indicate political leadership, but rather describes "objectively" which group is likely to act first, in whatever realm of activity is understood as the primary terrain of struggle. That terrain might be anything from a riot, to intellectual analysis of technologies of repression, to the arts, to the reproduction and defense of life. As Newton explained in 1967: "The identity of the first man who threw a Molotov cocktail is not known by the masses, yet they respect and imitate his actions. In the same way, the actions of the party will be imitated by the people – if the people respect these activities."[90]

In 1971, BPP members broadly agreed upon which sector of the population was the vanguard in the second sense of the term (the descriptive sense). However, because they differed over what kind of activity should be considered most revolutionary, they disagreed regarding which group of activists counted as the vanguard in the first sense of the term (the prescriptive sense). Many commentators have attributed the historical split in the Party to this kind of difference in views. However, it is crucial to note that the Party had long harbored internal ideological differences, as evidenced in the 1969 debate between Fred Hampton and Eldridge Cleaver/David Hilliard.[91] Others have identified tensions over the unequal distribution of financial resources as a catalyst for the split, especially as it affected members in New York City.[92] Yet, it is not clear that funds were ever truly equally distributed, in part because they came into the Party through a range of legal and illegal means.[93] It is also broadly acknowledged that reports about discontent over finances were amplified by FBI-aligned mainstream media outlets aiming to subvert popular support for the Party.

Arguably the greatest focus of dissent was the rising authoritarianism of the Central Committee, and especially the actions of David Hilliard and Huey Newton. Allegedly, the Central Committee ignored two years' worth of letters sent by New York Panthers to the leadership.[94] During a period when much of the rest of the Party leadership was in prison, Hilliard in particular carried out extensive purges, increasingly influenced by the writings of communist dictator Joseph Stalin.[95] While Newton was reading Isaac Deutscher's *The Prophet*, an anti-Stalinist biography of Russian socialist Leon Trotsky, he reportedly advised Hilliard: "No, you should not put Stalin on the cover [of the newspaper]."[96] However, purges were in fact imposed at multiple points in the history of the Party, a practice that even Eldridge Cleaver defended in 1971.[97] On the other hand, the reality of Newton's turn to authoritarianism was undeniable. It must be emphasized that this turn was deeply inconsistent with his prior character and behavior, however, and there is extensive evidence that even as Newton's rational capacities remained strong, his *emotional health* had begun a rapid decline, an effect of ongoing state surveillance and harassment, new chemical drug addictions, and the mind-altering procedures he was subjected to while imprisoned.[98] Ultimately, the paranoia and lack of trust that intensified within the Party cannot be grasped without a thorough understanding of Newton's change in health.

There had always been ideological differences among Party members, but the US government exacerbated the emotionally charged dimension of these differences by cultivating mistrust through extensive disinformation campaigns. The mistrust was sharpest between members who were geographically distant from each other, despite extensive Party efforts to manage this through traveling mediators and audio-recorded messages. Disturbingly, Cleaver was subject to a full year's worth of forged letters from the FBI about BPP members and Newton especially, many of which he came to "accept as bonafide."[99] The letters Newton received severely distorted his perceptions as well.[100] In March 1970, while he was still in prison, "the FBI initiated what the Senate Intelligence Committee labeled a 'concerted program' to drive a permanent wedge" between the two and their supporters.[101]

Standard interpretations depict the split as one between coasts – with a Newton-led West coast faction against armed struggle and a Cleaver-led East coast faction supporting armed struggle. However, this is an inaccurate picture in several regards. Most chapters on the East coast remained aligned with the Oakland-based Central Committee, and there were also members in California who either stood in opposition to or became targets of the Central Committee. Notably, George Jackson sided with the Newton faction, despite being an open advocate of armed struggle and enduring the death of his younger brother Jonathan in a failed, armed prison-break involving hostages in 1970.[102] It appears Newton sought to call off the action, and it remains unclear why Jonathan went through with it. Following the failure of Jonathan Jackson's action, police informants spread the rumor that Newton was to blame.[103] In January 1971, after further FBI efforts, the first prominent Panther to be expelled by Newton as a result of his developing paranoia was Deputy Minister of Defense Geronimo Ji-Jaga Pratt.[104] Pratt was a respected leader in the Los Angeles chapter and his past experience in the military had helped to save Panther lives in a city where police repression was the most lethal of anywhere in the country.[105] Pratt was also put in charge of organizing the underground military wing, but Newton, who had first called for this while in prison, came to fear Pratt would lead these forces against him.[106]

After Newton came to believe that individuals in the New York chapter intended to kill him as well, some members of the New York 21 – a group of Panthers targeted and jailed under false charges – wrote an open letter to the Weather Underground Organization defending the WUO's earlier position in the long-standing debate about armed struggle, strongly implying that the WUO was "the true vanguard."[107] They also criticized the Central Committee for what they interpreted as a developing tendency towards "arrogance," "dogmatism," "regionalism," and "fear" during the preceding months, in part because of the perceived abandonment of political violence.[108] Newton and the Central Committee responded by expelling them, though this would not be publicized in the paper until later, when two NY Panthers, Dhoruba bin Wahad and Michael "Cetewayo" Tabor, suddenly fled the country to join the Cleavers and Don Cox in Algeria, along with International Coordinator Connie Matthews, forfeiting $150,000 worth of bail in the process.[109] Having worked as Newton's personal secretary, Connie Matthews experienced at close proximity the very beginnings of his paranoia and rising authoritarianism.[110]

On February 26, 1971, during a live broadcast of a conversation between Newton and Cleaver, Cleaver called for the reinstatement of the expelled NY Panthers and the removal from the Central Committee of Hilliard, who was seen as the source of the authoritarianism and Newton's changing behavior.[111] On a subsequent call, which was secretly recorded by the group in Algiers, Newton lambasted Cleaver for airing Party business in public.[112] For years after, Newton placed ultimate blame on Cleaver for the split in the Party, scrutinizing his past interactions with him in search of what he had initially overlooked. In the following weeks, the Central Committee would begin the publication of an exposé on Cleaver, starting with "his sexual fascism and his ill-treatment of women" in the Party.[113]

Although Cleaver had used his position of leadership to speak out in defense of the NY Panthers, not all members of the NY chapter actually agreed with his ideas. According to Newton, "four Panther branches in New York and one in New Jersey" immediately sided with Cleaver.[114] However, since Cleaver had received forged letters in their name (in fact from the FBI) that referred to him as "the leading theoretician of the party's philosophy," he likely overestimated his own popularity.[115] In fact, when presented with an order from Cleaver to engage in open warfare, NY chapter leader Safiya Bukhari rejected it:

> Eldridge took the opportunity to tell me that it was time to escalate the struggle. He said it was time to take it to the streets and that's what I should tell people to do. I said, "No!" I was not going to tell people to do that. I told Eldridge that the conditions were not right, and I was not going to encourage our people to go out and take part in or become victims of a bloodbath. He told me if I didn't do it there would be a second split in the Black Panther Party. I held firm because I truly believed I was right. Eldridge didn't know what the objective conditions were. He was more than three thousand miles away, in Algeria.
>
> When Eldridge saw he was getting nowhere with me, he put Cetewayo [Tabor] on the phone. Cet told me I should do as Eldridge requested. I asked Cet, "Do you remember what you taught me? To deal with the principle and not the personality?" Cet said, in that deep melodious voice he possessed, "Yes." Then he was silent for a moment and after that made no further attempt to get me to do what Eldridge wished.[116]

It is worth pointing out that this international phone call was initiated by neither Cleaver nor Bukhari: "Neither of us had placed the call, but we knew who had. It seems the government or somebody wanted us to talk about something."[117] Bizarrely, Cleaver called for immediate armed struggle anyways. By March, violence would indeed erupt, though in a fratricidal manner, with BPP members dying at the hands of other BPP members.[118]

Whereas Newton and George Jackson's strategy of communal defense may be characterized as a form of *offensive defense* (or active defense), the approach taken by members of the decentralized guerrilla cells called the Black Liberation Army (BLA) was later described by NY Panther Jalil Muntaqim as *defensive offense*.[119] As members of the NY chapter, the NJ chapter, and other Panthers nationwide went underground, they deployed guerrilla tactics out of strategic necessity. Having become targets of open assassination attempts by the police, they engaged in expropriations to sustain themselves and invoked UN law to define themselves as enemy combatants and prisoners of war.[120] Observing the deaths of their comrades and facing an imminent threat of death when pulled over or encountered by police officers, some of these Panthers responded with pre-emptive acts of self-defense.

Some criticisms of the BLA have confused the political logic of retaliation that they sometimes practiced with a symbolic politics of revenge.[121] Like the actions undertaken by Don Cox on the West coast, the BLA logic of political retaliation was informed by the view that Black people as a community should "exact a political consequence" in order to stop violence within a societal environment that constantly devalued Black lives. BLA attacks on police followed the murders of Black people in the community, and BLA communiqués published throughout the 1970s explicitly affirmed this perspective.[122] It is also significant to note, as scholar Akinyele Umoja has established, that the BLA was originally not exclusively a splinter group of the BPP: "several Black revolutionary organizations contributed to the ranks of the Black underground which was collectively known as the Black Liberation Army."[123] Nonetheless, decades later, NY Panther leader Jalil Munitaqim acknowledged that "the commencement of armed struggle could be said to have been premature – premature in the sense that subjectively, our capacity to wage a sustained, protracted, national liberation war was not possible."[124]

Panthers on the West coast were sent underground as well, especially in Southern California where the aboveground chapter was shut down altogether. The rationale behind this decision was to limit casualties given the state violence they were enduring, but Newton's fears about Los Angeles Panthers siding with the BLA also played a part.[125] Former FBI agent Wesley Swearingen later stated that the FBI actively sought to create a split between Oakland and Los Angeles as well.[126] Accordingly, for many in the underground, the supposed "ideological differences" were less clear than initially appeared and some people switched sides, inflaming an "internal war."[127] On both coasts, going underground resulted in the loss of people available to run the social programs and connect with the broader community, a point that members across the board readily identified as a fatal flaw.[128]

Remarkably, no book-length treatment of the BLA exists today, though their communiqués have been recently collected and published, and video interviews have been produced online in recent years.[129] In identifying the similarities and overlaps between the BPP's factions, my intention is not to minimize the differences that arose, but to emphasize the extent to which the split was fundamentally an active construction and effect of the FBI's counterintelligence program. The Black Panther movement spawned a range of highly adaptive local strategies and tactics, developed by a myriad of exceptionally intelligent individuals, producing a powerful history that this book about one individual can at best only gesture towards.[130] Common to all members of the Black Panther movement, however, was a spirit of defiance, a valuation of self-defense, and a belief in Newton's axiom that *repression breeds resistance*.[131]

This phrase, uttered by Newton in an interview published in *The Black Panther* in January 1971, was the last open affirmation of armed struggle that he articulated.[132] Just a few months prior, Newton had officially offered to send BPP members as troops to aid the National Liberation Front (NLF) of South Vietnam in their war against the US army.[133] Apparently, the true intention behind this was to make use of members of the radical left who had gone underground (e.g. BLA, WUO) and could no longer operate politically aboveground in the United States.[134] While this was not revealed openly at the time, Newton did offer a glimpse into the strategic thinking involved: "We never broadcast our military maneuvers for military reasons. We might broadcast them for political reasons, which we've done in the past. . . . We operate on the axiom that in order to say what I want to say, I can't do what I want to do. To do what I want to do, I can't say what I want to say. Therefore, observe our actions and you'll know what I want to say."[135] The NLF graciously accepted the offer of international solidarity, but never called upon the troops.[136]

By the time of the "Intercommunal Day of Solidarity" event in Oakland in March 1971, however, all references to armed struggle by Newton would be either eliminated or coded.[137] In his speech that day, Newton emphasized the distinction between political actions and military actions and used the phrase "sterner stuff," which Party armorer Flores Forbes would later describe as "Huey's term for organized violence."[138] Newton had earlier affirmed: "Revolutions are made of sterner stuff."[139] That is, violence against the "forces" of the "ruling circle" would *someday* be a necessary part of the struggle to transform society, but, importantly "the vanguard party" would not be – could not be – the ones to carry it out. "We couldn't defend [an area], only the community could; we could teach them how."[140]

While Newton heavily criticized the guerrilla tactics that predominated on the East coast and in other expelled sections of the Black Panther movement in this period, he later conceded that the different lived experiences of the East coast Panthers likely informed their different political perspectives:

> When Dr. Martin Luther King was assassinated, people became disillusioned – especially the youth – with the old Civil Rights Movement. . . . As a consequence, the growth [of the Party] was very heavy, all over, but even more so – it was more prominent – on the East coast. It's probably because, on the East coast, living conditions, survival conditions, were much more dreadful than even on the West coast where the weather is much better.[141]

In asserting that climate and environment are conditions of oppression that themselves shape resistance, Newton's interview from 1989 suggested a measure of regret for the gap in understanding between the chapters.

Indeed, his own theory of intercommunalism should have – were its logic fully applied – encouraged a more decentralized approach to the management of the chapters and a recognition of their differentiated conditions of oppression.[142] According to Newton himself, the US was no longer a nation but a global empire, so liberated territories inside the US were not fundamentally different from liberated territories beyond its legal borders. In other words, Black Panther branches in New York City should not have been considered parts of one national organization any more than the British Black Panthers in the UK or the Polynesian Panther Party in New Zealand were. Instead, as the conditions in each locale differed, so should have their strategies and tactics. A restructuring of the Central Committee with leaders drawn from the chapters in Chicago and New York was considered as early as 1969 but never implemented.[143] Instead, power was consolidated in an Oakland-based core of members, and most of all in Newton, with decisions made from there, for all chapters in the country.

6

The Question of the Most Oppressed

Settle your quarrels, come together, understand the reality of our situation, understand that fascism is already here, that people are already dying who could be saved, that generations more will live poor butchered half-lives if you fail to act. Do what must be done, discover your humanity and your love in revolution.

George Jackson (1971)[1]

The Will of the Most Oppressed

In recent years, some scholars of Black Studies have expressed pessimistic or acquiescent views about the prospects for true freedom for Afrodiasporic people in the West. According to one prominent view, all people deemed Black are socially dead – not just denied the privileges of citizenship or excluded from the category of the human, but trapped *beyond being* itself. Faced with the Panther principle of self-defense, such pessimists might argue that not only are Black people not "allowed" to defend themselves from brutal violence and social control – as the disproportionate deaths of Black people from police violence, poverty, and medical neglect demonstrate – but in fact, no discourse that affirms the value of the life of a Black person is even comprehensible or acceptable in this world. Instead, the act of defending oneself is inevitably seen as an impossible monstrosity, a violent spectacle at worst, and a disordered and suicidal effort at best.

This view was not alien to Newton; in fact, he grappled with it directly. Consciously facing such realities, the lumpenproletarian insight – and Newton's existential insight – was to recognize that it is precisely because you cannot expect others to recognize, appreciate, or respect your humanity that you are in the best position to exercise will over your own life. As the worst-regarded person in society, you grasp that you cannot expect anyone to help or save you. The only person that you can count on is yourself, and so your destiny is completely in your own hands. In fact, even if all of dominant society is invested in your social death and seeks to produce your physical death, you can nonetheless decide to take it upon yourself to do anything you will to, including deciding to transform the whole of the world.

This is the insight from the standpoint of the hungry and abandoned, the "horde of rats," in Fanon's words, the "workless less-than-men" who become, through their own will, "rehabilitated in their own eyes and in the eyes of history. The prostitutes too, and the maids who are paid two pounds a month, all the hopeless dregs of humanity, all who turn in circles between suicide and madness."[2] According to Fanon, this will to live that persists among the "worst" people necessarily escapes description and language itself: "the peasant, the unemployed man, the starving native do not lay a claim to the truth; they do not say that they represent the truth, for they are the truth."[3]

This view, when put forth by Newton, has sometimes been misinterpreted as an echo of the philosophy of Friedrich Nietzsche, specifically his concept of the drive and *will to power* that treats health and life with utter abandon.[4] While Newton was indeed a close reader of Nietzsche, he was most fundamentally not a Nietzschean but a dialectical materialist and identified himself as such. As poet Alan Garrigan has rightly pointed out, Newton often engaged with Nietzschean positions but would usually seek to overcome them *dialectically*.[5] In a poem written in 1973, Newton began in a Nietzschean fashion, stating that "the desire for health is slavery," but he ended by affirming health, saying that "To will health is freedom."[6] We can also identify the same tendency to move beyond Nietzsche in Newton's very definition of power: "we recognize that the *will to power is the basic drive of man*. But it is incorrect to seek power over people."

Philosopher Joshua Hall has put it well: "In his autobiography, *Revolutionary Suicide*, Newton begins with Nietzsche but ultimately self-overcomes both himself and Nietzsche."[7]

To be clear, Black Panther Party members did learn to expect death, and Newton himself was existentially preoccupied with its inevitability (as the titles to his books *To Die for the People* and *Revolutionary Suicide* suggest). However, the striving for hope and dignity that Newton embodied and that the BPP pursued politically only *seems* like it is reducible to *power* and a *desire for death* from the point of view of the white world and the colonizer's system of norms – instead of the striving for life against all odds that it really is. This is precisely the point that Newton wanted to get across when he rejected the view among some psychologists in his time that Black radicals were suicidal: "Scholars and academics, in particular, have been quick to make this accusation. They fail to perceive differences."[8] "Revolutionary suicide does not mean that I and my comrades have a death wish; it means just the opposite. We have such a strong desire to live with hope and human dignity that existence without them is impossible."[9] "Our real desire is to live, but we will not be cowed, we will not be intimidated."[10] In the unpublished *These Graves Are All Too Young*, Newton discussed the unique and often misunderstood will of the most oppressed, and how it lent him and Seale confidence when they began organizing and recruiting in their community:

> We recognized that the people in Watts and so many other places were not resisting because they wanted to buy a new refrigerator or a new pair of shoes, they were fighting for their very existence and their dignity as human beings. This is what makes their will superior to the motives of the oppressor. . . . This is why we felt that in spite of the superior military might of the ruling circle the people would always be superior in their courage and strength.[11]

The distinct and indescribable character of the will of the oppressed remains as long as the colonial condition remains, contrary to any fads that might insist upon the impossibility of social change.

The philosophy of afropessimism comes closest to overcoming the colonizer's worldview when its supporters admit that its original inspirations have less to do with simple pessimism than with an attempt to describe experiences otherwise disregarded as madness. Founding theorist Frank B. Wilderson has hinted that afropessimism is about dealing with the technologically produced "madness" that being Black today can entail, but few have grasped this central aspect of his argument.[12] Black people are particular (though not exclusive) targets of remote technologies of neurowarfare that target the mind.[13] In identifying this, afropessimism thus provides a historical echo of the precursors faced by Black people and others in the 1960s, although it politically inverts Newton's point. That is, afropessimism is built upon the same phenomenology and experience of psychic isolation – akin to the madness of the soul breaker – but instead of forging a strong will from this place, pessimism constructs a totalizing hopelessness. This is precisely what Newton referred to as "reactionary suicide." Pessimism chooses to *reify* the status of social death, turning it into an inflexible limitation, whereas neither Fanon nor the Panthers saw this lived position as unchangeable. In the words of Black Studies scholars Hortense Spillers and Lewis Gordon: "It takes what *should be a point of departure* as a point of arrival [or] a moment of closure."[14] Instead, as Newton would say, "every determination is a limitation, and every limitation is a determination," setting up the conditions of possibility for further change.

What makes the lived position of the most oppressed valuable as a decolonial way of approaching life is precisely the fact that it *cannot be known* or *reduced to data*. The calculus of the colony, of governmentality, and of social control produces Blackness as one thing and it is precisely in that move that it perpetually fails. The self-conception of the colonized person, however, exceeds their observation from outside given the limits and blindness of the "white" subjectivity and its gaze, even if/when the colonizer is able to peer inside the very mind of the colonized. As Fanon put it, "in the eyes of the white, blacks have no ontological resistance."[15] This is the case even as Black life carves out whole spaces of resistance in solidarity with the rest of the oppressed. For Newton, crucially, this is done by first of all developing "a concrete analysis of concrete conditions."[16] Inevitably, this entails grasping coloniality not as a set of metaphysical abstractions, but as a set of people engaged in particular activities. In Elaine Brown's words: "The first question for Black people is to get past fear, to see past the monolith to the man."[17]

The idea that one might approach understanding phenomena from the point of view of the most affected – the most oppressed – has functioned in the mainstream as an inspiration for everything from critical race theory to electoral politics, from Black feminist thought to public health. Within the field of law, the concept of "legal empowerment" emphasizes the active participation of those most impacted by legal changes in the work of strategizing efforts to reshape those laws. Similar approaches within the field of education operate off the assumption that the oppressed have unique insights into how education in their own communities should look.[18] For Newton and the Panthers, who historically influenced and shaped so much of this discourse, their development of the concept of the "most oppressed" had a very particular history, hashed out through debate inside the Party and among the left more generally. It began with a claim about Blackness that, unsurprisingly perhaps, still evokes misunderstanding and backlash. In 1971, while at Yale, Newton explained:

> We say that black people are the vanguard of the revolution in this country, and, since no one will be free until the people of America are free, that black people are the vanguard of world revolution. We don't say this in a boasting way. We inherit this legacy primarily because we are the last, you see, and as the saying goes, "The last will be the first."[19]

Quoting Fanon, who himself was quoting a saying from the Bible, Newton made the claim that Black people (as the lumpenproletariat) are last within the hierarchy of statuses, and thereby first in their insight and grasp of the oppression that affects everyone as a whole. Crucially, however, Black people according to Newton are "last" (and thereby "first") not because of anything inherent in their being, but because they are positioned that way under white supremacy. Afrodiasporic people are only "Black" because colonizing Europeans decided to make them "black" and themselves "white." The unique insights that come with the Black standpoint are a structural effect and reflection of white supremacy's obsessions, fixations, and fetishes, not Black people's. As Newton noted: "There is no sacredness, there is no dignity, in either exploiting or being exploited."[20] This nuance is lost on critics (then and now) who misinterpret the Black Panther Party as having embraced a politics of Black exceptionalism. As Newton put it: "I knew the difference between white people and black people, of course, but the cue was always the way white people treated us, not the color itself."[21]

A Question Among Allies

As discussed in the last chapter, the vanguard was a concept used to identify which groups face the greatest oppressions and are thus likely to first rebel, but it also had a prescriptive dimension in referring to which political organizations were thereby likely to produce the most insightful strategies. Years later, however, Angela Davis would lament the dynamic that developed among some activists in which debates about the most oppressed would sometimes prevent coalitional work from taking shape.[22] Alongside asserting the fact of their own oppression, for members of the Black Panther Party the precise question of the relationship of Blackness to other oppressed people was a matter of constant reflection and open conversation. After all, the BPP allied with non-Black groups more than any other Black radical organization of the era. Throughout their history, the Panthers directly influenced the development of diverse organizations like the Puerto Rican Young Lords Party, the white and Appalachian Young Patriots Organization, the American Indian Movement, the Mexican American (Chicano) Brown Berets, and the Asian American I Wor Kuen. From the start, Newton and Seale explicitly sought to work with anyone who would work with them. This forced a constant theoretical grappling, throughout Party history, with the question of people's lived experiences of oppression, their insights, and their willingness to organize.

Within the Party, one prevailing perspective was that the incarcerated are the most oppressed, a subset of super-oppressed among the most oppressed. Kathleen Cleaver articulated this view when she explained that "the vanguard force in the liberation struggle at this present time is the imprisoned population," and she explicitly included political prisoners, common prisoners, and military prisoners.[23] There was also an awareness, however, that the official BPP position featured some ambiguity between the categories of Blackness, the lumpenproletariat, and the prisoner, which of course included many non-Black people.

Among prisoners, perhaps no theorist had his lived experiences held in higher regard than George Jackson, whose *Soledad Brother*, a collection of letters written to his family and supporters, sold 400,000 copies and traversed international borders. In his investigation into George Jackson's 1971 murder, Jo Durden-Smith described Jackson's book as advancing the argument that any effort towards political transformation "should have its roots in feeling."[24] That said, there was also a developing awareness at the time that emphasizing the lived experience of the most oppressed could result in romanticization. This argument was made explicitly regarding George Jackson, whose removed position in prison made him more susceptible to objectification and martyrdom when he died.[25] Indeed, Newton especially admired and looked up to Jackson, despite having never met him in person, referring to him as a "superman" who possessed "genius."[26] "George Jackson was my hero. He set a standard for prisoners, political prisoners, for people. He showed the love, the strength, the revolutionary fervor characteristic of any soldier for the people."[27] On the question of the will of prisoners to resist, Panther Ericka Huggins remarked years after her own incarceration that "the love among people in prison is particular," describing it as "the support of slaves, for one another."[28]

During his own imprisonment, Newton opened the question of the "most oppressed" to sincere open debate and radical questioning. In his 1969 letter to the Republic of New Afrika, he made room for the "the exception of the Indian" when discussing who suffers most from "the colonial plight."[29] Yet even his original Executive Statement No. 1, read out loud at the protest in Sacramento, acknowledged "the genocide practiced on the American Indians and the confinement of the survivors on reservations."[30] Indeed, from the Indigenous standpoint, the analysis of colonization is most clear and recognizable, and Indigenous Americans suffer the violences of police brutality, poverty, and medical neglect at the highest rates of any group, a dynamic eventually affirmed in Newton's later dissertation in 1980: "American Indians have been murdered, tortured, and isolated by the United States government longer than any other group of people in America."[31]

In the later years of the Party, Newton's observations during his travels to other parts of the world confirmed the intercommunalist hypothesis that rebellions are both more common and more likely to be successful at the edges of the empire where physical control is a primary means of oppression, whereas psychological colonization is greater at the center of the empire. When he and his fiancée Gwen Fontaine fled to Mexico (en route to Cuba) in the mid-1970s, Newton wrote in his journal: "The poverty we saw was very disturbing to Gwen and me. . . . The class situation in Mexico and the government's boss, the U.S. are responsible for this situation. The horrible ghettos of Detroit and New York were not as terrible as what we saw in Mexico."[32] Despite his strong sense of internationalism in theory, Newton's personal cultural tendency towards American exceptionalism would slowly be challenged throughout the 1970s as he traveled abroad.

While Newton was in Cuba between 1974 and 1977, the rest of the BPP would expand their conception of the "most oppressed" as well, though along a different dimension of lived experience. In April 1977, years after its peak, the BPP was the most prominent national organization to provide publicity and material support to disability activists engaged in an occupation of the federal Health, Education and Welfare offices in San Francisco, offering food, security, and tactical support against FBI harassment.[33] The disability activists, who included two BPP members, thereby ensured the passage of Section 504 of the Rehabilitation Act that barred discrimination against disabled people in all buildings and facilities receiving federal funding.[34] As disability studies scholar Sami Schalk has pointed out, BPP members were present on the first day of the occupation and described the activists' struggle as grounded in "self-determination" and "the right to survive."[35] Panthers also provided a critique of the marginalization by some in the movement of substance-addicted disabled persons.[36] Consistent with Panther ideals about the unique will to freedom generated by the most oppressed, disability organizer Judith Heumann would later ask rhetorically: "If I didn't fight, who would?"[37] Such welcome revisions regarding the composition of "the most oppressed" would not develop until much later, however, long after the Black Panther Party's membership and broader influence had considerably declined.

The Oppression of Sexuality

At the height of the Black Panther Party's national influence however, it was Newton's embrace of the gay liberation movement that would most significantly shift ideas about oppression. In August 1970, during a planning convention held at Howard University in Washington, DC (in advance of the Revolutionary People's Constitutional Convention that September), Newton seized the opportunity to push forward a critical conversation within the Party.[38] Theorizing and analyzing *homophobia* without employing the term – before the word or idea had entered mainstream discourse – he presented a layered argument for why it might be "the homosexual" who was the most oppressed in society:[39] "I know through reading, and through my life experience and observations that homosexuals are not given freedom and liberty by anyone in the society. They might be the most oppressed people in the society. . . . Maybe a homosexual could be the most revolutionary."[40] Newton drew from psychoanalyst Sigmund Freud's theory of repression to argue that repressed anxieties about how people relate to their gender roles (e.g. how men relate to the idea of being a man) are the source of the societal acceptance of physical violence towards queer people.[41] Critical of "the bourgeois treachery that tries to legislate sexual activity" between "adult people," Newton urged his fellow Panthers to challenge their own internal biases and change their language as initial steps in the bigger effort to "establish a revolutionary value system."[42]

Insisting that "we need as many allies as possible," Newton encouraged the BPP to build functional alliances with groups like the newly formed Gay Liberation Front (GLF) and

Radicalesbians, organizations that were invited to the convention by New York Panther Afeni Shakur.[43] GLF, and later also Third World Gay Revolution and Street Transvestite Action Revolutionaries (STAR), were originally inspired to become anti-racist, anti-capitalist, and anti-imperialist organizations after copying the practices of the Black Panther Party.[44] For their part, the BPP critiqued the homophobia of some Third World socialist movements.[45] In his statement, Newton asked of the queer organizations above all that they be "politically conscious"; at the convention, the Los Angeles branch of the GLF responded in turn, after internal debate, by affirming the Black Panther Party as the vanguard of the revolution.[46] The aim in examining the lived experiences of these various groups was not to focus on individual identities but to develop a "popular front" against the forces of oppression. The Black Panther Party, led by Newton's statement, was the first Black organization to stand in explicit support of liberation for queer people.

While some observers then and now might be surprised by the Party's alliance with the gay liberation movement, the idea that Black and queer communities exist as wholly separate entities is perhaps a reflection of middle- or upper-class cultural biases. From the lumpenproletarian standpoint – especially before queerness acquired mainstream respectability, when police harassment was more common – queer life *was* lumpen life and often vice versa; their spaces and lived experiences did not just overlap but were often simply the same. Among people abandoned by their families and the rest of society, the street-corner world of illegal hustles, sex work, communal living, and alternate approaches to defining "family" (i.e. street gangs and queer social scenes) points to a thorough interrelatedness of lived experience that was probably the inspiration for Newton's empathy. Such realities also help us realize that Newton's remarks about his "life experience and observations" likely referred to his time in the streets, when he "flirted with pimping for only about nine months" in his early twenties, an experience that likely involved interacting on the corners with queer people of various lifestyles.[47]

For related reasons, the prison was another space of overlap. During his time as a political prisoner, Newton had important conversations with "gay brothers who talked to him at length and were largely responsible for a change in his thinking about gay people."[48] At the same time, however, he was vigilant concerning what he felt was a particular vulnerability of queerness to political manipulation inside the prison.[49] In *Revolutionary Suicide*, he argued that, in prison, "love and vulnerability and tenderness were distorted into functions of power, competition and control."[50] He critically described a "pseudosexuality" that was actively, artificially, and coercively fostered by the prison authorities in order to better control inmates, with guards leveraging human connection and separation as a means of control and punishment.[51] Newton's acute awareness of this dynamic during his time at the jail at Alameda County Courthouse led him to end his relationship with his then-girlfriend LaVerne Williams, in order to spare her from police harassment and himself from having her leveraged against him.[52] He was clear that both homosexual and heterosexual relationships can be manipulated in this way, but he argued that homosexual relationships between prisoners were more easily and sadistically manipulated because of the confined status of both persons: "this is prison, where every desire is used against you."[53]

For Newton, such overlaps in lived experience inspired empathy and understanding, but for others such realities can instead inspire sharp, reactionary rejection and a desire to define oneself in exaggerated opposition. David Hilliard later remarked on the prevalence of queer people within the BPP:

> There were gay operatives in the Black Panther Party working at the highest levels of leadership. . . . Lesbian relationships were more acceptable in the party than homosexual relations between men. But the uneasiness over gay men was expressed primarily by men, most of whom were insecure with their own sexuality. Still, no one ever asked you to define your sexual orientation. We didn't divide ourselves like that. First and foremost you were a Black Panther.[54]

The most prominent upholder of homophobia in the Party was undoubtedly Eldridge Cleaver, whose famous 1968 *Soul on Ice* was for many in white America and its intelligentsia a principal draw to the Party, with 2 million copies in print by 1970.[55] The book – parts of which were first published in *Ramparts* and *Esquire* magazines starting in 1966, before Cleaver joined the Party – drew attention for its decolonial Marxism, its description of Cleaver's past as a rapist, and for its homophobic attacks against James Baldwin, the most prominent writer of the era to openly discuss queer life. According to Cleaver, Baldwin's political views were not radical enough and were a consequence of his queerness, as supposedly demonstrated in an alleged preferentiality towards white men.[56]

In 1972, Newton started drafting a book titled *Hidden Traitor*, the sole focus of which was a critique of Cleaver.[57] It was to feature an extensive discussion of Cleaver's troubled relationship to his own sexuality. The book never came to fruition, although multiple drafts are held in archive and, in 2002, the Dr. Huey P. Newton Foundation published an edited version of a late draft of a chapter titled "Eldridge Cleaver: He is No James Baldwin."[58] Drawing on a precise application of Freud's concept of paranoia, Newton argued that "Baldwin's *open homosexuality* threaten[ed] Cleaver's *repressed* homosexuality." He described an instance in which Cleaver passionately kissed Baldwin soon after the publication of Cleaver's vitriolic essays.[59] According to Newton, "The problems, difficulties, and internal conflict that Cleaver has within himself – because he is engaged in denial of his own homosexuality – is projected onto an eternal *self* (Baldwin) in order to defend his own threatened ego."[60]

Newton further argued that Cleaver's sexual assault of women was driven by his hatred and envy of femininity, and "not only envy of the female principle but contempt for blackness," evidenced by Cleaver's notorious writings about "practicing" rape on Black women before assaulting white women. Ultimately, Newton argued that Cleaver's "self-hatred and his sexual insecurity; his pitiful need for a clear love-hate dichotomy," were in part an effect of a failure to realize that "there is some masculinity in every female and some femininity in every male."[61] Black philosopher Tommy Curry has drawn attention to unpublished writings by Cleaver in which he is said to be more "candid and open about his homosexuality," suggesting that Cleaver's manuscript *The Book of Lives* represents a more authentic and self-reflective version of his approach to his same-sex desires while in prison.[62] Such interpretations must be reconciled, however, with the mounting evidence that Cleaver's sexuality was consistently expressed in a violent manner towards people of *all genders and ages* in the Party, as well as its supporters and the Black community at large.[63] These are matters that Cleaver was not honest about.

In *Hidden Traitor* and other texts, Newton argued that Cleaver was much less a sincere revolutionist interested in strategy than he was a writer interested in a romanticized view of insurrection. If that is so, it is perhaps Cleaver's consistent unwillingness as a writer to be *honest* about his lived experiences – as oppressed and oppressor – that had the greatest effect in guaranteeing the declining usefulness and circulation of his once famous writings in the decades since the 1960s.

The Oppression of Gender

During the first several years of the BPP's existence, Newton wrote very little regarding the lived experiences of women. Echoing this early silence, recorded discussions by Panther women about the relationship between their lived experiences and the question of "the most oppressed" were relatively limited early on as well, in part an effect of Newton's late incorporation of the issue into Party ideology as the organization's "chief theoretician." However, as historian Tracye Matthews has pointed out, by 1970, the BPP's ever-expanding coalitional work had increased opportunities for Black women in the Party to interact with and learn from others in the women's liberation movement and the beginnings of the Black feminist movement.[64]

The first extensive publication featuring Panther women discussing the matter of the experience of oppression appeared not in *The Black Panther* but in the SNCC's newspaper *The Movement* in September 1969.[65] This was a group interview with six female Panthers, their names anonymized. Its reprinting in *The Black Panther* later that month was cut off towards the end of the discussion without explanation.[66] In the original publication, it was the interviewer who first raised the issue in its most direct form: "Black women are considered to be the most oppressed group in the U.S., as blacks and as women. That special oppression gives them a special, even vanguard, role. Would you like to talk about that a little?"[67] One woman responded hesitantly, emphasizing the "sensitive," "kind of difficult and kind of touchy" dynamic of men in the Party who feared domination by women, though this very dynamic was identified by another as precisely "part of the special oppression of black women. Black women as generally a part of the poor people of the U.S., the working class, are more oppressed, as being black, they're super-oppressed, and as being women they are sexually oppressed by men in general and by black men also."[68] That respondent (most likely Berkeley Panther Roberta Alexander) further emphasized that "it's very important that black women understand and black men understand that black man's manhood is not dependent upon the subordination of black women."[69] The dominant tendency in the interview, however, was to emphasize unity among Black women and men and other oppressed groups, in contrast to the political separatism practiced by some white women's liberation movement groups. Male chauvinism was also analyzed in the discussion as being sustained by both men and women and as requiring the efforts of both in order to be effectively challenged. Ultimately, in the analysis of one of the women, "there's going to have to be an ideological struggle for decades and probably for centuries before male chauvinism is overcome."[70]

This analysis characterizing Black women's experiences of oppression as *unique* but also as an inseparably shared condition with men was echoed during the era by Angela Davis in her essay "Reflections on the Black Woman's Role in the Community of Slaves," from 1971. Still imprisoned, she argued that "the unbridled cruelty of this leveling process whereby the black woman was forced into equality with the black man requires no further explanation. She shared in the deformed equality of equal oppression."[71] Although Davis was writing about the experiences of past enslaved African Americans, she was also in effect writing about her present, putting into practice what she and James Baldwin called "the uses to which we could put the experience of the slave" during a time when state repression of radical publications was mounting.[72] It is difficult to overstate the innovative character of this essay, which has served as a foundation for so much later political activism, writing, and thought. Embedded in Davis's remarks about "deformed equality" was an early recognition that, under the dehumanizing conditions of chattel slavery, *gender* differences (between women and men) were essentially dissolved and replaced by *sex*-based differentiation (female and male), since the enslaved were treated as domesticated animals held as property.

Besides establishing a ground for solidarity in shared conditions of oppression, however, Davis also drew attention to the particular exposure of Black women to rape at the hands of the slave master. But even this seemingly highly gendered form of suffering Davis also characterized as an attack upon "the slave community as a whole."[73] Lastly, her analysis of the Black woman as uniquely oppressed led to the essay's most insightful point: its account of the domestic sphere as a place of resistant political activity, autonomy, and communal defense of the whole of the Black community under slavery. "As the center of domestic life, the only life at all removed from the arena of exploitation, and thus as an important source of survival, the black woman could play a pivotal role in nurturing the thrust towards freedom."[74] Davis's analysis notably converged with Newton's and Jackson's regarding the centrality of survival and communal care as the foundation of struggle. After Newton's release from prison, he became a very vocal defender of Davis, and especially so after Cleaver's expulsion.[75]

Sometime later, in 1974, as the Panther movement was in decline, a Black, anti-capitalist, and lesbian collective of activists, some of whom had been Panthers, formed the Combahee River Collective (CRC).[76] Coming out of many of the same debates, but also offering a critique of the patriarchal aspects of the Black liberation movement, their famous 1977 "Black Feminist Statement" specifically invoked and revised Newton's language from his 1971 Yale speech:

> [Newton, again:] We say that black people are the vanguard of the revolution in this country, and, since no one will be free until the people of America are free, that black people are the vanguard of world revolution. . . . We inherit this

legacy primarily because we are the last, you see, and as the saying goes, "The last will be the first."[77]

> [Combahee River Collective:] We might use our position at the bottom, however, to make a clear leap into revolutionary action. If black women were free, it would mean that everyone else would have to be free since our freedom would necessitate the destruction of all the systems of oppression.[78]

The indebtedness of the CRC's formulation to the thought of Newton has not been generally acknowledged. Affirming the Panther insight about the will of the most oppressed, the CRC also stated: "We realize that the only people who care enough about us to work consistently for our liberation is us."[79] Even some of the BPP's Maoist influence is evident in the CRC's statement, including the particular use of the language of "leap" and the concept of "criticism and self-criticism" later in the piece.[80] The Combahee River Collective affirmed the strategic analysis that described the most oppressed as being counterintuitively in a leading position to push forward change, though their analysis also featured a crucial difference in explicitly emphasizing that the most oppressed also have *conscious* and *rational* insights that others do not. This was a substantial intervention into, and clarification of, the debate about "the most oppressed." The CRC argued that "seemingly *personal experiences*" in fact reflect knowledge of *structures of oppression*.[81]

This was distinct from Newton's analysis, which rather implied more straightforwardly that the most oppressed are those most likely to rebel. Only George Jackson would write in passing of "lumpen intellectuals who possess revolutionary scientific-socialist attitudes."[82] While the idea that the Black community as lumpenproletariat is in fact the most *insighful* is not necessarily excluded by Newton's conceptualization, and was surely implicit in debates with allies, the Combahee River Collective made this aspect of intuition and analytic insight more explicit, allowing more room for forms of struggle that may not appear so clearly as forms of rebellion. Notably, both the BPP and the CRC exploded stereotypes that underestimated the strength of the intellect of the most oppressed, whether they were talking about the lumpenproletariat or Black women.

By making this aspect so explicit, Combahee also succeeded more thoroughly in encouraging people to openly discuss their lived experiences as a part of the development of strategy. Like Angela Davis, CRC was in this regard deeply inspired by the women's liberation movement's powerful tradition of openly discussing personal experiences of oppression, especially sexual violence. While the BPP developed theory by analyzing the experiences of the lumpenproletariat, and "self-criticism" was idealized as a part of everyone's political education, self-reflection and personal testimony were perhaps less often an explicit part of the rank and file's development of social analysis and political strategy.

In fact, in contrast with the feminist movement's motto that "the personal is political," Newton would articulate an apparent critique of exactly this view in 1971: "Sometimes there are those who express personal problems in political terms, and if they are eloquent then these personal problems can sound very political. We charge Eldridge Cleaver with this."[83] Interestingly, and counterintuitively, Newton used a critique of the feminist motto in order to critique the ideas of Cleaver, the rapist. This is counterintuitive because the motto had been used to lend political legitimacy to women's accounts of their personal experiences, including their experiences of being vulnerable to sexual violence. Newton's retort against Cleaver can be most easily understood if we consider Cleaver's infamous suggestion in *Soul on Ice* that his act of "rape was an insurrectionary act."[84] Newton was critically pointing out that Cleaver's misconception of his act as a form of political resistance was an effect of his "solipsism and narcissism," among other "personal problems."[85] That is, he "charged" Cleaver with disguising his personal problems as political ones. However, Newton's statement carried the flawed implication that there is no value in politically analyzing Cleaver's "personal problems" as a sign of larger structural problems. To the contrary, the feminist movement was in this period demonstrating precisely that talking about people's personal experiences was crucial for understanding what was going on societally. Furthermore, Cleaver's problems were not "just" personal – his actions directly impacted others, making his problems immediately social and indeed political after all.

Another reason why Newton's remark from 1971 was unusual was the fact that much of his work and writing up to that point had indicated clearly that he *did* see personal experience as reflective of political dynamics. Nonetheless, as the following sections argue, Newton seems to have often avoided discussing sexual matters *specifically* in political contexts, with this reticence being only gradually overcome over time. This avoidance hindered the development of his views on patriarchy, gender dynamics, and the relationship between sex and power in a way that would have repercussions for the whole of the Black power movement, given his enormous influence as a theorist. Eventually, his views did become *thoroughly* anti-patriarchal, but perhaps at a point too late for the movement as a whole. It is also among the most tragic of ironies in Newton's life that, just as he was developing a robust feminist philosophy, he would slip seemingly inexplicably ever deeper into an emotional dysregulation and madness that would see him enact the very patriarchal violence he had finally come to vigorously denounce. These are profound contradictions that require a full explanation.

In the remainder of this chapter, I attempt to identify and chronologize every significant discussion of women's oppression and the relationship between sex and power in Newton's body of published statements and completed unpublished works between 1966, when the Party was founded, and 1974, when Newton fled into exile in Cuba. In summary, I propose four phases in his relationship to gender and power: 1966–71 as a period characterized by an almost exclusive focus on men when discussing gender, sex, and power; 1972–74 as a period of deep critique of the entanglement of sex and power and a thorough anti-patriarchal turn in his thinking; 1974–77 as a time of tranquility while in Cuba; and 1977–82 (discussed in Chapters 7 and 8) as a period of striving for self-understanding in light of his slide into destruction of himself and others.

The Gendered Oppression of Black Men

Newton's "Fear and Doubt" (1967), discussed earlier, was focused exclusively on the lived experience and state of personal disorientation of the Black male. This essay has sometimes been accused by scholars of implicit misogyny, on the grounds that it supposedly affirms the 1965 Moynihan Report, a federal publication that argued that Black men's "pathologies" were caused by excessive domination by Black women, a view that Black feminists would subsequently label "the myth of the Black matriarch." However, a close look at Newton's essay makes it clear that Newton's figure of the Black male "blames himself" and not Black women in any way. As Lisa Corrigan has argued, "Newton's public speeches and writings like 'Fear and Doubt' charted another argument about black masculinity that acknowledged how both *structural violence* and *black male vulnerability* were caused by structures of white supremacy and *not black women*."[86] Rather than being misogynistic, the essay was instead concerned with Black men in a particularly insular way, a mode typical of Newton's writings during the early years of the Party's existence.

A weaker argument may be made that this mode was sexist in effect because it was androcentric (male-centric) within a society that was already patriarchal. Importantly, however, the only true "MAN" in this society, according to the Black male Newton describes, is the white male in power. "He feels that he is something less than a man, and it is evident in his conversation: 'The White man is 'THE MAN,' he got everything, and he knows everything, and a nigger ain't nothing.'"[87] Newton critiqued the mentality and practices of lumpenproletarian Black men who lack knowledge of the broader structures of power:

> He is confused and in a constant state of rage, of shame, of doubt. This psychological state permeates all his interpersonal relationships. It determines his view of the social system. His psychological development has been prematurely arrested. This doubt begins at a very early age and continues throughout his life.
>
> He may father several "illegitimate" children by several different women in order to display his masculinity. But in the end, he realizes that his efforts have no real effect.
>
> In a society where a man is valued according to occupation and material possessions, he is without possessions.

> He is ineffectual both in and out of the home. He cannot provide for, or protect his family. He is invisible, a non-entity. Society will not acknowledge him as a man. He is a consumer and not a producer.[88]

After identifying multiple spheres of life in which the Black male of his era felt inadequate, Newton ended his essay with an invocation of Louis Armstrong's song: "What did he do to be so Black and blue?" According to Newton's thinking in this period, the "brothers on the block" were the most oppressed, and Black women did not enter into his analysis.

In May 1968, while Newton was in jail, Joe Blum of the *Movement* newspaper interviewed him at length. The resulting text was published one month after the assassination of Dr. King and would circulate widely, serving as a major introduction to Huey Newton for many in this period.[89] Even more so than *The Black Panther* newspaper, at this point run without much input from Newton, this interview featured Newton as an individual expressing himself on everything from Black cultural politics to white radicals, from internationalism to armed struggle.[90] On the matter of gender dynamics, we see here for the first time the major influence of Cleaver, the Minister of Information, on Newton's thought. Newton read Cleaver's *Soul on Ice* in 1968 after meeting him in person. In the interview, Newton discussed the importance of having "a mind of our own," a phrase he borrowed from Cleaver, and offered an extended psychosexual metaphor that was drawn from the fourth and last section of *Soul on Ice*:

> The historical relationship between black and white here in America has been the relationship between the slave and the master; the master being the mind and the slave the body. The slave would carry out the orders that the mind demanded him to carry out. By doing this the master took the manhood from the slave because he stripped him of a mind. He stripped black people of their mind. In the process the slave-master stripped himself of a body. As Eldridge puts it the slave-master became the omnipotent administrator and the slave became the supermasculine menial.[91]

Newton went on to state that the slave master "discovered he had emasculated himself" through his disconnection from labor, and as a result projected an image of hypermasculinity onto the male slave: he "pictured the slave as being more of a man, being superior sexually," which he tried to compensate for through sexual violence and "access to the black woman."[92] At various times, the Black woman was included or excluded from this account of the master-slave dynamic. In addition, echoing Cleaver, Newton said of the slave master that "because he doesn't have a body, he doesn't have a penis, he psychologically wants to castrate the black man."[93] For this part of the discussion, the *Movement* editors themselves inserted the section heading "Penis Envy," misapplying Freud's concept.[94]

One of Newton's central points in this discussion revolved around the claim that the Black radicals of the late 1960s (presumed male) had "regained [the] mind that was taken away from us" and were now able to "decide the political as well as the practical stand that we'll take." In saying this, Newton was specifically referring to a dynamic common in Black social movement organizations earlier in the 1960s whose strategies were decided by white people; he sought to contrast this dynamic with the policies of the BPP.[95] Separately, he also drew attention to the violent sexual dynamics of slavery under which Black men and women were both frequently subject to various forms of sexual violence and brutality by slave masters. This section of the interview, like the comparable discussions in Cleaver's book, was sure to produce emotionally charged reactions from its readers, as it featured Black people testifying to realities that were a subject of taboo. However, to refer to these dynamics as "taboo" also obscures the fact that, historically, enslaved women were raped and enslaved men were castrated *in public*. These are realities that historians and scholars of Black studies and gender studies have worked hard to have this country come to terms with since then.[96] Newton's analysis suggested some sort of continuity between the physical castrations of the past and white men's actions towards Black men in his present.

However, his language also generated confusion about what this psychosexual dynamic meant practically in terms of liberation for Black people. In the following passage, in which he spoke of Black men reclaiming themselves, Newton could be interpreted as referring either to an aspect of the mind (the will to act) or to an aspect of the body: "If he can only recapture his mind, recapture his balls, then he will lose all fear and will be free to determine his destiny."[97] A similar ambiguity is present in other parts of the interview: "the vanguard group, the Black Panther Party along with all revolutionary black groups have regained our mind and our manhood."[98] Notably, against the developing trend among other members of the Party, Newton typically avoided vulgarity in his writings and published speeches, making the above remark all the more perplexing. Why use a reference to the sexual body to describe the reclaiming of the *mind*?

Newton goes on to assert that "we no longer define the omnipotent administrator as 'the Man' . . . because WE define them as pigs! . . . That's power itself. Matter of fact, what is power other than the ability to define phenomena and then make it act in a desired manner?"[99] The following statements from the interview continued then to fit more easily with Newton's broader system of thought:

> The white power structure today in America defines itself as the mind. They want to control the world. They go off and plunder the world. They are the policeman of the world exercising control especially over people of color.
>
> This is what is happening at this time with the rebellion of the world's oppressed people against the controller. They are regaining their mind and they're saying that we have a mind of our own. They're saying that we want freedom to determine the destiny of our people, thereby uniting the mind with their bodies.[100]

After this interview, to the best of my knowledge, Newton made no further public recorded statements about gender or sexual dynamics for two and a half years (1968–70).

This period of silence continued even during the internal struggle against sexism within the Party during the 1968–69 period. The fact that that struggle occurred was itself obscured by how Newton later narrated the Party's phases on its way to intercommunalism. Somewhere in his account of the shift from

Black Nationalism to the Revolutionary Nationalist effort to ally with other oppressed peoples there should presumably have been some mention of an internal Black womanist or feminist phase.

Decades later, Black feminist Patricia Hill Collins correctly identified that an "ill-defined manhood" hampered the Black liberation movement, burdening it with an ambiguous concept that, for some, equated *psychological* freedom with *sexual* power, but offered little acknowledgment of the importance of freedom from sexual violence.[101] Importantly, it must be stated, the term "manhood" had already been in heavy use in the Black community long before, deployed by figures like King, X, and Baldwin alike. And, crucially, the claim to manhood was arguably just as much about Black men refusing to be treated as children – called "boy" by white people – as it was about gender. However, Newton's early echo of Cleaver's theoretically troubled notion of manhood meant that ultimate responsibility for its use within the Party fell on Newton. The ambiguity was echoed even by Panther women, as in the "Panther Sisters on Women's Liberation" interview: "Our men have sort of been castrated, you know. The responsibilities that they rightfully should have had before, were taken away from them – to take away their manhood."[102] Castration was in that discussion, too, brought up in a seemingly metaphorical manner and associated with a lack of power.

Perhaps most easily overlooked in analyses of Newton's early language is the matter of why castration, a severe form of sexual violence against men, was invoked at all, but always seemingly as a metaphor. Why did members of the Black Panther Party so regularly invoke the reality of sexual violence done to Black men under slavery, but leave undefined what this meant in the present? By contrast, in Davis's writing, it was clear that her analysis of sexual violence done to Black women under slavery was meant to highlight their continued exposure to sexual violence in the present of the 1960s and 1970s. Contemporary Black Studies scholar Vincent Woodard has argued that Black men's experiences of sexual violence under slavery have had distinct social effects on Black men in the diaspora, hindering their ability to relate to sexuality, intimacy, and the self.[103] Coming from that history, sex and power were traumatically entangled. We are led then to hypothesize that these Black men's mentions of historical sexual violence may have been awkward gestures towards analyzing their own exposure to sexual violation and violence in their present.

A second look at Panther accounts reveals precisely these kinds of experiences. In 2006, Panther veteran Ericka Huggins recounted a story of being pulled over by police and held at gunpoint while pregnant; at the same time, another officer pointed a gun at her husband Panther John Huggins and kept his legs spread open while violently squeezing his testicles.[104] Such an episode encompasses both what Joy James has referred to as the genocidal attack on the *captive maternal* and what Tommy Curry has referred to as anti-Black *sexual racism*.[105] That is, all forms of Black care and the Black sexual body are targeted for violation, violence, and domination. On the night that Huey Newton was shot by Officer Frey and Frey ended up shot and killed, Newton was also sexually violated: "Frey frisked me in a degrading fashion, his hands probing my genitals."[106]

More common though than sexual violence at the hands of police was the sexual violence experienced in the prisons. All incarceration begins with sexual violence: a non-consensual exposure of the naked body, followed by a violation of its orifices, which is administered and normalized as part of our society's denigration of imprisoned human beings.[107] Even the public stripping, exceedingly normalized, has origins in the objectification, examination, and sale of enslaved Africans. As feminist philosopher Lisa Guenther writes: "in a strip search, one's body, the site of corporeal and intercorporeal mattering is literally put into the hands of another. The insistent message is that the body of the person being searched does *not* matter, that it does not even properly belong to that person, and that it can only bear the meaning that is imposed on it by the violence of others."[108] Newton, who went to prison in his early twenties, recounted precisely such experiences:

> At Vacaville I went through a ritual familiar to every inmate – the skin search. From that time forward, through my years in jail, I was never allowed to go from one building to another without this demeaning exercise. I took off all my clothes. Then they looked into my ears and nose, rubbed

> their hands through my hair, made me cough to prove there was nothing in my mouth; then I spread the cheeks of my buttocks while they searched my anus.[109]

Newton also described sexual harassment by guards during his three years as a political prisoner: "Often, as I showered, a guard would stand in the doorway, talking, looking not at my face but at my penis, and say, 'Hey Newton, how you doin' there, Newton? Want to have some fun, Newton?' I laughed at them."[110]

Black studies scholar and anthropologist Orisanmi Burton has identified the regularity of sexual assault by prison guards as a part of efforts to subjugate Black radicals in the era. In *Tip of the Spear*, a powerful examination of the 1971 revolt and commune at Attica Prison after the assassination of George Jackson, Burton draws attention to not just the homicidal massacre enacted by guards after the suppression of the commune, but also the organized mass sexual assault of prisoners.[111] Sexualized torture as a part of repression was common. Burton quotes Panther Albert Woodfox describing how, at the Tombs Prison in NYC, "They herded us like animals and forced us to lie [naked] on top of each other while guards made cruel and racist remarks, like 'Put that dick in him nigger.' Prisoners who refused to lie on the other men were beaten mercilessly."[112] In Burton's analysis, these assaults reflect an ongoing *war* against Black radical organizing. Feminist philosopher Linda Martín Alcoff has offered a helpful clarification, pointing out that "existing research counters the idea that rape is a 'natural' byproduct of war or even of militarism and suggests instead that sexual violence is *orchestrated*, occurring widely only under certain kinds of conditions, commanders, and commandment structures."[113] Legal theorist Valorie Vojdik has further affirmed that such "orchestrated" administrations of sexual violence tend to include other forms of sexual violation, including forced perpetration of sexual violence (for males), forced incest, and sexual torture.[114] And Frantz and Josie Fanon defined colonization as fundamentally a form of war continued, distinctly inclusive of sexual violence.[115]

The imposition of the concept of the criminal onto Black, poor, and colonized populations obscures the reality that the lumpenproletariat are *victims* of sexual violence more often than any other part of the population. In prisons, youth especially are a primary target for sexual violence, although all prisoners are subject to it as part of normalized procedures. The Black Panther Party, especially when it was first established, included many young men – such as Newton and Cleaver both – who had spent years as children imprisoned in the California Youth Authority's juvenile detention. As historian Donna Murch has written: "Youth Authority facilities could be brutal places, and many children and adolescents had experiences that marked them for life."[116] Despite understanding themselves as uniquely oppressed, these young men did not typically discuss their experiences of sexual violation. Instead, they spoke in vague terms about "psychological castration," "emasculation," and regaining "manhood" as a reclaiming of "the mind," invoking the specter of the sexual violation of Black men and boys under slavery as a point of reference but without discussing it directly. This was not grasped by others as a vulnerable acknowledgment of experiences of sexual violation, but perhaps it should have been. As with most people, Newton's avoidance of the matter of sexual violence may have been personal. In "Fear and Doubt," he wrote: "He is dependent and he hates 'THE MAN' and he hates himself. Who is he? Is he a very old adolescent or is he the slave he used to be?"[117]

Against the Gendered Oppression of Women

In 1970, after three years in solitary confinement and more than two years of not discussing sex, Newton made his public statement on "The Women's Liberation and Gay Liberation Movements." Yet, even in that statement, his recognition of the oppression of *women in particular* was limited. In both the published statement of August 15 and a related interview on August 14, he focused primarily on the oppression of queer people and homophobia, barely addressing women's liberation, despite the title of the statement.[118] He discusses the physical abuse of queer people and women, directly chastising the men in the Party for their insecurities – suggesting that "we want to hit the woman or shut her up because we are afraid that she might castrate us"

– but does not discuss sexual violence at all. Only when he was asked about it a few days later, in an interview with *Liberation News Service*, did he finally respond directly regarding the matter of women's oppression:

> LNS: What kind of reaction did you get to your letter to the Party about Gay Liberation and Women's Liberation?
> Huey: They were very happy that this should come from the Party, out of all people – the people seem to be very surprised.
> LNS: Who was that?
> Huey: The women's liberation people. They were very happy that the Party was attempting to relate to them. Within our Party we're not completely rid of male chauvinism (laughter). I think that we're trying, we're making an honest effort. Women in our Party can participate in any level in the Party. We're constantly fighting those bourgeois attitudes of male chauvinism. We are advancing, we try to keep our ranks open – there are women ministers in the Party. All women are trained, just as the men, with the revolutionary tool. At every level I think that the women should be included.
> LNS: How do you react to other Black groups that object to women's liberation on the grounds that it interferes with the self-assertion of the Black male?
> Huey: Well I think if we went along with that we'd be going along with the old values and we would be adhering to the old situation – which we are trying to break away from. This would be freedom for people you see. I think it would be backwards to try to build male chauvinism at this point.
>
> It's not really true but if the women in our ethnic group appear to have some objective superiority, being the head of families and so forth, it's a thing that we should also fight. I know that throughout our historical experience women have been the head of our families, a lot, but at the same time because of that you get male chauvinism among Blacks as a real problem. Because males come in with this attitude of "I have to show this woman that I am strong, and I won't follow that stereotype." So you really have a real problem

> of male chauvinism among us Blacks, because of our history. We're working on that, and I think we'll solve it.[119]

In this interview, in which he finally addressed the *internal* sexism within the Party, Newton dismissed the myth of the Black matriarch as "not really true," adding that, regardless, Panther men and Black men in general must strive to reject their male chauvinism. He did not publicly address the occurrence of coercive sexual dynamics among certain men in some chapters of the Party, but neither did Panther women publicly address the matter in this period either, following instead the Black activist norm of dealing with such problems internally.[120] It would not be until early 1971, with Cleaver's expulsion, that Newton finally denounced "sexual fascism" and "sexual chauvinism," articulating this as the official position of the Black Panther Party during the Intercommunal Day of Solidarity on May 5 of that year.[121]

In June 1971, Newton penned a long review in praise of a controversial film called *Sweet Sweetback's Baadasssss Song*. Produced by Melvin van Peebles, it has been variously described as the first blaxploitation film, as exploitatively pornographic, and as revolutionary. It tells the story of a Black man raised in a brothel who, after killing a police officer, is in continuous flight as a fugitive and is forced to have sex to survive. In an interview in April 1971, Peebles stated that "the theme of the film is 'you bled my mama, you bled my papa; won't bleed me.'"[122] Arguably the first film to feature an antagonistic Black protagonist, the film embraced the stereotype of the hypersexual Black male as a way to challenge mainstream depictions of Black characters as submissive, echoing some of the baggage and stereotypes that the Black Panther Party struggled with in its early years.

For our purposes, we are concerned with Newton's review of the film, which overwhelmingly praises it for its depiction of aspects of lumpenproletarian Black life, but does so by treating the film at an unusually removed level of abstraction. Whereas audiences reacted most strongly to the multiple, drawn-out scenes in which the protagonist is forced into sex, with the most disturbing of all being a scene where a boy is forced into sex with an adult woman sex worker, Newton instead argued that "People who look upon this as a sex scene miss the point completely, and people who look upon the movie as a sex movie miss the entire message of the film."[123] While it is correct that the film is saturated with political symbolisms, Newton's argument that the sex scenes are *only* and *purely* symbolic challenges common sense.[124] Accordingly, when he states that "whenever Sweetback engages in sex with a sister it is always an act of survival and a step towards his liberation," one is led to ask why sex – and always *being subject to forced sex*, sexual violence – is the means chosen to represent survival.[125]

In an extensive and sensitive interview conducted in 2007, Panther leader Ericka Huggins stated that, in her understanding, "Huey had been sexually abused by his father. We found out later, I don't know if it's true or not, but I'll say it because it touched my heart, that Huey had been sexually abused by his father. . . . That made things make sense to me."[126] This claim has not been affirmed by others. However, if true, such a tragic revelation might help explain Newton's perplexing analysis of the film and perhaps also more broadly his stilted approach to the topic of sexual violence. In the film review, his remarks about child sexuality specifically give pause, given his distinctive uses of the pronoun "we": "it is hard for us to remember our first sexual experience"; "Even though we may have sexual intercourse as children, we don't have a climax"; "we are all Sweetbacks and we are all united in his victimization."[127] It is also the case that Newton's father Walter was himself a child of rape.[128] Walter Newton's mother Alice Hilliard was a Black, teenaged houseworker who was raped by Walter's biological father, a German Jewish man named Solomon Simon, who was the son of a man who employed her.[129] Alice Hilliard later married a Black man, Ben Newton, from whom Walter received his surname. In the film review – Huey Newton's longest published text up to this point – he clearly struggled to conceptualize the multiple sexual scenes as violations, consistent with the broader societal blindness to understanding coercive sex imposed onto Black boys as sexual violence.

By 1972, there were signs that Newton was coming to terms with the entangled relationship between sex and power. In a talk delivered at Georgia State College on February 10, 1972, he finally affirmed the reality of the oppression that Black women are subject to. In response to a question from the audience, he stated:

> First I identify her as a Black woman and therefore a victim of oppression in more than one way. One way because she is Black and the second way because she's a woman. We realize that women are the most oppressed people in the world, and we can't help but support her efforts to bring about the freedom of the people. As far as her analysis and identification of the real conditions and the real objective facts, and her conclusion and whether certain avenues will get us that freedom, we have that under consideration, our Central Committee. We haven't concluded yet, but we support her in her drive for freedom.[130]

Newton makes a point of affirming this position *as an individual*, separately from the views of the rest of the Central Committee. Two months later, the Black Panther Party published an official revision to their Ten-Point Program, complete with changes to the gender of pronouns used in the text. Point 5 features just such a change:

October 1966: "If a man does not have knowledge of himself and his position in society and the world, then he has little chance to relate to anything else."

March 1972: "If you do not have knowledge of yourself and your position in the society and the world, then you will have little chance to know anything else."[131]

The talk Newton gave on May 20, 1972 to the Southern California Counseling Center, a radical and community-responsive center for psychiatry, was easily one of his most interesting and dynamic recorded presentations, touching on everything from the influence of Buddhism on Mao Zedong to Black author John A. Williams' novel *The Man Who Cried I Am*.[132] As part of his grappling with questions of sex and power, he explained a shift in his thinking about the relationship of the libido to the will to power. Specifically, he discussed the historical debate that arose between psychoanalysts Sigmund Freud and Alfred Adler on precisely the question of whether sexuality (*eros*) is or is not central to the human desire to overcome domination.[133]

> As you very well know Freud and Adler had some division in their school, their whole will to power theory was somewhat of an offshoot of Freud's theory of the libido sexual drive as the primary driving force of man. We say that we agree with Adler that the primary drive in man is the will to power, and we also agree with Freud's libido theory, the Oedipus. . . . We think that the will to power encompasses also the libido-psycho-sexual drive as being the primary drive of man's motivation. . . . With Adler's will to power this would give some credence to the fact that the basic struggle is man's will to gain power over himself, over his environment, so that he will have the freedom then to choose.[134]

Importantly, Newton emphasized that the sex drive is included in but *secondary to* a broader will to power that does not itself boil down to sex, a conclusion consistent with his original definition of power and the Black community's aim for self-determination.

He then went on to critique Freud's concept of the Oedipus complex, the Greek story according to which the future king Oedipus is only able to come to power by killing his father and sleeping with his mother. Ultimately Newton dismissed the Oedipus complex for being "ethno-centric," stating that its dynamics are not relevant to humanity in general – an echo of Fanon's critique of psychoanalysis in *Black Skin, White Masks*. Newton said of the myth:

> I don't think that it fits in with the origin of man or takes under consideration probably that the first man that anthropologists recognize was born in the cradle of Africa, where of course they were not touched or influenced by the kind of Greek mythology . . . The underlying guilt complex as they tragically expressed, that brought about the Oedipus [complex] and so forth. We'll reject that along with rejecting the whole psycho-sexual premise that the libido is the primary driving force of man. I think that it's better understood in

> the will to power that was expressed by Adler and Jung with his collective unconscious.[135]

In Panther leader Elaine Brown's autobiography, she described in more straightforward terms how Newton's view changed and gained clarity at this time: "He talked on through most of the rest of the night, about love and revolution, and about how 'fucking' had little to do with either."[136] This clarity was a great departure from the conflation between reclaiming one's "mind," one's "manhood," and one's "balls" that Newton had recited before. Near the end of his talk at the Counseling Center, he responded to an explicit question about women in the movement:

> As far as the woman's question, in our Party we make no distinction between the women and the men, we are for equality between the sexes, we realize we are all products of the bourgeois society and it's a constant problem for us to use introspection and examine ourselves and our motives in dealing with the females in the organization and our views towards females in this country and abroad. So philosophically we view women as equal, but I'm not going to lie. . . . A lot of the times that we make subconscious kind of moves and mistakes. And what has happened, we have enough women in our Party to be our conscience on that and it brings us back into order, so I think that the liberation movement, the women's liberation movement is a very significant one and the way that it operates in the black community, of course, the way it manifests is greatly different than in the white community.[137]

According to a handwritten note to Party fundraiser Marty Kenner, this "Will to Power" lecture was briefly considered for possible inclusion in the *Hidden Traitor* book, as of July 1972. It seems, then, that Newton's effort to re-analyze the relationship between sex and power, given the insights and shortcomings of his personal vantage point, had led him to finally come to terms with the distinct oppressions experienced by Black women.

Newton's developing critique of patriarchy and increasing willingness to grapple with his own past sexism took a mature form in his autobiography, published in 1973. He opened the narrative portion of *Revolutionary Suicide* with a description of the central place of sexual violence in his family tree, linking his personal history to "the history of all Black people. It is all of a piece. I have little knowledge of my grandparents or those who went before. Racism destroyed our family history. My father's father was a white rapist."[138] The opening makes clear that Newton was critiquing the entanglement of sex, racism, and power directly. At the same time, he also admitted to some ambivalence and uncertainty about what to make of other forms of power dynamics between the genders. He discussed how his father won his mother's heart through "charm," finding "him hard to resist"; they were both teenagers at the time, "some said too young to marry."[139] He drew attention to the complicated "patriarchal" control his father exercised over his mother.[140] Armelia was discouraged from working outside of the home for her protection, given Walter Newton's hyperawareness of the vulnerability of women to sexual violence at work.[141]

Newton's ability to grapple with the nuanced power dynamics between the genders was at its most refined in chapter 13 of his autobiography, "Loving." Here Newton made the difficult choice to be honest about some of his more troubled relationships with women during his youth, not just describing but actively inspiring empathy for those women who suffered because of his choices. He admitted to "conflicts in [his] feelings and involvements with women," wording this in more raw terms in earlier drafts of the chapter: "I had a guilt complex about the way I treated women. It was all pretty confusing."[142] The principal source of much of these tensions was the intensity of his desire to avoid the life his father led, "struggling to take care of a wife and seven children, having to work at three jobs at once, I began to see that the bourgeois family can be an imprisoning, enslaving, and suffocating experience."[143] In an interview with J. Herman Blake, Newton said his most persistent nightmares as a child were about his father's bills. In his youth, one of his family responsibilities was to go pay each bill in person – about twenty of them – and bring back the receipts.[144] "He early decided that as an adult he would not have any bills . . . He equated having a family with having bills and that is why he always felt trapped when he developed relationships with women."[145]

Instead, Newton chose a non-monogamous lifestyle – new in the Bay Area at the time – based on a "refusal to participate in the above ground capitalist economy" and the "bourgeois family structure" both, as scholar Andrew Lester has described it.[146] Newton admitted that with his looks and personality, he found himself in a position to "exploit" the women he dated: "Women paid my rent, cooked my food, and did other things for me, while any money I came by was mine to keep."[147] His feelings of guilt were so pervasive that he essentially confessed to the women: "I never forced or persuaded them. As a matter of fact, I said that in their place, I would not do it at all."[148] "The fact that I found it necessary to explain to women that they were at a disadvantage in their relationship with me indicated that I needed some kind of defense mechanism against the guilt I felt."[149] Intellectually inspired by philosopher Bertrand Russell's critique of marriage, and sincerely interested in questioning the concept, Newton was simultaneously well aware of the contradictions. He pointed out that one of his male collaborators in these non-monogamous practices, Richard Thorne, eventually went on to found "an interracial sex cult called Om Lovers."[150]

Newton was at his most conflicted in describing what happened when he took this exploitation to its logical end. While the young Newton did not interfere with the other relationships his romantic partners had, when he found himself in a position to extract money from their sexuality, he did so:

> For a time I tried the pimping life, but this caused altogether too much inner turmoil. Whenever I pimped a Black sister, my mind would be filled with flashes of the slave experience – the racist dogs raping Black women. I began to feel that if my conscience would not allow me to pimp Black women, perhaps I should pimp white women – the "enemy." But when I "turned out" a white woman and found there was still a crisis of conscience, I realized that I could never pimp for a living. With Black women the feeling was shame, because I was selling my sister's body. With white women

> the feeling was not shame but guilt, because I was now in the role of the oppressor.[151]

In earlier drafts, he elaborated that "I always ended up with a feeling of absolute worthlessness, and I gave it up rather quickly. I lost all self-respect."[152] At the other end of the spectrum of intimacy, he also went into detail about a woman named Dolores whom he "loved dearly," who attempted suicide because of her emotional struggles with his choice of non-monogamy. Writing with hindsight about his past years, he reflected: "By rejecting marriage and a family I held on to my 'freedom,' but I lost the intimacy and companionship of a woman – an experience that is probably as great as, perhaps greater than, the freedom I wanted."[153] Newton's ability to analyze his past patriarchal behavior represented major progress from his prior complete avoidance of public discussion of women's oppression during the first four years of the Party's existence, as well as his stilted discussion of sex and its traumas over an even longer period.

By the time he returned to college to pursue his bachelor's degree in the fall of 1973, his analysis of the relationship between sex and power had changed so drastically that he revised even the fundamental definition of *power* that had proven so influential for the Black Panther Party, recited by its members and activists on the left for years. That fall, he completed an essay titled "A Functional Definition of Politics, Revised," which he also submitted for a course in sociology taught by Walter Goldfrank at the University of California Santa Cruz.[154] In it, he redefined power as "the ability to define phenomena and make it act in a manner *willed*," replacing the word "desired."[155] This was a clear sign of his rejection of Freud's libido – *desire* and sex drive – as the prime mover of human nature. Notably, Newton finalized virtually all of the essays that he completed during his studies at the university with an indication of copyright, year of composition, and his name. Many of these unpublished essays are rich in ideas, but here I will only analyze those elements that deal with the matter of gender oppression.

For a philosophy class taught by William Emmanuel Abraham, a Ghanaian professor and close associate of President Kwame Nkrumah, Newton submitted an essay titled "Politics and

Myth."[156] Pointing out that the pre-historic Greeks originally "were matrilineal and matrilocal" – that is, socially centered on women's families and their lineages – he went on to argue that the rise of the Greek "heroic age" produced "one of the great world historical defeats of women."[157] He explained that the move away from tribal life in Athens and other Greek territories "usher[ed] in the age of nobility, monarchy, unequal wealth and, fatally, slavery."[158] For a course on world religions, Professor Noel Q. King wrote in his evaluation that he was "deeply moved" by Newton's essay "The First Hero of Literature," a "recension," or critical rewriting, of the ancient Mesopotamian *Epic of Gilgamesh*.[159] Newton's essay critiqued the marginalization of women's anger in the story and characterized the protagonist King Gilgamesh's "sexual appetite" as "especially oppressive."[160] His interests in this period were focused on anthropology, theology, and the behavioral sciences.

The next spring, in May 1974, Newton composed his most rigorous critique of gendered oppression, an essay titled "Eve, the Mother of All Living," a version of which is published in *The Huey P. Newton Reader* (2002). Newton's archives include an early outline of this essay, titled "Genesis of the Homosapien: A War Story," which was a more fictional and creative approach to the origins of patriarchy and its future possible demise.[161] Here, Newton expressed concern that the women's movement might result in a "coup d'état" rather than a true "revolution" if the technologies and infrastructure developed over the long existence of patriarchy were kept in place. The published form of the essay is more scholarly, evidence-based, and concerned most of all with analyzing why patriarchy came to power in pre-historic times and how it might be overcome in modern society. Newton wrote: "It is my argument that women were socially supreme as long as the size of population groups was relatively small," but "*the historical defeat of woman came by violence* – that must be admitted now."[162] His argument fit clearly within what has been called "third-wave feminism" in the US, a school of feminist thought that affirmed Third World, Indigenous, Black womanist, and decolonial feminist views of womanhood, as well as the long arc of women's struggle against tens of thousands of years of patriarchal power.

The essay combines anthropology, biology, and a study of creation myths, especially the story of Genesis: "*All* of the earliest mythology is univocal in the identification of creativity, power, and primacy with the female."[163] "Behind the iron reaction formation of the myth of Genesis stands a much older sensuous myth that enshrines woman as the center of creation."[164] Newton proposed that early men were initially ignorant about their role in procreation, but that once they came to understand it biologically, they leveraged women's vulnerability during pregnancy against them and enslaved them as a class. What followed was a psychological colonization: men "had to force on women a slave mentality and erase forever any intimations of her former glory."[165] Furthermore, because of men's own sexual insecurities, women "had to be desexualized" through the "age-old whore/madonna strategy."[166]

Newton also argued that modern technology has increasingly eliminated the need for men as fathers, providers, and lovers, a matter that seems to only exacerbate male insecurity: "In the era of doomsday weapons, his war-loving, chauvinistic, sexist male protests of power have become the scandal of history. Man, who cannot give life, has begun to take it by the billions in our century. He has revenged himself by desecrating Mother Nature and polluting Mother Earth."[167] In typically dialectical mode, Newton suggested that it seems to follow logically that feminist revolution might take some form of violence in order to eliminate the violence of the patriarchal state. In expressing this view, he seemed to be responding to the most militant, violence-advocating sectors of the white feminist movement of the time. The essay ends with the hope that the women's movement will ally with all oppressed groups, who are "merely 'women' to the ruling circle: cannon fodder, taxable objects, cogs in a wheel. It is a *human* liberation that makes a dialectic with every suffering member of the mass of humankind," against "the scarcity principle" perpetuated by capitalism.[168]

An affirmation of nature is consistent throughout all versions of the essay, from Newton's observation that "the first principle of nature itself seems to be female" to his call for resistance to the "antinatural tyranny" of patriarchy.[169] The essay also opens by citing the work of psychiatrist Mary Jane Sherfrey, who identified that "life in the uterus begins as female." Newton's invocation of this biological history was complicated slightly, however, by his clarification that "the fetus was defined by a rudimentary phallus," suggesting then not just an affirmation of female primacy, but also a scholarly gesture towards the uncertainty behind the sex binary itself. As he had stated earlier, "there is some masculinity in every female and some femininity in every male."[170]

There is much similarity in how the genitalia of Black and colonized men, intersexed people, and menstruating women broadly have been construed – as monstrous, unspeakable, and a danger to rational order – an effect of colonial and patriarchal efforts to control the natural human body.[171] Newton consistently rejected white supremacist myths about Black men's genitalia as being precisely myths.[172] All three populations, predictably, have been targets of sexual violence and genital mutilation. When Newton wrote in "Eve, the Mother of All Living" that "woman was slowly imprisoned in the very biology that had made her supreme," he identified a tension and a pattern that have been repeated historically for racialized, gendered, and sexed "others" under the coloniality of patriarchy. The whole of the human being is reduced to the materiality of the body, and then the body is seized for control, exploitation, and destruction. While imprisoned, Newton learned that the effort to regain control of the body for the colonized must start first of all with a reclamation of the mind against the dysphoria-producing effects of technologies of colonization.

The Gender of Revolution

Newton claimed he "loved" the Bible, especially the book of Ecclesiastes, and "read it frequently."[173] During 1973 and 1974, he wrote several essays on theology and, as mentioned above, increasingly integrated ideas from the Bible into his writings on patriarchy, politics, and myth. Despite common understandings, the Bible includes discussions of topics mistakenly considered unique to our modern day, such as the limits of the male-female binary. The New Testament Gospels make clear reference to intersexed human beings – that is, those born physically and physiologically at neither end of the sex spectrum. In the words of Jesus: "Not everyone can accept this teaching but only those to whom it is given. For there are eunuchs who have been so from birth, and there are eunuchs who have been made eunuchs by others, and there are eunuchs who have made themselves eunuchs for the sake of the kingdom of heaven. Let anyone accept this who can."[174] As an expansive and free thinker, Newton would have likely been able to "accept" such facts of nature without difficulty. Those who knew him personally have affirmed his embrace of both male and female "principles."

Ericka Huggins recalled that "Huey's main way of acknowledging human beings was almost androgynous. He was very masculine, yet he really enjoyed things that you think were feminine. . . . He loved how women were with each other. He would tell us all the time, 'I wish men were that way.'"[175] Newton explained how he himself faced ambiguous gendering as a child: "they often teased me when I was young, telling me I was too pretty to be a boy, that I should have been a girl. This baby-faced appearance dogged me for a long time, and it was one of the reasons I fought so often in school."[176] In a conversation Elaine Brown recalled, "At one point he said, 'I'm not a man, I'm not a woman, I'm just a plain-born child.'"[177] Ericka Huggins later affirmed that this line was the opening to a poem Newton once wrote.[178]

Claims to manhood and womanhood were unquestionably fundamental in the Black Panther Party. The Black men and women of the organization declared their manhood and womanhood precisely because they were denied this in a white supremacist society that devalued their humanity. Newton clarified that it was a "common misconception at the time that the Party was searching for badges of masculinity. In fact, the reverse is true: the Party acted as it did because we *were* men."[179] Black feminist writer Saidiya Hartman, in her writing on the exposure of enslaved women and men to sexual violence, has described "the elusiveness or instability of gender in relation to the slave as property."[180] While the enslaved were differentiated by *sex* – categorized as male and female, as animals are – they were disallowed access to the *gendered* status of men and women. Building upon the work of philosopher Sylvia Wynter, Tommy Curry has echoed that Black men have been just as disallowed from access to that abstract status of MAN as Black women have.[181] Wynter identified the status of Western, rational MAN as a colonial schema developed to dehumanize, dominate, and exclude the vast majority of humanity.[182]

Despite the existential importance of asserting manhood and womanhood, as the BPP developed, its members made the choice – in response to political necessity – to adapt gender roles in order to successfully continue pursuing the main goal of revolution. Women trained with arms, men cooked and served breakfasts, and the protection of life was a strategic focus. Later, Black Liberation Army veteran Dhoruba Bin Wahad would suggest of his old female comrade: "Assata was one of the better shooters in the Black Panther Party. Women tend to be better shooters than men – don't ask me why."[183] As Newton argued in his writings against patriarchy, modern technology would prove to be an equalizer. This was evident in the Third World, where decolonial movements relied on men and women alike out of necessity, inspiring the Black Panther Party in turn. A few resisted, but in the end it was more tactical to equalize gender roles than to expend energy imposing narrow roles on human beings who were naturally more divergent than the "bourgeois" categories they were colonized under. In the whirlwind of struggle, practical necessities tended to blur the distinctions, producing revolutionary approaches to gender in their wake.

Huey P. Newton, Elaine Brown, and Bobby Seale.
Used with permission by Dr. Huey P. Newton Foundation.

Black Panther Party delegation (Huey P. Newton, Elaine Brown, and Robert Bay) in China, September 1971.
Used with permission by Dr. Huey P. Newton Foundation.

Gwen (Fontaine) Newton and Huey P. Newton.
Used with permission by Dr. Huey P. Newton Foundation.

7

Contradictions of Power

Conventional wisdom would have one believe that it is insane to resist this, the mightiest of empires, but what history really shows is that today's empire is tomorrow's ashes, that nothing lasts forever, and that to not resist is to acquiesce in your own oppression. The greatest form of sanity that anyone can exercise is to resist that force that is trying to repress, oppress, and fight down the human spirit.

Mumia Abu-Jamal (1997)[1]

Global Power, Local Power

In the summer of 1971, after several years of expansion without an overarching strategy, a new, careful, and politically perceptive plan for how to build local power in a new global order had been diagrammed by Huey Newton and his supporters. It would avoid needless casualties, put the needs of the most oppressed first, and organize them in a revolutionary direction towards their own self-liberation against genocide. And yet, the Black Panther Party was simultaneously in crisis and split in two. And the more Newton tried to force control, the worse it got.

Several prominent leaders had been lost to assassination, exile, and controversial purges. Whole chapters were expelled, including the international embassy. In several cities, guerrilla warfare had begun: shoot-outs with police, bombings, and plane hijackings proliferated. In August, George Jackson was murdered in prison. Back in Algeria, an attempt by Eldridge Cleaver's group to take a delegation to China was rejected by the Chinese government. China still had no official diplomatic relationship with the US, given the conflict between the capitalist and communist states, and Cleaver's group in Algeria had hoped to leverage that. At the time, the rift between the Asian superpower and the Soviet Union was forcing socialists worldwide to choose sides, and the BPP had embraced China. Then, suddenly, as Kathleen Cleaver described it: "The revelation that [US] Secretary of State Henry Kissinger had secretly visited Beijing in July 1971 struck the revolutionary movements like a thunderbolt."[2]

Across the decade of the 1960s, as historian Robin Kelley has explained, "China offered Black radicals a 'colored' or Third World Marxist model that enabled them to challenge a white and Western vision of class struggle," although "China's role was contradictory and problematic in many respects."[3] In 1963, following the infamous bombing of a Black church in Birmingham, Alabama, Robert F. Williams sent out a call to several Third World leaders, seeking their solidarity against the act of domestic terrorism.[4] Mao Zedong was the only one to respond, publishing a robust statement "Calling Upon the People of the World to Unite to Oppose Racial Discrimination by U.S. Imperialism and Support the American Negroes in Their Struggle Against Racial Discrimination." He also invited Williams to China. In April 1968, Mao again reaffirmed China's support in "A New Storm Against Imperialism":

> Some days ago, Martin Luther King, the Afro-American clergyman, was suddenly assassinated by the U.S. imperialists. Martin Luther King was an exponent of nonviolence. Nevertheless, the U.S. imperialists did not on that account show any tolerance toward him, but used counter-revolutionary violence and killed him in cold blood. This has taught the broad masses of the Black people in the United States a profound lesson. It has touched off a new storm in their struggle against violent repression sweeping well over a hundred cities in the United States, a storm such as has never taken place before in the history of that country. It shows that an extremely powerful revolution-

ary force is latent in the more than twenty million Black Americans.[5]

Newton and Seale had sold copies of Mao's *Little Red Book* early on to college students to fund the Party.[6] Ironically though, at the time neither of them had even read Mao.[7] Newton would soon read all four volumes of Mao's writings, solidifying his "conversion" to socialism in the process.[8] The *Little Red Book* would prove deeply influential for the political education of Party members, and, while Newton was incarcerated, the organization became deeply internationalist. Besides cultivating feelings of solidarity with the revolutionary struggles of other oppressed people, Party leadership also hoped to develop relationships that would allow them to receive real material aid, as they eventually would in the form of institutional support in Algeria.

According to David Hilliard, however, Newton was skeptical: "Our emphasis on foreign events drives Huey crazy. 'Who are we selling papers to?' he asks us in one of his tapes. 'The Black community, or the Chinese or the Koreans? I think that they should give us some money to print it.'"[9] Hilliard claimed that China would have offered aid if not for the likelihood of US government interception. While the strategies Newton proposed were directly Maoist in inspiration – with their emphases on local power, survival programs, and communal defense – he was nonetheless seriously critical of the excessive focus on foreign allies, feeling that the paper should "echo the will and aspirations of the people in the community" instead. By the time Newton returned from prison in 1970, international topics would be confined to a separate section of the newspaper.[10]

Soon after his release, the Chinese People's Association for Friendship with Foreign Countries offered Newton an invitation to China.[11] It would not be until late September 1971 though, once he became aware that President Nixon planned to visit the following February, that he, Elaine Brown, and Newton's bodyguard Robert Bay took the opportunity to visit for ten days and deliver the "People's Petition."[12] The petition called for China to negotiate with President Richard Nixon on behalf of the oppressed people of the United States.[13] Its original version had focused on the stalemate between the incarcerated rebels who seized control of Attica Prison on September 9 and New York Governor Nelson Rockefeller who was backed by Nixon. However, once the Attica rebels were defeated, the document was changed to serve as a more general act of diplomacy.[14] Newton's account of the visit in *Revolutionary Suicide* is very positive, but he did not get to meet Mao as originally promised. According to Newton, there was "concern . . . within the Central Committee of the Chinese Communist Party whether that would spoil the Nixon intended visit, and because I'm not a head of state, that that visit was more important on a state-to-state relation."[15] The reception the Panthers were invited to included ambassadors from many nations, but also several other groups of US citizens.[16] Newton had wanted to visit before China established diplomatic relationships with the US government, but although Nixon had not yet arrived, the Panthers were already too late.

The arrival of the Panthers was nonetheless publicly celebrated and incorporated into the festivities for National Day on October 1, 1971. Newton met twice with Premier Zhou Enlai, including one six-hour meeting also attended by Jiang Qing, wife of Mao Zedong.[17] According to Newton, the Chinese leaders were particularly interested in his interpretation of Marxism, and they explicitly affirmed his theory of intercommunalism: "So they accepted it, said yes they accepted the concept. They said it was sound."[18] "They agreed that they can only call themselves liberated territory because they said the world belongs to the people and . . . they have a universal identity with all of the oppressed people of the world."[19] Undergoing a retrial at the time for the murder of Officer Frey, Newton was also offered political asylum.[20] This was in itself a generous offer, given the turn China was taking towards de-escalating tensions with the US. But perhaps it was also a reflection of low expectations that the Black Panther Party would be able to regain its momentum after the split. Newton graciously declined and affirmed that his struggle was in the United States.

On his return, Newton was relatively tight-lipped during the press conference at the airport.[21] In his talk in 1972 at the Southern California Counseling Center, however, he was more frank about China's problems. For one, he was critical of the lack of free speech in China: "They don't even have first amendment rights of freedom of speech, they are afraid of that."[22] This was a notable remark, given the truly violent repression of speech that the BPP had to deal with in the US. In addition, Newton pointed out, when he offered philosophically rigorous critiques of dialectical materialism itself, he was disappointed to find little honest engagement: "Many people say that I'm rather idealistic, including the Chinese, when I said that: . . . [if] contradiction is the ruling principle of the universe, is it possible the contradiction itself will be resolved in the future? And of course, they rejected that and they have a way of not talking about, with visitors anyway, about things they don't agree with. They said that no it's impossible."[23] Elaine Brown later worded Newton's inquiry more succinctly: "'If, under a dialectical materialist analysis, nothing 'stood outside' of the process, did that negate the process itself?'"[24] Newton had also been influenced early on by what he believed was a hands-off approach on China's part towards its internal ethnic minorities.[25] However, by 1973, when pressed, he admitted that Tibetans and other ethnic minorities in China were indeed treated in a genocidal manner, comparable with the fate of Black people and other ethnic groups under British and American rule.[26]

Ultimately, China would not be an ally the Party could count on. Nonetheless, the organization continued to draw upon their strategies. For China, the aim would be the maximization of what Marx called "the productive forces," in order to bring about a socialist transformation in the long run. They would be able to dominate global manufacturing through low labor costs, a way of seizing power from capitalists on their own terms in a global order dictated by free trade. According to Newton's account of his conversation with Zhou Enlai, however, their ultimate goal was the "dissolution of the state."[27] At times, Newton described the BPP's aim similarly, in terms of pursuing strategies that would eventually "negate our necessity for existing."[28] In other words, the organization itself should ideally be treated only as a means to an end, not as the goal in itself.

Much as Newton had earlier echoed Mao's line in arguing that the BPP was against war but could only abolish war through war, so did the Oakland Central Committee mimic China in their willingness to take up capitalist practices and engage with liberal political institutions, despite their fundamentally socialist views. It was this kind of approach that encouraged Newton to adjust the organization's prior "blanket condemnation of the small victimized Black capitalists found in our communities."[29] In fact, in actual practice, the Panthers in many chapters had already long been accepting donations from Black businesses and collaborating with them as part of the work of developing the second wave of social programs. From the earliest days even, Black businesses also bought and sold the Party newspaper in their stores.[30] Applying the logic of dialectical materialism to reinterpret these practices, Newton came to the conclusion that these businesses were in fact doing more revolutionary good than harm: "When we say that we see within Black capitalism the seeds of its own negation and the negation of all capitalism, we recognize that the small Black capitalist in our communities has the potential to contribute to the building of the machine which will serve the true interests of the people and end all exploitation."[31] In addition, applying an intercommunalist analysis, he figured that the "Black bourgeoisie . . . is something of an illusion. It's a fantasy bourgeoisie, and this is true of most of the white bourgeoisie too."[32] In the bigger picture, it was rather the massive transnational businesses that were the true exploiters. Just as the Panthers had stated that they would ally with anyone who would ally with them, in their effort to build greater local power in their communities, they cultivated stronger relationships with Black businesses. Nonetheless, Newton maintained that "capitalist exploitation is one of the basic causes of our problem."[33] "There is no salvation in capitalism, but through this new approach, the Black capitalist will contribute to his own negation."[34]

By this point, Newton had long consolidated his position as the dominant voice on the Central Committee. The wave of expulsions earlier in 1971 had made clear that anyone who criticized his decisions would likely find themselves isolated. Notably, the new posture towards Black businesses also reflected this domineering impulse. In Oakland, the Party required a regular contribution from all Black businesses in the community. Any that did not comply faced bad press, protests, boycotts, and, at the worst, strong-arming.[35] The logic of dialectical materialism, when applied, meant figuring out who might be friend or foe by pushing at the population in question until they were forced to choose sides though their actions. Another important part of the strategy included the pursuit and control of territory, and to this end the Party acquired over twenty-one properties mostly in the Bay Area.[36] They also pursued an effort to take control of the Port of Oakland, the second largest port in the world at the time in terms of container tonnage.[37] Newton and the Party produced research on the economics of the port, and in an unpublished 1974 essay titled "Oakland: An All-American Example," Newton critiqued the disproportionately minor fraction of port revenues that contributed to the city budget.[38]

From the outside, the BPP's shift on engaging with capitalists was disorienting for some, but former allies were most baffled by the Party's sincere entrance into electoral politics. Elaine Brown later explained that this, too, was influenced by the People's Republic of China, which did not hesitate to use all available means to build socialist power: "China's recent entrance into the U.N. was neither contradictory to China's goal of toppling U.S. imperialism nor an abnegation of revolutionary principles. It was a tactic of socialist revolution. It was a tactic, Huey concluded, that offered us a great example. Those were the roots of Huey's new idea: to have Panthers run for political office."[39] In 1972, Panthers won four seats on the Berkeley Community Development Council, and thereafter aimed at city-wide positions.[40] Interestingly, Newton did not publish a justification for the decision to pursue electoral campaigns, as he had done previously on other issues through essays such as "Re-analyzing Black Capitalism" and "On the Relevance of the Church." However, in his unpublished essay "A Functional Definition of Politics, Revised," he did explain part of the rationale. In it, he echoed some of the very lines of thought that had inspired the police patrols:

> what we admitted when Bobby Seale ran for Mayor: actual power underlies *all* symbolic power. So first we have to destroy the symbols by exhausting all symbolic means of power. There is too little stress given to the dialectical process of qualitative and quantitative change, and to the dynamic of "exhausting all legal and political means" in the liberation struggle.[41]

So, it seems that the intention was to attain electoral positions, and in the process expose the inadequacy of electoral politics. This was in essence what Newton had said earlier about electoral politics given reactionary intercommunalism: "no party or government can step outside the framework of the corporate system and its politics and embark on a course which consistently threatens the power and privileges of the giant corporations."[42] When Seale ran for mayor and Brown for city council, the argument was that the Panthers would then be in a better position to both denounce the inadequacy of the electoral system and mobilize the citizenry. They would be using the electoral system to "negate" it, in an open fashion, through practice.

In 1972, as part of the initial preparations for the campaign, Newton made the stunning decision to contract the national chapters – about forty at the time – in order to completely divert their resources, as well as the BPP's most talented organizers, to this task.[43] Decades later, one of the first members sent to Oakland, Boston Panther Michael Fultz, reflected:

> Personally I thought it was a good thing; that's my view now and frankly that was my view of the time ... Staying in Boston and building on the base we had in Boston would have been plausible; we had a very strong chapter and a strong base in the Boston black community. We had a good relationship with people. ... But, rather than having these various chapters with variable effectiveness, you could create a base, see what you could do in one city, in Oakland, which was a more plausibly organizable city, than, say, Boston, New York City, or Baltimore.[44]

Ever since "Correct Handling of a Revolution," Newton had affirmed the importance of "face-to-face" relationships for the vanguard party.[45] However, it is easy to identify in this extreme act more evidence of Newton's developing paranoia about the size of the organization, as well as his continuing desire to exert control. It also appears that he simply failed to grasp the depth and strength of the national chapters beyond Oakland, most of which he never visited.[46] Importantly, many chapters had in fact grown out of local organizations – some even preceding Newton and Seale's Party – and had simply taken up the Panther name and program in pursuit of local goals. Ironically, after deciding to contract these largely autonomous organizations to the Oakland electoral campaign, Newton was completely absent from the campaign itself.[47]

One of the jobs of early core member Elbert "Big Man" Howard was to travel to different chapters and help with legal assistance for jailed members. That work gave him a greater appreciation of just how much the Party had grown. Many years later, he stated:

> [The electoral campaign] was viable, but, at the same time, I don't think [Huey] wanted to deal with the responsibility of a nation-wide organization and all the things that had to be done. So, in my opinion, he did a disservice to the people who had followed the Panther philosophy and worked their tails off to develop programs, to gain resources to do that in their communities. And all of a sudden you tell them to close down the chapters, and there were people in the communities that benefited from what happened in those chapters.[48]

Even as the survival programs in Oakland expanded, the dismantling of programs elsewhere in order to build the political campaign in Oakland was an early sign of shifting priorities. Boston captain Audrea Jones called the change "a major mistake," observing that in these other communities "people felt abandoned by that."[49] Bobby Seale was originally against the contraction as well.[50] And then, despite a strong showing – Seale's mayoral campaign got 40 percent of the vote – the BPP did not win any elected positions in Oakland in 1973. In addition, as historian Robyn Spencer-Antoine has pointed out, the campaign exhausted the Party both financially and in terms of morale.[51]

The survival programs in Oakland also suffered because of the singular attention given to the electoral campaign. Not only were fewer resources made available to sustain them, but the strategic project intended for them that they should serve as a structured vehicle – was not supported either. Sometimes community members were recruited to help run the programs themselves.[52] However, the programs more often than not functioned as straightforward charity services or publicity for the electoral campaign. In Spencer-Antoine's analysis: "The Panthers touted their survival programs as a strategic measure; however, they failed to actively engage in community-based political education to teach Oakland residents about the politics behind these programs. As a result, though these programs achieved many successes, they were rarely a catalyst for community political action."[53] The strategy of communal defense developed collaboratively with George Jackson was never put into practice. Slowly, the well-being of the people was decreasing in importance. Interestingly, in this, too, the Black Panther Party seemed to be following the trend of the policies practiced in China.

As part of its integration of capitalist methods, the People's Republic of China increasingly leveraged the population itself as a resource in order to bring Chinese technological power up to par with that of Western powers. Much as American capitalism had relied upon the free labor of Africans to develop its economy, so would the Chinese economy strategically leverage its own world-leading population. In a similar vein, Newton often referred to the Party membership as "an ox for the people." In his essay "On the Relevance of the Church," he explained matter-of-factly that the survival programs would face minimal labor costs because the Party would be forcing its members to work for free. Newton used the word "exploit," but placed the word in euphemistic quotation marks. In practice, however, this was precisely what happened, as members who had left their own communities in order to build the Oakland "stronghold" later faced expanding obligations that only intensified as the Party struggled financially in the late 1970s.[54] Whereas the BPP's earlier efforts to channel the lives of the oppressed had been motivated by a deep feeling of empathy and identification with the people, being the lumpen themselves, in the 1970s Newton's Oakland organization instead increasingly treated both its members and the community at large as objects in a technocratic plan.

The Harm of Self and Community

At the same time, Newton was increasingly falling prey to addiction. When the Black Panther Party began, they were, at least in principle, anti-drug. The very first rule of conduct was, "No party member can have narcotics or weed in his possession while doing party work," and rules two and three essentially reiterated the same point. Not only was there an expectation of disciplined behavior while conducting Party duties, but members also had reason to be wary of police harassment. Furthermore, the Panthers' appreciation for the life of Malcolm X meant that many of them were inspired by the sobriety he developed through his time in the Nation of Islam. And yet, Party members were often less invested in the idea of a complete conversion from lumpen life than Malcolm had been. Whereas the original rules had differentiated the BPP from some other groups during an era when experimentation with drugs was widespread, that discipline increasingly went by the wayside in the 1970s. When asked about what strategies Panthers had for coping psychologically with the constant surveillance, harassment, and assault at the hands of police and federal agents, Panther Norma Armour Mtume recalled:

> Drinking and drugging (laughter). . . . But no, I mean we – when we had a chance to cool down we might have a party or a birthday party. . . . It is, it's high, high stress. . . . I mean, we – I recognized early that there was a lot of folks who had alcohol problems, and later on started using different types of drugs. But then, we have to remember that these are people that came in from the community. People that joined the Party, they were already doing those kinds of things. When they came into the Party, they were directed, clean up, because it wasn't allowed. You couldn't be a drug head and alcoholic every day and do the work that you needed to do. So, that wasn't condoned. But because we were who we were, some of us slipped back into those habits.[55]

Panther Bill Brent claimed that alcohol, marijuana, and synthetic pills were used by some Party members when he was a member in the late 1960s.[56] Flores Forbes wrote about smoking five to six joints of marijuana a day at times in the mid-1970s.[57] David Hilliard later described extensively his alcoholism during his time with the Party, his subsequent cocaine usage, and his much later addiction to crack.

Newton himself was introduced to cocaine at parties after he was released from prison, and he started using as he traveled the country celebrating his freedom.[58] It is important to recognize that, at the time, cocaine was misconceived as harmless, criminalization was not enforced, and the drug was sometimes even openly distributed by businesses as a gift.[59] Phyllis Jackson, who worked in security for the Party, has offered the additional context that, as full-time revolutionaries who held fast to the view that "sleep is the cousin of death," anything that could keep you awake and active was seen as an advantage.[60] Elaine Brown and J. Herman Blake observed that, for a while, Newton often took Ritalin, as did some other Panthers.[61] Interestingly, in *Revolutionary Suicide*, Newton insisted that the Black Panthers were "dead set against" "the advocacy of drugs" and that their use was "absolutely forbidden," statements that perhaps reflect some degree of ethical conflict on his part.[62] Once the Party acquired a nightclub in Oakland called the LampPost, Newton frequented it and consumed cocaine on a nightly basis, in extreme amounts.[63] In the later 1970s, he consumed it with former Party members who were "into cocaine full-time in West Oakland."[64] Panther Aaron Dixon described in his memoir how Newton changed in the years after his imprisonment: "Prior to Huey's arrest and imprisonment, he had not indulged in drugs, nor had he disrespected party members. But when he came out of prison, all the elements were there, waiting to ensnare him. . . . For Huey, next to the US government, cocaine became his greatest enemy."[65]

In most accounts of this period in Party history, the exclusive focus has been on the organization' "criminality" – the fact of their law-breaking – with relatively little attention paid to the normalized self-harm they engaged in. Drug addiction and substance abuse are diseases of colonialism, and the drug trade is the capitalist exploitation of this condition, itself driven, in a cyclical manner, by poverty and more addiction. In addition, comparably little attention has been paid to the fact that, in participating in the drug trade, the Panthers were doing harm to the community of the most oppressed. In other words, the focus on "criminality" reflects a punitive approach and the aim to villainize and place blame rather than address harms through care and social defense. Newton's personal addiction to cocaine was clearly the main cause of his choice to pull the Party into the drug trade, which was itself a sign of his further succumbing to the disease.

Easily overlooked in Newton's re-examination of Black capitalism is that he had always included in his understanding of it both "legitimate" and "illegitimate" capitalists.[66] He described illegitimate capitalists as those who "play the game" of capitalism but do so in a manner criminalized by the state and the capitalists in power – in essence, those who make money through the black market. Accordingly, although Newton and the BPP did not state this openly, the plan in engaging Black capitalism broadly was to also leverage and then "negate" Oakland's black market and capitalist underworld. Party veteran Flores Forbes, who came to develop a close relationship with Newton, was eventually included in the inner circle of bodyguards and security personnel that Newton termed the "Buddha Samurai." In his autobiography, Forbes attested to the Party's imposition of a tax on after-hours nightclubs, pimps, sex workers, and drug dealers, sometimes through the use of physical force.[67]

Bobby Seale later exclaimed that he was surprised to find out that the Party was involved in the drug trade in May of 1974, though at another point he stated that this had begun as early as January.[68] In conversation with Forbes, Newton hedged that the Panthers were "not Bible thumpers" and that he did not intend to altogether eliminate drug dealers.[69] This was noteworthy, since he did claim to want to altogether eliminate capitalists. Forbes described the organizational goal as "coming as close to destroying them as possible without depleting their revenue stream."[70] In his autobiography, Hilliard described a "meeting with the Ward Brothers," major figures in Oakland's drug and sex work trades, about unionizing the sex workers and pimps and about their "obligation to help and contribute to the black community."[71] According to Hilliard, "Our thrust was to organize an illegitimate economic resource, connect it with our community programs, and put the money into our programs," while also in turn lending some positive reputation to these lumpen populations. Forbes later explained that there were Party members whose specific job was dealing with drug dealers, taxing them at a 23 percent rate, and even dealing drugs themselves.[72] Much later, in Newton's detailed 1980 dissertation, *War Against the Panthers*, he does not explicitly deny the government documentation suggesting that he used drugs and got the Party involved in the drug trade, using instead vague words like "possible" and "might."[73] However, he does remark upon the creation of a new independent agency within the State Department of Justice – the Organized Crime and Criminal Intelligence Board – which acquired its financial backing through "laundered funds" bypassing congressional appropriations processes, and whose specific purpose was to target the Black Panther Party.[74]

In many regards, the Party's simultaneous pursuit of targeted violence, black-market economic control through provision of social services to the community, and political backing of candidates for office can be easily compared with the historical practices of many other groups throughout nineteenth- and twentieth-century American history – political parties, ethnic community organizations, labor unions – that eventually gained mainstream political legitimacy. Chicago, New York City, and San Francisco stand out as prominent historical examples bearing these kinds of political histories.[75] In this vein, between 1974 and 1977, while Newton was in exile but in bi-weekly contact by phone, Party Chair Elaine Brown led the Party in producing a sophisticated political apparatus that resulted in seats on major city committees and the election of the first Black mayor of Oakland, Lionel Wilson. Although Seale had not been elected, Wilson was an ally of the BPP and collaborated closely with them.[76] These accomplishments built upon the Party's empirical research and grassroots fieldwork. In early 1977, there were even plans underway to begin the re-expansion of the Party into cities like Las Vegas and East St. Louis.[77]

Accordingly, although Newton's approach made clear sense in *rational* and strategic terms, and produced real successes, it also seemed to reflect an uncharacteristic decline in *emotional* regard for the lumpenproletarian populations that were being exploited, physically assaulted, and treated as a means to a political end. These were the very populations whose well-being had first inspired Newton's initial pursuit of communal care, social defense, and revolutionary change. How is progress made, one wonders, if one is feeding a child in the morning and then funneling poison to their parents at night? According to Forbes, "Huey used to say that the line between the state and us was very thin."[78] Historian Errol Henderson later reflected:

> It was the service to the community that transformed peoples of all classes, from college students to gang members. As these projects, especially in California, came to be extortionist plans and strong-arming attempts, they lost their capacity to transform folk in a constructive way. In fact, they further legitimized the unprincipled lumpen activities of the BPP and reduced its capacity to substantively transform its members and the larger community.[79]

Somehow, the lumpen came to be regarded, by Newton himself, as disposable. Against the standard view, then, that the Party fell into "criminality" in this period – given that the Panthers were always outlawed in one sense or another – it is more accurate to identify the primary change as a shift from caring for and defending their own community to actively exploiting and harming it, at least in part.

In 1974, the Party's Central Committee, having been slowly reduced to include only people Newton felt he could trust, increasingly came to resemble the structure of a family organization, with relatives of core Panthers filling its ranks. The proportion of women in the Party also decreased, back to about 40 percent of the membership, which had by this point been reduced to a few hundred in total.[80] Among the traumatized and increasingly substance-dependent membership, internal violence reproduced itself.[81] "Because of the military posture of this organization, the BPP had embraced the street gang-style of discipline popularized by Bunchy Carter."[82] The use of physical discipline on members became formalized into a board of Methods and Corrections. The board "usually consisted of two Panthers (male and female) who served on a rotating basis."[83] "Punishment" "was always an act of violence," with the rationale being that "if we had been in

Bolivia with Che, we told ourselves, we would be shot for violations of rules or orders," Forbes explained.[84] "We were trained to believe we were at war and that, during wartime, soldiers get shot for, say falling asleep on guard duty."[85]

Consistent with a military logic, even dedicated members were treated as disposable, as exhibited in the policy that members would be expelled if their underground actions failed, not out of malice but in order to preserve the public face of the organization.[86] People would be provided with aid to go underground, but there would be no legal defense. Consistent with this, Panthers who ended up in prison were deprioritized.[87] By contrast, members of the Black Liberation Army on the East coast took the opposite approach during the same period, striving often to free imprisoned comrades. Safiya Bukhari later wrote about the prevalence of trauma disorders in the Party, in light of everything its members underwent. In her brilliant essay, "We Too Are Veterans: Post-Traumatic Stress Disorders and the Black Panther Party," she drew upon the experiences of her ex-military brother and her comrades in the Party to analyze the prevalence of symptoms such as startle responses, recurrent dreams, survivor's guilt, emotional isolation, and substance abuse.[88]

Problems of Power

It is clear that Newton disliked being in a position of leadership, a point he repeated constantly. In *These Graves Are All Too Young*, he stated frankly: "I don't like to lead things."[89] During the 1972 talk in Southern California, he said: "In the first place I hate to view myself in a leadership role because I personally don't think that I am a leader, the whole goal is to eliminate the leaders of course."[90] In an interview, he lamented of his supporters and followers: "I know that I can't give them all those things that an idol is supposed to."[91] "It was obvious that they viewed me then more as a symbol because there was much more hero-worship than I had experienced when I walked among the people before I was imprisoned."[92] Newton was clearly distressed by all of this.

Soon after Newton was released from prison, David Hilliard led the Central Committee in changing his title from "Minister to Defense" to "Supreme Commander."[93] At the Revolutionary People's Constitutional Convention that fall, after New York Panther Cetewayo Tabor introduced him as the "Supreme Commander," Newton began by affirming that "the power is with *you*, and as soon as we realize that, we will make many changes."[94] He later described his disappointment at his perpetual objectification:

> As I talked, it seemed to me that the people were not really listening or even interested in anything I had to say. Almost every sentence was greeted with loud applause, but the people there were more concerned with phrase mongering than with ideological development. I am not a very good public speaker – I tend to lecture and teach in a rather dull fashion – but the people were not responding to my ideas, only to an image, and although I was very excited by all the energy and enthusiasm I saw there, I was also disturbed by the lack of serious analytical thought.[95]

Elaine Brown later elaborated that "he hated speaking in public because he could not be honest. It was a show and he was not a good performer."[96] An emotional confidant for Newton, she observed: "he had neither the patience nor the ability to dress up those ideas for public consumption. If he continued trying to place them in a big arena, people would, he predicted, ultimately come to hate him – and worse, the ideas. Most people preferred fantasy truths and fantasy heroes; and he hated the former and refused to be the latter."[97] Newton eventually succeeded in getting the "Supreme Commander" title dropped; he replaced it with "Servant of the People," which the Central Committee responded to with "Supreme Servant."[98] They eventually settled on the less grandiose but still objectifying title of "the Servant."[99]

One way Newton seems to have responded to the idolization was through avoidance and escapism. Panther captain Aaron Dixon recalled that, in the 1970s, "Many of us rarely saw Huey. He seldom came to Central Headquarters, as the Central Committee met at his home."[100] Flores Forbes claimed that Newton knew only ten or so members by name and would often disappear for days at a time.[101] Elaine Brown described Newton as fundamentally a free-spirited individualist, who usually preferred to move without the security guards that the Central Committee required for him.[102] Surveillance and harassment by government agents and police also led the Central Committee to place Newton in a high-rise apartment with its own security system. The apartment was owned by a lawyer ally of the Party, contrary to rumors that the organization was paying for it.[103] In retrospect, we can see that, during 1970 and 1971, the Central Committee made impositions upon Newton against his wishes, while also submitting to him in the manner that they preferred. Elaine Brown later critiqued this ironic dynamic: "It was by its own desire that the Central Committee had become a euphemism, a body of men with titles but no power. If there were no more Central Committee decisions, it was because they had begged Huey to lead them, guide them, take charge of their party and their lives."[104]

The concept of a Central Committee was drawn from Leninist thought and the various Third World socialist movements that inspired the Panthers. In theory, a Central Committee could be said to be "democratic" insofar as its officers subject themselves to self-examination and critique in consultation with a rank-and-file membership who actively participate in shaping their institutions.[105] In an interview from September 1970, Newton described the Central Committee as it had functioned while he was still in prison:

> After the policy is decided among the Party, it's presented to the Party members in a dialectical way. We have a dialectical argument – we argue back and forth, to try to enlighten, to show the pros and cons of the particular policy, and we invite criticism, self-criticism, criticism of the Party, and, if the Party members reject the Central Committee's conclusions, proposals, then it would not be put into effect until through dialectical argument everyone is satisfied.[106]

In that extensive interview, interviewer Mark Lane specifically remarked upon Newton's active desire for debate and push-back in Central Committee discussions.[107]

Newton explained that his main intention behind establishing an "Ideological Institute" for the Party was to decenter himself as "chief theoretician" and create a "dynamic program to remove the need for a leader."[108] "I was not happy with being the only one developing ideas, I wanted to see the analytical approach developed by the other comrades so that they would be able to develop new ideas as they encountered new conditions."[109] For the first version of the Ideological Institute, in August 1970, two to three dozen Panther organizers from across the country were invited for a series of courses led by Minister of Education Raymond "Masai" Hewitt, Bobby Seale, and Newton.[110] The texts and thinkers to be read were, however, chosen by Newton, predetermining the "system of reasoning" to be internalized by Party members.[111] In the assessment of scholar Robin Kelley, "unfortunately, the Ideological Institute did not amount to much; few Party members saw the use of abstract theorizing or the relevance of some of these writings to revolution."[112] Perhaps the only exception was the teaching of Plato's "allegory of the cave." According to Blake, "Panther leaders were energized by reading this work of a Greek philosopher and discussing its significance for the lumpenproletariat."[113]

Later, Newton described alternative plans for a student body composed of fifty lumpenproletarian youths – "brothers and sisters off the block." "Most of them are kick-outs and dropouts; most of them left school in the eighth, ninth, or tenth grade. . . . But now they are dealing with dialectics and they are dealing with science – they study physics and mathematics so that they can understand the universe . . . They are the ones who will bring about change, not us alone."[114] Newton was optimistic, but the Institute did not last long. Instead, the Oakland chapter's school for younger children, which was not led by Newton, proved to be a greater success. Initially called the Children's House in 1969, the school was renamed the Intercommunal Youth Institute in 1971, and then restructured as the Oakland Community School from 1973 until it closed in 1982.[115]

Despite these efforts, Newton not only failed to stop the concentration of power in his hands, but even worsened it through many of his own actions. Brown wrote of his relationship with the Central Committee: "Their surrender of will had, paradoxically, generated his own surrender to the isolation of absolute leader."[116] Panther Don Cox later attempted a close analysis of the psychological dynamics at play that led to Newton's eventual authoritarianism. In part, he affirmed that Cleaver's actions contributed greatly: "Huey and Eldridge were, for many of us Messiahs. The very campaign to free Huey, as conceived by Cleaver, was in fact a cult of personality."[117] Newton's idolization, according to Cox, was also profoundly connected to the Black community's traumas following the losses of Martin Luther King, Jr. and Malcolm X: "Because we did not want to see any more of our leaders eliminated, we launched a massive campaign to assure that Huey would not be condemned to the death penalty. A cult of his personality was created. Huey was elevated to the status of the gods, and his every word became gospel."[118] With time, Cox concluded, "The *actual* Huey could not survive the Huey that we had created. How many could have resisted."[119]

In a memo circulated in March 1968, FBI Director J. Edgar Hoover established that one of the FBI's primary goals was to "prevent the rise of a 'messiah' who could unify and electrify the militant black nationalist movement."[120] Hoover continued: "Malcolm X might have been such a 'Messiah'; he is the martyr of the movement today. Martin Luther King, Stokely Carmichael, and Elijah Muhammed all aspire to this position." King was murdered a month later, Carmichael left the country in 1969, and Muhammed was already considered "less of a threat because of his age." Arguably, Newton became this kind of figure for both the Black community's aspirations and the government's surveillance operations. On February 2, 1971, a memo from Hoover to FBI city offices described the impact of Newton's declining emotional health on BPP operations: "Primary cause of internal problems appears to be dictatorial, irrational and capricious conduct of Huey P. Newton." The memo would go on to advocate for more counterintelligence proposals and actions.[121]

Historian Robyn Spencer-Antoine notes that the Black Panther Party filed a federal civil rights action in 1976 detailing years of "burglaries, raids, unlawful opening of mail, false arrests, auditing of Newton's tax returns, [and the] placing of an undercover agent in the apartment next to Newton in 1971."[122] Newton also recounted a shoot-out that occurred just outside of his door, coming from that apartment. Much of this harassment was conducted in a visible manner, a sign of the FBI's intention to cause psychological distress. Also included in the Party's civil rights claim were charges of: "infiltrating the BPP with provocateurs, murdering the Chicago Panther Fred Hampton, sabotaging and discrediting BPP programs, suppressing the party's right to free speech, and other acts of general harassment." While Newton's paranoia was thus based on real experiences, it also produced an emotional crisis that caused him to perceive threats everywhere. At the same time, while he faced regular false arrests for criminal acts, it was also the case that he engaged in anti-social and sometimes recklessly illegal behaviors while intoxicated. As Spencer-Antoine carefully describes it: "allegations of repression supplanted self-criticism."[123]

Regarding the concentration of power, it is important to emphasize the ironic fact that Newton himself offered a robust critique of authoritarianism. In his insightful 1974 essay, "Eliminate the Presidency," he identified the kernel of latent authoritarianism – the right to "prerogative" – which is enshrined in the Constitution and creates an exception in American law for the Office of the President.[124] Written while the Senate's Investigation Committee was conducting hearings on the Watergate scandal and Nixon's surveillance of the Democratic Party, "Eliminate the Presidency" is a sophisticated text that presents a nuanced understanding of the historical link connecting the legal concepts underlying medieval European monarchy to their later echoes in American Constitutional law: "What monster have we created, who by turning the phrase 'Divine Right' [into] 'Executive Privilege' shall destroy a tradition which began in opposition to absolute despotism?"[125] In this text, Newton proposed the complete elimination of the offices of the Executive branch and a delegation of all relevant powers to Congress, the more democratic branch.

Accordingly, it is paradoxical that Newton pursued a military-style political structure for the Party, even if this was to some degree urged on him from below. Several Panthers have identified this centralization as being part of an effort, led by Masai Hewitt, to organize underground military activities that had been decentralized and undisciplined – "organized guns that can respond to one voice," as Forbes put it.[126] This was also the rationale behind Newton's praise for Mario Puzo's novel *The Godfather*, which boiled down to affirming a model of secrecy within the chain of command.[127] These decisions were not impulsive and irrational, but clearly weighed and considered. At the same time, though, it was all a far cry from a collective decision-making process growing out of dialectical discussion.

In the bigger picture, what has most strained historical understanding in the decades since has been less Newton's political strategies – which can be readily grasped as rational if one cares to understand them – than his interpersonal behaviors. He increasingly demonstrated an emotional impulsiveness that had been completely uncharacteristic for him. Before his imprisonment, John Seale was one to attest, it was unusual to see Newton get upset.[128] One crucial change after 1970 was that he engaged in acts of personal violence, always while intoxicated on alcohol or cocaine, or both. Elaine Brown recounts an instance when he slapped her after being awake for two days straight, high on cocaine, and exhibiting uncontrolled eye movements.[129] The drugs worsened a hazardous lack of sleep.[130] He became so paranoid that he accused even his brother Melvin of trying to kill him.[131] Masai Hewitt was demoted for being one of the few to speak up, and left the Party soon after. "You could see in his eyes the hurt, the disappointment, and the humiliation he felt."[132] In the spring and summer of 1974, Newton expelled David Hilliard and his brother June. Bodyguard Robert Bay left as well.[133] When even Bobby Seale was reportedly beaten and expelled, one had to wonder about how Newton's mind was functioning.[134]

Aaron Dixon later wrote:

> Since its inception, the organization had attracted some of the best young people in Black America, and, I would argue, some of the brightest, toughest and most dedicated citizens in America altogether. . . . Gradually many would leave the fold, some voluntarily, some on Huey's orders. Some would even flee the party in an attempt to put distance between themselves and the madness going on in Oakland.[135]
>
> I wondered what had happened to him between our first meeting and his release from prison . . . But some-

> thing had happened to him. Huey used to joke, "A funny thing happened on the way to the forum. . ." In the case of Huey P. Newton, whatever happened was deadly serious. . . . There would be speculation that the government used some form of mind control or psychological experimentation on Huey while he was locked up in the California penal system.[136]

That summer of 1974, in August, Newton allegedly beat a tailor by the name of Preston Callins almost to death. And then, one night, during a heated argument in the street with a sex worker and her pimp, Newton's impulsive brutality hit a new peak. The victim's name was Kathleen Smith. She was seventeen, and died after being in a coma for three months. Unbelievably, just two months prior to the battering of Kathleen Smith, Newton had written "Eve, Mother of All Living." In the days surrounding the altercation, several chapter locations in Texas were raided, Newton was beaten by police to the point of concussion, and another attempt was made on his life by unknown parties.[137] Across the previous three months, the Oakland headquarters had been raided, the LampPost was raided and burglarized, Newton's home was raided, and the Oakland chief of police told him there was a contract out on his life.[138] Facing one charge of assault and another for murder, Newton went underground and fled to Cuba with his fiancée Gwen Fontaine.

A year later, when Elaine Brown visited him in Cuba, Newton could not remember the events of the night of the attack on Smith. "Her death punished him in more ways than that. 'I don't even know her face,' he said quietly in the beer bistro."[139] For Newton, who was so used to his photographic memory, not recalling even her face was hard to make sense of. Worsening the matter, when he returned to stand trial in 1977 for the death of Smith, it was taken as evidence of his guilt that a key witness was almost killed. However, Panther Flores Forbes has since taken the blame for that action, which he and his partner undertook independently after becoming intoxicated.[140] The witness, Crystal Gray (given name Raphaelle Gary), Smith's pimp, later refused to deny that she was offered money and immunity by the police to testify against Newton.[141]

In the decades since, the macabre fascination of some with piecing together the details of Newton's anti-social behavior during his severe struggles with addiction and mental health in the 1970s and 1980s has largely contributed to his continuing villainization, as well as the persistent denigration of the Black Panther Party as a whole. During the same period, despite constant state harassment, the organization continued its achievements, setting up the award-winning Oakland Community School and leading a national effort to bring attention to sickle cell anemia.[142] Even Newton's consistent legal acquittals in the 1970s reflect the impressive power of the political and legal apparatus the Party had developed. Some of the worst actors in the pervasive effort to discredit the BPP have been the authors of publications claiming to expose Newton at his worst, often without substantiating their sources. Hugh Pearson's *Shadow of the Panther* is emblematic of this approach and has been characterized by scholar Charles E. Jones as a "flawed" and "biased journalistic account" of Newton's decline in health.[143] In her review of Pearson's book, Lori Robinson, founder of *Emerge* magazine, wrote: "The FBI, which undermined Black activists such as Newton, almost seem like the good guys. . . . This book *might* be capable of discrediting the uplifting legacy of Panthers who struggled, sacrificed and died for Black Power."[144] Decades later, the terrain of struggle over information has shifted to search engines, online articles, and digital media. The technologies for discrediting the Black Panther Party and other social movements today may very well be more sophisticated and algorithmic than we are inclined to imagine.

In 2001, scholar of ethnic studies and former member of the American Indian Movement Ward Churchill published the exceptionally rigorous article, "To Disrupt, Discredit and Destroy." Complete with 410 footnotes, the essay detailed the extent of the state's repressive efforts against the Black Panther Party, from disinformation to assassination. Churchill's concluding remarks remain insightful for understanding ongoing struggles over thought itself:

> We are in a war, whether we wish to be or not, and the only question before us is how to go about winning it. Here too,

the legacy bequeathed by the Black Panther Party provides invaluable lessons. By studying the techniques with which the counterinsurgency war against the Party was waged, we can, collectively, begin to devise the ways and means by which to counter them, off-setting and eventually neutralizing their effectiveness.

The current prospects for liberatory struggle in the United States are exceedingly harsh, even more than was the case a generation ago. Far harsher, however, is the prospect that the presently ascendant system of elite predation might be allowed to perpetuate itself indefinitely into the future, exploiting and oppressing the preponderance of the population in the midst of every moment along the way. We owe it to ourselves to abolish the predators, here and now, or as rapidly as possible, enduring whatever short-run sacrifice is required to get the job done, reaping the longer-term rewards of our success. We owe it to those who sacrificed before us to fulfill the destiny they embraced. Most of all, we owe it to our coming generations to free them from that against which we must struggle. Thankfully, the fallen warriors of the Black Panther Party have left us many tools with which we may at last complete their task.[145]

8

Technology of Madness

We have seen how the ruling circle shows its disrespect for the people through deceit and duplicity. We will not let this continue even if it means that we will not live to see its final destruction. The ruling circle does not respect nor understand the people. They feel that if they can keep the chains on their minds which are placed there in the schools, the churches and other institutions of the tyrant, then they will be able to carry out their evil designs indefinitely.

Huey P. Newton (1972)[1]

The Mind is Flesh

Perhaps the most influential essay Newton ever published was "Prison, Where is Thy Victory?," written in the summer of 1969.[2] Despite being confined to solitary yet again, through his ingenuity and with the help of supporters, Newton managed to author and sneak out a philosophical critique of the prison itself.[3] The essay was Newton's demonstration that, just as he had defeated the soul breaker, he could overcome whatever prison he was put into. Philosopher Brian Sowers has drawn attention to the essay's implicit references – both theological (Pauline Christian and Hebrew) and philosophical (Platonic) – to argue that Newton's remarks about the prison should be understood as claims about life in American society in general – what Malcolm X called the "prison within a prison."[4]

Newton disparaged the creators of prisons for believing that humans can be easily analyzed and reduced to knowable entities. Using mathematical metaphors, he contrasted the certainty of knowledge that exists in the study of geometry with the unknowability of the whole of the human being:

> The prison cannot have a victory over the prisoner because those in charge take the same kind of approach and assume if they have the whole body in a cell that they have contained all that makes up the person. . . . In the case of humanity the whole is much greater than its parts because the whole includes the body which is measurable and confinable and the ideas which cannot be measured nor confined.[5]

Newton explained that the *common prisoner* is not truly controlled because they only pretend to follow the rules, treating it as a game to overcome. Furthermore, the *political prisoner* cannot be truly controlled either, because they reject altogether the basic premises of the prison, never internalizing the project of "rehabilitation." For the political prisoner especially, their perpetual spirit of defiance means that, even as they are held against their will, they in fact continue to resist politically. "Ideas move from one person to another by the association of brothers and sisters who recognize that a most evil system of capitalism has set us against each other, although our real enemy is the exploiter who profits from our poverty."[6] Ultimately, Newton saw the shortcomings of the prison as consistent with the shortcomings of the mind-state and gaze of those who control it: "those who operate the prisons have failed to examine their own beliefs thoroughly, and they fail to understand the types of people they attempt to control. Therefore, even when the prison thinks it has won, there is no victory."[7] In the decades since, Newton's essay has remained a classic of prison literature, as well as a more general testimony to the strength of the human spirit.

In his article "The Shadow of the Soul Breaker: Solitary Confinement, Cocaine, and the Decline of Huey P. Newton," historian Joe Street argued against Newton's analysis. Drawing from Newton's earlier descriptions of his suffering in the soul breaker during his youth, Street speculated that it was the effects of solitary confinement that led to his psychological collapse and turn to interpersonal violence in the 1970s. While Street's article at first glance might appear helpful because it directly addresses the matter of Newton's mental health, it also argued, without strong evidence, that his decline was due *primarily* to the effects of solitary confinement. This line of argument is at odds with accounts from multiple people – J. Herman Blake, John Seale, Newton's brother Lee Edward, and more – who visited Newton in prison.[8] As journalist George Williams attested after a visit in May 1970: "I cannot emphasize enough how fresh he appeared, mentally, physically, spiritually – as if he were a monk just emerging from years of meditation in a mountaintop monastery."[9] Street's line of argument reflected a disconnect, too, from Newton's own account of his second imprisonment:

> I could not have handled the Penal Colony solitary without the soul breaker behind me.[10]
>
> It was the easiest solitary confinement I ever pulled because I was allowed to have reading material there. . . . Unlike the soul breaker, my cell contained a bunk, toilet, washbasin, chair, and tin desk.[11]
>
> The isolation of lock-up was bearable, really more than that. My brain was active; there were many things to think about, and I filled the days working out ideas I had begun to develop back in Oakland City College. Furthermore, my family was able to visit me often.[12]
>
> They could lock up my body but not my spirit; that was with the people.[13]

Street's argument relies heavily upon Newton's account of his first experience in solitary but completely dismisses his account of his later experience. Street also erroneously conflates the two experiences.[14] Pointing to Newton's description of his disorientation in the hours immediately after his release from prison in 1970, Street argued that "these symptoms indicate that his descent into crime and drug addiction was firmly enmeshed in his prison experience," referring specifically to the effect of solitary confinement.[15] However, SHU ("security housing unit") syndrome does not in fact typically include violence towards others as one of its most common symptoms.[16] Notably, since the 1960s, many Panthers and their allies have spent decades in solitary confinement, and though some have eventually exhibited mental decline, there have been no accounts of the sort of impulsive violence that Newton exhibited. Regrettably, Street's article also places comparatively little blame for Newton's decline on state repression and harassment.

Newton's collapse, which was marked by such a change in his personal character, defies easy explanation. Importantly, he later grappled with doubt about the powers of the mind to overcome, after all. However, this skepticism came not from a change of heart concerning the power of solitary confinement to affect his mind, but from a frightening new awareness of a completely different set of techniques that explicitly targeted the materiality of the brain itself. The historical realities that inspired Newton's shift in thinking would prove disturbing.

Rarely discussed by scholars, Huey Newton's brilliant 1974 essay "The Mind is Flesh" is a key to the puzzle. It begins with a critique of modern philosophy, declaring that the "Cartesian concept of mind" has been vastly surpassed by advances in the sciences.[17] According to the seventeenth-century philosopher Descartes, the body and the soul are two fundamentally different kinds of substances, represented in the idea of the "polar opposition between mind and matter." This view was a cornerstone of Western thought for centuries. As Newton's essay argues in several ways, however, mind-body dualism had always been logically unsound, as it makes causal relations between experiences in the mind (e.g. thoughts) and events in the world (e.g. actions) impossible.[18] Newton proposed overcoming this binary through dialectical materialism, incorporating modern science and philosophy both. He argued that the mind is *not in space*, but must nonetheless have a "spatial reference."[19] It can also, through abstraction, infinitely overcome physical limits, but it may just as easily be burdened by that capacity, as when memory itself causes us to suffer.[20] In turn, Newton provocatively suggested that it is, ironically, the very materiality and practicality of our bodies that helps us overcome the pain and burden of memory. "Thus soul-help means body-help in the most generous sense of the term."[21]

The physicality of our bodies keeps us from losing ourselves in abstraction – as Newton discovered in the soul breaker.

At this point, however, the essay makes a sharp turn: a "nightmare," created by American empire and its "superindustrial state," "attempts to manipulate the mind-brain (exclusive of the body and the environment) in order to 'socialize' modern-day Americans."[22] Newton quotes a report from the Department of Health, Education, and Welfare, titled "Development and Legal Regulation of Coercive Behavior Modification Techniques with Offenders," which discussed plans for the remote cognitive manipulation, or "mind control," of the American population:

> A miniaturized radio transmitter, implanted inside the brain or body, can monitor and transmit the conversations, locations, even the sexual responses of the subject twenty-four hours a day. The report explains that sewed up inside the subject's body along with the transponder would be a radio-controlled electric-shock device. This device could deliver punishment to the "offender" anywhere in the world.[23]

Newton's essay laid out extensive evidence of the involvement of scholars at Harvard University, Yale School of Medicine, and Berkeley's School of Criminology, in cooperation with the National Security Agency, in projects aimed at directly and forcibly controlling the social, economic, and political behaviors of criminals and citizens in general through "behavioral engineering."[24] "Electrical impulses injected into the brain can induce, inhibit, or modify such phenomena as movement, desire, rage, aggression, fear, pain, and pleasure."[25] Writing in 1974, Newton noted that "computers have already been tested on subjects in mental 'hospitals'."[26] He cites especially the work of Yale neurophysiologist José Delgado, who in 1969 published a philosophical justification for mind control in *Physical Control of the Mind: Toward a Psychocivilized Society*.[27] During testimony in front of Congress in 1974, Delgado stated: "The individual may think that the most important reality is his own existence, but this is only his personal point of view. This lacks historical perspective. Man does not have the right to develop his own mind. . . . We must electrically control the brain. Some day armies and generals will be controlled by electric stimulation of the brain."[28]

In Newton's assessment, "the unstated motive of this domestic counterrevolution is nothing less than control of *bodies*. And the techniques are extrapolated worldwide wherever tyranny and the American Empire hold sway."[29] Newton expressed concern over what was an intentional effort at absolute control over human agency, propelled, he argued, by the most narrow-minded versions of science and progress: "Here we may see clearly the subjective misunderstanding of objective phenomenon at the very origin of the modern method: complete ethnocentrism; class blindness; and the seeds of modern, 'enlightened' colonization and enslavement."[30] Against technological colonization and slavery, Newton insisted on our full humanity: "Our field is real life where each arbitrary order of abstraction (mind-brain-body) is always a function of human flesh and blood. And the sum of these abstractions is the soul. . . . Thus dialectical materialism presses, always, toward a structuralism of *dynamic process*."[31] Demanding that "new controls of mind not be applied by the few without the prior conscious consent of the many," Newton exclaimed in defiance that we are neither mere bodies, nor simply spirit: "The mind is flesh!"

Newton's essay is better understood when placed within a broader historical context. Mind control research in the United States began two decades earlier with its roots in Nazi science. Although during World War II the Office of Strategic Services (OSS) – predecessor to the CIA – had begun to imitate Nazi research into "truth serums" and hypnosis, it was not until after the war that the US made substantial advances by directly recruiting Nazi scientists.[32] Beginning in 1945 and continuing up to the 1980s, Operation Paperclip was a covert military effort to recruit 1,800 German scientists, engineers, and their families.[33] Nazi doctors had been experimenting with mind control drugs on prisoners in the concentration camps, and this work directly informed US research begun in 1947 under the US Navy's Project CHATTER and continued in 1949 under the CIA's Project BLUEBIRD (later renamed ARTICHOKE), under which behavior modification drugs were tested without consent on military personnel and prisoners.[34] BLUEBIRD used experiments on humans to develop techniques for brainwashing, mind control, and psychological torture. The project continued through the 1970s under the names MKULTRA, MKSEARCH, MKDELTA, MKNAOMI and other headings. Subjects were rendered entirely unaware of the experiments performed on them, which included the forced administration of drugs, electroshocks, hypnosis, sensory deprivation, isolation, psychosurgery, implantation of electrodes in the brain, physical and sexual abuse, and torture. In 1975, the US Senate Select Committee to Study Governmental Operations with Respect to Intelligence Activities, also known as the Church Committee, exposed a portion of these programs to public scrutiny. However, a close examination of scholarly publications from the era in the fields of psychiatry, psychology, and neurology shows that "the climate [among scholars] was permissive, supportive and approving of mind control experimentation" involving "the most influential figures in American psychiatry in the second half of the twentieth century," although awareness of this fact has been lost in the relative silence since then within both academia and public discourse.[35]

In her recent article "Erasing Minds: Behavioral Modification, the Prison Rights Movement, and Psychological Experimentation in America's Prisons, 1962–1983," historian Zoe Colley sets out extensive evidence demonstrating federal funding for a range of behavior modification research and mind control experimentation on prisoners.[36] She quotes one participating professor, James McConnell, who wrote in his article "We can Brainwash Criminals – Now": "No one owns his own personality. Your ego, or individuality, was forced on you by your genetic constitution and by the society into which you were born. You had no say about what kind of personality you acquired, and there's no reason to believe you should have the right to refuse to acquire a new personality."[37] While researchers consistently relied on the dehumanization of the figure of the criminal to justify the expansion of their projects, Colley's research affirms that support for the use of behavior modification on political prisoners was widespread.

Colley identifies the federal Marion Penitentiary in Illinois as a key site where "even one of the former wardens . . . Ralph Aron, testified in court that 'the purpose of [Marion] . . . is to control revolutionary attitudes in the prison system and in the society at large.'"[38] Taking in political prisoners from across the country throughout the early 1970s, Marion's inmates included members of the Black Panther Party, the Republic of New Afrika, the Nation of Islam, and even participants in riots. Eventually, the concentration of political prisoners at Marion contributed to the radicalization of the prison population as a whole.[39] Rebel prisoners established a chapter of the Federal Prisoners' Coalition, engaged in work strikes, and in 1972 submitted a report to the United Nations Economic and Social Council protesting their conditions. According to Colley, the report "described how men who refused to take part in the behavior modification program were injected with tranquilizing drugs and placed in solitary confinement . . . Stripped naked and strapped to a steel bed, men were forced to eat and defecate where they lay."[40] As repression intensified in the form of beatings and more intense forms of solitary confinement, the Political Prisoners Liberation Front filed lawsuits against the prison, eventually, in 1973, managing to win the first federal court ruling that prisoners had suffered cruel and unusual punishment.[41] In 1974, the Law Enforcement Assistance Administration admitted that it had funded at least 400 behavior modification programs in prisons, but they could not confirm the funding as "no records had been kept."[42]

In *Body and Soul*, scholar Alondra Nelson identifies that Newton's concern about these projects began in 1973, during his work with lawyer Fred J. Hiestand to protest the establishment of a "Violence Center" at the University of California, Los Angeles. According to Nelson, the proposed Center for the Study and Reduction of Violence aimed to employ "brainwashing, hypnosis, and sleep deprivation," as well as "psychosurgery (the removal or alteration of an area of diseased brain tissue thought to cause aggressive behavior)," to "control violence," which was described by researchers as "a form of mental illness or brain dysfunction that could be controlled and monitored by psychiatrists and neuroscientists."[43] These plans explicitly identified as target populations "black males, the incarcerated," intersex people (with the "XYY chromosome syndrome that was then believed to cause aggressive conflict"), menstruating women, and "black and Chicano" high school students.[44]

Among the researchers slated to work at the Center was one Dr. Frank R. Ervin, who had argued in his book *Violence and the Brain* for the permanent insertion of electrodes in the brains of targeted patients in order to remotely control their behavior. Also lined up to join the Center were Governor Reagan's Secretary of Health Dr. Earl Brian and counterintelligence advisor William Hermann.[45] Hermann worked with both the FBI and the CIA and had been a part of the psychological operations unit in Vietnam and Cambodia.[46] According to journalist Gordon Thomas, patients and prisoners at Saigon's Bien Hoa Hospital in 1966–68 were subject to CIA experiments that included the implantation of "tiny electrodes" in their brains that allowed psychiatrists to "arouse their subjects to violence" by "pressing control buttons on their handsets."[47] In response to the proposed Center at UCLA:

> The Black Panther Party joined forces with civil rights, feminist, prisoners' rights, and students organizations – made up of the western region chapter of the NAACP, the National Organization for Women (NOW), the Mexican American Political Association (MAPA), Committee Opposing Psychiatric Abuse of Prisoners (COPAP), United Farm Workers Organizing Committee (UFOC), and the California Prisoners' Union (CPU) – to attempt to block public funding to the violence center and thereby impede its formation.[48]

Nelson details how the original funding plans fell through, only to be replaced by funding from the university itself through its Neuropsychiatric Institute. Eventually, however, UCLA students and faculty stepped forward to protest and managed to end the plan for the Center altogether.

Nevertheless, similar projects continued elsewhere. Already, during a six-month span during 1967 and 1968 alone, between 400 and 1,000 prisoners had been subjected to "clinical testing of behavioral control materials" at the prison at Vacaville, officially known as the California Medical Facility. Vacaville was the main facility through which newly convicted prisoners in the state were processed and psychiatrically assessed before being sent to other prisons.[49] In 1968, experimentation was conducted at Vacaville under Subproject 3 of MKSEARCH (replacing MKULTRA Subproject 140), as confirmed in a letter dated October 18, 1978 from CIA Deputy Director Frank Carlucci to Democratic Representative Leo J. Ryan.[50] A legal affidavit written by a former prisoner attested that research occurred on the third floor of the facility (in section B3), and drug testing at the facility was described in scholarship as late as 1971.[51] According to a 1972 article in *The Washington Post*, at least three prisoners were subjected to psychosurgery while at Vacaville.[52] This involved a procedure known as an amygdalotomy, where a long electrode is inserted into the brain to "burn out electrically" the rear portions responsible for emotions, affects, and basic human behaviors.[53] In February 1972, a project to implant brain electrodes for "remote tracking," immobilization, and control of discharged prisoners was cancelled following public protest.[54] Importantly, although Newton's writing focused on implantations, procedures such as the amygdalotomy were simpler to accomplish and could with much less effort have severe effects on a mind. As bioethicist Nita A. Farahany has explained, "ablating the amygdala can . . . cause profound personality changes," including "lack of remorse," "lack of fear response," and the "blunting [of] emotions to such an extent that the person becomes a psychopath."[55]

Eldridge Cleaver spent time at Vacaville before the Party's formation, as did Huey Newton and David Hilliard during the existence of the Party, before they were transferred to other prisons. Hilliard described so-called "high-violence potential" inmates being forcibly medicated with the anti-psychotic Prolixin while there.[56] Emory Douglas has stated that early Party member Charles Bursey was subject to electroshock treatment while in prison.[57] In an interview in 1969, Kathleen Cleaver confirmed that Eldridge, too, had been subject to electro-shock treatments before the Party.[58] Scholar Orisanmi Burton has demonstrated that inmates convicted of sex crimes, like Cleaver, were particular targets of MKULTRA experiments in the early 1960s, but, as he and Colley have both shown, so too were Black political activists.[59]

In the early 1970s, as Newton's mental health declined, rumors circulated among those who knew him best that something had been done to him while he was in prison, too.[60] During a speech at UCLA in October of 1971, Kathleen Cleaver discussed the matter openly:

> We feel, from the information we've received, that the present status of Huey P. Newton – many of you are aware of this, many of you are not – is that of a "Manchurian Candidate," that the man *was* a revolutionary, who was arrested and taken into the California Department of Corrections penal system. [. . .] When he was released, he was no longer the same person. And during this period of time, he had been subjected and programmed to many types of various drug treatments and distortions [. . .] in these brain-twisting, people-killing centers that are run [. . . .] at Atascadero, and Vacaville and CMC East.[61]

It seems as well that Newton was aware of these speculations. In 1973, *Christian Century* magazine published an interview conducted with Newton that discussed the rumors: "Some have even hinted that he must have been the victim, while in prison, of a macabre behavior-altering medical experiment – a 'clockwork orange' type of treatment."[62] It merits notice that the author's suggestion that "the prison authorities" may have "inflict[ed] psychosurgical or biomedical 'therapy' upon Huey" was enough of a public concern at the time to be remarked upon by a mainstream publication.[63] Notably, Newton completed his "The Mind is Flesh" essay in May 1974, precisely the same time that he was falling into increasingly violent cycles of harm towards those around him, just before he expelled Seale, Hilliard, and so many others from the Party, and right before the murder of Kathleen Smith.

The Black Panther newspaper was persistent in its coverage of these matters, as well. A January 6, 1973 article titled "Tearing Out Our Thoughts: Psychosurgery and the Black Community" explained the distinctions made by researchers between procedures targeting higher- and lower-level cognitive functions: "There is the cingulotomy in which fibers connecting the frontal lobes of the brain to the mid-brain are destroyed. The second operation is the amygdalotomy, which destroys the clump of cells in the brain that controls a person's emotions."[64] Scholar of Black studies and disability studies Sami Schalk has produced detailed scholarship about a series of articles in the Party newspaper in 1977 that focused on the tragic case of Lou Byers, a Black former member of the military who underwent an "experimental brain operation" without his consent during a stay at the Veterans Administration Hospital in Menlo Park, California. In the callous words of the operating doctor, the procedure was designed to leave Byers to "live as a vegetable."[65] As a result of the operation, Byers lived thereafter emotionally muted, unable to count above twenty, and only vaguely able to recognize his own mother. According to Los Angeles Panther Wayne Pharr, the wife of Los Angeles Panther Paul Redd later claimed that a similar procedure, "a lobotomy to reduce his tendency for violence," was conducted on her husband as well.[66] "Whatever happened in the joint, Paul never recovered from it. He became reclusive and hard to get a hold of. At one point, he was homeless." The variety of effects observed indicates the high level of sophistication already at that point in the ability to produce specific behavioral and emotional outcomes within the targeted populations.

In his 2023 book *Tip of the Spear*, Orisanmi Burton introduced the term *cognitive war* to describe the use of these kinds of procedures in the 1960s and 1970s as part of the effort to stifle "revolutionary minds" and the political movements of the Black and oppressed.[67] Burton does not explicitly define cognitive war, but we can infer that it is to be distinguished from *psychological war*, being more physiological than the latter, while also including it. Cognitive war might accordingly be the most violent mode of war of all, insofar as it aims not just at bodies but at the very "flesh" of what Newton called the "mind-brain-body."[68] Burton's groundbreaking research on behavior modification experiments conducted at New York Dannemora State Hospital for the Criminally Insane (later Adirondack Correctional Treatment Education Center – ACTEC) also revealed the practice of "sex experiments" at the facility. One of his interviewees, Masia Mugmuk, claimed that prisoners were fed drug-infused food to "make us want to rape each other."[69] As Burton has explained:

> Using incarcerated deviants, militants, and malcontents as raw material, ACTEC functioned as a laboratory where

> respected members of the academic community experimented with scientific forms of sexual grooming and rape. After violently reducing them to a childlike state, they subjected those over whom they exercised asymmetrical power to coercive medical and scientific techniques that aimed to cultivate sexual desires, orientations, and practices that were contrary to their will and suited the needs of those who aimed to control them.[70]

Burton also uncovered further documentary evidence that MKULTRA mind control and sex experiments were conducted at the Vacaville Medical Facility in California.[71] "Against the dominant conception of the prison as a site of criminal justice that is marginal to global concerns, these experiments illuminate the prison as a site of incubation for technologies that are central to the reproduction of empire."[72]

Investigative journalist Tom O'Neill's 2019 book *Chaos: Charles Manson, the CIA, and the Secret History of the Sixties* helpfully elucidates more of the history behind these experiments.[73] MKULTRA programs were conducted at colleges, hospitals, prisons, and military bases all over the US and Canada, with the help of 185 researchers, across eighty-nine known institutions (including forty-four universities and colleges), not including multiple false "front" organizations and companies created by the CIA.[74] O'Neill focuses in particular on the research of one Dr. Louis Jolyon West, whose experiments confirmed that "hypnosis could make people so pliable that they'd violate their moral codes."[75] West claimed that "he knew how to replace 'true memories' with 'false ones' in human beings without their knowledge."[76] MKULTRA's goals explicitly included the "creation of hypno-programmed assassins" and "induced psychosis."[77] Dr. West was also slated to lead the "Violence Center" at UCLA, along with Dr. Jose Delgado.[78] When the existence of MKULTRA was exposed by Congress in 1975, O'Neill explains, most of the information about West's research was illegally hidden from the investigators. The CIA instead falsely claimed that their experiments had been failures.[79]

West was in fact building upon already established work conducted under operation ARTICHOKE. In their respective researches and writings, former foreign service officer of the US Department of State John D. Marks, and, later on, psychiatrist Colin Ross (whose expertise is in dissociative identity disorder, previously termed multiple identity disorder) amassed and presented extensive government documentary evidence that, already in the 1950s, precisely these kinds of conditions had been intentionally and successfully produced by scientists in multiple experiments, through "depatterning" and the creation of "new identities," with "amnesia barriers" triggered by words or other sounds "used in simulated or actual operations."[80] Ross has referred to these conditions as *iatrogenic* (psychiatrist-made) dissociative identity disorders. Subjects could be led to undertake violent actions at odds with their personal ethics.[81] According to one unclassified and today digitally accessible CIA document titled "Hypnotic Experimentation and Research, 10 February 1954," a test subject

> was instructed that her rage would be so great that she would not hesitate to kill [redacted] for failing to awaken. Miss [redacted] carried out these suggestions to the letter including firing the (unloaded pneumatic pistol) gun at [redacted] and then proceeding to fall into a deep sleep. After proper suggestions were made, both were awakened and expressed complete amnesia for the entire sequence.[82]

In her book *Surviving Evil: CIA Mind Control Experiments in Vermont*, former test subject Karen Wetmore describes the procedures she was subjected to, starting at age thirteen, as one among thousands. She reconstructed her experiences as best as she could through extensive research and requests for documentation through the Freedom of Information Act.[83]

Perhaps the most unsettling aspect of the research of Marks, O'Neill, Ross, and others is their effort to reach towards a better understanding of the possible relationship between these government programs and the unprecedented surge in the 1970s of virtually altogether new profiles of social violence, including the still unexplained historical appearance of "serial killers," particularly in Northern California. Remarkably, details in Angela Davis's 1974 autobiography *With My Mind on Freedom*, provide a case in point. Davis's book, which chronicles her life as an activist in the 1960s and early 1970s, includes an account of her bizarre experiences with an apartment building manager who developed what she described as "psychosis."[84] The man, who heard voices in his head that he said were coming from his apartment, falsely claimed that Davis was forcibly keeping him as a "prisoner in his own house."[85] Davis recounted how he attempted to run her over in his car, but during "moments of lucidity" would confess to her his mental health struggles and experience of "stumbling into madness."[86] He claimed to feel "brainwashed" and "hypnotized" and was convinced that Davis was the cause. She "felt sorry for this man and wondered how much of his illness was the product of being Black in a racist, anti-Communist world."[87]

Also remarkable were events that took place in the small Northern California beach-town of Santa Cruz, which endured a sudden surge of twenty-eight murders within an eight-month period during 1972 and 1973, despite having a population of only 120,000.[88] Author Emerson Murray quotes one resident's summation of the murderers: "They were nice-looking, middle-class, law-abiding citizens. They also shared another common trait: they were all former mental patients released from California State hospitals."[89] For political activists of the period, however, perhaps no phenomenon was stranger than the dynamics surrounding the Symbionese Liberation Army (SLA). Although originally formed out of a Black cultural association of inmates at Vacaville prison, this predominantly white group of purportedly left-wing "radicals" infamously engaged in murders of Black progressives and kidnapped the daughter of an elite publishing magnate. The SLA added Huey Newton "to their hit list after the BPP openly condemned the organization for ruthlessly assassinating Oakland school superintendent Marcus Foster."[90] Newton was convinced at the time that the highly publicized SLA was a government operation.[91] Journalist Brad Schreiber has since argued this explicitly in his award-winning book *Revolution's End*, laying out clear evidence that the group was indeed unknowingly following a leader who had been subjected to chemical cognitive manipulation.

Throughout the 1970s, mainstream news was filled with concerns about unethical, open-air experiments conducted by the military on civilian populations, mind control research, and Congressional hearings about it all.[92] Yet, despite the supposed halting of MKULTRA programming in 1973, there is evidence that scientists were still producing research under its heading as late as 1996.[93] In the 1980s, CIA front organizations shifted from mind control techniques to mind control technologies, pursing research into "intelligence electronic warfare" and "the physiological and biological effects of magnetic fields."[94] Political scientist and scholar of security studies Armin Krishnan has helpfully introduced the terms "neurowarfare" and "neuroweapons" to describe the most contemporary developments, which include technologies for accessing and controlling minds remotely, established in the decades since the "cognitive war" techniques of the 1960s.[95] In *The Battle for Your Brain*, bioethicist and philosopher Nita A. Farahany makes considerable progress in parsing and lending some legitimacy to the concerns of some who fear they have been targeted or made test subjects of new and unimaginable technologies.[96] Ultimately, Krishnan argues, the evidence points to the likelihood of projects aiming for "neurowarfare proper – a direct attack on the brains and consciousness of entire populations in order to either cause internal political chaos, or to change their political identity, way of life, and allegiance in a stealth conquest without violence."[97] In fact, described more accurately, such methods would represent the height of violence, what psychoanalyst Joost Meerloo termed "the rape of the mind" in his analysis of the link between mind control techniques and modern authoritarian governments.[98] The dangers laid out in such scholarship urge us towards a paradigm shift and the opening of a discussion about the contemporary repercussions of the past atrocities Huey P. Newton warned about, as well as the technologies pursued by those in power in the decades since.

Casualties of Cognitive War

Entering the prison meant showing press identification, signing in, and getting my wrist invisibly stamped, waiting for a series of steel gates to slide open, with no two ever opening at the same time, showing more identification,

> signing more slips of paper, going through more steel doors, until I was in the prisoner's area. . . . I was finally led to a small office to wait for Huey Newton, who, I was told, was with his psychologist Dr. Sorenson. . . . We waited and waited, meanwhile making several somewhat half-hearted attempts to point out the time to various officials, one of whom politely informed us that Mr. Sorenson's work was just as important as ours. . . . Before using the phone to contact the official who had arranged for us to see Huey, we were warned to dial quickly because any phone left off the hook for longer than 10 seconds would set off an alarm.[99]

This was how radio journalist Denny Smithson described his experience, on October 17, 1968, of entering Vacaville prison where Newton was transferred after his conviction in September. Interviewing Newton with journalists Joe Blum of *The Movement* and Karen Wald of *The Guardian*, Smithson expressed his shock at seeing Newton without his afro, "his head practically shaved." "It was completely bald," Newton said with a laugh. His explanation was that it was actually his second haircut since arriving, after an earlier "bad haircut."[100]

Joe Blum, who knew Newton from their time together at Merritt College, later recalled a conversation with an official at the prison:

> We talked to this pretty high-up honcho. He said, "The inmates, they have this really hard shell, but if you break into that shell, then you can sort of mold what's inside." And I thought, my god, what are you doing to their brains? What kind of chemicals are you using? I'm glad I could still see the stamp on my hand, so I could leave. I felt like I was dealing with a sadistic monster. When I saw Huey after he was in that place, and he was in there for a while, I felt that some of the changes might have been related to that. It was a very scary place.[101]

Newton and the reporters went on to discuss the mandatory battery of tests – aptitude, IQ, and more – and meetings with psychologists, psychiatrists, and sociologists that Newton was subjected to during his stay at Vacaville. His visit with Dr. Sorenson was his first, and the doctor had asked Newton about how he controls his emotions.[102] In *Revolutionary Suicide*, Newton described his experiences with the psychiatrists:

> It has been my experience in prison that psychiatrists are among the most rigid and inflexible members of the staff. They are programmed and computerized like robots and cannot approach inmates as human beings. With their tests and questionnaires they seem to have a preconceived idea of what an "adjusted" human being is. Any deviation from this mold is a threat to them.[103]

Newton would often fake his performance on the various tests, only occasionally performing honestly if he found the test interesting: "I explained to them that I refused to relate to these tests because they are routinely used as weapons against Black people in particular and minority groups and poor people generally. . . . Since we are taught to believe that the tests are infallible, they have become a self-fulfilling prophecy that cuts off our initiative and brainwashes us."[104]

Newton explained further that, "during this testing, the authorities puzzled over where to put me. There was much speculation in the prison about that, and through the grapevine I heard that they had some trouble deciding."[105] Prisoners typically stayed at Vacaville for sixty days, so Newton was surprised to be moved after only twenty-five.[106] Upon arriving at California Men's Colony East Facility in San Luis Obispo (known by inmates as "California Penal Colony"), he quickly noticed that the prison was 90 percent white and 80 percent gay. It was in this prison that he would develop a critique of his own homophobia, but also where he would develop his analysis of the prison as a place where sexuality is intentionally and coercively manipulated. As described earlier, in Newton's analysis, "these men were exploited and controlled by the guards and the system. . . . The system was the pusher in this case, and the prisoners were forced to become addicted to sex."[107]

* * *

Ericka Huggins had been a Party organizer in Los Angeles, but did not meet Newton until after he had left prison. They empathized over their shared appreciation of meditation, which had helped both of them during their experiences of incarceration.[108] Huggins remained in the Party until the late 1970s, and observed Newton's decline: "Everybody and their brother wanted to kill him or get to him – the police, the people who weren't well, and also curiosity seekers. But Huey was private, and, get this, a shy person. When a certain level of drugs was running, he wasn't shy at all. But there was a part of him, that when he would enter a room full of people he didn't know, he would want to hide."[109] Newton's second wife, Fredrika, whom he married in 1984, affirmed his shyness:[110] "What most intrigued me about Huey was the difference in how he was perceived publicly and how he was privately. At the apartment, he was really shy, making awkward kind of moves on me. He wasn't smooth at all."[111] Panthers George "Bunchy" Crear and Phyllis Jackson, who worked in Oakland through the late 1970s, agreed that Newton was shy.[112] Jackson added that he was also an awkward dancer. In Newton's words: "My problem was that I could not dance, and when the music began, I felt self-conscious. If I did not leave when the dancing started, I would begin discussions or recite poetry."[113] In a later interview, he described himself as having "a timid personality."[114] J. Herman Blake, who met Newton during his trial and got to know him well, described him as a "warm, friendly, and gentle man."[115] Interviewer Make Lane wrote of Newton's tendency to "almost always depersonalize any question that is directed at him," adding that in conversation his "integrity and warmth and candor were apparent."[116]

Contrary to the kind of behavior he would eventually fall into, then, Newton was not at his core a violent person. Neither, however, was he a self-deprecating or meek person. "What Huey had was a sense of his own self-worth outside of what other people thought," said Phyllis Jackson.[117] He transformed his sense of self, through effort, into the spirit of defiance that came to inspire so many. What had been a willingness to defend himself as a boy turned, in adulthood, into a politics of Black self-defense and dignity. In describing Newton's broad appeal to Black Americans, Black Studies scholar Judson Jeffries has drawn upon the slavery-era origins of the concept of the "bad nigger."[118] Under slavery, the enslaved African who refused to act as the slave master demanded inevitably earned the label of "bad nigger"; this label, in turn, came to be a term of admiration and praise among the enslaved. "When one is referring to a 'ba-ad' nigger, the more one prolongs the 'a', the greater is the homage." Unfortunately, this aspect of Newton's personality, which he himself described in rational, existential, and political terms, has allowed for an easy conflation, through the racist logic underlying the American idea of the criminal, with his quite different acts of impulsive violence in the 1970s. That is, it has been typical to regard Newton's violence as related to his Blackness rather than as a symptom of what he underwent. And, perhaps also, at some level of his semi-consciousness, there was a convergence between his personal principle of pre-emptive defense on the one hand and a hypersensitive, paranoid aggressivity connected to his cognitive unwellness on the other. According to witnesses in the 1970s, Newton's acts of violence towards those around him typically followed from minor slights that he responded to disproportionately, always while intoxicated.[119]

Publicly available videos of Newton are limited, in part because of his incarceration and in part because of his avoidance of publicity. That said, observing and analyzing what is available, a comparison of videos from before and after his processing at Vacaville does allow one to identify some differences in his physical behavior. In all the available videos of Newton during his jailing in 1967 and 1968, across several interviews, he is tranquil, composed, and speaks smoothly, despite his confinement and the stresses of the trial.[120] By contrast, an extended video interview conducted on August 4, 1970, one day before his release, shows him exhibiting sudden, jerky movements and apparent excessive energy.[121] In another video recorded at a news conference in the fall of 1970, Newton speaks slowly and smoothly, like his prior self, but stops the interview after complaining of a headache from the brightness of the lights.[122] In a video of his press conference in September 1971, upon returning from China, he exhibits some signs of sudden movements, but to a lesser degree.[123] Footage of Newton speaking in Georgia in September of 1971 shows him calm and somewhat timid.[124] The hour-long video of Newton's 1973 debate with conservative public intellectual William F. Buckley records his speech as calm, if somewhat slurred at points, and he appears to exhibit some physical restlessness.[125]

Newton also exhibited what Fredrika Newton has termed manic depressive behaviors. According to Fredrika, who met him after his prison release: "He'd call me and threaten to jump off the balcony. 'I'm going to fly like a bird. I'm so depressed, I'm going to kill myself. I need you to come see about me.'"[126] An FBI memo dated January 25, 1971 takes credit for "counterintelligence projects now in operation" for their success in "undermin[ing] Huey's mental stability."[127] And a handwritten note attached to an FBI airtel memo from Director Hoover dated January 28, 1971 reads: "Newton responds *violently* to any question of his actions or policies or reluctance to do his bidding. . . . It appears Newton may be on the brink of mental collapse and we must intensify our counterintelligence."[128] Hoover had been made aware of state projects in "experimental use of hypnotism" on prisoners as early as 1937.[129] Elaine Brown has stated that she learned from her contact in the CIA not only of Hoover's plans to target potential "Black messiahs," but also about an ongoing effort to shape a false one:

> "There's something I want to tell you that you may not know," Jay said with solemnity, after a minute. "Are you aware that Hoover issued a directive about black militants, instructing all FBI offices to eliminate or prevent the rise of another black 'messiah' figure, as Malcolm X and Martin Luther King were perceived to be? Well, the shocking thing is contained in the other part of that directive. It states that an alternative or related plan is for the FBI *itself* to *develop* such a black messiah."[130]

Brown's source was a romantic partner named Jay Richard Kennedy. There is clear documentary evidence that Kennedy was at minimum an informant for both the CIA and the FBI, though Brown described him as having worked for the OSS and CIA directly.[131]

In an era when so many prominent political leaders globally were subject to assassination, Newton's escape of the same fate – paired with his bizarre decline into madness – rightly arouses suspicion. However, some of these mind control procedures – complete with "amnesia barriers" – were designed to hide the fact of their hold on the targeted individual. Armin Krishnan's theorizations on military technologies today suggest a line of consideration: "Indeed, it might be most prudent for a belligerent using a neurowarfare approach to hide the attempt of mental or psychological manipulation and coercion. Ideally, the victims of brain interference should never be aware of covert attacks on their perception, decision-making and behavior."[132] After the morbid spectacle of the assassinations of the 1960s, was Newton in 1970 the target of a newly unfolding strategy and mode of warfare? Consistent with the techniques of colonialism, the bodies and minds closest to the center of empire are sometimes targeted for capture, control, and tactical manipulation rather than outright destruction.

Orisanmi Burton has suggested that, ironically, the largest archive of Black radical knowledge today is held by the US government and its massive surveillance apparatus.[133] Yet, as Newton pointed out, "when the BPP filed its federal civil rights lawsuit against, *inter alia*, the CIA in 1976," hundreds of CIA domestic files on "Black dissidents" had already been destroyed before the Congressional Committees were able to pursue inquiries.[134] At a conference held at the University of New Mexico and broadcast on C-SPAN in 2006, Elaine Brown affirmed this, speaking on the records available, "Most of those are obliterated, names are taken out, things are changed around and so forth. I've attempted to get my records again, and the first time I had them [while] in the Party, I had over 12,000 pages or something ridiculous like that and when I went back, ten years [later], they didn't even have 600 pages available. So, it goes to show, that stuff gets written out."[135] In 1973, CIA Director Richard Helms ordered the destruction of all files related to the MKULTRA program.[136] In his dissertation, Newton concluded:

> The likelihood that the truth about CIA efforts to neutralize the Party will never be fully known is great. Aside from the admitted destruction by the CIA of files concerning the BPP and failure to respond to civil discovery efforts,

> one man who had first-hand knowledge of the operation noted, "If they i.e., the CIA had gotten exposed, then it would have been the CIA versus the Black Panthers and all Black Americans – they [would] have had a lot of Americans against them. The agency would have been exposed, open to attack."[137]

* * *

In the late summer of 1974, Newton fled to Cuba with his partner, fellow Panther Gwen Fontaine. On the way, they first spent several months in Mexico while a boat was organized for their transit. The archives at Stanford University include a typed manuscript referred to as part of a journal.[138] In it, Newton reflects that his relationship with his partner improved while they lived outside of the United States:

> Gwen and I had been together about six years by August 1974 but during those six years we had spent very little time alone together. There was always an entourage wherever we went – on speaking engagements, Party meetings, working on books and articles, etc. This was a time when we really got to know each other very well and we clung to each other and became very close. Though, as other couples, we had fought before and have fought after this three or four months' ordeal, we don't remember arguing or fighting at that time.[139]

In a later interview, Newton reported feeling calm while in Cuba: "I felt free and safe and comfortable for the first time in my life."[140] Calling Cuba a "liberated territory," he remarked on the limited reach of American radio and other technology: "It's all blacked out, but every once in a while something would go wrong and you'd get 'Soul Train' for a few minutes."[141] Elaine Brown has pointed out that there was "no cocaine at all in Cuba,"[142] and Huggins later stated that Newton was "not just sober, alcohol and drugs," but "very focused and clear and so on."[143] Bill Brent, who had only met Newton once before, in 1968 – before Vacaville – corroborated this after they met on the island: "his relaxed manner put me at ease."[144] Over three years in Cuba,

Newton read 400 books.[145] Newton and Fontaine had their wedding ceremony there. In later interviews, Gwen's sister Demetra Gayle recalled that "Huey and Gwen were happy in Cuba."[146] During their time in Mexico, they even danced together.[147]

At earlier points, too, Newton had seemed to be at his best when outside the United States. He wrote of experiencing a "psychological liberation" when he visited China in 1971.[148] Robyn Spencer-Antoine has also noted Newton's positive experiences abroad, highlighting a speech he delivered in Denmark and remarking that, in 1973, "Newton remained a charismatic and functional leader despite rumors of misconduct that began to swirl around him."[149]

Notably, even while he was in the US, Newton's capacity for rational analysis did not seem significantly compromised. During 1973 and 1974, he pursued and acquired his bachelor's degree from the University of California Santa Cruz, where he composed several essays, including the earlier mentioned "Politics and Myth," "The First Hero of Literature," and "The Mind is Flesh." In fact, his essays increased in complexity and intellectual range throughout the 1970s, at the same time that his emotional health declined. In the spring of 1974, Newton was accepted into a doctoral program at UC Santa Cruz. From Cuba, he deferred his acceptance with the intention of enrolling when he finally returned to the US. When questioned by his brother Melvin about the events of the summer of 1974, "he said he had a mental breakdown. I accepted what he said, and what that did, of course, was end that conversation, so I couldn't get on his case."[150]

Soon after Newton's return in the late summer of 1977, he was lured in again by the psychological and chemical draw of cocaine. It is unclear when he first developed an addiction to crack. George "Bunchy" Crear has suggested that Newton may have started using after the case of Kathleen Smith ended in a mistrial in March 1979, and that he was suffering with severe addiction by the time the Party folded in 1982.[151] David Hilliard has confessed to essentially introducing Newton to the drug, at one point suggesting this happened in 1978 but at another time saying it was in 1985.[152] Despite its common association with the Black poor, the plague of crack affected countless people in the 1980s, across classes and ethnic groups.[153]

Hilliard, who struggled with multiple forms of addiction himself, summarized Newton's description of crack: "Huey is absolutely right. The drug obliterates any sanction in your personality; everything that's evil in me emerges and tries to destroy all my relationships."[154] Despite Newton's severe addictions, he rejected rehabilitation programs and even "escaped a couple of times from drug-treatment facilities."[155] "All kinds of loving, caring things had been done but he would a find a reason not to stay," Ericka Huggins recalled.[156] In prison, Newton had maintained healthy habits and a daily workout routine, allowing him to "exercise and practice control of my thoughts," as he put it.[157] In sharp contrast, while in the throes of addiction he reportedly stated to Hilliard: "I don't even know myself from one day to the next. The man I sleep with is not the man I wake up with."[158]

Hilliard's *This Side of Glory* offers deep insight into the power that drug addiction – undoubtedly its own form of mind control – exercises over people: "I tell you that there will come a time when your willpower alone won't carry you through your problems."[159] For Huey Newton, who had overcome so much through the exercise of his will, drugs proved to be a psychological trap and cognitive shackle that intensified the harms of all the other stressors and oppressions he carried. Hilliard worded it ominously: "I cannot trust my mind because my mind is programmed to self-destruct . . . *That sure smells good*, a voice inside says when a friend pours a cognac. *You can have a beer today*, another voice tells me soon as I awake. The [rehabilitation] program says everybody has a committee in his or her mind of different voices. I have a whole government."[160]

Several of Newton's friends described him as a single human being seemingly split into "two halves."[161] Flores Forbes invoked the gothic horror character "Jekyll and Hyde," adding, "I've never seen someone switch like that on coke."[162] While at the university, Newton befriended the world-renowned evolutionary biologist Robert Trivers, who became an honorary member of the Party. Trivers also used the phrase "Jekyll and Hyde" to describe him:

> At his best, he was like a king, and therefore if you were a friend of his and in his presence, you were like a prince. It

> was a very heady experience. But he ranged the full gamut from a wonderful person to be with, brilliant, stimulating, very gentlemanly, almost courtly and old-fashioned in his manners when he was ready to be. On the other hand, he could be one of the more frightening creatures you would ever run into.[163]

In his dissociative state, Newton both physically assaulted people himself and gave orders to his personal security circle to inflict harm. Insisting that Newton was not sadistic, Trivers did "not know how to reconcile the warm, brilliant man I knew with these brutal acts."[164] Many have described how Newton indulged in endless, drug-induced nights, awake for days on end, possessively disallowing his guests from leaving and sometimes threatening them if they did.[165] Bizarrely, this appears to have sometimes been triggered by alcohol alone. And yet, when Newton in the 1960s used to enjoy wine on the street corners, talking with the "brothers on the block" about philosophy, the experience was completely different. Now, intoxicating substances seemed to affect him like a trigger, transforming his personality. In December 1982, his beloved wife Gwen left him. "She couldn't deal with her alcoholic addict husband. It was Huey P. Newton, alcoholic addict. When she left, she was exhausted."[166]

According to Trivers, "when he was at his best was during periods when he was drying out, where he had done the drugs so hard that he would go on six weeks where he would just drink tea and meditate."[167] Discussing the differences between a healthier Newton and the one in his altered state, Ericka Huggins elaborated: "When he would call me to his apartment, he wasn't loaded. That was the real Huey, the one in between the two extremes. Huey was depressed in his apartment. This wasn't when he was in his manic mode. This was [him] quiet, sitting on his bed, pondering what his life was about. I don't know how many people got to see him like this."[168]

* * *

In 1977, soon after Newton returned from Cuba, Elaine Brown left the Party.[169] "Over the next several weeks," Forbes recalled, "other people left or were expelled from the Party. It was reminiscent of the purge of 1974."[170] Forbes also described a tension that finally boiled over about a rule that had taken hold despite waves of anti-sexist organizing.[171] Other than women leaders, women in the BPP were not allowed to date men outside of the Party. "The reasons given for this prohibition were as varied as the men who might have answered the question. The rule was made to control the influx of men into the Party, as far as I was concerned. So if you asked me why we practiced this caveman policy, my response would be for reasons of security."[172]

As critical as Newton had been in *Revolutionary Suicide* of the communal romantic dynamics he engaged in when he was younger, he did not in that book offer any critique of the sexism entangled with the BPP's non-monogamous practices, stating simply in 1973 that the "communal life of the Black Panther Party" had "resolved" and "displaced problematical individual relationships."[173] In his youth, at least, Newton had imposed no restraints on the sexual lives of his female partners. According to Spencer-Antoine, over a period of a couple of months, the rank and file submitted multiple criticisms of "the unspoken policy of Panther women dating solely within the organization."[174] According to Forbes, Ericka Huggins took charge of the women's campaign, thereby becoming the most prominent female leader in the Party.[175] Forbes' account of a difficult Central Committee meeting makes it clear that Huggins directly challenged Newton, while also seizing the opportunity to raise questions about Brown's departure.

Despite their intimate friendship, Huggins and Newton never had a romantic relationship. Decades later, in an extended oral history interview, Huggins explained that in late 1979 Newton raped her:

> When Huey came in, he was crazy. I don't mean he was saying words that were crazy. He was crazy. He then, I don't know how much he had been using or for how long, but he was on some kind of binge . . . I can give you the details, moment by moment, of how it occurred, but I will say that rape, we all know never has anything to do with sex and this certainly didn't. It was violent. I was violated. I'm saying it matter-of-factly because I know that it's true.[176]

Shocked by Newton's actions, which occurred more than once, Huggins left the Party sometime after. There are rumors that he raped another woman.[177] Huggins says it was her consistent practice of meditation that allowed her to cultivate the consciousness to heal. Beyond that, she also built upon her ability to see the human being beyond Newton's fall:

> This is the nature of addiction. This is also the nature of the craziness that the external forces and the internal forces in resonance with one another can create.[178]

> It was almost like a possession. I know that there are people who were raised in my mother's Pentecostal church who talk about possession and demons; I'm not talking about it from that standpoint. I just remember at one point at the very end of my life in the Party, in 1980, '81, where I would look into Huey's eyes and there was no Huey there anymore. I didn't know what was in there, but it was not Huey.[179]

> The thing about Huey Newton is this: he was a good man too. So how I remember him is for the good things that he did do. I don't choose to remember him as a horrible person because I feel like we all have demons, and I don't excuse a person for the things that they do, operating from their demons, I don't mean that, but I don't hold anybody in place, because I don't want to be held in place either. We can all transform.[180]

In his insightful book *Rethinking Rufus: Sexual Violations of Enslaved Men*, Black historian Thomas A. Foster provides unique research into the rarely discussed experiences of African-American males who, under the regime of slavery, were coerced by their masters into the rape of others. Because of persistent myths perpetuated about the supposed hypersexuality of Black people, these orchestrated violations of women and men alike have proven resistant to sensitive analysis, so Foster's work is important. "The men were violated, as their bodies were used to violate the bodies of others."[181] Often, these brutalities served the economic, biopolitical calculus of increasing the reproduction of more enslaved human beings. Other times, enslaved men were used as blunt objects of punishment to violently control the behavior of women. Foster writes: "enslaved men were at times psychologically tortured by being forced to assist in sexualized punishments. Attackers understood the anguish this would cause and the divisiveness it could engender within a victim's community."[182] Sowing division within the Black community through sexual violence and the orchestration of rape cultivated chaos, "physiological wretchedness," and trauma among a colonized people.[183] The dynamic created by the slave master cunningly displaced ultimate blame for the rape onto the Black male, obscuring what was rather "a multilayered sexual assault perpetrated by white men on both black men and white and black women."[184]

In *Rape and Resistance: Understanding the Complexities of Sexual Violation*, feminist philosopher Linda Martín Alcoff put forth a definition of violation itself:

> To violate is to infringe upon someone, to transgress, and it can also mean to rupture or break. Violations can happen with stealth, with manipulation, with soft words and a gentle touch . . . Violence is not determinative of what we are after. What we are concerned with is a violation of sexual agency, of subjectivity, of our will. We should also be concerned with the ways in which our will has been formed.[185]

As far as we have been able to understand, Newton increasingly lost his ability to determine and form his own will over time. Something happened to him during his imprisonment at Vacaville, with its inhuman experiments, which combined with the snare of drug addiction to distort his mind. It is appropriate to remember, then, not just Newton's writings about the reality of mind control, but also his writings about the sexual violations, manipulations, and experiments imposed in the prison, where men "were forced to become addicted to sex" and "every desire is used against you."[186] In these ways and more, the prison violates the minds and bodies of the incarcerated, whose experiences inevitably repeat and reverberate out of the prison into the broader society.

The People's Control

One may wonder about how Newton processed his experiences through all of this. Some of his essays from this late period offer clues. In his unpublished "Thoughts on the Will to Power" (1978), Newton argued again for a profound rejection of the all-too-common linking of sex and power. Grappling with the "left and right wings" of "depth psychology" and "human nature," he focused on the work of psychoanalyst Sigmund Freud as key to Western civilization's understanding of itself.[187] In his creative analysis, Newton argued that, for the later Freud, the key concept of *eros* came to be reconceptualized as less about individuals' sexual impulses than about the relationality between people in terms of *love*. "Life, love, and growth are one and the same, more deeply rooted and fundamental than sexuality and 'pleasure.'"[188] Newton points out, however, that it was in fact the sexual aspects of Freud's ideas which were easiest for Western civilization to accept, internalize, and deploy in its project of military domination. He quotes from Freud's 1933 "Why War?" in which Freud states: "There is no need for psychoanalysis to be ashamed to speak of love in this connection, for religion itself uses the same words: 'Thou shalt love thy neighbor as thyself.' This however, is more easily said than done."[189] Elevating "the power of Eros, the love force against the machines of death," Newton's analysis reflects a rejection of the elevated tie between sex and power, but also an awareness of the ease with which they are linked. During periods of war, conquest, and colonization, sex-and-power are traumatically imposed on the colonized in a way that then has staying power in their culture, framing their reality. However, just because the relation between the genders and the rest of life's phenomena may be analyzed in terms of war, this does not mean that natural reality is itself a war. This is part of the frame of coloniality.

In the late 1970s and 1980s, Newton became also distinctly interested in the psychology underlying how people come to deceive themselves. His 1978 essay "On Truth and Sanity" features a discussion of the effects of hypnosis on people's inability to remember their own actions, the relationship to the unconscious, and "research that suggests that both 'true' and 'false' perceptions, in human reasoning, may be inherent functions of the same process."[190] Newton's approach to these matters gained greater sophistication through his collaboration with Robert Trivers between 1978 and 1983. As historian Erika Lorraine Milam has shown, Newton and Trivers worked as equal partners in the development of their theory of the observable behavior of "self-deception" in animals, publishing an article in *Science Digest* in 1982 and working for several years on a proposed book.[191] In brief, the theory was that organisms unconsciously engage in psychological self-deception in order to more effectively accomplish the deception of others; one is, after all, more convincing if one believes one's own lies. In Trivers' assessment, Huey Newton "fell down, as so many of us do, when it came to his own self-deception."[192]

In recent decades, several of Newton's loved ones have emphasized that he suffered from bipolar disorder. Ericka Huggins has pointed this out, and Hilliard stated that Newton was diagnosed in the 1980s as bipolar or manic depressive.[193] Frederika Newton also later stated: "I'm convinced Huey was bipolar and could have benefited greatly from the meds that are now available."[194] Due to the conditions of his unwellness, Newton at a certain point lost the capacity to care even for himself and was in need of intervention. Fredrika Newton reflected: "I should have had him committed, because he was so psychotic. It was drug-induced psychosis and he was out of his mind, and he needed help."[195] In *The Protest Psychosis*, psychiatrist Jonathan Metzl has critically questioned the ease with which the label of madness is today imposed on the Black population, identifying the 1960s as a period when Blackness and madness came to be associated for the first time.[196] In the case of Newton and others like him, however, perhaps the most pressing question is whether or not his psychosis was indeed *iatrogenically* produced. Between 0.015 percent and 0.1 percent of people develop psychosis each year, and of those almost all develop it as teenagers or in their early twenties – not in their mid-thirties as Huey Newton did.[197] Frighteningly, if Newton's mental illness was indeed man-made, most deceptive of all was the fact that the misdeed came to be effectively hidden by the very madness of the victim.

In the broadest picture, then, Metzl is correct to propose that we "use diagnosis to better understand not the patient, but the society."[198] While what is sometimes called "madness" has its genetic biophysiological causes, scholars of mental health have also labored to demonstrate that most mental health struggles are, at root, caused by the cultural logic undergirding how our current society is organized, which disregards and devalues anyone who does not fit its ideal of usefulness to racial capitalism.[199] There exists a societal culture of eugenicism, exemplified in anti-Black racism but not limited to it, which lies at the root of the social practices that regard the poor, the racially oppressed, and the mentally unwell as not just disposable but as an active threat to the social body.[200] Efforts to resist this culture of objectification and disposal through depathologization and inclusion are crucial, but, as for all the oppressed, the primary solution is healing, communal defense, and social change.

While some forms of madness have always been with us, many of the ailments we encounter today are clearly unique to our technological society. As Frantz Fanon argued, colonial society intentionally manufactures madness among the most oppressed, all the better to make use of them for its own ends, to set them against one another, and to feed moral panics among the more privileged.[201] For humanity, the cure is the elimination of the colonial structures and technologies at hand. To this end, the very experiences of the mad can provide insights to us all for the work of spearheading societal care, healing, and defense. In *Black Madness :: Mad Blackness*, philosopher Therí Alyce Pickens uses the palindrome-like phrasing of her book's title as "a critical alternative to 'mental illness' or 'disorder,'" "while resisting an uncritical celebration of madness as experience or as metaphor."[202] Above all, Pickens' work urges us to question how much of the "madness" suffered today is in fact actively produced, caused by techniques and technologies unimaginable. By building upon pivotal scholarship like that of Pickens, and developing a rigorous historical account of how we got to our present, the prospects for revolutionary social healing can become reality.

Newton fled from the rehabilitation centers that his loved ones brought him to. Such reactions are common. "[H]e had been given a bipolar diagnosis and refused to take medication. He just refused and I don't blame him because the medications at that time were horrible."[203] Writing in the 1950s as a physician and psychiatrist, Fanon produced stunning insights that allow us to pierce through "the haze of the organic confusion" that often arises for the mad when they are confronted with the puzzle of trying to find true, decolonial healing in the labyrinth of colonial society.[204] Fanon did not hesitate to openly acknowledge the sinister histories. Writing in 1959 of the "electric shocks" and "truth serums" used by colonizer doctors, he validated the fears of the colonized: "We must not be surprised to find that doctors and professors of medicine are leaders of colonialist movements."[205] "The doctor sometimes proves himself as the most sanguinary of colonizers. . . . So he becomes the torturer who happens to be a doctor."[206]

Vitally, however, Fanon insisted that the solution could not be an utter rejection of doctors, psychotherapy, and medication, but must be rather a decolonial recapture of institutions of medicine that could allow for communal defense. In "Medicine and Colonialism," describing the resistance movement in Algeria, he wrote:

> It found itself faced with the necessity of setting up a system of public health capable of replacing the periodic visit of the colonial doctor . . . to supervise the people's health, to protect the lives of our women, of our children, of our combatants.[207]
>
> The Algerian nurse or doctor is able to win the patient's family over to a complete cooperation: . . . regular administration of medications, prohibition of visits, isolation, and strict observance of diet for several days.[208]
>
> These medications which were taken for granted before the struggle for liberation, were transformed into weapons. And the urban revolutionary cells faced with the responsibility of supplying medications were as important as those assigned to obtain information as to the plans and movements of the adversary.[209]

Fanon ends the essay by describing how people successfully took "their destiny into their own hands" by coming to terms with the necessity of embracing the use of "the most modern forms of technology" for their side of the struggle.[210]

When the Black Panther Party revised its Ten-Point Program in 1972, it was precisely the matter of technology that was added to the tenth and final point: "We want land, bread, housing, education, clothing, justice, peace, and *people's community control of modern technology*." In an essay from that year titled "A Citizen's Peace Force," published in the scholarly journal *Crime and Social Justice*, Newton described "domestic counter-insurgency [as] a 'growth industry'" and wrote of a "computer intelligence system" developed to target activists in an "electronic battle field."[211] With a foresight that resonates into our present day, he projected that "every man, woman, and child will have a secret dossier of their life locked in the new national data banks."[212] Newton paints a bleak picture, but concludes with an optimistic insight: "An electronic net will descend on huge urban populations," "but technology is a knife that cuts both ways and the state's overdependence on hostile technology suggests the way out."[213]

9

Life of the Mind, Politics of the Street

I do not know enough about myself
Because you do not know enough about yourself
Would you help me know

Huey P. Newton (1975)[1]

It is a stunning achievement and a reflection of Newton's intellect that, despite the measures orchestrated against him, he was somehow able to keep *thinking* and *philosophizing*, producing innovative ideas, essays, and complete books. His thought throughout the 1970s was increasingly nuanced and incisive, reflecting his enduring humanism, ethical refusal of human suffering, and spirit of resistance. Most of this writing remains, however, unpublished.

Encountering it for the first time, one may be taken aback at just how well-read Newton was in the canon of Western thought and across multiple fields, ranging from anthropology to theology, political economy to evolutionary biology. At a time when Black Studies and Ethnic Studies were just gaining footholds in the universities as a result of the efforts of social movements of the left, including the efforts of the Black Panther Party, Newton was following in the footsteps of other Third World theorists of his era by drawing upon and leveraging European traditions of knowledge against their own limits.[2] Newton's thought is crucial for us because it allows us to trace the principal pressure points, so to speak, of the colonial systems of thought that define our world today. Newton's thought addresses the human condition broadly, but also grapples with the historical specificity of the colonized American condition, a condition that is, in turn, relevant for all because of the global reach of American empire. For the project of charting a path out of a system integrated into the very ways we think, Newton's work remains important.

The University

Newton's range of thought was so vast that his late writings often present a challenge to readers. In the early 1970s, his thought straddled the especially unruly space between self-taught expertise and the scholastic standards of the university. In 1972, Newton humbly reflected:

> I'm not an intellectual, I am alienated. Because of my history and because of the experience that produced me, I would fall squarely into the area of the unemployables or the proletarian that is unemployed. But, at the same time, because of some realizations, I can realize, I probably realize more, generally, than most people in the working category who haven't indulged in abstracting and investigating man's relationship to each other and nature. So, I think that I suffer a double alienation from my class generally speaking . . . I don't think I fit squarely into either category as far as on an academic level.[3]

By this point, Newton had already delivered speeches at several universities, but he was "intimidated" by the vast cultural differences between academia and the lives of the Black and the poor.[4] In 1971, he returned to Merritt College, where he had earned his associate's degree, to deliver a semester's worth of philosophy lectures titled "A Primary Introduction to Phenomena."[5] As discussed earlier, these lectures were quite dense, and Newton struggled to effectively communicate to his students the range of ideas that went into his thinking, often assuming too much background knowledge from them. He was determined, however, to continue growing intellectually, and in the fall of 1972 he applied to study for a bachelor's degree at the University of California

Santa Cruz (UCSC). His application was supported by a letter of recommendation from the President of Merritt College, Norvel Smith.[6]

Newton's two years at UCSC were highly productive. Historian and founding provost Page Smith considered him "an eccentric genius" but was "puzzled . . . as to why a man of such obvious stature and renown would want to attend the University of California Santa Cruz."[7] Newton had in fact been granted an honorary doctorate in political science from UCSC in 1969 by a vote of the students, but once there he specifically refused requests to get involved in campus politics.[8] Instead, he quickly developed relationships with prominent faculty at the institution, including J. Herman Blake, Norman O. Brown, William E. Abraham, Noel Q. King, Michael Caspi, Donald Nicholl, Paul Lee, and Burney Le Boeuf. He took multiple courses in the History of Consciousness department, which approaches philosophical and social questions through the merger of multiple disciplines. Newton also taught a course on intercommunalism in the Education department.[9] That syllabus included readings on Hegel, Nietzsche, Sartre, Mahatma Gandhi, psychologist Erik Erikson, Austrian ethologist Konrad Lorenz, German phenomenologist Max Scheler, and several of Newton's own books. He graduated from UCSC's Oakes College, its most ethnically diverse college, in June 1974.[10] On his way to graduating, he applied to join the doctoral program in the History of Consciousness. As the university's first graduate department, it bears a radical history and was originally organized along egalitarian principles. Newton reportedly reasoned that, in the modern age, leaders of revolutionary organizations should have PhDs.[11]

At UCSC, he had about a dozen loyal faculty supporters. In the spring of 1974, several faculty collaborated with him to sketch out a plan to integrate the BPP's Oakland Community School with the History of Consciousness department as part of an overarching intercommunalist "learning center."[12] There were plans also to establish another Panther liberation school in the predominantly Mexican American town of Salinas, develop an exchange program between the Oakland school and the University's Coastal Science Campus, and for Newton to offer further lectures on intercommunalism.[13] This project was halted before gaining much more momentum, however. A letter from acting chairperson Jerome Neu intervened: "Because communications from persons unauthorized to speak for History of Consciousness may have misled you, we should perhaps also mention that though some special relationship between some members of the History of Consciousness program or the program itself and your Intercommunalism project may develop, no commitment is being made by us at this time."[14] Nonetheless, Newton was accepted into the doctoral program in April, and he and Provost Page Smith discussed holding a public conversation for the bicentennial of the American Revolution in 1975, likely inspired by Smith's reading of Newton's "Eliminate the Presidency."[15]

Newton's plans for graduate school were derailed when he fled to Cuba for three years, but, after returning to the US in 1977, he followed through with his original plan to continue his studies at Santa Cruz. Anthropologist Triloki Pandey met Newton at the time and came to regard him as "a sensitive person" and "really an intellectual."[16] Pandey later highlighted "the depth of his introspection and the force of his logic."[17] Mathematician Ralph Abraham referred to Newton as "a brilliant mind . . . [and] a very misunderstood intellect."[18] In the assessment of Robert Trivers, "Huey Newton was a natural-born genius, one of five or six I have met in my lifetime. Each is unique, of course, but Huey was unique in the explosive and persuasive power of his personality."[19] Trivers considered Newton in particular a "master logician."[20] Some, like Newton's original advisor, esteemed political theorist Peter Euben, felt that he "has a sharp mind, but it needs more focus and restraint."[21] Literary theorist Eugenio Donato concluded that Newton's unique style as an "essayist" subverted "the strict protocols of academic discourse."[22] During his first year of doctoral study, Newton's scholarship included bold attempts at conceptualizing the limits of Western philosophy in essays titled "Thucydides' Opening," "The Rise of a Non-Aristotelian System," and "De-constructing the Object."

Things in Santa Cruz did not go as well this time, however. According to William Moore, a Black student activist and graduate student in the department, some faculty attempted to bar Newton's entry into the doctoral program. They questioned his intentions in pursuing a doctoral degree, despite his ability to publish successfully without it, and they questioned his "reputed 'violent' nature."[23] Moore argued that this questioning reflected racism on the part of the faculty, who had subjected his own application to similarly critical questioning a few years prior. In May 1978, Newton was arrested after an altercation at a bar in nearby Aptos, California. Newton, Moore, and Newton's bodyguard Robert Heard had stopped in momentarily to pick up food, but within minutes were assaulted. Media portrayals in the white suburban community quickly blamed Newton and Heard for the altercation, invoking Newton's other court trials. But according to research by William Charles Ford, the bar was in fact a particularly racist establishment. "Anti-Black and anti-Newton graffiti reading 'Hang Niggers' and 'Kill Huey' was found in the bathroom of the bar, dating earlier than the incident, indicating a history of tolerated race hatred at the location."[24] Later that summer, one of the customers, a man named Kenny Hall, "came out and admitted having instigated the fight with Newton." "Hall's injuries were determined to have occurred when Hall pushed Newton through a plate glass window," but by that point Newton had already been vilified for months.[25] Ford's analysis of the court proceedings includes speculation about COINTELPRO involvement.[26] According to Trivers, some faculty supporters were also subject to state surveillance and harassment.[27] In October 1978, the department sent a letter to Newton notifying him that a subpoena had been received requesting access to his student records.[28]

It is also the case that the political character and administrative structure of the History of Consciousness department was to change dramatically, starting in the fall of 1978.[29] Whereas the position of chair had previously rotated on a quarterly basis, beginning in 1978, new faculty member and historian Hayden White became chair for several years.[30] In spring of that year, Newton had taken an independent study with White, but was given a grade of Incomplete for it, his first non-passing grade. White refused to give Newton a passing grade, semester after semester, for almost two years.[31] In his multiple drafts for "The Roots of Existential Philosophy in Western Thought" Newton was at one point assisted by Professor Paul Lee. Lee provided Newton with philosopher Søren Kierkegaard's archival lecture notes on F. W. J. Schelling's famous Berlin lectures (1841–42) – understood as foundational to existentialism – but White still insisted that Newton's work was academically inadequate.[32] Two months before his graduation, in April 1980, White even attempted to block the acceptance of Newton's dissertation, despite not being on his committee.[33] Notably, Newton seemed to experience more interpersonal success at Peralta Community College, where he worked as a teaching assistant for General Psychology and Afro-American Sociology classes and received positive evaluations for his improved teaching.[34] Despite the obstacles, his output at Santa Cruz in 1978 included the essays "Eclipse of Community: The Making of the English Working Class," "Science, Codes and Myths," "Truth and Sanity," "New Educational Models," "The Historical Origins of Existentialism and the Common Denominators of Existential Philosophy," and "Thoughts on the Will to Power."

In the view of his fellow graduate students, Newton's struggles were clearly "political."[35] Several of them described warm, positive, and supportive interactions with him.[36] According to Ford, Newton's success at UCSC was hampered by a climate of extreme racism.[37] Combined with his increasingly dysregulated mental state, the outcome was inevitably bleak. His dissertation committee was often in flux, affected in part by administrative rule changes, and Pandey eventually took over as chair of the committee in the spring of 1979.[38] According to both Pandey and Trivers, Newton sometimes did not respond well to scholarly criticism and increasingly came to class intoxicated. Decades later, political theorist Robert Meister claimed: "people really tried."[39] On Newton's part, he had expressed hope that "all of the disciplines would be able to sit down with each other and work out some systematic way to talk about our universe," but "this did not happen."[40]

In 1980, instead of a philosophical treatise, for his dissertation Newton submitted an overview of the range of government techniques deployed to destroy the Black Panther Party titled *War Against the Panthers*. Opening with a broad history of the suppression of grassroots social movements in the US, it argued for the need to recognize the dangers posed to democracy by the increasing power of the intelligence agencies. Newton wrote:

"the claim is to be made that repression of selected sectors of mass society is extremely difficult to carry out, if not impossible, without a resulting loss of cherished freedoms for the entire society."[41] The text relied on 2 million pages of documentation produced by the Freedom of Information Act, leading teacher and friend Paul Lee to describe Newton as "the most hounded man in the history of mankind, as documented by the hounders."[42] Newton's sense of disappointment belied, however, his remarkable intellectual productivity during his time at the university. Later on, and for several years, UCSC held an "annual Huey P. Newton Memorial lecture at Merrill College."[43] The university work that he left behind remains available today to engage with and learn from.

I Am We

"We're seeking the birth of the new man, the man that will create the new order, where wars and violence will no longer exist."[44] From early on, Newton was optimistic that one day human beings would, in practice, realize our common interest and essential unity with each other and nature. "There will be a coming together and a unity of man. . . . That complex whole where man finally reaches a unity with himself and with every other living thing within the universe."[45] At the same time, as a dialectical thinker, Newton identified that "man is nature" but "is also in contradiction to nature."[46] Accordingly, human beings are perpetually inclined to dominate and overcome nature. Newton saw this as unavoidable, but hoped that, in that process, humanity would come to grasp its unity with nature and strive to preserve those very characteristics that reflect our origins in it. "It must also learn to generate a new sort of man, capable of preserving, amplifying, and passing to our human or posthuman followers the striving for mastery of reality, while preserving its elements of intellect, character, freedom, and joy."[47]

In the process of creating a new version of the human, we would also, Newton hoped and projected, cast aside the old divisions we have instituted among ourselves, producing a universal human identity in the process:

> If we do not have universal identity, then we will have cultural, racial, and religious chauvinism, the kind of ethnocentrism we have now. So we say that even if in the future there will be some small differences in behavior patterns, different environments would all be a secondary thing. And we struggle for a future in which we will realize that we are all Homo sapiens and have more in common than not.[48]

To convey this idea, Newton sometimes invoked a philosophical idea from ancient Africa. This idea came to be preserved in the modern Zulu language as *ubuntu*, which is sometimes translated as "we are human only through the humanity of others." "There is an old African saying, 'I am we.' If you met an African in ancient times and asked him who he was, he would reply, 'I am we.' This is revolutionary suicide: I, we, all of us are the one and the multitude."[49] For Newton, as individual human beings we find our greatest purpose when we act for, live for, and commune with others. That form of being makes it clear that we are in fact *of a whole*. In a poem, Newton wrote: "One day I suddenly realized I had forgotten: name / age / sex / address / race / I had found myself."[50]

In Newton's view, dialectics do not predetermine the future, but they can help us understand the range of possibilities. So, just as we might eliminate our contradiction with nature through greater awareness, we might also come to erase the contradiction by destroying ourselves: "man opposes nature, but man is also the internal contradiction in nature. Therefore, while he is trying to reverse the struggle of opposites based upon unity, he might also eliminate himself."[51] Expanding upon Newton's writings on nature, Black feminist philosopher Romy Opperman affirms that "capitalism and white supremacist settler states cannot be relied upon to ensure the survival and the flourishing of racialized people, nor that of the environments in which we live."[52] Dialectically then, it is nature's minor element – the mass of humanity itself – which must step up to provide care for and militant defense of the Earth. And because "man is nature," this would be, in effect, the Earth defending itself.[53] This must be a global effort. In "Dialectics of Nature" Newton explained: "Intercommunalism is founded on the basic concept of the unity of nature underlying and transcending all arbitrary national and geographic divisions."[54]

In the process of overcoming borders, boundaries, and divisions, love becomes the dominant principle: "Because in the new world, people will only live to love each other anyways, you see. We won't be concerned about those material things and so forth. I'm contending that what sustains the revolutionist is the love that he has for the people."[55] Love is not just aspirational, but already present as a part of us, and primordial. "We haven't found out really what makes a man a man other than love and consciousness. But still we haven't found out because it's difficult to define love and maybe we'll never be able to. Maybe it evades words because words corrupt."[56]

As a philosopher, Newton criticized Western philosophy for allowing words (labels) to let us lose sight of the felt wholeness of experiences like love. Experiences are more than words can describe, but are reduced to words by the psychological power of language. A handwritten note by Newton reads:

> The object is not the event or process. (The process is constant change)
> The label is not the object.
> *The object is the identifiable part of the event or process.
> <u>The label is the value that we place upon the object.</u>
> The object is mutable in time and space.
> It is never the same at any given time.[57]

In brief, labels reduce our grasp of the perpetual process of change by becoming attached to objects, which are themselves only snapshots of phenomenal experience in process. In "The Roots of Existential Philosophy in Western Thought" (1978), Newton argued that this tendency, although rooted in our psychologies and some aspects of pre-historic culture, was worsened by the philosophies of Plato, Aristotle, Kant, and Hegel, who "reified" the lived reality of existence and furthered the "binding of space-time" through the elevation of the idea of static "essences."[58] The "use of rational consciousness as an instrument" and the "definitory" effects of written language have encouraged the idea that the abstract "essence" of a thing is more substantial than its actual felt reality, Newton argued.[59] "As long as logic is given absolute pre-eminence in philosophy, and the logical mind placed first in the hierarchy of human functions, reason seems inevitably caught up in the fascination of static and self-identical essence . . .; so as far as he logicizes, man tends to forget existence."[60] These conclusions that Newton came to in the late 1970s about the limits of logic were a radical departure from his earlier belief in the necessity of rationalism.

However, being a dialectical thinker and not inclined to discard Western thought altogether, he also took seriously Fanon's claim that "All the elements of a solution to the great problems of humanity have, at different times, existed in European thought."[61] Specifically, Newton felt that existentialism developed historically in Europe as a counterbalance to the intensification of rationalism and essentialism during the industrial age. He praised this strain of Western philosophy for its elevation of the concept of freedom. Bringing together "philosophical," "literary," and "theological" existentialism, Newton felt that the claim that "existence must be the primary category" signaled a "revolt against traditional philosophy," producing in effect "the most radical doctrine of freedom in the history of Western thought."[62] To be more precise, he argued that "in the struggle between essence and existence is born the *sense* of freedom."[63] In other words, it is *because* we have an understanding of both the limits and the movement of life that we have the gift of the idea of freedom itself.

For Newton, philosophical systems have direct effects on how we structure our societies. In "Rise of a Non-Aristotelian System" (1977), he asserted that "the closed logical system becomes the exact paradigm for the closed political system."[64] It produces "personal, national, international tragedies based on either/or ideologies, racial and national stereotypes and the systematized insanity of the Nation State."[65] "Aristotle's laws of identity, of either/or, of 'A or non-A', are a working definition of psychological dysfunction."[66] "In Aristotle's system as applied, the split becomes complete and institutionalized, with jails for the 'animal' and churches for the 'soul.' . . . Today the real Aristotle might be a political prisoner or denied 'security clearance.'"[67]

Newton believed that these old philosophies still have real impacts today on our ability to embrace the discoveries of contemporary science, which have far outstripped the old ideas. "We are the people of 'Process' and 'Progress', but the entelechy of Aristotle, the fixations of Euclid, the 'laws' of Newton are a logical cage from which, so far, we cannot escape, in which we are literally starving to death and going mad."[68] Newton was aware of advances in theoretical physics that had debunked standard understandings of cause and effect, space and time, and the separation between subject and object. He quotes from the theoretical physicist Werner Heisenberg: "it is very difficult to modify our language so that it will be able to describe these atomic processes, for words can only describe things of which we can form mental pictures and this ability, too, is a result of daily experience."[69] The problem then, Newton argued, is that these limitations do not just come from Western philosophy, but are also side effects of how we experience in the first place. "For instance, only since Einstein and Minkowski do we begin to understand that 'space' and 'time' cannot be split empirically, otherwise we create for ourselves delusional worlds. Only since their work has modern sub-microscopic physics with all its accomplishments become possible."[70] Newton quotes Albert Einstein in order to critique Kantian philosophy: "I am convinced that the philosophers have had a harmful effect upon the progress of scientific thinking in removing certain fundamental concepts from the domain of empiricism, where they are under our control, to the intangible heights of the *a priori*."[71] In the twentieth century, it was the scientists, Newton proposed, who have more often been radicals, both in thought and in political practice. "The new audacious thinkers – the Einsteins, Heisenbergs, Russells, Whiteheads – all spoke *scientific truth to power*."[72]

It should not be surprising that Newton was deeply interested, too, in the biological sciences, a fact exemplified by his final publication. In 1982 he co-authored with Robert Trivers "The Crash of Flight 90: Doomed by Self-Deception?"[73] The paper closely examined the conversation between a pilot and co-pilot on a flight that crashed soon after takeoff, drawing attention to the way the pilot ignored all signs of malfunction and even managed to convince his more cautious co-pilot to do the same, resulting in their mutual doom. Trivers and Newton had been developing their theory of the evolutionary development of self-deception for some time, observing the seemingly paradoxical tendency in insects and other animals. "How could natural selection simultaneously favor ever-more-refined sensory organs and perception only to favor systematically distorting the information once it had arrived in the brain?"[74] In brief, as they state in the article: "The benefit of self-deception is the more fluid deception of others. The cost is an impaired ability to deal with reality."[75] It is easier to deceive others if you truly believe your own lie. The publisher with whom Newton and Trivers contracted their book went out of business before they could complete it, but Trivers published the book after all, decades later, in 2011.[76] *Deceit and Self-Deception: Fooling Yourself the Better to Fool Others* was dedicated "In memory of Dr. Huey P. Newton, Black Panther and dear friend."[77]

Both Newton and Trivers saw broader social and political implications to their theory. As they observed in their article: "Certain types of adventurous men are especially prone to this form of self-deception. Both pilot, age 34, and co-pilot, age 31, had been military pilots before turning to commercial work."[78] In Trivers' later book, he devoted a whole chapter to war, stating: "Modern war is conducted against an out-group by powerful people who have an exaggerated opinion of themselves and their degree of morality, are overconfident, often have an illusion of control, enjoy taking risks, and are almost always male."[79] Newton and Trivers saw the workings of empire as clear social signs of exactly this phenomenon. Nonetheless, the hope they held on to was that knowledge and self-awareness could help people change course and take actions that would be in the greater interest of both themselves and their communities. An early draft of the book in Newton's archives includes the statement: "Contrary to common belief, a biological argument is not deterministic. We choose the lives we lead and knowledge of biology should merely improve the choice."[80]

Newton had clearly been reflecting on these kinds of dynamics years before meeting Trivers. In 1970 he said: "We contend that even the ruling circle isn't really in control, because if they were in control of their own lives they wouldn't be bent on the suicidal course they are now on."[81] White supremacy is exemplary of what Newton and Trivers would have described as "self-deception in the service of deceit." This particular lie harms everyone. "We, the people," Newton once declared, "are threatened with genocide because racism and fascism are rampant in this country and throughout the world."[82] He took seriously the argument that genocide was unfolding in his present, and in internal Party discussions while he was imprisoned he proposed submitting a petition to the United Nations to bring charges of genocide against the United States.[83]

In considering this, the Black Panther Party was following a prior tradition: in 1951, the Civil Rights Congress, an organization led by Black socialists, submitted a petition to the United Nations titled "We Charge Genocide: The Crime of Government Against the Negro People," accusing the US of multiple acts of genocide. This petition built upon the UN's Convention on the Prevention and Punishment of the Crime of Genocide, passed unanimously by its General Assembly in 1948. Its second article defined genocide as acts committed with intent to destroy, in whole or in part, a national, ethnical, racial, or religious group, including:

> (a) Killing members of the group;
> (b) Causing serious bodily or mental harm to members of the group;
> (c) Deliberately inflicting on the group conditions of life calculated to bring about its physical destruction in whole or in part;
> (d) Imposing measures intended to prevent births within the group;
> (e) Forcibly transferring children of the group to another group.[84]

In 1964, Malcolm X revived this pursuit, seeking support from multiple foreign heads of state to bring a case against the United States for having violated the human rights of Black Americans.[85] Malcolm sought to shift the struggle from an appeal to national civil rights to an invocation of human rights through the United Nations and humanistic principles in general. In 2021, a US-based coalition called In the Spirit of Mandela, led in part by former New York Panthers Jalil Muntaqim and Sekou Odinga, helped facilitate the International Tribunal on Human Rights Abuses Against Black, Brown and Indigenous Peoples, held at the Malcolm X and Dr. Betty Shabazz Memorial and Educational Center in Harlem, NY.[86] While legally non-binding, the tribunal nonetheless found the US guilty of genocide.

Newton's final public speeches in 1986 and 1987 addressed directly the incredible strength and spirit that Black people in the Western hemisphere have cultivated through centuries of genocidal treatment. Facilitated by Emory Douglas and delivered at the Uhuru house of the African People's Socialist Party in Oakland, Newton's speeches exemplified what Nietzsche called the "transvaluation of values."[87] Inspired by his study of evolutionary biology, Newton argued that Black people as a group have cultivated distinct strengths as a direct result of undergoing the worst treatment over centuries. In the final analysis, it is truly the oppressor group that is the most fearful, the most weak, and the most enslaved. In December 1986, he told the audience of proud, Black people:

> We fight because we are free; we fight against slaves. I can imagine that sometime a group of slaves will get shackles and put them on a free person and our job is to be released from those shackles, and perhaps we can make the slaves free also.
>
> That puts us in a position to know who we are and who we are fighting against. We're fighting against unconscious people, blind people and slaves. We have to fight from a strong attitude and know that we're free, and we'll break the shackles in order to free everyone else. That's the nature of the struggle. It's not truly a race struggle. Some slaves turn it into that but we must see the light.[88]

Concerning the Spirit

In Newton's view, a healthy and fulfilling education is fundamental to the struggle for freedom.[89] His late writings on education are emphatic about the harm done to the youth in the US as part of the broader workings of colonial empire. In the late 1970s, he collaborated extensively with Professor Arthur Pearl, an accomplished educator and activist, and author of *The Atrocity of Education*. For a course with Pearl, Newton submitted "New Educational Models" (1978), a presentation of the pedagogy practiced by the BPP's Oakland Community School (OCS). The paper focused especially on the Party's comprehensive programming for infants, with attention paid to cognitive development and how they learn to relate to their own bodies.

> OCS is the realization of a dream, then, to repair disabled minds and the disenfranchised lives of this country's poor communities, to lay the foundations [so] as to create an arena for the world without such suffering. Our aim is to provide the young of these communities with as much knowledge possible and to provide them with the ability to interpret that knowledge with understanding. For we believe without knowledge there can be no real understanding and that understanding is the key to liberation of all.[90]

Newton was known at the school for his joyful relationship with the students, even during the bad times in his life. According to David Hilliard, "when Huey visited the Oakland Community School, he couldn't get two steps into the building before the children surrounded him and hugged him. He spoke to each one. Inside the school he felt safe. Among the presence of children, no one could harm him."[91] Ericka Huggins recalled: "Huey always loved being there because there was a part of him that was like a big kid. I don't mean he never grew up. I mean he was just childlike. He loved it there and the children loved him."[92] Newton's first wife Gwen had two children, Jessica and Ronnie, for whom Newton served as a kind stepfather. His last partner Fredrika spoke also of Newton's relationship to her boy Keiron: "because Huey was so childlike, he was wonderful to my son."[93]

As a child, Newton himself was suspended from school thirty-eight times.[94] Because of his own traumas, he grasped that it is often the very children who get labeled "bad" or "troubled" who harbor hidden brilliance and ability. For the OCS, the reality of colonization meant that Black children, poor children, and those of other oppressed groups need extra support to grow in a healthy manner. Newton wrote: "As we involved ourselves more with each family, the pressing need for program expansion was evident."[95] "New Educational Models" argues that these children's vibrant energies should not be suppressed but rather nourished and fostered. "It was our belief that the oral culture of the poverty ghetto was a sign of survival energy, not non-literate regression."[96] In Newton's view, this energy reflected their greater capacities, born of their very impulse to survive despite their conditions. "We equate creativity, or any other descriptive word for meaningful energy, with survival."[97] The children's energy was seen at OCS as a sign of their humanity – rather than a lack thereof – and Newton understood their great capacity for love as the clearest indication of that humanity. "We believe that children learn for love and that then they love to learn. Love and survival are synonymous in our vocabulary."[98]

Evident in Newton's writings on education but also present throughout his body of work in the 1970s was a deep belief in a concept of *energy* that could not be reduced to biological life. In his unpublished essay "Utopia: Universal Life Energy" (1974), he conceptualized energy as the dialectical overcoming of the concept of the will to power. "In nature power is energy."[99] Newton's concept of energy was influenced by theoretical physics, psychoanalysis, and dialectics, and it implied an elimination of the separation between the human subject and inanimate objects. This was a theory of energy as relation, and as material immanence, or omnipresence. "Nietzsche is trying to produce a new metaphor of the over-man, a redistribution of energy. This redistributive motive may also be laid to Marx, Freud, and Einstein. . . . The 'eternal return,' the 'dialectic,' the 'unconscious,' all, in their way, are a cancellation of the subject/object non sequitur."[100] In other words, he saw universal energy as present in all and humanity as striving to relate to this reality, despite our limits. "[S]ince nature in its essence is pure energy itself, and since we are an integral part of nature, for all of our famous alienation, our utopia is (not) nowhere and no place, it is *everywhere* and *everyplace*."[101] This may be grasped as Newton's dialectical materialist approach to spirituality.

By contrast, he was often carefully critical of organized religion, especially in the West. In 1970 and 1971, during his East coast speaking tour, he spoke extensively on his view of religion at the time. At a speech at a community college in New York, he stated:

> So when we start talking about one thing is absolute, we're acting very much like the Europeans did when they created their god. Because they said my god is absolutely good, my god is absolutely antisexual, my god has nothing that resembles the characteristics of man. So therefore he alienated himself from his god, and because man created god in his own image, he alienated himself from himself. The African developed a dialectical method even to deal with his god, and therefore he can accept himself as a man. So his religion led to self-acceptance instead of self-rejection.[102]

Newton was consistent through much of his life in his rejection of the existence of an independent entity called "God," instead identifying god as a concept and part of humanity's dialectical relationship to itself. In a speech at Georgia State College, he described god as the shifting unknown:

> The boss that we call ignorance is everything that man does not know, that he does not understand, that he feels he has no control of. And as we analyze that, that's the boss of all religions which we call God, which man is not. But as technology moves on and education moves on, . . . we see that we take more and more control of things . . . But as soon as we found out the secrets of the universe, we incorporated those things that used to be called the big boss into ourselves – in other words, the attributes of God, that man acquired. The trend goes on, man will get larger and God will get smaller. But in the final analysis we will see that God will not get smaller because God is within. So we'll have man-god, we'll have heaven on earth and peace for all men.[103]

At his most strident and atheistic in 1971, Newton asserted simply that God is a function of humanity and that, in the future, humanity will aspire towards "godliness" through greater knowledge and technology.[104] "In the metaphysical sense, we based the expression all power to the people on the idea of man as God. I have no other God but man, and I firmly believe that man is the highest or chief good."[105]

As the 1970s progressed and Newton reworked his views on religion so as to foster a better relationship between the BPP and Black churches, he returned to the Bible. The Party even established a center called the Son of Man Temple, although, as scholar Vincent Lloyd has identified, soon its "resemblance to a religious institution faded, and it became a more conventional cultural center" with an emphasis on humanism and human expression.[106] Newton wrote several essays on religion while at UCSC in 1973–74. Some of these, such as "The Son of Man" (1973), offer a political analysis of Jesus' rebellion against the Roman empire.[107] According to Newton, the power of myth and messianism came to produce material, historical effects through Jesus' movement. He contrasts this with a prior Judaic tradition that had identified man as powerless to change history, a point he argued in his essay "'Second Isaiah' and the Mystery of the Servant" (1974).[108] Newton's writings on Jewish and Christian theology reflected a rigorous engagement with scholarly debates within those fields at the time.[109]

As Newton struggled to overcome the harm done to his mental health, it is clear that he increasingly came to value the study of theology as both a spiritual resource and a practical expression of his love of education. He was ordained in 1973 as a reverend in the liberal, non-denominational First Church of Universal Life, and later expressed interest in becoming ordained as a Lutheran minister, given the extensive urban outreach Lutherans did at the time.[110] He also dove into the study of Zen Buddhism and affiliated himself with the San Francisco Zen Center.[111] As he was completing his doctorate in 1980, he applied to the Graduate Theological Union through the University of California, Berkeley but was rejected.[112] He had also hoped to apply for UCSC's Ethnic Studies Program but missed the deadline.[113] Around the same time, he volunteered extensively with the National Guard and considered applying to that as well.[114]

There is also, however, considerable evidence that, when Newton was at his most unwell, his interest in spirituality converged in extremely dangerous ways with his dysregulated cognitive state, producing unhealthy delusions. Elaine Brown recalled him saying during one of his worst bouts: "I shall will myself to fly one day."[115] Fredrika Newton has discussed, too, his "florid delusions."[116] Delusions can include not just false perceptions, but also problematic connections, extrapolations, and conceptions about true perceptions. This tendency was sometimes exacerbated by the praise of those around him, resulting in self-aggrandizement and misconceived notions of self-sacrifice.[117] As Ford observed, at UCSC, "the theological bent of Newton's work is what attracted many people to him, including Page Smith, Paul Lee, and Noel Q. King."[118] Trivers tells of being particularly inspired once – while in conversation with Newton's brother Melvin after Huey had died – by the "extraordinary sight" of two rare hummingbirds, called the "doctor bird" and the "god bird" by the Indigenous: "It was almost as if Huey were alive, only in some other dimension."[119] Even after his death, he has increasingly been associated, by some, with the messianic. Perilously, even the spiritual can be colonized, turned into yet another technology of domination; a "religious awakening" may be a double-edged sword and discernment is a necessary practice.[120] Even Newton seems to have grasped this eventually, despite the forces he struggled against, and in his later years he did not give credence to such delusions.

These dynamics are rendered all the more complex by the fact that many personal accounts lend credibility to the view that Huey P. Newton *was*, in fact, an extraordinary human being. In his own telling, ideas came to him in part through hard work, but also through difficult-to-describe sudden inspirations: "Actually the concept of intercommunalism came to me one morning almost as in a vision, but it was the culmination of an intellectual search which began with my release from prison."[121] Newton clearly possessed impressive natural abilities, but was also extremely determined. And yet, at the same time, he struggled with what he insisted was undiagnosed dyslexia.[122] All three of these aspects of his personality are encapsulated in the story of his feat of graduating high school while illiterate. During his life, some expressed skepticism that this truly happened, but Newton was emphatic: "One of my closest comrades called me a liar to my face, but it's the truth and I'm going to tell it. That is, that I didn't learn to read words like 'house' and 'see' and 'it' until I was past 16 years old and in the 12th grade."[123] The marvel of limited literacy and profound literate knowledge existing within the same person is a familiar one in the Black Radical tradition, exemplified by Malcolm X, who took it upon himself to read the whole dictionary, word by word, while in prison. Malcolm's story is itself an echo of the legend according to which the prophet Muhammed received the holy Quran from God while fully illiterate.

Mumia Abu-Jamal later speculated that, "like most illiterates," Newton "developed an extraordinary memory" as a coping mechanism, allowing him to memorize symbols without understanding them:

> Illiterates . . . devote a significant amount of mental energy to memorize important data, especially to avoid the shame of discovery. This is no mean feat. One must by sheer necessity develop a way of knowing that is based on hearing and retaining data that early writers and readers never actualize. Moreover, illiterates must develop original ways of seeing and interpreting and categorizing the world. For unlike your literate colleagues, you are unable to relay and store data on a page; you must store data on your internal mental template – and then develop the machinery for retrieval.[124]

What Abu-Jamal describes is common also among immigrants who, without learning the language of the country they have moved to, nonetheless navigate complex social environments for years. The cognitive relationship between acquired literacy and memory is as yet unclear, but studies suggest that some memory functions improve with acquisition of literacy among adults.[125] In line with this, Abu-Jamal extrapolated that Newton's mental resources became freed up once he learned to read. Combined with the fact that he naturally had a strong memory, we can see how reading may have enhanced his capacities. Specifically, he clearly exhibited an ability to recall and connect distant ideas across disciplines, feeling, after all, that "everything is connected."

In contemporary terms, Newton was clearly *neurodivergent*. Although he overcame his inability to read, he continued to struggle with writing throughout his life. His first wife Gwen (Fontaine) Newton transcribed some of his dense academic writings in the 1970s, but even his signature was often penned by her.[126] Fredrika Newton claimed that his anxiety about writing was at its worst in public, and, when anxious, he apparently also walked with a limp, indicating a deeply embodied way that his mind processed stress.[127] Newton did not carry himself with the charisma typically expected of a political leader, and yet people nonetheless described him as possessing a unique interpersonal "magnetism."[128] Elaine Brown later described the popular effect Newton had in his hometown: "It was actually quite an amazing thing to behold Huey walking down an Oakland street. He drew large crowds of eager children and teary-eyed women with flowers and men reaching out to shake his hand."[129] Even in New York, after his release, "Elderly men and women . . . rushed up to him on the streets of the Manhattan ghetto. Many cried as they told him that they never expected to see him again."[130] Some of this was an effect of the social impact of the Black Panther Party, as well as a product of people's expectations, but some of it was unique to Newton. Professor Burney Le Boeuf later reflected that "Newton's effect on other people was what I imagine it was like for Alexander the Great."[131] These realities ask that we develop better understandings of the psychological and physiological dynamics underlying how leadership functions in human society.

In his autobiography, Newton described how, long before the Black Panther Party even existed, "some people got the notion that I had mystical powers."[132] He even played with hypnotizing others at parties, explaining that he "used it for 'styling' in the community," but eventually became bored with it.[133] Several BPP members have written of having inexplicable experiences in his presence. Seale said that Newton "could detect whether you were honest or dishonest . . . He's got some kind of intuition that he can detect this stuff about certain kinds of people."[134] Forbes described "this recurring belief I had about Huey that he could read my mind."[135] George Robinson, one of Newton's bodyguards, explained: "Huey was a reader. He could sit down, and when he wanted to, or if he had the energy, he could be with a person he had never met and tell them what was in their bedroom, for example. I had never seen anything like it. He did say that anybody could do it, but that it takes a lot of energy and something about using all (the powers of) your brain."[136] When Elaine Brown first met him, she had an experience that felt as if he was "stopping time" itself.[137] She later came to conclude, with clarity, that "Huey was not a god."[138] Newton himself affirmed, "I don't want to be Jesus or any other god."[139]

Leadership

When the great political theorist Cedric Robinson published his masterwork *The Terms of Order: Political Science and the Myth of Leadership*, it would have been difficult to read the book and not think about Huey Newton. Published in 1980 but written in 1971 as a dissertation, the book examined the concept of leadership as it is experienced by human beings.[140] Robinson would have known Newton personally through their work together in the Afro-American Association in 1962, as Newton was one of the ten original founders of the influential Black nationalist study group.[141]

In the book, Robinson made a distinction between extraordinary persons, political authority, and political leadership. A person with *extraordinary* qualities may or may not become a leader, he explained. As "a deviant," "the extraordinary person" possesses rare qualities but this very fact, "rather than attract, may repulse."[142] As for the notion of *authority*, Robinson described it as basic to "human consciousness," whether experienced in relation to a parent, an expert, a ritual, or a political figure.[143] Whether it occurs in a centralized or democratized fashion, authority functions to "absorb the circumscribed 'responsibility' of the community."[144] Lastly, concerning political *leadership*, Robinson argued at length that "the leader is actually a social construction; an expedient use of the social, psychological, and phenomenological materials contained in an individual" by their community.[145] Societies and communities *make leaders* in order to address their needs, and then endow them with expectations, responsibilities, and power.

Given that Robinson was a Black organizer in the Bay Area in the 1960s and 1970s, it is hard to imagine that he would not have read Newton's writings. And, indeed, a close look at his definition of leadership strongly suggests Newton's influence:

> I believe that the empirical function of the leader is to *define* the situation of the community, and to *choose* and organize *activity* in the situation which will benefit the community. The leader is an instrument of rational action where rational action is understood as collective action which extends the *survival of the community*. The leader is thus an element in

> the *logical-positivist model of reality*. The situation of the community is an *objective* situation accessible to the decoding, rearrangement, and *definition* of its objects by the leader.[146]

Robinson's definition of the leader bears a strong resemblance to Newton's definition of power: "Power is the ability to define phenomena and make them act in a manner willed." Additionally, with its emphasis on *defining* reality, community *survival*, and even *logical positivism*, Robinson's definition echoes several of Newton's ideas. However, for Robinson, the point of analyzing leadership was to develop a way to avoid its pitfalls. For him, societies and communities not only *make leaders* but possess the power to make them differently, or even to choose to function without them. Robinson advocated the complete redistribution of *political authority* from the one to the many. Through the "development of each group member" with a new culture of "maturity," authority may be cultivated and redistributed. In fact, Robinson saw this new culture as possibly following from changes in technology, "as the demography and technology of the community become increasingly elaborate and complex, which has at its base the interiorization of authority and the consequent absence of external political authority."[147] The democratization of technology and the elimination of singular leaders would encourage the disappearance of "exclusionist authority and social ideologies of natural superiority."[148]

Such a redistribution of authority would require much intentionality and effort. Decades later, Angela Davis offered her own reflections on the process of the production of leadership:

> I used to feel embarrassed by it, because I felt the vast difference between who I felt myself to be and what was projected onto the image, the representation, the icon. And I came to terms with it by recognizing precisely that it was a production of a people in struggle. So, I don't identify so much with the images, . . . but they are the creation of people who struggle with and for me.[149]

Davis described coming to terms with her elevation as a function of the power of the community. However, according to Robinson, the important thing is that *the people themselves* come to understand this. What would it take for a people as a whole to understand that they are the ones with the *extraordinary* abilities? Newton was hopeful that this realization would one day come:

> I think in the future people will realize more and more that they are responsible for creating leadership just as they are responsible for creating God. Groups create leaders just as they create other things, but they usually lose their awareness that this is so and begin to feel that the leaders are external to them, somebody to whom they must submit. . . .
>
> So I would think that in the immediate future leadership will take more the form of the "chairmanship" – and in the distant future, although I can't really visualize it yet, leadership will become a coordinated effort among people and maybe even titles or statuses will no longer be necessary.[150]

What is most important then is not the effort to reduce the influence of individual leaders, but instead for everyday people to grasp and cultivate their ability to function themselves as leaders at various times, deploying their different skills and trusting their lived knowledge.

The failures of individual leadership that defined Newton's generation produced the fertile soils in which the "leaderless" movements of today developed, characterized by the power of the masses. It is both ironic and dialectical that, at the same time that the mass of humanity has become less and less important in the eyes of the elites, it has become all the more important that we enact among ourselves the principled ideals of leadership that those elites, in their corruption, have altogether abandoned. Newton insisted that, at all times throughout history, "the people are the real power," and this is truer now than ever. Whatever we have expected from leaders – be it courage, determination, or extraordinariness – we should instead expect from ourselves and from each other collectively.

Huey P. Newton never called himself a genius. Instead, he used that word to describe the will of the people together: "The authentic revolutionary does not see himself, alone, as the instrument of destruction and reconstruction. He exists in the cortex of the combined genius of the great oppressed masses of humankind. That racial cortex and bosom is the genius loci of revolution."[151]

For Newton, the revolutionary transformation, liberation, and defense of our society must be made by all of us together.

* * *

"He must have known something was about to happen. A couple of weeks before Huey died, he told me in the kitchen, 'You better get some insurance out on me.'"[152] Newton had started giving all of his possessions away. He had had a premonition about his own death – or perhaps he heard something on the streets.[153] According to Emory Douglas, Huey had been making progress towards sobriety in the late 1980s, managing long stretches without drugs.[154] Fredrika affirmed that he was sober during the last few months of his life: "When people talk about him being on drugs in West Oakland, it's not true. Huey got really calm. He was easy to be around. . . . I knew he was sober, since it was no secret when he was using. . . . Huey was calm and helpful with the children."[155] But then, one night, his will and hope faltered. A plan for a film had fallen through and, given Newton's legal and tax problems, the couple had been left in a financial hole.[156] Fredrika recalled: "Huey never picked up my son, and that's when I knew that Huey had gone off again."[157] In the account of a friend named Pat Wright who saw him that night: "He said he was fighting a battle, and he kept saying that two or three times. I told him I understood but I could tell something was wrong."[158]

The story told by the police was that the grip of addiction had once again led Newton into an argument on the streets of Oakland late at night. He was known for invoking his past reputation in order to obtain free drugs. Some have concluded that he chose that night to commit what he had once called "reactionary suicide" – giving up on life altogether – by exposing himself to violence in the streets: death by drug dealer. According to police, a man named Tyrone Robinson claimed "that he killed Newton in self-defense after Newton tried to shoot him during an argument over cocaine," though forensic investigation would later show that Newton was not in possession of a weapon at any point.[159] The prosecution claimed that Robinson shot Newton to bolster his position with the since-corrupted Black Guerrilla Family prison gang. However, according to the Huey P. Newton Foundation, Robinson had recently arrived in Oakland and had no awareness of Newton's name or history.[160] Members of Robinson's family who knew Newton's family were even apologetic afterwards.[161] Complicating matters further, scholars Churchill and Vander Wall have raised doubts about Robinson's involvement in the drug trade altogether.[162] In their view, "the death of Huey P. Newton bears every sign of having been a political assassination."[163] The prosecutor at the trial, Kenneth Burr, later stated to the press: "My contention is that he killed Newton and he later bragged about doing it. Why he did it may or may not be relevant."[164] Newton was shot once in the jaw, and then twice more in the head.[165] One witness who lived nearby claimed she heard Newton refuse an order to get in a car with his assailant. She quoted the last words she heard him say before the gunfire: "Man, I ain't getting in your car."[166] Though Robinson would be found guilty, the events of that night remain in question.

Huey P. Newton arose out of the lived conditions of the Black, poor, and oppressed. He spoke from that position and acted from it, forging Black dignity, revolutionary love, and militant defense against the machine of American empire. He acted for all of us. In the end, he was lost to those same colonial machinations. It is just to remember Huey Newton as an extraordinary person, because he was one. However, rather than see him as an individual, he might have preferred that we see him as part of the power of the people – a product both of oppression and of the people's collective desire to be free from it. After all, as he himself explained, the Black Panther Party "arose *from within the community*, motivated by the needs and conditions of the people." In the years since his death, friends and comrades have imagined Newton's last words, and myths have been created.[167] Today those words have caught on and continue to be repeated by people far and wide, ending up even in the US government's National Archives.[168] Indeed, they sound very much as if Huey had in fact uttered them, facing those who tried to have him erased from history: "You can kill my body, and you can take my life, but you can never kill my soul. My soul will live forever!"

Free Huey!
Free all political prisoners!
Free us all!

THE ROOTS OF EXISTENTIAL PHILOSOPHY IN WESTERN THOUGHT

by

Huey P. Newton

I. The Argument:

A. "Co-Conscious Man" or the "pre-individual" are furthest from "Rational Man" but, as in Nietsche, time and space are circular.

B. Further comparison to Heidegger, Buber, Kierkegaard and other seminal existentialists.

C. Thus, seeds of modern philosophy start before writing and continue through to the "Atomic Age."

II. Co-Conscious Man:

A. The world view and Gemeinshaft of first pre-individuals.

B. Control of fire and speech: Ur-Prometheus.

C. Reconstruction of paleolithic mythos.

D. Treatment of past, present, future. Similarities and differences with existential corpus.

III. The Prato Individual:

A. The rise of syntax.

B. Pre-literacy and neolithic mythos.

C. Ritual language and minatory speech.

D. The Rise of the City:

1. Sumer, 10,000 B.C.
2. The Ur-myths
3. Old testament precursors
   a. Hebrew existentialism

"The Roots of Existential Philosophy in Western Thought" (Outline Version) (page 1 of 4), 1977–1978.
Used with permission by Dr. Huey P. Newton Foundation.

Huey P. Newton's doctoral graduation from the University of California, Santa Cruz, 1980 (Dr. Triloki Pandey, Huey P. Newton, adopted daughter Jessica Newton, and Ericka Huggins).
Used with permission by Dr. Huey P. Newton Foundation.

Huey P. Newton with a child.
Used with permission by Dr. Huey P. Newton Foundation.

Huey P. Newton delivering a speech at Uhuru House of the African People's Socialist Party in Oakland, California, 1986–1987.
Used with permission by Dr. Huey P. Newton Foundation.

Appendix: The Intellectual Legacy of Huey P. Newton

The next opportunity for socialist revolution, based on newer and stronger forms of communalism growing in the matrix of an overdeveloped capitalism, is still yet to come. But when it comes, it will be constructed on a "felt cohesion in the community" which "the working people, in antagonism to their labour and to their masters" will build for themselves.

Huey P. Newton (1978)[1]

It is its own kind of care work to restore humanity to members of the human community who have passed away and whose memory has been fragmented by colonial narratives and forces. To do real justice to Newton's life and work will require the collective labor of many scholars. In one regard, Newton's scholarship requires expertise in the Western canon. At the same time, however, it requires the generosity of spirit that only Black/New Afrikan and sincerely anti-racist scholars can provide. To aid in that work, I have listed below all of the unpublished or out-of-print writings of Newton's that I have been able to identify. These are additional to the writings currently available in the published books and collections: *To Die for the People*, *In Search of Common Ground*, *Revolutionary Suicide*, *Insights and Poems*, *War Against the Panthers*, and *The Huey P. Newton Reader*.

Bibliography of Unpublished or Out of Print Works

Poems

General Famine
Lord of the Poison

Essays

A Consistent Ideology (1971)
Intercommunalism: A Higher Level of Consciousness (1971?)
A Citizen's Peace Force (1972)
Politics and Myth (1973)
The First Hero of Literature (1973)
The Son of Man (1973)
A Functional Definition of Politics (Revised) (1973)
Genesis According to Science (1974)
"Second Isaiah" and the Mystery of the Servant (1974)
John and the Servant (1974)
Energy and Aggression (1974)
Utopia: Universal Life Energy (1974)
Intercommunalism (1974)
Oakland: An All-American Example (1974)
Thucydides' Opening (1977)
The Rise of a Non-Aristotelian System (with introduction) (1977)
De-constructing the Object (1978)
The Roots of Existential Philosophy in Western Thought (1978)
Common Denominators of Existential Philosophy (1978)
Eclipse of Community (1978)
Science, Codes and Myths (1978)
On Truth and Sanity (1978)
New Educational Models (1978)
The Historical Origins of Existentialism and the Common Denominators of Existential Philosophy (1978)
Thoughts on the Will to Power (1978)

Book Manuscripts (Drafts)

These Graves Are All Too Young
War Without Terms: The Death of George Jackson
Deceit and Self-Deception
Hidden Traitor
War Against the Panthers (at least three very different versions, one written in exile in Cuba (1975), one written for qualifying exams at UCSC (1978), and one submitted for the dissertation (1980))
Blues for Huey (co-written with Trivers)
Journal of Exile to Cuba

Notes

Note Abbreviations

DHPNC: M0864, Dr. Huey P. Newton Inc. collection, Department of Special Collections, Green Library, Stanford University.

FA: Freedom Archives, Berkeley, CA.

JHBEMP: M1357, J. Herman Blake and Emily L. Moore Papers, Stuart A. Rose Manuscript Archives and Rare Book Library, Emory University.

RHR: M1048, Random House Records, Rare Book and Manuscript Library, Columbia University Libraries.

PAP: TAM.517, Philip Agee Papers, Tamiment Library and Robert F. Wagner Labor Archives, Elmer Holmes Bobst Library, New York University.

Acknowledgments

1 bell hooks and Cornel West, *Breaking Bread: Insurgent Black Intellectual Life* (New York: Routledge, 2016). Used with permission.

1 Consciousness

1 Scott Forter and Dan Pulcrano, "Newton Presents his Philosophy," *City on a Hill Press*, June 8, 1978, Series 1, Box 39, Folder 19, DHPNC. Used with permission by Dr. Huey P. Newton Foundation.

2 "Interview with Huey P. Newton, September 17, 1970, by Mark Lane," Series 1, Box 57, Folders 9–10, DHPNC, 73–4.

3 "Interview, Sept 17, 1970, by Mark Lane," Series 1, Box 57, Folders 9–10, DHPNC, 73.

4 Huey P. Newton, *Revolutionary Suicide* (New York: Penguin, 1973/2009), 11. According to his older brother Melvin in 1970, Huey Newton was born in the small town of Mer Rouge ("Interview with Melvin Newton, July 5, 1970," Series 1, Box 1, Folder 7, JHBEMP, 16–17). Based upon much later interviews with Newton's family, author Lise Pearlman identifies the town of Oak Grove (Pearlman, *Huey P. Newton's Family: Roots of a Revolutionary Suicide* (Berkeley,

CA: Regent Press, 2025), xiii). Most sources, however, list the larger city of Monroe, which appears to have been the last place the Newtons lived before they left Louisiana for California.

5 "Interview, Sept 17, 1970, by Mark Lane," Series 1, Box 57, Folders 9–10, DHPNC, 73–4. In his autobiography, Newton stated that his family moved when he was three years old (Newton, *Revolutionary Suicide*, 12). In earlier sources, however, Newton stated that he was one year old ("Interview, Sept 17, 1970, by Mark Lane," Series 1, Box 57, Folders 9–10, DHPNC, 73–4). Edward M. Keating, *Free Huey! The True Story of the Trial of Huey P. Newton for Murder* (Berkeley, CA: Ramparts Press, 1970), 144–5.

6 Mumia Abu-Jamal, "The Genius of Huey P. Newton," *Prison Radio*, January 6, 2016. Newton, *Revolutionary Suicide*, 140. Pearlman, *Huey P. Newton's Family*, 165.

7 Bobby Seale, *Seize the Time: The Story of the Black Panther Party and Huey P. Newton* (1968) (New York: Random House, 1970), 13.

8 *All Power to the People! The Black Panther Party and Beyond*, dir. Lee Lew Lee, Electronic News Group, 1996.

9 Huey P. Newton, "The Technology Question: 1972," *The Huey P. Newton Reader*, ed. David Hilliard and Donald Weise (New York: Seven Stories Press, 2002), 256.

10 Huey P. Newton, "Speech at Boston College: November 18, 1970," *To Die for the People: The Writings of Huey Newton*, ed. Toni Morrison (San Francisco: City Lights, 2009), 20.

11 Newton, "The Technology Question: 1972," *The Huey P. Newton Reader*, 256.

12 Huey P. Newton, "Hidden Traitor Renegade Scab: Eldridge Cleaver" (1972), Series 1, Box 50, Folder 3, DHPNC.

13 "Huey Newton Talks to *The Movement* about the Black Panther Party, Cultural Nationalism, SNCC, Liberals and White Revolutionaries," *The Black Panthers Speak* (1970), ed. Philip S. Foner (Chicago: Haymarket Books, 2014), 61.

14 "Prisoners," *The Jericho Movement*, https://thejerichomovement.com/prisoners.

15 Robert Trivers, *Wild Life* (New Brunswick, NJ: Biosocial Research Publications, 2015), 153.

16 Tim Findley, "Huey Newton Twenty-Five Floors from the Street," *Rolling Stone*, August 3, 1972, 31.

17 Huey P. Newton, *These Graves Are All Too Young*, Series 1, Box 55, Folder 5, DHPNC, 311.

18 David Hilliard and Lewis Cole, *This Side of Glory* (Boston: Little, Brown, and Company, 1993), 179. Founding Party member Emory Douglas, too, has described Newton's evident unease the day the original photograph was taken (Phone interview with Emory Douglas, June 16, 2025).

19 Fredrika Newton, "Fredrika Newton, Widow of Black Panther Party Co-Founder, Reacts to 'The Big Cigar' (Guest Column)," *The Hollywood Reporter*, June 18, 2024. "Special Agent Wesley Swearingen," *What We Want, What We Believe: The Black Panther Party Library*, Roz Payne Archives and Newsreel Films, AK Press Video, 2006.

20 Ward Churchill and Jim Vander Wall, *Agents of Repression: The FBI's Secret War Against the Black Panther Party and the American Indian Movement* (1990)

(Baltimore: Black Classic Press, 2002). Ward Churchill and Jim Vander Wall, *The COINTELPRO Papers: Documents from the FBI's Secret Wars Against Dissent in the United States* (1990) (Baltimore: Black Classic Press, 2002).

21 Billy X Jennings, "Remembering the Black Panther Party newspaper, April 25, 1967–September 1980," *San Francisco Bay View National Black Newspaper*, May 4, 2015.

22 Newton, *Revolutionary Suicide*, 17.

23 Ibid., 18.

24 Ibid., 19.

25 David Hilliard, Keith Zimmerman, and Kent Zimmerman, *Huey: Spirit of the Panther* (New York: Basic Books, 2008), 277.

26 Huey P. Newton, "New Educational Models" (1978), Series 1, Box 40, Folder 10, DHPNC, 1–2.

27 Newton, *Revolutionary Suicide*, 20.

28 Ibid., 54.

29 "Interviews and other recordings, August 12, 1968" (1 of 2), Series 1, Box 1, Folder 2, JHBEMP, 22–4.

30 Newton, *Revolutionary Suicide*, 55.

31 "7/17/70," Series 1, Box 1, Folder 6, JHBEMP. "David Hilliard: Oct 9, 1970," Series 1, Box 2, Folder 11, JHBEMP, 20–1. Brian P. Sowers, "The Socratic Black Panther: Reading Huey P. Newton Reading Plato," *Journal of African American Studies* 21 (2017), 26–41. Sowers compellingly argues that much of *Revolutionary Suicide* is structurally based upon several concepts in Plato's writings, including the elevation of philosophy over poetry.

32 Newton, *Revolutionary Suicide*, 77.

33 "Interview with Melvin Newton, July 5, 1970," Series 1, Box 1, Folder 7, JHBEMP, 80–8.

34 Newton, *Revolutionary Suicide*, 69.

35 Newton, *Revolutionary Suicide*, 58. "Interview, Sept 13, 1970," Series 1, Box 2, Folder 5, JHBEMP, 36–7.

36 "Interview with Melvin Newton, July 5, 1970," Series 1, Box 1, Folder 7, JHBEMP, 46–7. "Interview, Sept 13, 1970," Series 1, Box 2, Folder 5, JHBEMP, 9.

37 "Interview, Sept 13, 1970," Series 1, Box 2, Folder 5, JHBEMP, 11. Pearlman, *Huey P. Newton's Family*, 165, 189.

38 "Interview with Melvin Newton, July 5, 1970," Series 1, Box 1, Folder 7, JHBEMP, 250–5.

39 James Baldwin, *No Name in the Street* (New York: Bantam Doubleday Dell Publishing, 1972), 173.

40 Phone interview with Joe Blum, January 16, 2025.

41 Seale, *Seize the Time*, 14.

42 "3/27/70," Series 1, Box 1, Folder 6, JHBEMP. "Interview, Sept 13, 1970," Series 1, Box 2, Folder 5, JHBEMP, 20–1. Newton, *Revolutionary Suicide*, 9–11, 16. "Interview with Alex Hoffman, October 3, 1970," Series 1, Box 2, Folder 10, JHBEMP, 11. Keating, *Free Huey!*, 144–5. Pearlman, *Huey P. Newton's Family*, 74–5, 81–2, 100–1, 107–9.

43 "3/27/70," Series 1, Box 1, Folder 6, JHBEMP. Newton, *Revolutionary Suicide*, 9. "Interview with Melvin Newton, July 5, 1970," Series 1, Box 1, Folder 7,

JHBEMP, 163. The children of the family were, from eldest to youngest: Lee Edward, Myrtle, Leola, Walter Jr., Doris, Melvin, and Huey ("Interview with Leola Carr, sister of Huey P. Newton, July 15, 1970," Series 1, Box 1, Folder 8, JHBEMP).

44 Newton, *Revolutionary Suicide*, 10–11, 16. "Brief Memorandum: Reporting on a Brief Visit with Mrs. Armelia Newton at her Home," Series 1, Box 3, Folder 3, JHBEMP.

45 Newton, *Revolutionary Suicide*, 10.

46 Ibid., 22.

47 Abu-Jamal, "The Genius of Huey P. Newton," *Prison Radio.*

48 Newton, *Revolutionary Suicide*, 75.

49 Seale, *Seize the Time*, 15.

50 Documents and Notes, Series 1, Box 37, Folder 2, DHPNC.

51 "It's About Time Black Panther Party feat. Mr. Billy X Jennings," *Things Fall Apart*, podcast, March 18, 2021. Philip Shenon, "Working Profile D: Lowell Jensen. A Gentleman in Line of Fire at Justice Dept.," *New York Times*, January 13, 1986, A 12. Flores Forbes, *Will You Die With Me?* (New York: Atria Books, 2006), 26.

52 Newton, *Revolutionary Suicide*, 79–92.

53 "Interviews and other recordings, August 12, 1968" (1 of 2), Series 1, Box 1, Folder 2, JHBEMP, 22–4. Seale, *Seize the Time*, 26, 21.

54 Seale, *Seize the Time*, 20.

55 "Herman Blake: March 21, 1969," Series 1, Box 1, Folder 5, JHBEMP, 7.

56 "Interview, Sept 17, 1970, by Mark Lane," Series 1, Box 57, Folders 9–10, DHPNC, 43. Newton, *Revolutionary Suicide*, 60–7. Seale, *Seize the Time*, 14.

57 Robin D. G. Kelley, *Freedom Dreams: The Black Radical Imagination* (Revised and Expanded) (Boston, MA: Beacon Press, 2022), 73, 77, 82, 85.

58 Henry Hampton and Steve Fayer, *Voices of Freedom: An Oral History of the Civil Rights Movement from the 1950s through the 1980s* (New York: Bantam Books, 1990), Ch. 20.

59 Seale, *Seize the Time*, 13.

60 Joshua Bloom and Waldo E. Martin, *Black Against Empire: The History and Politics of the Black Panther Party* (Berkeley: University of California Press, 2013), 105–6. Robyn Spencer, *The Revolution Has Come: Black Power, Gender, and the Black Panther Party in Oakland* (Durham, NC: Duke University Press, 2016), 57–9. "Evolution of A Black Panther Part 2," *The Real News Network*, October 3, 2015, https://therealnews.com/cleavertwo0930.

61 Huey P. Newton, *War Against the Panthers: A Study of Repression in America* (New York: Harlem River Press, 1996), 3.

62 Abu-Jamal, "The Genius of Huey P. Newton," *Prison Radio.*

63 Churchill and Vander Wall, *The COINTELPRO Papers*, 123.

64 Newton, *War Against the Panthers*, 10. William Charles Ford, "Hounded: Huey P. Newton in Santa Cruz: 1973–1974, 1977–1980" (May 24, 1991), *Hip Santa Cruz 6: First-Person Accounts of the Hip Culture of Santa Cruz in the 1960s, 1970s, and 1980s*, ed. T. Mike Walker and Ralph H. Abraham (Rhinebeck, NY: Epigraph Books, 2023), 214.

65 Lise Pearlman, *The Sky's the Limit: The People v. Newton. The Real Trial of the Century?* (Berkeley, CA: Regent Press, 2012).

66 Judson Jeffries, *Huey P. Newton: The Radical Theorist* (Jackson: University Press of Mississippi, 2002).
67 Hilliard, Zimmerman, and Zimmerman, *Huey*, 159.
68 G. Louis Heath, *Off the Pigs! The History and Literature of the Black Panther Party* (Metuchen, NJ: The Scarecrow Press, 1976), ix.
69 Newton, *All Too Young*, Series 1, Box 55, Folder 5, DHPNC, 314.
70 Newton, "On the Peace Movement: August 15, 1969," *To Die for the People*, 152.
71 Huey P. Newton and Erik Erikson, *In Search of Common Ground* (New York: W. W. Norton & Company, 1973), 35, 41–2.
72 Ibid., 40.
73 Therí Alyce Pickens, *Black Madness :: Mad Blackness* (Durham, NC: Duke University Press, 2019), 113.

2 The Defense of Life

1 Safiya Bukhari, excerpt from "This is Worth Fighting For," from *The War Before: The True Life Story of Becoming a Black Panther, Keeping the Faith in Prison, and Fighting for Those Left Behind*. Copyright © 2010 by the Estate of Safiya Bukhari. Reprinted with the permission of The Permissions Company, LLC on behalf of the Feminist Press at the City University of New York, feministpress.org.
2 Newton, *Revolutionary Suicide*, 77.
3 Ibid., 218.
4 Donna Murch, *Living for the City: Migration, Education, and the Rise of the Black Panther Party in Oakland, California* (Chapel Hill: University of North Carolina Press, 2010).
5 Newton, *Revolutionary Suicide*, 281.
6 Ibid., 74, 81.
7 Ibid., 82.
8 Ibid. "Interview, Sept 13, 1970," Series 1, Box 2, Folder 5, JHBEMP, 36–7. The young Newton read also Dostoevksy's *The Devils* and *The House of the Dead*.
9 Newton, *Revolutionary Suicide*, 82. "Interview, Sept 13, 1970," Series 1, Box 2, Folder 5, JHBEMP, 36–7.
10 Newton, *Revolutionary Suicide*, 83.
11 Ibid.
12 Ibid., 80, 281.
13 "3/13/70," Series 1, Box 1, Folder 6, JHBEMP.
14 Seale, *Seize the Time*, 72.
15 Newton, *Revolutionary Suicide*, 70.
16 Seale, *Seize the Time*, 59–62.
17 Andrew Fearnley, "The Black Panther Party's Publishing Strategies and the Financial Underpinnings of Activism, 1968–1975," *The History Journal* 62:1 (2019), 195–217, 214.
18 The interview transcripts are held among the J. Herman Blake and Emily L. Moore Papers in Special Collections at Emory University. Despite the quality of Blake's work, it merits mentioning that his relationship with the

Black Panther Party soured before the book was published over a financial dispute that arose once other editors were brought on board. Blake was also dealing at the time with poor health following surgery, as well as professional pressures over his relationship with the Party (Various Documents, Series 1, Box 5, Folder 1, JHBEMP).

19 J. Herman Blake, "The Caged Panther: The Prison Years of Huey P. Newton," *Journal of African American Studies* 16 (2012), 245. "Interview with Lee Edward Newton, Older Brother of Huey P. Newton, November 1, 1970," Series 1, Box 3, Folder 7, JHBEMP, 1. The book Armelia Newton was referring to: Gene Marine, *The Black Panthers* (New York: Signet Books, 1969).

20 Interviews with Flores Forbes, Fall 2023. Newton did write his own notes at times. See the cover of the republication of Newton's 1972 collection of essays *To Die for the People* (San Francisco: City Lights, 2009).

21 Phone interview with Emory Douglas, June 26, 2025.

22 Eldridge Cleaver, "On the Ideology of the Black Panther Party: Part 1" (1969), *Target Zero: A Life in Writing*, ed. Kathleen Cleaver (New York: Palgrave, 2006), 171.

23 Ibid., 172. Newton later affirmed the essay's overarching arguments (Newton, "Speech at Boston College," *To Die for the People*, 26); that said, he was skeptical of the distinction made by Cleaver of a "left wing" and "right wing" of the proletariat ("7/17/70," Series 1, Box 1, Folder 6, JHBEMP).

24 Cleaver, "On the Ideology," *Target Zero*, 175. Newton explained: "We sometimes have a problem because people do not understand the ideology that Marx and Engels began to develop. People say, 'You claim to be Marxists, but did you know that Marx was a racist?' We say, 'He probably was a racist: he made a statement once about the marriage of a white woman and a black man, and he called the black man a gorilla or something like that.' The Marxists claim he was only kidding and that the statement shows Marx's closeness to the man, but of course that is nonsense. So it does seem that Marx was a racist" (Newton and Erikson, *In Search of Common Ground*, 26).

25 Karl Marx and Frederick Engels, *Manifesto of the Communist Party* (1848), trans. Samuel Moore (1888), 20, *Marxists Internet Archive*. Cleaver, "On the Ideology," *Target Zero*, 181.

26 Kathi Weeks, "The Lumpenproletariat and the Politics of Class," *Crisis and Critique* 10:1 (2023), 324–47. Peter Stallybrass, "Marx and Heterogeneity: Thinking the Lumpenproletariat," *Representations* 31, Special Issue: The Margins of Identity in Nineteenth-Century England (1990), 69–95. James Ingram, "Lumpenproletariat," "Marx from the Margins: A Collective Project, from A to Z," *Krisis* 2 (2018).

27 Cleaver, "On the Ideology," *Target Zero*, 177.

28 Karl Marx, *The Class Struggles in France, 1848–1850*, *Marxists Internet Archive*. Karl Marx, *The Eighteenth Brumaire of Napoleon Bonaparte*, trans. Saul Padover (1869) (Moscow: Progress Publishers, 1937), *Marxists Internet Archive*. J. Sakai, *The "Dangerous Class" and Revolutionary Theory: Thoughts on the Making of the Lumpen/proletariat* (Montreal: Kersplebedeb, 2017), 21, 52–79. Hal Draper, *Karl Marx's Theory of Revolution, Vol. 2: The Politics of Social Classes* (Delhi: Aakar Books Press, 2011). Frank Bovenkerk, "The Rehabilitation of the Rabble:

How and Why Marx and Engels Wrongly Depicted the Lumpenproletariat as a Reactionary Force," *The Netherlands Journal of Sociology* 20:1 (1984), 13–41. Peter Hayes, "Utopia and the Lumpenproletariat: Marx's Reasoning in The Eighteenth Brumaire of Louis Napoleon Bonaparte," *Review of Politics* 50:3 (1988).

29 Karl Marx, *Capital Volume 1: A Critique of Political Economy* (1867), trans. Ben Fowkes (London: Penguin Books, 1990), 797.

30 Ibid., 797, 798. Marx was at his most empathetic when describing the insidious function of the "absolute general law of capitalist accumulation" in disallowing "regular co-operation between employed and unemployed" (ibid., 798, 793).

31 Marx stated explicitly in a newspaper editorial: "The classes and the races too weak to master the new conditions of life must give way." Karl Marx, "Forced Emigration: *New York Daily Tribune*, March 22, 1853," *Marx-Engels on Britain* (Moscow: Progress Publishers, 1953), *Marxists Internet Archive*. Erik van Ree, "Marx and Engels's Theory of History: Making Sense of the Race Factor," *Journal of Political* Ideologies 24:1 (2019), 54–73. Kevin B. Anderson, *Marx at the Margins: On Nationalism, Ethnicity, and Non-Western Societies* (Chicago: University of Chicago Press, 2016). I am using the word "racialism" in the sense used by Cedric Robinson in *Black Marxism* (London: Zed Books, 1983), as distinguished from modern racism but comparable in its essentializing dehumanization of people of the lower classes.

32 Huey P. Newton, "Intercommunalism (1974)," ed. Delio Vásquez, *Viewpoint Magazine*, June 11, 2018.

33 "The Supreme Court 'Master of Trickery,'" *The Black Panther*, July 11, 1970, *Marxists Internet Archive*.

34 Cleaver, "On the Ideology," *Target Zero*, 173, 176.

35 Seale, *Seize the Time*, 25–6.

36 Josie Fanon, a white-passing woman of Romani ("gypsy") background, also transcribed *Black Skin, White Masks*. See Nicole Yokum, "A Call for Psycho-Affective Change: Fanon, Feminism, and White Negrophobic Femininity," *Philosophy and Social Criticism* 50:2 (2024), 343–68.

37 Frantz Fanon, *The Wretched of the Earth*, trans. Constance Farrington (New York: Grove Press, 1968/New York: Ballantine Books, 1973).

38 Frantz Fanon, *The Wretched of the Earth*, trans. Constance Farrington (New York: Grove Press, 1963), 37. Frantz Fanon, *Les damnés de la terre* (1961) (Paris: La Découverte/Poche, 2002), 42.

39 Newton, "Reply to Roy Wilkins re: Vietnam: September 26, 1970," *To Die for the People*, 190.

40 Huey P. Newton, "In Defense of Self-Defense," *The Black Panther*, June 20, 1967, *Marxists Internet Archive*.

41 Immanuel Wallerstein, "Fanon and the Revolutionary Class," *The Capitalist World Economy* (Cambridge: Cambridge University Press, 1979), 259.

42 Fanon, *Wretched*, trans. Farrington, 129.

43 Ibid., 131.

44 Cleaver, "On the Ideology," *Target Zero*, 176.

45 John W. Finney, "2% of Businesses in U.S. Owned By Blacks in 1969, Survey Says," *New York Times*, August 5, 1971, 46.

46 Huey P. Newton, "The Will to Power," Series 1, Box 48, Folders 17–18, DHPNC, 17.

47 Elaine Brown, *A Taste of Power* (New York: Doubleday, 1992), 136.

48 Charles E. Jones and Judson L. Jeffries, "Don't Believe the Hype," *The Black Panther Party Reconsidered*, ed. Charles E. Jones (Baltimore, MD: Black Class Press, 1998), 44–6.

49 Donna Murch, *Assata Taught Me: State Violence, Racial Capitalism, and the Movement for Black Lives* (Chicago: Haymarket, 2022), 25. As Murch explains: "This duality, merging different strata from 'college and community', remained a hallmark of the Black Panther Party throughout its history" (28).

50 Baldwin, *No Name in the Street*, 166–7.

51 Michael "Cetewayo" Tabor, "Capitalism Plus Dope Equals Genocide," San Francisco: Black Panther Party Ministry of Information, 1969, 11.

52 Harris Poll, "The Black Mood: More Militant, More Hopeful, More Determined," *TIME*, April 6, 1970, 28.

53 "Gallup/Newsweek Poll: Negro Survey, Question 86," *Newsweek*, May 1, 1969, Gallup Organization (Cornell University, Ithaca, NY: Roper Center for Public Opinion Research, 1969). Former Panther Flores Forbes has referred to a poll of black males ages of 18–42 indicating an 80% approval rating (Forbes, *Will You Die With Me?*, 4), and former Panther Geronimo Ji-Jaga Pratt referred to a poll indicating that "92% supported not only the Black Panther Party, but nationhood; national independence" ("Pacifica Radio Broadcast of Talk by Geronimo Ji Jaga," October 1997, Geronimo Ji-Jaga (Pratt) Collection, FA). Historian Howard Zinn cited "a secret FBI report to President Nixon in 1970" indicating that "approximately 25% of the black population has a great respect for the BPP, including 43% under 21 years of age" (Zinn, *A People's History of the United States: 1492–Present* (New York: Harper Perennial, 2005), 464). While Forbes' and Pratt's figures may be overstatements, Zinn's cited figures likely underestimate the actual case, as members of the Black community in this period were often cautiously avoidant when asked in public by surveyors about their awareness of the Black Panther Party. For a clear demonstration, see "Black Panther Newspaper," *KQED News*, February 22, 1970, Bay Area Television Archive, https://diva.sfsu.edu/collections/sfbatv/bundles/188923.

54 Stuart Hall, "The Politics of Mugging," *Policing the Crisis: Mugging, the State, and Law and Order* (London: Palgrave, 1978), 397, 357, 396. In 1971, Caribbean historian C. L. R. James wrote in praise of imprisoned Panther theorist George Jackson: "where [W. E. B.] Du Bois and myself were observing a situation, taking part [. . .] but guided by theoretical and intellectual development, the generation to which Jackson belonged has arrived at the profound conclusion that the only way of life possible to them is the complete intellectual, physical, moral commitment to the revolutionary struggle against capitalism" (C. L. R. James II, "George Jackson," *Radical America* 5:6 (1971), 54, 56).

55 Cleaver, "On the Ideology," *Target Zero*, 175–6.

56 "Huey P. Newton at New York Community College" (November 19, 1970), Series 1, Box 57, Folder 12, DHPNC, 17.

57 George L. Jackson, *Blood in My Eye* (Baltimore: Black Classic Press, 1990), 139.

58 Baldwin, *No Name in the Street*, 174–5.
59 "Elbert 'Big Man' Howard Oral History Interview Conducted by David P. Cline," June 30, 2016, Library of Congress, https://www.loc.gov/item/2016655436.
60 James Johnson, "Transcription of Interview with Aaron Dixon," July 11, 1970, Special Collections Library, University of Washington. Forbes, *Will You Die With Me?*, 4. Seale, *Seize the Time*, 99–106. Fred Hampton, "Power Anywhere Where There's People!" 1969, *Marxists Internet Archive*. Trivers, *Wild Life*, 151. Murch, *Assata Taught Me*, 28.
61 "Eyes on the Prize II; Interview with Huey P. Newton," May 23, 1989, Film and Media Archive, Washington University in St. Louis, American Archive of Public Broadcasting (GBH and the Library of Congress), http://americanarchive.org/catalog/cpb-aacip-3277bf8bccb. Edited for clarity.
62 Seale, *Seize the Time*, 105.
63 Newton, "In Defense of Self-Defense," *The Black Panther*, June 20, 1967, 3. This original version published in the newspaper differs from the later version published in *To Die for the People* ("In Defense of Self-Defense I: June 20, 1967," *To Die for the People*, 80). In 1970, Newton rephrased his point more simply: "Laws should be made to serve people. People should not be made to serve laws. When laws no longer serve the people, it is the people's right and the people's duty to free themselves from the yoke of such laws" (Newton, "Eulogy for Jonathan Jackson and William Christmas: August 15, 1970," *To Die for the People*, 226).
64 Mark 2:27–8 (KJV).
65 "Elbert 'Big Man' Howard Oral History Interview," Library of Congress.
66 "Eyes on the Prize II; Interview with Bobby Seale" (November 4, 1988), Film and Media Archive, Washington University in St. Louis, American Archive of Public Broadcasting (GBH and the Library of Congress).
67 "Interviews and other recordings, August 12, 1968" (1 of 2), Series 1, Box 1, Folder 2, JHBEMP, 26–7. "It won't only be a grievance board. This board would set up policy for the police; they would be elected by the people, then this board will hire the policeman. But the board will also have the requirements down, the policy of how the police are supposed to act. The board will have the power to fire the police as well as hire them, you see. . . . They would have to live in whatever community they patrol, and of course they would have to show a great understanding of the psychology and the values of the people in that community."
68 Cameron Vanderson and J. Herman Blake, "'Look'n M' Face and Hear M' Story': An Oral History with Professor J. Herman Blake," December 2, 2014, https://escholarship.org/uc/item/4m01p3bz.
69 Joy James and K. Kim Holder, "In the Presence of Agape, Battles for Life Ensue," *Millenials Are Killing Capitalism*, podcast, February 16, 2023.
70 Newton, *War Against the Panthers*, 34. In *Revolutionary Suicide*, Newton wrote: "The system, in fact, destroys us through neglect much more often than by the police revolver. The gun is only the *coup de grâce*, the enforcer" (202).
71 "Interview, Sept 17, 1970, by Mark Lane," Series 1, Box 57, Folders 9–10, DHPNC.
72 Newton, *Revolutionary Suicide*, 128.

73 Ibid., 148.
74 Murch, *Living for the City*, 145.
75 Newton, *All Too Young*, Series 1, Box 55, Folder 3, DHPNC, 56.
76 Eldridge Cleaver, "Introduction," *The Genius of Huey Newton*, San Francisco: Black Panther Party Ministry of Information, January 1970, 5.
77 Later on, Sam Napier, Elaine Brown, Ericka Huggins, Judi Douglass, David Graham Du Bois, Michael Fultz, and JoNina Abron would work as principal editors.
78 "Cointelpro Black Extremist 100–448006, Section 22 [October–December 1970]," Black Freedom Struggle in the United States, *Proquest*, https://blackfreedom.proquest.com/wp-content/uploads/2020/09/blackpanther11.pdf.
79 Keating, *Free Huey!*, 169. Seale, *Seize the time*, 102–6. "Interviews and other recordings, August 12, 1968" (1 of 2), Series 1, Box 1, Folder 2, JHBEMP, 68–70.
80 Muhammad Ahmad, *We Will Return in the Whirlwind: Black Radical Organizations 1960–1975* (Chicago: Charles Kerr Publishing Company, 2007), 176.
81 Newton, *Revolutionary Suicide*, 197.
82 Hampton and Fayer, *Voices of Freedom*, Ch. 20.
83 "5/15/70," Series 1, Box 1, Folder 6, JHBEMP. "3/27/70," Series 1, Box 1, Folder 6, JHBEMP. "Interview with Leola Carr, sister of Huey P. Newton, July 15, 1970," Series 1, Box 1, Folder 8, JHBEMP.
84 "Interview, Sept 17, 1970, by Mark Lane," Series 1, Box 57, Folders 9–10, DHPNC, 77.
85 "Eyes on the Prize II; Interview with Bobby Seale," Library of Congress.
86 Newton, *Revolutionary Suicide*, 55. Bloom and Martin, *Black Against Empire*, 59. Emory Douglas, "Some American History," By the People, for the People: A Black Panther Party Celebration, California Museum, June 14, 2025.
87 "Capitol is Invaded," *Sacramento Bee*, May 2, 1967, 1.
88 Newton, *Revolutionary Suicide*, 155, 157–9.
89 Ibid., 356.
90 Ibid., 155, 157.
91 *All Power to the People*, dir. Lee.
92 Huey P. Newton, "Executive Mandate No. 1," *The Black Panther*, May 15, 1967, *Marxists Internet Archive*. This is the first text with Newton's name on it in the *Black Panther* newspaper, first read aloud at the Panther's protest at the state capitol on May 2, 1967. See also Newton, "Executive Mandate No. 1: May 2, 1967," *To Die for the People*.
93 Newton, *Revolutionary Suicide*, 158.
94 Ibid., 157.
95 Seale, *Seize the Time*, 31.
96 Newton, "Executive Mandate No. 1," *The Black Panther*, May 15, 1967.
97 "Eyes on the Prize II; Interview with Bobby Seale," Library of Congress.
98 Huey P. Newton, "Functional Definition of Politics, Revised," Series 1, Box 38, Folder 11, DHPNC.
99 Chela Sandoval, *Methodology of the Oppressed* (Minneapolis: University of Minnesota Press, 2000).
100 Jane Rhodes, *Framing the Panthers* (Chicago: University of Illinois Press, 2007).

101 David Marriott, "On Revolutionary Suicide," *Diacritics* 49:4 (2021), 101–33.
102 Revolutionary Action Movement, "The World Black Revolution (1966)," *Viewpoint Magazine*, December 29, 2017.
103 Cleaver, "On the Ideology," *Target Zero*, 172.
104 Huey P. Newton, "A Functional Definition of Politics," *The Black Panther*, May 15, 1967, *Marxists Internet Archive*. In *The Huey P. Newton Reader* "A Functional Definition of Politics" is erroneously dated as first published January 17, 1969.
105 "Image of Huey P. Newton from National Archives Footage," Department of Justice, Federal Bureau of Investigation, 65.27, uploaded by Disembodied Territories, November 8, 2021, https://vimeo.com/643486440.
106 Newton, "In Defense of Self-Defense," *The Black Panther*, June 20, 1967.
107 Newton, "A Functional Definition of Politics," *The Black Panther*, May 15, 1967.
108 "An interview with Huey P. Newton," Pacifica Radio Archives, American Archive of Public Broadcasting (GBH and the Library of Congress), http://americanarchive.org/catalog/cpb-aacip-28-b853f4m063.
109 *Huey P. Newton: Prelude to Revolution* (1971), dir. John Evans, Xenon Entertainment Group, February 28, 1998. This interview was recorded in early 1968.
110 Newton, "A Functional Definition of Politics," *The Black Panther*, May 15, 1967.
111 Newton, "In Defense of Self-Defense," *The Black Panther*, June 20, 1967.
112 Ibid.
113 Frances Fox Piven and Richard A. Cloward, *Poor People's Movements* (New York: Pantheon Books, 1977), 24.
114 Ibid., 37.
115 Douglas McAdam, *Political Process and the Development of Black Insurgency, 1930–1970* (Chicago: University of Chicago Press, 1999).
116 Bobby Seale, "The Coming Long Hot Summer," *The Black Panther*, June 20, 1967, 4, 7, *Marxists Internet Archive*. As Bloom points out, the phrase was originally Malcolm X's (Bloom and Martin, *Black Against Empire*, 419 n38).
117 In an interview conducted years later, Newton outlined his thought process behind cancelling plans for a bank robbery: "We were printing up a little mimeographed leaflet with the Ten-Point Program at the time, and we planned to staple money to the leaflet and drive through the community, throwing the leaflets out. And we were hoping that the community would read the leaflet, that the money would encourage them to read it. . . . At that time I was reading Frantz Fanon, and I decided that the people that were involved with me was more important than the money. So while I would insist on being executed if I were wounded in the bank, I didn't think I could execute them. Which upset them very much, and they became violent towards me, because it took them a lot of fortitude to agree to that plan in the first place. They had gotten themselves used to the plan, then I withdrew the action, and they were very upset" (Hampton and Fayer, *Voices of Freedom*, Ch. 20).
118 Huey P. Newton, "The Correct Handling of a Revolution," *The Black Panther*, July 20, 1967, *Marxists Internet Archive*.
119 Newton, "In Defense of Self-Defense," *The Black Panther*, June 20, 1967.

120 Ibid.

121 Newton, *Revolutionary Suicide*, 3. It was less known in the 1960s, when Newton read the essay from which the line is taken, that *Catechism of a Revolutionary* was in fact composed by Sergey Nechayev. See Megan C. Thomas, "Secrecy's Use: Using Bakunin to Theorize Authority and Free Action," *Contemporary Political Theory* 15 (2016), 264–84.

122 *Huey P. Newton: Prelude to Revolution* (1971), dir. Evans. Interview from February 1968.

123 Newton, *Revolutionary Suicide*, 355.

124 Ibid., 159.

125 Bloom and Martin, *Black Against Empire*, 100. Newton, *Revolutionary Suicide*, 244.

126 Robert H. Brisbane, *Black Activism: Racial Revolution in the United States, 1954–1970* (Valley Forge, PA: Judson Press, 1974), 207.

127 Newton, *Revolutionary Suicide*, 189–93.

128 Denny Smithson, "A Visit with Huey Newton: Vacaville Prison Facility; October 17, 1968," Pacifica Radio Archives, American Archive of Public Broadcasting (GBH and the Library of Congress), http://americanarchive.org/catalog/cpb-aacip-28-d795718160.

129 "Pigs Run Amuck: Executive Mandate No. 3," *The Black Panther*, March 16, 1968, 1, *Alexander Street*.

130 Huey P. Newton, "In Defense of Self-Defense: An Exclusive Interview," *The Black Panther*, March 16, 1968, 14, *Alexander Street*.

131 "Draft Perspective for Newton-Seale Campaign," Huey Newton Collection, FA.

132 "Interviews and other recordings, August 1968," Series 1, Box 1, Folder 2, JHBEMP, 85.

133 "Speeding up Time," *The Black Panther*, March 16, 1968, 1, *Alexander Street*.

134 Years later, Newton attributed the phrase "speeding up time" directly to Eldridge Cleaver ("Interview, Sept 17, 1970," Series 1, Box 2, Folder 1, JHBEMP, 54). Cleaver may have written this article anonymously so as to avoid conflict with the terms of his parole.

135 "Speeding up Time," *The Black Panther*, March 16, 1968, 8, *Alexander Street*.

136 Newton, *Revolutionary Suicide*, 222. Hilliard and Cole, *This Side of Glory*. Though his family was disturbed by the leaflet, Newton eventually allowed it, placing the expansion of the movement above his own well-being ("Interview with Lee Edward Newton, Older Brother of Huey P. Newton, November 1, 1970," Series 1, Box 3, Folder 7, JHBEMP, 48).

137 Cleaver, "Uptight in Babylon" (1971), *Target Zero*, 80.

138 Don Cox, *Just Another Nigger: My Life in the Black Panther Party* (Berkeley: Heyday, 2018), 37–46. Hilliard and Cole, *This Side of Glory*, 195.

139 Cox, *Just Another Nigger*, 63.

140 William Lee Brent, *Long Time Gone: A Black Panther's True-Life Story of his Hijacking and Twenty-Five Years in Cuba* (New York: Random House, 1996), 118–21. Bloom and Martin, *Black Against Empire*, 342.

141 Kit Kim Holder, "The History of the Black Panther Party, 1966–1971," dissertation, University of Massachusetts, 1990, 46.

142 Hilliard and Cole, *This Side of Glory*, 152.

143 Ibid., 181. Newton, *Revolutionary Suicide*, 208.
144 Brent, *Long Time Gone*, 124.
145 Hampton and Fayer, *Voices of Freedom*, Ch. 27. Hilliard and Cole, *This Side of Glory*, 184–5. Cox, *Just Another Nigger*, 69.
146 Hampton and Fayer, *Voices of Freedom*, Ch. 27. Bloom and Martin, *Black Against Empire*, 119. Hilliard and Cole, *This Side of Glory*, 193. Cox, *Just Another Nigger*, 69.
147 Cox, *Just Another Nigger*, 70.
148 Newton, *All Too Young*, Series 1, Box 55, Folder 3, DHPNC, 28; Folder 4, DHPNC, 134–5, 189–90; Folder 5, DHPNC, 265, 306. Newton, *Revolutionary Suicide*, 210, 276. "On the Contradictions within the Black Panther Party," *Right On!* April 13, 1971, 9.
149 Hilliard and Cole, *This Side of Glory*, 194.
150 Hampton and Fayer, *Voices of Freedom*, Ch. 27.
151 "Interview with Huey Newton" (1975), *AFRO News*, https://afro.com/afro-exclusive-interview-with-huey-p-newton.
152 "George Jackson and Huey P. Newton Interviews" (Side B), June 7, 1968, PM 211B, George Jackson Collection, FA. See also "Huey Newton on Guns & Gun Control (1968)," *YouTube*, uploaded by AfroMarxist, April 26, 2018.
153 Newton, *All Too Young*, Series 1, Box 55, Folder 5, DHPNC, 303.
154 Cleaver, "Uptight in Babylon," *Target Zero*, 80.
155 Hilliard and Cole, *This Side of Glory*, 285.
156 Bobby Seale Speech at MIT (February 2, 1995), private recording. Alondra Nelson, *Body and Soul: The Black Panther Party and the Fight Against Medical Discrimination* (Minneapolis: University of Minnesota Press, 2011), 17.
157 Forbes, *Will You Die With Me?*, 56.
158 John Peterson, "The Panthers Sheathe Their Claws," *National Observer*, February 12, 1972, Series 2, Box 1275, Folder 5, RHR.
159 Trivers, *Wild Life*, 146.
160 Newton, *Revolutionary Suicide*, 201.
161 Ibid., 202, 258.
162 Celia Rosebury, "Black Liberation on Trial: The Case of Huey Newton," Bay Area Committee to Defend Political Freedom (Berkeley, California, 1968), Huey Newton Collection, FA.
163 Pearlman, *The Sky's the Limit*, 455. *American Justice on Trial: People v. Newton*, dir. Andrew Abrahams and Herb Ferrette, Open Eye Pictures, 2022.
164 *All Power to the People*, dir. Lee.
165 Rosebury, "Black Liberation on Trial: The Case of Huey Newton," Bay Area Committee to Defend Political Freedom.
166 *People v. Newton*, 8 Cal. App. 3d 359 (Ct. App. 1970).
167 Newton, *Revolutionary Suicide*, 224–6, 247–8.
168 Ibid., 261.
169 Bloom and Martin, *Black Against Empire*, 199.
170 Ibid., 212.
171 Ward Churchill, "To Disrupt, Discredit and Destroy," *Liberation, Imagination, and the Black Panther Party*, ed. Kathleen Cleaver and George Katsiaficas (New York: Routledge, 2001). Newton, *War Against the Panthers*, 78–81. Brad Schreiber, *Revolution's End: The Patty Hearst Kidnapping, Mind Control,*

and the Secret History of Donald DeFreeze and the SLA (New York: Skyhorse Publishing, 2016), 15–17.

172 "Special Agent Wesley Swearingen," *What We Want, What We Believe: The Black Panther Party Library*, Roz Payne Archives and Newsreel Films, AK Press Video, 2006.

173 Blake, "Caged Panther," 247.

174 M. Wes Swearingen, *FBI Secrets: An Agent's Exposé* (Boston: South End Press, 1995), 82–4. FBI Director J. Edgar Hoover stated: "It is felt that a substantial amount of the unrest is directly attributable to this program" (84).

175 Newton, *Revolutionary Suicide*, 277.

176 According to Los Angeles Panther Wayne Pharr, two months after the murders, Us members continued to shoot at BPP members; in response, Deputy Minister of Defense Geronimo Ji-Jaga Pratt had some individuals operating in an underground manner "put in some work, and the killing stopped" (Pharr, *Nine Lives of a Black Panther* (Chicago: Lawrence Hill Books, 2014), 131–4).

177 "Breakfast for Black Children," *The Black Panther*, September 7, 1968, 7, *Marxists Internet Archive*. See also Bloom and Martin, *Black Against Empire*, 437 n8.

178 Bloom and Martin, *Black Against Empire*, 182.

179 "Ruth Beckford (1925–2019)," *WendyPerron*, https://wendyperron.com/ruth-beckford-1925-2019. Bloom and Martin, *Black Against Empire*, 188.

180 Newton, *Revolutionary Suicide*, 70.

181 Huey P. Newton, "To Feed Our Children," *The Black Panther*, March 26, 1969, *Marxists Internet Archive*.

182 "Mark Lane interview, Tape 10," Series 1, Box 57, Folders 9–10, DHPNC, 5.

183 "Elbert 'Big Man' Howard Oral History Interview," Library of Congress. Richard Philbrick, "Panther Free Meals 'Threat' to Hoover," *Chicago Tribune*, May 8, 1976, 81.

184 Daniel Walker, *Rights in Conflict: Convention Week in Chicago, August 25–29, 1968*, A report submitted to the National Commission on the Causes and Prevention of Violence (New York: E. P. Dutton, 1968).

185 Brown, *A Taste of Power*, 198.

186 "Fred Hampton: 'The Lost Interview' (Chicago, October 1969)," *YouTube*, uploaded by Hezakya Newz & Films, January 29, 2026.

187 "Eyes on the Prize II; Interview with Bobby Seale," Library of Congress. John Kifner, "Explosion in Chicago Rips Statue of a Policeman," *New York Times*, October 6, 1970, 28.

188 "Fred Hampton: 'The Lost Interview,'" *YouTube*. Concerning the role of white allies, Hampton continued: "I believe that basically they [SDS-WUO] believe that white people need to learn how to struggle. They believe that these white workers need to learn how to struggle through confrontation. I have to say that I believe basically that this is incorrect. I believe white workers *have* been struggling; they're some of the most violent people in the world. I believe what they need is a *redirection* in their ideology and their politics. They need to know who to struggle against. The workers need to start to begin to learn that their job is to struggle against the bosses. And until they do this, their struggle is incorrect; it's like no struggle at all."

189 David Hilliard, Elaine Brown, Ericka Huggins, and Fredrika Newton, "The Origins of the Black Panther Party: History, Facts, Goals, Platform," February 18, 2006, University of New Mexico, *C-Span: American Perspectives*. Brown mentions that the funeral for Walter Toure Pope had just occurred. He was murdered on October 18, 1969.

190 Ibid.

191 Fred Hampton, "You Can Murder a Liberator, But You Can't Murder Liberation," *The Movement* 5:12 (The Movement Press, January 1970), *Marxists Internet Archive*.

192 "Eyes on the Prize II; Interview with Bobby Seale," Library of Congress.

193 "Eyes on the Prize II; Interview with Huey P. Newton," Library of Congress.

194 Brown, *A Taste of Power*, 201. In 1982, with the City of Chicago, Cook County, and the federal government named as defendants, a $1.85 million settlement would be issued, at that point the largest ever in a civil rights case.

195 Newton, *All Too Young*, Series 1, Box 55, Folder 5, DHPNC, 274–8. *Eldridge Cleaver, Black Panther*, dir. by William Klein, O.N.C.I.C., 1969, *YouTube*, uploaded by Said Bouchelaleg, October 14, 2018. Brown, *A Taste of Power*, 222–4.

196 Bobby Seale, *A Lonely Rage* (New York: New York Times Books, 1978), 177.

197 "Sisters' Section: Sisters Unite," *The Black Panther*, May 25, 1967, 6, *Marxists Internet Archive*.

198 Billy X, "Photo Gallery," *It's About Time Black Panther Party*.

199 Spencer, *The Revolution Has Come*, 47.

200 Ahmad, *We Will Return*, 195. Bloom and Martin, *Black Against Empire*, 343–4.

201 *Comrade Sister* (1996), prod. Phyllis J. Jackson and Christine L. Jordan (unreleased).

202 Bloom and Martin, *Black Against Empire*, 194.

203 Regina Jennings, "Why I Joined the Party: An African Womanist Reflection," *The Black Panther Party Reconsidered*, 259.

204 Phone conversation with Phyllis Jackson, January 14, 2025. Brown, *A Taste of Power*.

205 "Civil Rights History Project: Norma Mtume," June 27, 2016, Smithsonian Museum of History, Library of Congress, https://www.loc.gov/item/2016655429.

206 Safiya Bukhari, "On the Question of Sexism Within the Black Panther Party," *The War Before*. "Roberta Alexander Oral History Interview by David P. Cline in San Diego, California," June 29, 2016, https://www.loc.gov/item/2016655433.

207 Newton, *All Too Young*, Series 1, Box 55, Folder 5, DHPNC, 263.

208 Phone conversation with Phyllis Jackson, January 14, 2025.

209 *Comrade Sister* (1996), prod. Jackson and Jordan.

210 Stephen Shames and Ericka Huggins, eds., *Comrade Sisters: Women of the Black Panther Party* (Woodbridge, UK: ACC Art Books, 2022), 116.

211 Mary Phillips and Angela LeBlanc-Ernest, "The Hidden Narratives Recovering and (Re)Visioning the Community Activism of Men in the Black Panther Party," *Spectrum* 5:1 (2016), 72, 77–8. *All Power to the People*, dir. Lee.

212 The Dr. Huey P. Newton Foundation, *The Black Panther Party Service Programs*, ed. David Hilliard (Oakland, CA: Dr. Huey P. Newton Foundation, 2008).
213 Suzun Lucia Lamaina, *Revolutionary Grain: Celebrating the Spirit of the Black Panthers* (Brisbane, CA: Susan Lamaina Photography, 2025). Pharr, *Nine Lives of a Black Panther*, 79.
214 Newton, *All Too Young*, Series 1, Box 55, Folder 3, DHPNC, 78–80. Hilliard and Cole, *This Side of Glory*, 171. "July 24, 1970," Series 1, Box 1, Folder 6, JHBEMP.
215 "July 24, 1970," Series 1, Box 1, Folder 6, JHBEMP.
216 "Eyes on the Prize II; Interview with Huey P. Newton," Library of Congress. Newton, *All Too Young*, Series 1, Box 55, Folder 3, DHPNC, 79–80: "SNCC had the skills and we respected them very greatly, yet we felt that they were headed for a decline because the thrust of the movement had moved out of the South and into the cities of the North and West. So we felt that SNCC and the Black Panther Party really needed each other, and Black people needed us both. We voted to give the leadership of the Party over to SNCC. That is how I view the situation now that I look back on it because we made Stokely the Prime Minister which meant that he was head of the Party. We even thought that we could move our headquarters to Atlanta and be under SNCC in their building there because they had the kinds of duplicating equipment and other materials we needed. . . . Eldridge and Bobby both agreed to this and I was in full agreement with this position because I was not interested in a Party as such: I was most interested in the revolution and the freedom of Black people and I wanted to see the best personnel possible to bring that about in positions of authority."
217 According to former FBI agent M. Wesley Swearingen: "FBI officials saw a strengthening coalition within the black community that they felt had to be stopped immediately. The FBI framed Stokely Carmichael as an informer for the CIA by planting an informant report in his car where other members could find it, with the help of another FBI informer. The report was discovered and the Panthers sent a 'hit team' after Carmichael, who as a result departed immediately for an extended period in Africa" (Swearingen, *FBI Secrets*, 82).
218 Keating, *Free Huey!*, epigraph. This interview, conducted by Joy Johnson, was originally published in September 1970 in *Ramparts* magazine.
219 Nelson, *Body and Soul*.
220 Shames and Huggins, *Comrade Sisters*, 84.
221 Nelson, *Body and Soul*, 77, 223 n10.
222 Ibid., ix.
223 "Civil Rights History Project: Norma Mtume."
224 Shames and Huggins, *Comrade Sisters*, 127.
225 "Amen!" *The Black Panther*, January 4, 1969, 19, *Marxists Internet Archive*. "Thoughts for Negroes," *The Black Panther*, March 9, 1969, 4. "The Anatomy of Extermination," *The Black Panther*, March 31, 1969, 16. *The Black Panther*, May 31, 1969.
226 "Birth Control," *The Black Panther*, February 7, 1970, 7, *Alexander Street*.
227 "Sterilization: Another Part of the Plan of Black Genocide," *The Black Panther*, May 8, 1971, *Alexander Street*.

228 "Youth Makes the Revolution," *The Black Panther*, August 2, 1969, *Alexander Street*.
229 "Civil Rights History Project: Ericka C. Huggins," Smithsonian Museum of History, Library of Congress, June 30, 2016, *YouTube*, February 21, 2020.
230 Kiran Garcha, "Children and Childhood in Black Panther Party Thought and Discourse: 1966–1974," *Journal of African American Studies* 23 (2019), 320–34.
231 Benjamin R. Young, "Imagining Revolutionary Feminism: Communist Asia and the Women of the Black Panther Party," *Souls* 21 (2019), 1–17.
232 Brown, *A Taste of Power*. Fiona Thompson, "An Oral History with Ericka Huggins" (2007), Oral History Center, Bancroft Library, UC Berkeley, 2010.

3 The Theory of Intercommunalism

1 Huey P. Newton, excerpt from "The Mind is Flesh" from *The Huey P. Newton Reader*, edited by David Hilliard and Donald Weiss. Copyright © 2002 by Fredrick S. Newton and David Hilliard. Reproduced with the permission of The Permissions Company, LLC on behalf of Seven Stories Press, sevenstories.com.
2 Eldridge Cleaver, "On Meeting the Needs of the People," *The Black Panther*, August 16, 1969, 4, *Marxists Internet Archive*.
3 Frank Bardacke, "Who Owns the Park?" *Verso Books Blog*, October 31, 2011. Left in the Bay, "Who Owns the Park?" *Verso Books Blog*, August 11, 2022.
4 For the Black United Front of Nova Scotia, see Jennifer Smith, *An International History of the Black Panther Party* (New York: Garland, 1999). For the Bahamas: John T. McCartney, "The Influences of the Black Panther Party (USA) on the Vanguard Party of the Bahamas (1972–1987)," *Liberation, Imagination, and the Black Panther Party*, ed. Cleaver and Katsiaficas. For New Zealand, Polynesia, India, and Israel-Palestine: Risdon N. Slate, ed., *Black Power beyond Borders: The Global Dimensions of the Black Power Movement* (New York: Palgrave Macmillan, 2012). For more on Polynesia, see also Angelique Stastny and Raymond Orr, "The Influence of the US Black Panthers on Indigenous Activism in Australia and New Zealand from 1969 onwards," *Australian Aboriginal Studies* 2 (2014); and Shames and Huggins, *Comrade Sisters*. For more movements and sources, see Jones and Jeffries, "Don't Believe the Hype," *The Black Panther Party Reconsidered*, 37, 52–3 n54.
5 Kathleen Cleaver, "Back to Africa: The Evolution of the International Section of the Black Panther Party (1969–1972)," *The Black Panther Party Reconsidered*. Frank J. Rafalako, *MH/CHAOS: The CIA's Campaign Against the Radical New Left and the Black Panthers* (Annapolis, MD: Naval Institute Press, 2011).
6 Bloom and Martin, *Black Against Empire*, 318.
7 Judson Jeffries, ed., *Comrades: A Local History of the Black Panther Party* (Bloomington and Indianapolis: Indiana University Press, 2007). Judson Jeffries, ed., *On the Ground: The Black Panther Party in Communities Across America* (Jackson: University Press of Mississippi, 2008). Judson Jeffries, ed., *The Black Panther Party in a City Near You* (Athens: University of Georgia Press, 2018).

8 Yohuru Williams and Jama Lazerow, eds., *Liberated Territory: Untold Local Perspectives on the Black Panther Party* (Durham, NC: Duke University Press, 2008), 24. Newton, *Revolutionary Suicide*, 206.
9 Brown, *A Taste of Power*, 135.
10 Murch, *Assata Taught Me*, 15.
11 "Interview, Sept 17, 1970, by Mark Lane," Series 1, Box 57, Folders 9–10, DHPNC, 84.
12 Ibid., 21.
13 Ollie A. Johnson III, "Explaining the Demise of the Black Panther Party," *Black Panther Party Reconsidered*, 410 n4.
14 "On May 29, 1970, the Court of Appeal in San Francisco reversed Huey Newton's conviction. The court held that the trial court in Oakland had committed prejudicial error in not instructing the jury to acquit if it found that Newton was unconscious at the time police officer Frey was shot. . . . The appellate court in San Francisco also found it an error not to have given Newton a hearing on his claim that a felony conviction several years earlier was unconstitutional and invalid inasmuch as he was not represented by counsel at the time. The appellate court also declared error that the Oakland court had not reopened the trial when the defense discovered that the only eyewitness to the shooting of Frey had said, an hour and a half after the incident, that he had *not* seen the assailant's face. (At the trial, this same witness had testified that the assailant was Newton)" (Kay Boyle, "No One Can Be All Things to All People," *Evergreen*, No. 81, August 1970, Huey Newton Collection, FA).
15 "Unforgettable Change: 1960s: Black Panther Party: A Black Power Alternative," Picture This: California Perspectives on American History, Oakland Museum of California. "Huey Newton interview," August 30, 1970, prod. Colin Edwards, Colin Edwards Collection, CE 055, FA. "Huey Newton Release," August 5, 1970, Huey Newton Collection, KP 461B, FA. When asked why he took off his shirt that day, Newton replied: "People thought it was some grand gesture or something; but it was just hot" (Tim Findley, "Huey Newton Twenty-Five Floors from the Street," *Rolling Stone*, August 3, 1972, 30).
16 Huey P. Newton, "Intercommunalism: A Higher Level of Consciousness," Series 1, Box 48, Folder 4, DHPNC, 6.
17 Newton, *All Too Young*, Series 1, Box 55, Folder 5, DHPNC, 251–2.
18 Newton, "Speech at Boston College," *To Die for the People*, 30.
19 "Huey Newton Speaks, July 4, 1970, by Mark Lane," Series 1, Box 57, Folder 7, DHPNC, 5. Video of this press conference is also available at: "Huey P. Newton Speaks at a 1970 News Conference," *YouTube*, uploaded by Satanico Pandemonium, July 25, 2014, https://www.youtube.com/watch?v=NplrUhW79b8.
20 Newton, "Intercommunalism: 1974," ed. Delio Vásquez, *Viewpoint Magazine*, June 11, 2018. Also available in: Newton, "Who Makes U.S. Foreign Policy?," *The Huey P. Newton Reader*, 295–303.
21 Newton, "The Technology Question: 1972," *The Huey P. Newton Reader*, 261.
22 Ibid.

23 Newton, "Intercommunalism: 1974," *Viewpoint Magazine*, June 11, 2018.
24 Mohammed Hussein and Mohammed Haddad, "Infographic: US Military Presence around the World," *Al Jazeera*, September 10, 2021.
25 Newton, "Intercommunalism: A Higher Level of Consciousness," Series 1, Box 48, Folder 4, DHPNC, 5, 9.
26 Newton, "Speech at Boston College," *To Die for the People*, 35.
27 "Huey P. Newton interview," August 1, 1971, prod. Grenada TV, Huey Newton Collection, PM 065, FA.
28 Newton, "Speech at Boston College," *To Die for the People*, 37.
29 Brown, "Foreword" (2009), in Newton, *To Die for the People*, xx.
30 Kai T. Erikson, "Introduction," Newton and Erikson, *In Search of Common Ground.*
31 Abu-Jamal, "The Genius of Huey P. Newton," *Prison Radio.*
32 Newton and Erikson, *In Search of Common Ground*, 38.
33 Mumia Abu-Jamal, *We Want Freedom: A Life in the Black Panther Party* (Brooklyn, NY: Common Notions, 2016), 74.
34 Blake, "Caged Panther," 244.
35 Assata Shakur, *Assata* (Chicago: Lawrence Hill Books, 1987), 226.
36 Tim Findley, "Huey Newton Twenty-Five Floors from the Street," *Rolling Stone*, August 3, 1972, 33.
37 "A Conversation with Huey Newton," *Oui Magazine*, March 1978, 71–2, 132–4.
38 Newton, "Speech at Boston College," *To Die for the People*, 31.
39 "Huey Newton Talks to the Movement," *The Black Panthers Speak*, ed. Foner, 50–66.
40 Newton, "To the Republic of New Afrika," *To Die for the People*, 96.
41 Newton, "Speech at Boston College," *To Die for the People*, 33.
42 Huey P. Newton, "Utopia: Universal Life Energy" (1974), Series 1, Box 39, Folder 1, DHPNC, 8–9.
43 Huey Newton, "Vanguard of the People's Struggle" (1970), *Off the Pigs*, 227, 229. This text is a version of an interview of Newton conducted on KPFA-FM Radio on August 14, 1970, edited and mimeographed by BPP Headquarters, Oakland CA.
44 Newton, "Speech at Boston College," *To Die for the People*, 33.
45 Newton, "Uniting Against a Common Enemy: October 13, 1971," *To Die for the People*, 217.
46 "Huey Newton Interview," August 30, 1970, CE 055, prod. Colin Edwards, Colin Edwards Collection, FA.
47 Newton, "Intercommunalism: A Higher Level of Consciousness," Series 1, Box 48, Folder 4, DHPNC, 4.
48 "Huey P. Newton at New York Community College" (November 19, 1970), Series 1, Box 57, Folder 12, DHPNC, 16.
49 "Huey Newton Speaks, July 4, 1970, by Mark Lane," Series 1, Box 57, Folder 7, DHPNC, 5.
50 Newton and Erikson, *In Search of Common Ground*, 41. Emphasis added.
51 Ibid., 30.
52 Kwame Nkrumah, *Neo-Colonialism: The Last Stage of Imperialism* (London: Panaf Books, 1970).

53 Newton, "On Pan-Africanism or Communism: December 1, 1971," *The Huey P. Newton Reader*, 252.
54 Nayla Tozin, "Intercommunalism vs. Pan-Africanism: A Comparison of Two Approaches to International Liberation," *Confluence*, May 2, 2025.
55 Cedric G. Johnson, "Huey P. Newton and the Last Days of the Black Colony," *African American Political Thought: A Collected History*, ed. Melvin L. Rogers and Jack Turner (Chicago: University of Chicago Press, 2021).
56 Newton, "Speech at Boston College," *To Die for the People*, 37.
57 "Huey Newton Speaks, July 4, 1970, by Mark Lane," Series 1, Box 57, Folder 7, DHPNC, 5.
58 Newton, "Intercommunalism: A Higher Level of Consciousness," Series 1, Box 48, Folder 4, DHPNC, 9–10.
59 Newton, *Revolutionary Suicide*, 6.
60 "Chapter 28: The Chicago Campaign," *The Autobiography of Martin Luther King Jr.*, ed. Clayborne Carson (Warner Books, 1998), https://kinginstitute.stanford.edu/publications/autobiography-martin-luther-king-jr/chapter-28-chicago-campaign.
61 Martin Luther King, Jr., "Chicago Plan" (January 7, 1966), *Civil Rights Movement Archive*. Martin Luther King Jr.'s time in Chicago is also fascinating for the Southern Christian Leadership Conference's extensive collaborative work with gangs of various types. For more on King's analysis of colonization, see James H. Cone, "Martin Luther King, Jr., and the Third World," *The Journal of American History* 74:2 (1987), 455–67.
62 Robert Blauner, "Internal Colonialism and Ghetto Revolt," *Social Problems* 16:4 (1969), 393–408.
63 Frantz Fanon, "French Intellectuals and Democrats in the Algerian Revolution," *Toward the African Revolution*, trans. Haakon Cheavlier (1964) (New York: Grove Press, 1967), 81. Originally published in December 1957 in *Moudjahid* 90.
64 Newton, "To the Republic of New Afrika: September 13, 1969," *To Die for the People*, 94–5.
65 Newton, "In Defense of Self-Defense," *The Black Panther*, June 20, 1967.
66 Note from Toni Morrison to Jim Silberman (October 11, 1971), Series 2, Box 1275, RHR. "Look'n M' Face and Hear M' Story: An Oral History with Professor J. Herman Blake," University of California Santa Cruz Library, 2014. Newton, "In Defense of Self-Defense: June 20, 1967," *To Die for the People*, 80–1.
67 Huey P. Newton, "Eclipse of Community: The Making of the English Working Class" (1978), Series 1, Box 38, Folder 9, DHPNC, 7.
68 Ibid., 5.
69 Ibid., 7. He adds: "Whether their destiny was chattel slavery or wage-slavery, preindustrial populations had to be conquered and colonized first."
70 Ibid., 8–9.
71 Ibid., 6.
72 Ibid., 2.
73 Ibid., 16–17. Notably, Newton places the term "colonies" in euphemistic quotation marks, once again critiquing the use of the word given his analysis of empire, while nonetheless affirming that the people are colonized.

74 Fanon, *Les damnés*, 41–2. Fanon, *Wretched*, trans. Farrington, 38. Translation edited.
75 Bloom and Martin, *Black Against Empire*, 110.
76 Emory Douglas, "On Revolutionary Culture," *The Black Panther*, September 15, 1969, *Marxists Internet Archive*.
77 Newton, "On the Peace Movement: August 15, 1969," *To Die for the People*, 152.
78 Huey P. Newton, "Message from the Minister of Defense Huey P. Newton on the Peace Movement," *The Black Panther*, September 27, 1969, 30, *Alexander Street*.
79 Historian Marcus Rediker's argument that the radical liberalism of the "Founding Fathers" was a watered-down version of ideologies emanating from the actions of rebellious slaves, sailors, and mobs lends further credence to such a project (Marcus Rediker, "A Motley Crew in the American Revolution," *Outlaws of the Atlantic* (Boston: Beacon Press, 2015), Ch. 6. See also Vincent Brown, "Black History's Warning to the World," UCSC Interdisciplinary Humanities Center, February 20, 2025, https://www.ihc.ucsb.edu/event/black-historys-warning-to-the-world.)
80 Bobby Seale claims on a couple of occasions that this part of the Ten-Point Program was his idea. See *All Power to the People*, dir. Lee. "Eyes on the Prize II; Interview with Bobby Seale," Library of Congress.
81 George Katsiaficas, "Organization and Movement: The Case of the Black Panther Party and the Revolutionary People's Constitutional Convention of 1970," *Liberation, Imagination, and the Black Panther Party*.
82 Abu-Jamal, *We Want Freedom*, 72.
83 Huey P. Newton, "Eliminate the Presidency," *The Black Panther Party Service Programs*, ed. Hilliard, 94.
84 Newton, *War Against the Panthers*, 5.
85 Ibid., 7, 6.
86 Newton, "Speech at Boston College," *To Die for the People*, 27–8.
87 Ibid., 27.
88 Newton and Erikson, *In Search of Common Ground*, 37.
89 John Narayan, "The Wages of Whiteness in the Absence of Wages: Racial Capitalism, Reactionary Intercommunalism and the Rise of Trumpism," *Third World Quarterly* 38:11 (2017), 2482–500, 2487–8.
90 Newton, "The Dialectics of Nature: 1974," *The Huey P. Newton Reader*, 312.
91 Notes, Series 1, Box 47, Folder 5, DHPNC.
92 James Boggs, *The American Revolution: Pages from a Negro Worker's Notebook* (1963) (New York: Monthly Review Press, 2009), 41.
93 Newton, "Speech at Boston College," *To Die for the People*, 29.
94 Newton and Erikson, *In Search of Common Ground*, 111.
95 Ibid., 31.
96 Ibid., 68.
97 "Real and nominal value of the federal minimum wage in the United States from 1938 to 2024," *Statista Research Department*, July 26, 2024.
98 Tula Connell, "Precarious Work Rises, Incomes Fall Around the World," *SolidarityCenter.org*, May 19, 2015, https://www.solidaritycenter.org/ilo-precarious-work-rises-incomes-fall-around-the-world.

99 Weeks, "The Lumpenproletariat and the Politics of Class," 332. She adds: "Rather than choose between the categories [of proletariat and lumpenproletariat], however, there are even better reasons to reject them both" (342).

100 Robert L. Allen, "Reassessing the Internal Neocolonialism Theory," *The Black Scholar* 35:1 (2005), 2–11.

101 Ruha Benjamin, *Imagination: A Manifesto* (New York: W. W. Norton and Company, 2024), 39.

102 "Interview with Alex Hoffman, October 3, 1970," Series 1, Box 2, Folder 10, JHBEMP, 21, 33.

103 Ibid., 34.

104 "Study: Poor Are More Charitable Than the Wealthy," *National Public Radio*, August 8, 2010. Lau Lilleholt et al., "Does Resource Scarcity Increase Self-Serving Dishonesty? Most People Wrongly Believe So," *Journal of Experimental Psychology* 152:7 (2023), 1887–1906. Suparee Boonmanunt et al., "Does Poverty Negate the Impact of Social Norms on Cheating?" *Games and Economic Behavior* 124 (2020), 569–78.

4 The Soul Breaker

1 Brown, *A Taste of Power*, 319.

2 Newton, *Revolutionary Suicide*, 104.

3 Grassian, "Psychopathological Effects of Solitary Confinement," *American Journal of Psychiatry* 140:11 (1983), 1450–4. Lisa Guenther, *Solitary Confinement: Social Death and Its Afterlives* (Minneapolis: University of Minnesota Press, 2013).

4 Newton, *Revolutionary Suicide*, 105–6.

5 Newton, *Revolutionary Suicide*, 106–7. See also Huey P. Newton, "Prison, Where is Thy Victory?" *The Black Panther*, January 3, 1970, 13, *Marxists Internet Archive*.

6 Jeffries, "Postscript: Literary Criticisms of Newton's Work," *Huey P. Newton: The Radical Theorist*.

7 Newton, *All Too Young*, Series 1, Box 55, Folders 3–5, DHPNC. This document lacks the early chapters about Newton's personal life and starts with a "Section 3," which appears to be analogous to chapter 14 in *Revolutionary Suicide*. It also contains line edits and the note "suggested new title," from which one can derive that it was a relatively late draft.

8 Nasrullah Mambrol, "Analysis of Shelley's Adonais," *Literary Theory and Criticism*, February 17 2021.

9 Newton, *All Too Young*, Series 1, Box 55, Folder 3, DHPNC, 3.

10 Brown, *A Taste of Power*, 244.

11 Newton, *Revolutionary Suicide*, 106.

12 Later, while a political prisoner, he made the decision to remain in solitary so as to avoid being murdered by prisoners sent by guards. However, he explicitly advised against taking such a decision lightly: "I cannot tell inexperienced young comrades to go into jail and into solitary, that that is the way to defy the authorities and exercise their freedom. I know what solitary can do to a man" (Newton, *Revolutionary Suicide*, 107).

13 Newton, *Revolutionary Suicide*, 58. "Interview, Sept 13, 1970," Series 1, Box 2, Folder 5, JHBEMP, 15. He also read George Berkeley ("Interview with Melvin Newton, July 5, 1970," Series 1, Box 1, Folder 7, JHBEMP, 85).
14 Newton, *Revolutionary Suicide*, 57.
15 Newton, *Revolutionary Suicide*, 69. "7/17/70," Series 1, Box 1, Folder 6, JHBEMP.
16 The first text with Newton's name on it is "Executive Mandate No. 1," first read out at the Panther's protest at the state capitol building in Sacramento on May 2, 1967, but Seale has stated that this was composed collectively by himself, Newton, and Cleaver (*All Power to the People*, dir. Lee). It is also possible that Seale's wife Artie Seale played a role in editing it. "Herman Blake: October 14, 1970, Memorandum to the File: Richard M. Aoki," Series 1, Box 2, Folder 15, JHBEMP.
17 By the time Newton was arrested in 1967, three books of Fanon's were available in English: *Wretched of the Earth* (1963), *A Dying Colonialism* (1965), and *Black Skin, White Masks* (January 1967). A physician by the name of Dr. Aguilar recounted "marveling" at Newton's ability to "paraphras[e] the concepts set forth in Dr. Fanon's books in a dozen brilliantly succinct sentences" (Newton, *Revolutionary Suicide*, 191).
18 Newton, *Revolutionary Suicide*, 283.
19 Frantz Fanon, *Black Skin, White Masks*, trans. Charles Lam Markmann (New York: Grove Press, 1967), 109; Frantz Fanon, *Black Skin, White Masks*, trans. Richard Philcox (New York: Grove Press, 2008), 89.
20 Newton, "Fear and Doubt," *To Die for the People*, 77.
21 Christopher L. Hill, "Crossed Geographies," *Representations* 128:1 (2014), 93–123.
22 Bernard Flynn, "Maurice Merleau-Ponty," *The Stanford Encyclopedia of Philosophy* (Summer 2016), ed. Edward N. Zalta (2020).
23 Dan Zahavi, *Husserl's Phenomenology* (Stanford, CA: Stanford University Press, 2003), 55.
24 G. W. F. Hegel, "Independence and Self-Dependence of Self-Consciousness: Lordship and Bondage," *Phenomenology of Spirit*, trans. A. V. Miller (Oxford: Oxford University Press, 1952). Hegel's analysis of this relationship was inspired by the Haitian Revolution, which abolished slavery in its struggle for national independence. See Susan Buck-Morss, *Hegel, Haiti, and Universal History* (Pittsburgh: University of Pittsburgh Press, 2009).
25 For Fanon's thematic invocation of Descartes, see *Black Skin, White Masks* (trans. Philcox), 90–2. By contrast, Hegel treated skepticism as the principal problem of philosophy to be overcome. See Michael N. Forster, *Hegel and Skepticism* (Cambridge, MA: Harvard University Press, 1989).
26 Newton and Erikson, *In Search of Common Ground*, 24.
27 Ibid., 23.
28 Edmund Husserl, *Cartesian Meditations: An Introduction to Phenomenology*, trans. Dorion Cairns (Dordrecht: Kluwer Academic Publishers, 1993). Diogenes Laertius, "Pyrrho," *Lives of the Eminent Philosophers*, trans. Pamela Mensch, ed. James Miller (New York: Oxford University Press, 2018).
29 Newton, "Speech at Boston College," *To Die for the People*, 22–3.
30 Newton, quoted in Brown, *A Taste of Power*, 246.

31 "Interview, Sept 17, 1970, by Mark Lane," Series 1, Box 57, Folders 9–10, DHPNC, 120.

32 "Most human behavior is learned behavior. Most things the human being learns are gained through an indirect relationship to the object. . . . Those things learned indirectly many times stimulate very effective responses to what might be later a direct experience. At this time the black masses are handling the resistance incorrectly" (Newton, "In Defense of Self-Defense," *The Black Panther*, July 20, 1967, 3).

33 "Huey P. Newton at New York Community College" (November 19, 1970), Series 1, Box 57, Folder 12, DHPNC, 5. "Empiricism," *Online Etymological Dictionary*, ed. Douglas Harper, 2024.

34 "Empiric," *Online Etymological Dictionary*, ed. Douglas Harper, 2024.

35 Newton, *Revolutionary Suicide*, 76.

36 "Huey Newton Talks to the Movement," *The Black Panthers Speak*, ed. Foner, 61.

37 "Interview, Sept 17, 1970, by Mark Lane," Series 1, Box 57, Folders 9–10, DHPNC, 71. In the 1970s, Newton subscribed to the newsletter of the William James Association, an organization created by UC Santa Cruz professors Page Smith and Paul Lee (Newsletter, Series 1, Box 37, Folder 12, DHPNC. Jack Bowers, "The William James Association Prison Arts Project," *Hip Santa Cruz 5*, ed. T. Mike Walker (New York: Epigraph Publishing Service, 2020), Ch. 6).

38 Cornel West, *The American Evasion of Philosophy: Genealogy of Pragmatism* (Madison: University of Wisconsin Press, 1989).

39 Huey P. Newton, "Merritt Lecture Series 1–3: A Primary Introduction to Phenomena (Lecture 1)," Series 1, Box 59, Folder 4, DHPNC. "Idealism and the Rational Method," Series 1, Box 4, Folder 20, JHBEMP. "Ideology and Philosophy," Series 1, Box 4, Folder 20, JHBEMP.

40 Immanuel Kant, *Critique of Pure Reason* (1781), trans. Paul Guyer and Allen W. Wood (Cambridge: Cambridge University Press, 1998).

41 Newton, *Revolutionary Suicide*, 58, 76.

42 David Hume, *A Treatise of Human Nature* (1739) (2nd ed.), ed. L. A. Selby-Bigge (Oxford: Oxford University Press, 1978), 252 (Book 1, Part 4, Section 6).

43 Ibid., 207 (Book 1, Part 4, Section 2).

44 R. A. Mall, *Experience and Reason: The Phenomenology of Husserl and its Relation to Hume's Philosophy* (The Hague: Martinus Nijhoff, 1973), 28. Adolf Reinach, "Kant's Interpretation of Hume's Problem," trans. J. N. Mohanty, *The Southwestern Journal of Philosophy* 7 (1976), 161–88.

45 Tom Rockmore, "Hegel and Husserl: Two Phenomenological Reactions to Kant," *Hegel Bulletin* 38:1, Special Issue: Hegel and Phenomenology (2017), 67–84. See also Zahavi, *Husserl's Phenomenology*, 69.

46 Newton and Erikson, *In Search of Common Ground*, 24.

47 Newton, "Speech at Boston College," *To Die for the People*, 23–4.

48 Jonathan Friedman, "Marxism, Structuralism and Vulgar Materialism," *Man* 9:3 (1974), 444–69.

49 Karl Marx, "Theses on Feuerbach" (1845), *The Marx-Engels Reader* (2nd ed.), ed. Robert C. Tucker (New York: W. W. Norton and Company, 1978), 145.

50 Hampton and Fayer, *Voices of Freedom*, Ch. 20. "Huey P. Newton, Interviewed by Louis Massiah," *Eyes on the Prize: America at the Racial Crossroads 1965–1985*, recorded May 23, 1989, Washington University Film and Media Archive, Henry Hampton Collection.
51 Newton, "Merritt Lecture Series 1–3: A Primary Introduction to Phenomena (Lecture 1)," Series 1, Box 59, Folder 4, DHPNC.
52 "2/6/70," Series 1, Box 4, Folder 20, JHBEMP.
53 "1/16/71," Series 1, Box 4, Folder 20, JHBEMP. These are notes from Blake's attendance at the Black Panther Party's Ideological Institute.
54 Newton, "Merritt Lecture Series 1–3: A Primary Introduction to Phenomena (Lecture 1)," Series 1, Box 59, Folder 4, DHPNC.
55 John T. Blackmore, *Ernst Mach: His Life, Work, and Influence* (Berkeley: University of California Press, 1972). Denis Fisette, "Phenomenology and Phenomenalism: Ernst Mach and the Genesis of Husserl's Phenomenology," *Axiomathes* 22 (2012), 53–74. For more on Newton's reading of Einstein, see Chapter 9.
56 V. I. Lenin, *Materialism and Empirio-Criticism: Critical Comments on a Reactionary Philosophy, Collected Works*, Vol. 14, ed. Clemens Dutt, trans. Abraham Fineberg (Moscow: Progress Publishers, 1908), 138. See also Helena Sheehan, *Marxism and the Philosophy of Science: A Critical History* (Atlantic Highlands, NJ: Humanities Press, 1993).
57 Lenin wrote: "We have seen that Marx in 1845 and Engels in 1888 and 1892 placed the criterion of practice at the basis of the materialist theory of knowledge. 'The dispute over the reality or non-reality of thinking which is isolated from practice is a purely scholastic question,' says Marx in his second Thesis on Feuerbach. The best refutation of Kantian and Humean agnosticism as well as of other philosophical crotchets (Schrullen) is practice, repeats Engels. 'The success of our action proves the conformity (Uebereinstimmung) of our perceptions with the objective nature of the things perceived,' he says in reply to the agnostics" (*Materialism and Empirio-Criticism*, 138).
58 In the same series of lectures, Newton also critiqued British Communist Party member and philosopher Maurice Cornforth on similar grounds as he did Lenin. In his book *Science Versus Idealism: In Defence of Philosophy against Positivism and Pragmatism*, Cornforth rejected the "logical empiricism" of Rudolf Carnap and the "radical empiricism" of William James. Critiquing Cornforth, Newton explicitly credited philosophers Charles Peirce and William James for their impact on the scientific method through their introduction of "logics" to materialism (Newton, "A Primary Introduction to Phenomena," Series 1, Box 59, Folder 4, DHPNC, 10–11, 14. See also Newton, *All Too Young*, Series 1, Box 55, Folder 4, DHPNC, 101).
59 The cautious approach informing logical positivism and later logical empiricism should be distinguished from the social scientific tradition of positivism established by August Comte.
60 Newton, *Revolutionary Suicide*, 68.
61 Alfred Jules Ayer, *Language, Truth, and Logic* (New York: Dover Publications, 1952).
62 Newton, *All Too Young*, Series 1, Box 55, Folder 4, DHPNC, 94.

63 Newton, "Merritt Lecture Series 1–3: A Primary Introduction to Phenomena (Lecture 1)," Series 1, Box 59, Folder 4, DHPNC, 6.
64 Newton, *Revolutionary Suicide*, 173–80. Newton, *All Too Young*, Series 1, Box 55, Folders 4–5, DHPNC, 94–8.
65 Newton, *Revolutionary Suicide*, 173–4.
66 Ibid., 174, 129.
67 Newton, "On the Relevance of the Church: May 19, 1971," *The Huey P. Newton Reader*, 222.
68 Newton, *Revolutionary Suicide*, 166–7.
69 William James, *Essays in Radical Empiricism* (1912), ed. H. G. Callaway (Lanham: Lexington Books, 2022), 35.
70 Nietzsche, *Thus Spoke Zarathustra*, ed. Adrian Del Caro and Robert Pippin (Cambridge: Cambridge University Press, 2006), 161.
71 Huey P. Newton, "Let Us Hold High the Banner of Intercommunalism and the Invincible Thoughts of Huey P. Newton, Minister of Defense and Supreme Commander of the Black Panther Party," *The Black Panther*, January 23, 1971, *Marxists Internet Archive*, 22.
72 Newton, *Revolutionary Suicide*, 3.
73 Ibid., 68. "7/24/70," Series 1, Box 1, Folder 6, JHBEMP. "Interview with Melvin Newton, July 5, 1970," Series 1, Box 1, Folder 7, JHBEMP, 86–88.
74 "Interview, Sept 13, 1970," Series 1, Box 2, Folder 5, JHBEMP, 36–7.
75 Various documents, Series 1, Box 43, Folders 6–9, DHPNC.
76 Abu-Jamal, "The Genius of Huey P. Newton," *Prison Radio*. Judson Jeffries "Newton's View of People and the State," *Huey P. Newton: The Radical Theorist*, 42–52. Newton, "The Will to Power" (1972), Series 1, Box 48, Folders 17–18, DHPNC, 10. Huey P. Newton, "Thoughts on the Will to Power" (1978), Series 1, Box 40, Folder 2, DHPNC.
77 Newton, "Statement: May 1, 1971," *To Die for the People*, 23.
78 Huey P. Newton, "Black Capitalism Re-Analyzed by Huey P. Newton, Minister of Defense Black Panther Party, Servant of the People," *The Black Panther*, June 5, 1971, 13–14, *Alexander Street*. "5/15/71," Series 1, Box 4, Folder 20, JHBEMP.
79 Peniel E. Joseph, "The Black Power Movement: A State of the Field," *The Journal of American History* 96:3 (2009). For more definitions of Black Power from the period, see James H. Cone, *Black Theology and Black Power* (New York: The Seabury Press, 1969); James Boggs, "Black Power: A Scientific Concept Whose Time Has Come" (1970), *E-flux Journal* 79 (2017) (this text first appeared in *Racism or Class Struggle: Further Pages from a Black Worker's Notebook* in 1970). See also Patrick King, "Introduction to Boggs," *E-flux Journal* 79 (2017).
80 Newton, "Repression Breeds Resistance: January 16, 1970," *To Die for the People*. Newton, "On the Middle East: September 5, 1970," *To Die for the People*.
81 "Huey Newton Talks to the Movement," *The Black Panthers Speak*, ed. Foner, 61. "Interview, Sept 17, 1970, by Mark Lane," Series 1, Box 57, Folders 9–10, DHPNC, 79.
82 Jean Genet, who authored *The Thief's Journal* and the introduction to George Jackson's *Soledad Brother* (1970), smuggled BPP newspapers to the

activist community in France and to Foucault in particular (Jason Demers, "Prison Liberation by Association: Michel Foucault and the George Jackson Atlantic," *Atlantic Studies* 13:2 (2016). Robert Sandarg, "Jean Genet and the Black Panther Party," *Journal of Black Studies* 16:3 (1986). Stuart Elden, *Foucault: The Birth of Power* (Cambridge: Polity, 2017), 137). Foucault starts employing the concept of power extensively in 1969 and 1970, but does not put forth his own definition of the term until 1978. Foucault's definition remained vague, however; he described power as "an intrinsic part of all these relations and, in a circular way, . . . both their effect and cause" (Michel Foucault, "Lecture One," *Security, Territory, Population: Lectures at the Collège de France, 1977–1978*, trans. Graham Burchell (New York: Palgrave, 2007), 2). For evidence that Foucault drew many of his ideas from Newton and the Black Panther Party, see Brady Thomas Heiner, "Foucault and the Black Panthers," *City* 11, June 6, 2008; Delio Vásquez, "Illegalist Foucault, Criminal Foucault," *Theory and Event* 23:4 (2020), 935–72; Jason Demers, "Unmasking Currents: Thinking Power and War with Foucault and the Black Panthers," *Transatlantica* 2 (2022).

83 In "Utopia: Universal Energy" (1974), Newton emphasized that associating Nietzsche with "the Hitler-Nazi regime when we talk about the will to power" is "an incorrect view" (Newton, "Utopia: Universal Life Energy," Series 1, Box 39, Folder 1, DHPNC, 5).

84 Newton, "Speech at Boston College," *To Die for the People*, 35.

85 Newton and Erikson, *In Search of Common Ground*, 35, 41–2: "One of the greatest contributions of Freud was to make people aware that they are controlled much of their lives by their unconscious. He attempted to strip away the veil from the unconscious and make it conscious: that's the first step in feeling free, the first step in exerting control. It seems to be natural for people not to like being controlled. Marx made a similar contribution to human freedom, only he pointed out the external things that control people." Newton's fusion of Marx and Freud may come from his reading of Erich Fromm's *Beyond the Chains of Illusion* (1962), which he mentions reading in 1968 while imprisoned (Smithson, "A Visit with Huey Newton: Vacaville Prison Facility; October 17, 1968," Library of Congress).

86 Newton and Erikson, *In Search of Common Ground*, 34–5.

87 Ibid., 41–2.

88 In Newton's early essay "In Defense of Self-Defense" (1967) he stated that "The people must oppose everything the oppressor supports, and support everything that he opposes." However, he continued by clarifying that this simply means that one should not allow one's terms of resistance to be determined by others: "If Black people go about their struggle for liberation in the way that the oppressor dictates and sponsors, then we will have degenerated to the level of groveling flunkies for the oppressor himself." Newton's increasing focus on dialectical materialism over time reflected an emphasis on agency in determining one's mode of resistance (Newton, "In Defense of Self-Defense," *The Black Panther*, June 20, 1967, 3).

89 Newton and Erikson, *In Search of Common Ground*, 24–5.

90 Newton, *Revolutionary Suicide*, 277, 282.

91 Ibid., 291.

92 Ibid., 284.
93 As a concept or method, dialectical materialism was, strictly speaking, not Marx's innovation but rather derived from discussions and debates among early socialists contemporary with Marx who creatively employed the ideas of Hegel. Dialectical materialism was first theorized at length in Engels' *Dialectics of Nature* (1883), published after Marx's death.
94 Newton, "Speech at Boston College," *To Die for the People*, 31.
95 Ibid.
96 Newton and Erikson, *In Search of Common Ground*, 25.
97 Newton, *Revolutionary Suicide*, 329.
98 Robin D. G. Kelley and Betsy Esch, "Black Like Mao: Red China and Black Revolution," *Afro Asia: Revolutionary Political and Cultural Connections between African Americans and Asian Americans*, ed. Fred Ho and Bill V. Mullen (Durham, NC: Duke University Press, 2008), 126.
99 Newton, "The Method of Dialectical Materialism in Equation Form," Series 1, Box 47, Folder 3, DHPNC.
100 *The Murder of Fred Hampton*, dir. Howard Alk, prod. Mike Gray, Facets Multi-Media Chicago Film Group, 1971.
101 Newton, "Statement: May 1, 1971." *To Die for the People*, 56. I credit my former student Rosa Petterson for drawing my attention to the importance of this essay.
102 Ibid., 58.
103 For a comparison and analysis of some contemporary ideas about the Party relative to those of theorists of the late 1960s, see Marcelo Hoffman, "Sources of Anxiety About the Party in Radical Political Theory," *Theoria* 63:149 (2016), 18–36.
104 Newton and Erikson, *In Search of Common Ground*, 26.
105 Rodrigo Nunes, *Organisation of the Organisationless: Collective Action After Networks* (PML Books & Mute, 2014). "The Siege of the Third Precinct in Minneapolis: An Account and Analysis," *CrimethInc*, October 6, 2020. Alex Farrington, "Reorienting *The Production of Space*: Rhythmanalysis, Desire, and 'The Siege of the Third Precinct,'" *Politics and Space* 39:5 (2021), 938–54. Nicolas Jabko and Adam Sheingate, "Practices of Dynamic Order," *Perspectives on Politics* 16:2 (2018), 312–27.
106 Newton, "The Defection of Eldridge Cleaver from the Black Panther Party and the Defection of the Black Panther Party from the Black Community," *To Die for the People*, 47.
107 Ibid.
108 Newton and Erikson, *In Search of Common Ground*, 27. Newton called this historical materialism.
109 Newton, *Revolutionary Suicide*, 359.
110 Newton and Erikson, *In Search of Common Ground*, 103.
111 "Herman Blake: March 21, 1969," Series 1, Box 1, Folder 5, JHBEMP, 9–10.
112 Newton, "The Defection," *To Die for the People*, 49.
113 "How Does It Go with the Black Movement?" January 23, 1973, Firing Line Broadcast Records, Hoover Institution Library & Archives, Stanford, CA,

https://digitalcollections.hoover.org/objects/6257/how-does-it-go-with-the-black-movement.

114 Newton, "The Defection," *To Die for the People*, 49.

5 The Structured Vehicle and the Revolutionary Defense of Community

1 Newton, *All Too Young*, Series 1, Box 55, Folder 5, DHPNC, 305. Used with permission by Dr. Huey P. Newton Foundation.

2 Newton, "The Defection," *To Die for the People*, 50.

3 "Interview, Sept 17, 1970, by Mark Lane," Series 1, Box 57, Folders 9–10, DHPNC, 85.

4 Newton, "Statement: May 1, 1971," *The Huey P. Newton Reader*, 210. Emphasis added.

5 "Mark Lane interview, Tape 10," Series 1, Box 57, Folders 9–10, DHPNC, 1.

6 Jalil Muntaqim, *We Are Our Own Liberators: Selected Prison Writings* (Portland: Arissa Media Group, 2010).

7 Fanon, *Wretched*, trans. Farrington, 130.

8 Ibid., 129–30.

9 Ibid., 137.

10 Ibid.

11 María José Méndez, "The Violence Work of Transnational Gangs in Central America," *Third World Quarterly* 40 (2018), 373–88. Kyle Edwards, "Violence Work: Central America's Illicit Economies," October 25, 2019, Political Science, College of Liberal Arts, University of Minnesota.

12 Seale, *Seize the Time*, 30.

13 Bunchy Carter, as paraphrased in Brown, *A Taste of Power*, 145.

14 Fanon, *Wretched*, trans. Farrington, 35; Fanon, *Les damnés*, 39. Emphasis added.

15 "Decolonization, which sets out to change the order of the world, is, obviously, a program of complete disorder" (Fanon, *Wretched*, trans. Farrington, 36).

16 If this interpretation is rare, it is in part an effect of mistranslation. Take, for instance, the first sentence of chapter 1 of *Les damnés de la terre*: "Commonwealth, quelles que soient les rubriques utilisées ou les formules nouvelles introduites, la décolonisation est toujours un phénomène violent." Farrington's 1963 translation renders the end of the sentence with the phrase "decolonization is always a violent phenomenon," whereas Philcox's 2004 translation renders this as "decolonization is always a violent event." There are in fact thirty uses of the word "phenomenon/a" in *Les Damnés*; a majority (twenty) are properly translated in the original Farrington translation, but the word only appears about eleven times in the Philcox. Concerningly, there are other words that disappear altogether from the Philcox translation, such as the reference to Blackness in "the village of the colonized, . . . the village of the native, the Negro village, the medina, the reservation." Contrast Fanon, *Wretched*, trans. Farrington, 39 and Fanon, *Les damnés*, 42 against Fanon, *Wretched*, trans. Philcox, 4.

17 George Jackson, *Soledad Brother* (New York: Lawrence Hill Books, 1994), 16.

18 *Look For Me in the Whirlwind: The Collective Autobiography of the New York 21* (New York: Random House, 1971), 171.
19 Ibid., 290.
20 Newton, *Revolutionary Suicide*, 81.
21 Ibid., 78.
22 Ibid., 134–5.
23 Brown, *A Taste of Power*, 328.
24 Angela Y. Davis, "Political Prisoners, Prisons and Black Liberation" (1971), *If They Come in the Morning. . .: Voices of Resistance* (London: Verso, 2016), 27.
25 Ibid., 35.
26 Ibid., 36.
27 Ibid., 32.
28 Malcolm X, "Speech to Peace Corps Workers (December 12, 1964)," *Malcolm XFiles.com*.
29 Malcolm X, "Message to the Grass Roots," *Malcolm X Speaks* (New York: Pathfinder Press, 1965). Malcolm X, "Message to the Grassroots" (November 10, 1963), *YouTube*, uploaded by Onchocerciasis, May 15, 2020. While Malcolm X's speeches were available on vinyl, Newton stated that he accessed them mostly through the Socialist Workers Party newspaper *The Militant* and Bobby Seale's collection of copies of the Nation of Islam's newspaper *Muhammed Speaks* ("Interview, Sept 15, 1970," Series 1, Box 2, Folder 7, JHBEMP, 23).
30 Malcolm X, "Message to the Grass Roots," *Malcolm X Speaks*.
31 Newton, "Speech at Boston College," *To Die for the People*, 22.
32 "Huey P. Newton interview," prod. Grenada TV, PM 065, Huey Newton Collection, FA.
33 Newton, *Revolutionary Suicide*, 117.
34 Robert F. Williams, *Negroes with Guns* (1962) (Chicago: Third World Press, 1973).
35 Newton, *Revolutionary Suicide*, 117–18.
36 "Interview, Sept 13, 1970," Series 1, Box 2, Folder 5, JHBEMP, 68.
37 Newton, *Revolutionary Suicide*, 119. Trivers, *Wild Life*, 155.
38 Joy James, "The Womb of Western Theory: Trauma, Time Theft, and the Captive Maternal," *Carceral Notebooks* 12 (2016), ed. Bernard E. Harcourt, 255.
39 Joy James, "The Captive Maternal is a Function, Not an Identity Marker," *Scalawag Magazine*, April 28, 2023.
40 Ibid.
41 Newton and Erikson, *In Search of Common Ground*, 62.
42 "Interview, Sept 17, 1970, by Mark Lane," Series 1, Box 57, Folders 9–10, DHPNC, 123.
43 Huey Newton and Ericka Huggins, *Insights & Poems* (San Francisco: City Lights, 1975), 19.
44 Newton and Erikson, *In Search Of Common Ground*, 68.
45 Bukhari, "This is Worth Fighting For," *The War Before*, 94.
46 Newton, "Speech at Boston College," *To Die for the People*, 20–1.
47 Fanon, *Wretched*, trans. Farrington, 308. Fanon, *Les damnés*, 296. Translation edited.

48 Newton, "The Will to Power," Series 1, Box 48, Folders 17–18, DHPNC. "Eyes on the Prize II; Interview with Huey P. Newton," Library of Congress.
49 Robyn Spencer, "Communalism and the Black Panther Party in Oakland, California," *West of Eden: Communes and Utopia in Northern California*, ed. Iaian Boal (Oakland: PM Press, 2012), 92–121.
50 Jackson, *Blood in My Eye*, 82.
51 Phone conversation with Phyllis Jackson, January 15, 2025. Pharr, *Nine Lives of a Black Panther*, 205. Phone interview with Emory Douglas, June 26, 2025.
52 "Liberated Zones," *Community Movement Builders*, 2023. "Our Projects," *Solidarity Research Center*, 2024. *Cooperation Jackson*, 2024.
53 Newton, *Revolutionary Suicide*, 177–8.
54 Fearnley, "The Black Panther Party's Publishing Strategies and the Financial Underpinnings of Activism." Brown, *A Taste of Power*, 244, 362–5, 393. Spencer, *The Revolution Has Come*.
55 Brown, *A Taste of Power*, 244.
56 Newton and Erikson, *In Search of Common Ground*, 30.
57 Newton, "The Technology Question: 1972," *The Huey P. Newton Reader*, 260.
58 Fanon, *Wretched*, trans. Farrington, 50. Fanon, *Les damnés*, 52. Translation edited.
59 Jackson, *Blood in My Eye*, 113.
60 Newton, "Vanguard of the People's Struggle," *Off the Pigs*, 219–20.
61 "Mark Lane interview, Tape 11," Series 1, Box 57, Folders 9–10, DHPNC, 4.
62 Newton, "Statement: May 1, 1971," *To Die for the People*, 54.
63 Michel Foucault, Catherine von Bülow, and Daniel Defert, "The Masked Assassination," trans. Sirène Harb, *Warfare in the American Homeland*, ed. Joy James (Durham, NC: Duke University Press, 2007), 154–5. Newton, *Revolutionary Suicide*, 355–6. Group d'Information sur les prisons, "The Assassination Coverup, after the Assassination, and Jackson's Place in the Prison Movement," *Intolerable: Writings from Michel Foucault and the Prisons Information Group (1970–1980)*, ed. Kevin Thompson and Perry Zurn, trans. Perry Zurn and Erik Beranek (Minneapolis: University of Minnesota Press, 2021), 155–6. I have combined text from both translations here.
64 Azadeh Zohrabi, "Resistance and Repression: The Black Guerrilla Family in Context," *Hastings Race and Poverty Law* 9:1 (2012), 167–90. Hilliard and Cole, *This Side of Glory*, 379 (description by Kumasi, co-founder of Black August Prison Movement).
65 "Huey Newton interview," prod. Grenada TV, PM 092, Huey Newton Collection, FA. Phone interview with Emory Douglas, June 26, 2025.
66 Untitled letter dated "Sunday 28/71," Series 1, Box 54, Folder 10, DHPNC. See also letter dated "2/21/71," Series 1, Box 48, Folder 17, DHPNC.
67 Jackson, *Blood in My Eye*, 41.
68 Angela Y. Davis, Gina Dent, Erica R. Meiners, and Beth E. Richie, *Abolition. Feminism. Now.* (Chicago: Haymarket Books, 2022). Mariame Kaba, *We Do This Til We Free Us* (Chicago: Haymarket Books, 2021).
69 Angela Y. Davis, *Abolition: Politics, Practices, Promises*, Vol. 1 (Chicago: Haymarket Books, 2024), xii.
70 Jackson, *Blood in My Eye*, 42.

71 Ibid., 24–5.
72 Ibid., 42.
73 Ibid., 81.
74 Art Goldberg, "Conversations: The Panthers After the Trial," *Ramparts Magazine*, March 1972, 26.
75 Newton, "The Defection," *To Die for the People*, 52.
76 Newton, *All Too Young*, Series 1, Box 55, Folder 3, DHPNC, 17. "Interview, Sept 13, 1970," Series 1, Box 2, Folder 7, JHBEMP, 5.
77 Newton, "The Defection," *To Die for the People*, 49.
78 Garrett Epps, "Huey Newton Speaks at Boston College, Presents Theory of 'Intercommunalism,'" *The Harvard Crimson*, November 19, 1970. For more on cooperation and cooperatives, see Bernard Harcourt, *Cooperation: A Political, Economic, and Social Theory* (New York: Columbia University Press, 2023).
79 Newton, "Vanguard of the People's Struggle," *Off the Pigs*, 220, 229. "Interview, Sept 15, 1970," Series 1, Box 2, Folder 7, JHBEMP, 14. See also "Huey Newton: Proportional Representation in a Socialist Framework, 8/12/70," Series 1, Box 1, Folder 10, JHBEMP.
80 Jackson, *Blood in My Eye*, 122–3.
81 Lorenzo Kom'boa Ervin, *Anarchism and the Black Revolution* (London: Pluto Press, 2021). See also William C. Anderson, *The Nation on No Map: Black Anarchism and Abolition* (Edinburgh: AK Press, 2021). Zoe Samudzi and William C. Anderson, *As Black as Resistance: Finding the Conditions for Resistance* (Chico, CA: AK Press, 2018).
82 Angela Y. Davis, *Are Prisons Obsolete?* (New York: Seven Stories Press, 2003).
83 Newton, "On the Relevance of the Church," *To Die for the* People, 71.
84 Newton, "Correct Handling of a Revolution," *The Black Panther*, July 20, 1967. "Huey Newton Talks to the Movement," *The Black Panthers Speak*, ed. Foner.
85 Bloom and Martin, *Black Against Empire*. Leslie Feinberg, "Lavender and Red Pt. 75: Early Left-Wing liberation: 'Unity with all the oppressed,'" *Workers World*. Emily K. Hobson, *Lavender and Red: Liberation and Solidarity in the Gay and Lesbian Left* (Oakland: University of California Press, 2016), 32.
86 Brown, *A Taste of Power*, 124.
87 Newton, "The Defection," *To Die for the People*, 47–8.
88 Fanon, *Wretched*, trans. Farrington, 129.
89 Newton and Erikson, *In Search of Common Ground*, 37–8.
90 Newton, "The Correct Handling of a Revolution," *The Black Panther*, July 20, 1967.
91 "Kathleen Cleaver speaking at UCLA 10/22/1971," *YouTube*, uploaded by UCLA Irv and Xiaoyan Drasnin Communication Archive, April 15, 2014.
92 "On the Contradictions within the Black Panther Party [CD]," March 5, 1971, prod. Bruce Soloway, Black Panther Party general collection, CD 985, FA. Hilliard and Cole, *This Side of Glory*. Bloom, *Black Against Empire*, 355 (citing Martin Kenner).
93 Fearnley, "The Black Panther Party's Publishing Strategies and the Financial Underpinnings of Activism." Spencer, *Revolution Has Come*. Hilliard, Zimmerman, and Zimmerman, *Huey*.

94 "On the Contradictions within the Black Panther Party [CD]," March 5, 1971, prod. Bruce Soloway, Black Panther Party general collection, CD 985, FA.

95 Don Cox, "An Insider's Take on How the Black Panther Party was Hurt by its Own Ideals," *Time*, February 13, 2019.

96 Hilliard and Cole, *This Side of Glory*, 261.

97 *Right On!* April 13, 1971, 10–11. Bloom and Martin, *Black Against Empire*, 345. Hilliard and Cole, *This Side of Glory*.

98 Ahmad, *We Will Return*, 210. Some members of East coast chapters of the Party believed that Newton's shift away from insurrectionary violence might have been an effect of these mind-altering procedures, but, as argued in Chapter 2, Newton had taken a stand against offensive armed actions against police already in early 1968, while he was still jailed in Alameda County, and before he was taken to Vacaville, a primary site of these experiments.

99 Newton, *War Against the Panthers*, 65.

100 "CIA Dirty Tricks Against the BPP," *The Black Panther*, January 11, 1975, 6–9, *Alexander Street*. Abu-Jamal, *We Want Freedom*, 212.

101 Churchill and Vander Wall, *The COINTELPRO Papers*, 148.

102 After George Jackson's death, some his supporters came to be critical of Newton and blamed him for Jackson's death as well (Forbes, *Will You Die With Me?*, 252; Ahmad, *We Will Return*, 209). However, Newton's personal papers include his own *extensive* writings on and investigations into the causes of Jackson's assassination. Some of this material appears in alternative versions of Newton's *War Against the Panthers*, as well as in various stand-alone book drafts titled *War Without Terms: The Death of George Jackson* held in archive at Stanford University (DHPNC).

103 Churchill and Vander Wall, *Agents of Repression*, 96. Ahmad, *We Will Return*, 203. Pharr, *Nine Lives of a Black Panther*, 227. In an interview afterwards, a sorrowful Newton defended the spirit behind Jonathan's action, calling it "a pure political act" reflective of the popular will to "pick up the gun," and comparing it to urban guerrilla struggle in Brazil ("Huey Newton Interview," August 30, 1970, CE 055, prod. Colin Edwards, Colin Edwards Collection, FA).

104 "Special Agent Wesley Swearingen," *What We Want, What We Believe: The Black Panther Party Library*, Roz Payne Archives and Newsreel Films, AK Press Video, 2006.

105 Huey P. Newton, "On the Purge of Geronimo from the Black Panther Party," *The Black Panther*, January 23, 1971, 7, *Marxists Internet Archive*. Holder, "The History of the Black Panther Party, 1966–1971," 59. Bloom and Martin, *Black Against Empire*, 360. Hilliard and Cole, *This Side of Glory*. Churchill, "To Disrupt, Discredit and Destroy," *Liberation, Imagination, and the Black Panther Party*.

106 Akinyele Umoja, "Repression Breeds Resistance: The Black Liberation Army and the Radical Legacy of the Black Panther Party," *New Political Science* 21:2 (1999), 137, 139. Ollie A. Johnson III, "Explaining the Demise of the Black Panther Party," *Black Panther Party Reconsidered*, 414 n68.

107 "1971: Open Letter to the Weather Underground by the New York Panther 21," *Breakthrough*, 59–65.

108 The open letter includes advocacy of guerrilla actions undertaken by "twos and threes," a direct reference to and citation of Newton's language in "Correct Handling of a Revolution."

109 Bloom and Martin, *Black Against Empire*, 360–1. Robyn C. Spencer, "Conny Matthews," *The Black Panther*, Special Commemorative Issue: 5, "It's About Time Black Panther Party," October 16, 2011. According to Newton in the unpublished *These Graves Are All Too Young*: "The New York 21 had written an open letter to the Weathermen saying that they felt the leadership of the Party had lost its revolutionary fervor and that they saw the Weathermen as the vanguard of the revolution. That was alright with us if they wanted to take that position but the Central Committee took the position that the New York 21 had resigned from the Party with that statement and the expulsion was simply a Party recognition of that fact" (Newton, *All Too Young*, Series 1, Box 55, Folder 5, DHPNC, 260).

110 "On the Contradictions within the Black Panther Party [CD]," March 5, 1971, prod. Bruce Soloway, Black Panther Party general collection, CD 985, FA. In Elaine Mokhtefi's autobiographical *Algiers, Third World Capital* (London: Verso, 2018), she states that, while Newton was in a manic state brought on by cocaine usage, he forcibly detained Matthews (121), a claim echoed by others (phone conversation with Orisanmi Burton, November 25, 2025). Mokhtefi also claims that Newton attempted to sexually coerce Panther and Young Lords member Denise Oliver, a claim I have not encountered affirmed elsewhere. Mokhtefi's account of events in New Haven and New York contains several clear errors that put the veracity of her narrative about Newton, with whom she had no contact, into question. That said, it is clear that at times while in New Haven and New York in particular, Newton was extremely paranoid, intoxicated, and acted impulsively. Regarding allegations of his enacting sexual violence, see Chapter 8. In Newton's account of events in New Haven and New York, he stated that he believed Matthews had been sent by Cleaver to disrupt Party operations. See Newton, *These Graves Are All Too Young*, Series 1, Box 55, Folder 5, DHPNC, 256–62.

111 Bloom and Martin, *Black Against Empire*, 362.

112 Cox, *Just Another Nigger*, 178–9. "On the Contradictions within the Black Panther Party," *Right On!* April 13, 1971, 9.

113 Newton, *All Too Young*, Series 1, Box 55, Folder 5, DHPNC, 263. The planned series was more extensive than what was ultimately published.

114 Ibid., 262.

115 Newton, *War Against the Panthers*, 67. Shakur, *Assata*, 231–2.

116 Bukhari, "This is Worth Fighting For," *The War Before*, 92.

117 Ibid.

118 Holder, "The History of the Black Panther Party, 1966–1971," 60. Bloom and Martin, *Black Against Empire*, 363–4. Panther Naima Major later recalled an order to attack against any "SF [San Francisco] Panthers and left adventurists" (Abu-Jamal, *We Want Freedom*, 181).

119 Muntaqim, *We Are Our Own Liberators*, 27–40. Umoja, "Repression Breeds Resistance," 144.

120 Umoja, "Repression Breeds Resistance." Kuwasi Balagoon, *A Soldier's Story: Writings by a Revolutionary New Afrikan Anarchist* (Montreal: Kersplebeded, 2003).
121 Holder, "The History of the Black Panther Party, 1966–1971," 45, 50–1.
122 Umoja, "Repression Breeds Resistance," 144. *Collected Works of the Black Liberation Army, Vol. 1* (Rookery Press, 2003).
123 Umoja, "Repression Breeds Resistance," 132.
124 Muntaqim, *We Are Our Own Liberators*, 35.
125 Flores, *Will You Die with Me?*, 56. Pharr, *Nine Lives of a Black Panther*, 234, 237, 259.
126 "Special Agent Wesley Swearingen," *What We Want, What We Believe: The Black Panther Party Library*, Roz Payne Archives and Newsreel Films, AK Press Video, 2006.
127 Flores, *Will You Die with Me?*, 57. Some formerly purged California panthers rejoined the movement as part of the Cleaver faction on the West coast (Brent, *Long Time Gone*, 128–9).
128 Umoja, "Repression Breeds Resistance," 146. Muntaqim, *We Are Our Own Liberators*, 28, 35–6. In *These Graves Are All Too Young*, Newton states, "We understand that the final transformation may require underground action but it will develop very slowly, it will be very tight knit, and it will always need an open front. Any underground action needs above-the-ground action to feed it" (Newton, *All Too Young*, Series 1, Box 55, Folder 5, DHPNC, 296).
129 *Collected Works of the Black Liberation Army, Vol. 1.*
130 Williams and Lazerow, *Liberated Territory: Untold Perspectives of the Black Panther Party*. Jeffries, ed., *Comrades*. Jeffries, ed., *On the Ground*. Jeffries, ed., *The Black Panther Party in a City Near You*.
131 Newton, "Repression Breeds Resistance: January 16, 1970," *To Die for the People*.
132 Adding to the confusion during the era was the misdating of this text by the editors of the 1972 collection of Newton's writings *To Die for the People* as if it had been written in 1970 rather than in 1971. See "Repression Breeds Resistance: Huey Newton Talks to *Sechaba*," *The Black Panther*, January 16, 1971, *Alexander Street*. Newton, "Repression Breeds Resistance: January 16, 1970," *To Die for the People*.
133 Newton, "To the National Liberation Front of South Vietnam: August 29, 1970," *To Die for the People*.
134 Interviews with Flores Forbes, Fall 2023. "Huey P. Newton on the Eve of his Release (1970)," Digital Information Virtual Archive, San Francisco State University, 2009–2024.
135 "Huey Newton Speaks, July 4, 1970, by Mark Lane," Series 1, Box 57, Folder 7, DHPNC, 5.
136 Letter, Series 1, Box 47, Folder 24, DHPNC. Newton, "Letter From Nguyen Thi Dinh: October 31, 1970," *To Die for the People*.
137 "Intercommunal Day of Solidarity" (1971), *YouTube*, uploaded by AfroMarxist, February 12, 2022.
138 Forbes, *Will You Die With Me?*, 73.
139 Newton, "Speech at Boston College," *To Die for the People*, 21.
140 "Interview, Sept 15, 1970," Series 1, Box 2, Folder 7, JHBEMP, 36.

141 "Eyes on the Prize II; Interview with Huey P. Newton," Library of Congress. In a televised interview in 1988, Newton also lauded the Detroit-based Republic of New Afrika: *People Are Talking*, KPIX-TV, January 15, 1988, Bay Area Television Archive, *YouTube*, uploaded by Reelblack One, June 2, 2020.

142 Delio Vásquez, "Intercommunalism: The Late Theorizations of Huey P. Newton, 'Chief Theoretician' of the Black Panther Party," *Viewpoint Magazine*, June 11, 2018.

143 "Eyes on the Prize II; Interview with Bobby Seale," Library of Congress. Curtis Austin, *Violence in the Making and Unmaking of the Black Panther Party* (Fayetteville: University of Arkansas Press, 2006), 300.

6 The Question of the Most Oppressed

1 George L. Jackson, *Blood in My Eye* (Baltimore: Black Classic Press, 1990). Used with permission.

2 Fanon, *Wretched*, trans. Farrington, 129.

3 Ibid., 48. Translation modified.

4 David Marriott, "On Revolutionary Suicide," *Diacritics* 49:4 (2021), 101–33. Abu-Jamal, "The Genius of Huey P. Newton," *Prison Radio*.

5 Alan Garrigan, "Political Challenges in a Selected Section of 'Insights and Poems' (1975) by Huey Newton and Ericka Huggins," *Literary Heist*, June 20, 2022.

6 Newton and Huggins, *Insights & Poems*, 21.

7 Joshua Hall, "Newton Contra Alt-Right Nietzsche: Dionysus as Androgynous Black Panther," *The Pluralist* 15:2 (2020), 110–28. See also Howard Caygill, "Philosophy and the Black Panthers," *Radical Philosophy* 179 (2013), 7–13.

8 Newton, *Revolutionary Suicide*, 5.

9 Ibid., 3.

10 Newton, "Speech at Boston College," *To Die for the People*, 22.

11 Newton, *All Too Young*, Series 1, Box 55, Folder 3, DHPNC, 25.

12 Wilderson identifies some of the symptoms: "The fluorescent lights pierced my eyes like daggers of ice" (Frank B. Wilderson III, *Afropessimism* (New York: Liveright Publishing Company, 2021), 5). And he offers a brief analysis: "A psychotic episode is no picnic . . .; it cannot be called madness because madness assumes a change in the weather" (Frank B. Wilderson, "Afropessimism and the Ruse of Analogy," *Antiblackness*, ed. Moon-Kie Jung and João H. Costa Vargas (Durham, NC: Duke University Press, 2021), 37).

13 Pickens, *Black Madness :: Mad Blackness*.

14 Hortense Spillers and Lewis Gordon, "Afro-Pessimism and its Others," May 24, 2021, *YouTube*, uploaded by Soka University of America. Emphasis added.

15 Fanon, *Black Skin, White Masks*, trans. Philcox, 89.

16 Newton, "The Defection," *To Die for the People*, 47, 49.

17 Brown, *A Taste of Power*, 253.

18 Paolo Freire, *Pedagogy of the Oppressed* (New York: Herder and Herder, 1970).

19 Newton and Erikson, *In Search of Common Ground*, 37–8.

20 Newton, "Prison, Where is Thy Victory?" *The Black Panther*, January 3, 1970, 13.

21 Newton and Erikson, *In Search of Common Ground*, 135–6.
22 "Eyes on the Prize II; Interview with Angela Y. Davis," May 24, 1989, Film and Media Archive, Washington University in St. Louis, American Archive of Public Broadcasting (GBH and the Library of Congress), http://americanarchive.org/catalog/cpb-aacip-5ebb23748d8.
23 "Kathleen Cleaver speaking at UCLA 10/22/1971," *YouTube*.
24 Jo Durden-Smith, *Who Killed George Jackson?* (New York: Alfred A. Knopf, Inc., 1976), xv.
25 Ibid. Dan Berger, *Captive Nation: Black Prison Organizing in the Civil Rights Era* (Chapel Hill: University of North Carolina Press, 2014).
26 Brown, *A Taste of Power*, 270, 294. Newton, *Revolutionary Suicide*, 336, 331.
27 Newton, *Revolutionary Suicide*, 335.
28 "Civil Rights History Project: Ericka C. Huggins," Smithsonian Museum of History, Library of Congress, June 30, 2016, *YouTube*, February 21, 2020.
29 Newton, "To the Republic of New Afrika: September 13, 1969," *To Die for the People*, 94–5.
30 Newton, "Executive Mandate No. 1," *The Black Panther*, May 15, 1967.
31 Newton, *War Against the Panthers*, 23.
32 "August 17, 1974?," Series 1, Box 47, Folder 13, DHPNC, 6. See also Hilliard, Zimmerman, and Zimmerman, *Huey*, 221.
33 Sami Schalk, "Misfitting: Disability Broadly Considered" (April 6, 2019), *YouTube*, uploaded by Iowa City Public Library, April 24, 2019.
34 "The 504 Protests and the Black Panther Party," December 19, 2021, *Disability Social History Project*.
35 Sami Schalk, *Black Disability Politics* (Durham, NC: Duke University Press, 2022), 29.
36 Ibid.
37 Judith Heumann and Kristen Joiner, *Rolling Warrior* (Boston: Beacon Press, 2021).
38 Newton, *All Too Young*, Series 1, Box 55, Folder 5, DHPNC, 246.
39 The term *homophobia* first appears in print in 1969 and in scholarship in 1971. George Weinberg, "Behavior: The Homosexual: Newly Visible, Newly Understood," *Time*, October 31, 1969. Vern L. Bullough, "Homophobia," *glbtq: An encyclopedia of gay, lesbian, bisexual, transgender, and queer culture*, 2015.
40 Huey P. Newton, "The Women's Liberation and Gay Liberation Movements: August 15, 1970," *To Die for the People*, 157–8.
41 Newton, "Vanguard of the People's Struggle," *Off the Pigs*, 226. "Huey Newton Interview" (August 14, 1970), *YouTube*, uploaded by AfroMarxist, June 2, 2018.
42 Newton, "Vanguard of the People's Struggle," *Off the Pigs*, 226. "Huey Newton Interview" (August 14, 1970), *YouTube*, uploaded by AfroMarxist, June 2, 2018. Newton, "The Women's Liberation and Gay Liberation Movements," *To Die for the People*, 157.
43 Samuel Galen Ng, "Trans Power! Sylvia Lee Rivera's STAR and the Black Panther Party," *Left History* 17:1 (2013), 11–41.
44 Ibid. Lisa Corrigan, "Queering the Panthers: Rhetorical Adjacency and Black/Queer Liberation Politics," *QED: A Journal in GLBTQ Worldmaking* 6:2 (2019), 1–25.

45 Corrigan, "Queering the Panthers," 11.

46 Newton, "The Women's Liberation and Gay Liberation Movements," 157. Feinberg, "Lavender and Red Pt. 75: Early Left-Wing Liberation," *Workers World*.

47 Newton, *Revolutionary Suicide*, 96.

48 Hobson, *Lavender and Red*, 32.

49 In her autobiography, Angela Davis makes the same observation. Angela Davis, *With My Mind on Freedom: An Autobiography* (New York: Bantam Books, 1974), 56.

50 Newton, *Revolutionary Suicide*, 273.

51 Ibid., 271.

52 Blake, "Caged Panther," 240–1.

53 Newton, *Revolutionary Suicide*, 271–2.

54 Ronald K. Porter, "A Rainbow in Black: The Gay Politics of the Black Panther Party," *Counterpoints* 367 (2012), 373 n2.

55 Ray Lewis White, "Eldridge Cleaver's *Soul on Ice*: A Book Review Digest," *CLA Journal* 21:4 (1978), 556–66.

56 Eldridge Cleaver, *Soul on Ice* (New York: Dell Publishing Co., 1968).

57 Fearnley, "The Black Panther Party's Publishing Strategies and the Financial Underpinnings of Activism, 1968–1976."

58 Various documents, Series 1, Box 43, DHPNC. Various documents, Series 1, Box 48, Folders 15–17, DHPNC. Various documents, Series 1, Box 50, DHPNC. Various documents, Series 1, Box 55, Folder 9, DHPNC. Newton, "Eldridge Cleaver: He is No James Baldwin," *The Huey P. Newton Reader*.

59 Newton, "Eldridge Cleaver: He is No James Baldwin," *The Huey P. Newton Reader*, 287–8.

60 Ibid., 288. In an early draft of this chapter, Newton cites Freud at length: "Freud's theory of a homosexual wish fantasy at the root of paranoia was not only a stroke of psychological genius but a linguistic discovery as well. The formulation of the paranoid system was as follows: A) 'I (a man) love him.' This painful homosexual proposition is contradicted by a series of defenses. 1) Delusions of persecution: 'I do not *love* him – I *hate* him': This reformulation still does not satisfy the demand of the ego (the I) that it be treated as an object, or in this case a passive victim. 2) Thus, 'I hate him' because 'He *hates* (persecutes *me*), thus justifying my hatred of him.' B) In summary the result is 'I do not *love* him – I *hate* him, because he persecutes me!' It is necessary to look at this prime tactic of projection first practically and then psycho-sexually. While forbidden feelings of love are translated into variations of hate, at the same time another major defense is at work: 'I do not love *him* – I love *her* because she loves me!' In the anecdotes to follow it can be seen that Cleaver vacilated [*sic*] between these mechanisms of denial of homosexual panic and pseudo-sexuality directed not at women so much as the *idea* of women, and white or forbidden, hateful women at that. Cleaver's gyroscopic poetic-critical imagination swings between these vicissitudes of self love and homosexual love" (Newton, "Hidden Traitor Renegade Scab: Eldridge Cleaver" (1972), Series 1, Box 50, Folder 3, DHPNC, 2–3).

61 Newton, "Eldridge Cleaver: He is No James Baldwin," *The Huey P. Newton Reader*, 289.

62 Tommy Curry, *The Man-Not: Race, Class, Genre, and the Dilemmas of Black Manhood* (Philadelphia: Temple University Press, 2017), 73–86.

63 Despite his claims of remorse in *Soul on Ice*, after his release from prison Cleaver continued to rape. While in the Party, he attempted to hide his activities, until a local Black mother complained to the Party about his rape of her fourteen-year-old daughter, after which Cleaver retorted, "I only wish that she had been 12 years old." He also advocated the creation of an academy, "like the one in Plato's Republic," in which he could train young boys at ages as young as six in how to have sex. While in Algiers, he also allegedly beat his pregnant wife, Kathleen Cleaver, planned to abandon her in Korea, and engaged in a relationship with a local teenager (Malika) whom he referred to as his "last love" (Hilliard, Zimmerman, and Zimmerman, *Huey*, 154–6. "I Louise Wibecan am making this report . . .," "Chairman Bobby on the Hidden Traitor . . . May 7, 1972," Series 1, Box 48, Folders 17–18, DHPNC; "VI. Hidden Traitor," Series 1, Box 47, Folder 11, DHPNC, 41–9, 56–7; "Hidden Traitor," Series 1, Box 48, Folders 16–17, DHPNC; Series 1, Box 50, Folder 3, DHPNC; Elaine Mokhtefi, *Algiers, Third World Capital* (London: Verso, 2018)). During the peak of the split in the Party, in a 1971 response to claims that she was abused by Eldridge, Kathleen Cleaver did not deny the claims, but criticized them as "scandalous" and "personal" ("On the Contradictions within the Black Panther Party [CD]," March 5, 1971, prod. Bruce Soloway, CD 985, Black Panther Party general collection, FA).

64 Mary Phillips, Robyn C. Spencer, Angela D. LeBlanc-Ernest, and Tracye A. Matthews, "Ode to Our Feminist Foremothers: The Intersectional Black Panther Party History Project on Collaborative Praxis and Fifty Years of Panther History," *Souls* 19:3 (2017), 241–60, 248.

65 "Panther Sisters on Women's Liberation," *The Movement* 5:8 (The Movement Press, September 1969), FA, 8–9.

66 "Sisters," *The Black Panther*, September 13, 1969, 12–13, *Alexander Street.*

67 "Panther Sisters on Women's Liberation," *The Movement*, 8.

68 Ibid.

69 Ibid. During a speech in July earlier that year at the United Front Against Fascism Conference, Roberta Alexander made almost exactly the same statement: "Black women, interestingly enough, are oppressed as a class, part of the super-oppressed class of workers and unemployed in this country. Black women are oppressed because they are black, and then on top of that, black women are oppressed by black men. And that's got to go. Not only has it got to go, but it is going" (Bloom and Martin, *Black Against Empire*, 303–4). She is also referred to by name by another respondent in the interview.

70 "Panther Sisters on Women's Liberation," *The Movement*, 8.

71 Angela Davis, "Reflections on the Black Woman's Role in the Community of Slaves," *The Black Scholar*, December 1971, 6.

72 James Baldwin, "An Open Letter to My Sister, Angela Davis," *If They Come in the Morning*, 20.

73 Davis, "Reflections," 12.

74 Ibid., 11.

75 According to Newton, "Indeed, two loyal and worthy comrades were driven out of the party because they refused to submit to his sexual fascism. They

were UCLA Philosophy professor Angela Davis and Julia Wright, the daughter of the late Richard Wright. In our attack we concentrated on his behavior in Algiers and his brutal treatment of Kathleen" (Newton, *All Too Young*, Series 1, Box 55, Folder 5, DHPNC, 263).

76 The Combahee River Collective, "A Black Feminist Statement" (1977), *The Second Wave: A Reader in Feminist Theory*, ed. Linda Nicholson (New York: Routledge, 1997), 67.

77 Newton and Erikson, *In Search Of Common Ground*, 37–8.

78 The Combahee River Collective, "A Black Feminist Statement," 67.

79 Ibid., 65.

80 Ibid., 70.

81 Ibid., 64. Emphasis added.

82 Jackson, *Blood in My Eye*, 113.

83 Newton, "The Defection," *To Die for the People*, 51. Spencer, *The Revolution Has Come*, 198.

84 Cleaver, *Soul on Ice*, 14.

85 Newton, "Hidden Traitor Renegade Scab: Eldridge Cleaver" (1972), Series 1, Box 50, Folder 3, DHPNC, 4.

86 Corrigan, "Queering the Panthers," 13. See also Bloom and Martin, *Black Against Empire*, 95.

87 Newton, "Fear and Doubt," *To Die for the People*, 79.

88 Ibid., 78–9.

89 Conversation with Joe Blum, San Francisco, October 2023.

90 "Huey Newton Talks to the Movement," *The Black Panthers Speak*, ed. Foner, 50–66.

91 Ibid., 58. "4/10/70," Series 1, Box 1, Folder 6, JHBEMP.

92 "Huey Newton Talks to the Movement," *The Black Panthers Speak*, ed. Foner, 58.

93 Ibid., 58–9.

94 Phone interview with Joe Blum, January 16, 2025.

95 Ibid., 55, 57.

96 Davis, "Reflections." Saidiya Hartman, *Scenes of Subjection* (Oxford: Oxford University Press, 1997). Jennifer Morgan, *Reckoning with Slavery* (Durham, NC: Duke University Press, 2021). Erin Gray, "Laughing at Meat and Fury: A Materialist Critique of U.S. Lynching Culture," dissertation, University of California, Santa Cruz, 2017, *Proquest*.

97 "Huey Newton Talks to the Movement," *The Black Panthers Speak*, ed. Foner, 59.

98 Ibid., 61.

99 Ibid.

100 Ibid., 59.

101 Patricia Hill Collins, *Black Feminist Thought: Knowledge, Consciousness, and the Politics of Empowerment* (London: Routledge, 2000), 7.

102 "Panther Sisters on Women's Liberation," *The Movement*, 8.

103 Vincent Woodward, *The Delectable Negro: Human Consumption and Homoeroticism within U.S. Slave Culture* (New York: New York University Press, 2014).

104 "The Origins of the Black Panther Party," *C-Span: American Perspectives*.

105 James, "The Womb of Western Theory." Curry, *The Man-Not*.
106 Keating, *Free Huey!*, 159. Newton, *All Too Young*, Series 1, Box 55, Folder 5, DHPNC, 117.
107 Corey Devon Arthur, "I've Been Strip-Frisked Over 1,000 Times in Prison. I Consider It Sexual Assault," *The Marshall Project*, February 4, 2021.
108 Guenther, *Solitary Confinement*, 190.
109 Newton, *Revolutionary Suicide*, 267. Newton, *All Too Young*, Series 1, Box 55, Folder 5, DHPNC, 210.
110 Newton, *Revolutionary Suicide*, 252.
111 Orisanmi Burton, *Tip of the Spear: Black Radicalism, Prison Repression, and the Long Attica Revolt* (Oakland: University of California Press, 2023).
112 Ibid., 129. Albert Woodfox, *Solitary* (Toronto: HarperCollins, 2019), Ch. 12.
113 Linda Alcoff, *Rape and Resistance* (Cambridge: Polity, 2018), 25. See also Kerry F. Crawford, Amelia Hoover Green, and Sarah E. Parkinson, "Wartime Sexual Violence is Not Just a 'Weapon of War,'" *The Washington Post*, September 24, 2014.
114 Valorie K. Vojdik, "Sexual Violence Against Men and Women in War: A Masculinities Approach," *Nevada Law Journal* 14 (2014), 923–52.
115 Fanon, "French Intellectuals and Democrats in the Algerian Revolution," *Toward the African Revolution*, 83. Fanon, "Colonial War and Mental Disorders," *Wretched*.
116 Murch, *Living for the City*, 65.
117 Newton, "Fear and Doubt," 79.
118 "Huey Newton Interview" (August 14, 1970), *YouTube*, uploaded by AfroMarxist, June 2, 2018. Newton, "The Women's Liberation and Gay Liberation Movements," *To Die for the People*.
119 "The Whole World Revolution Will Be Kicked Off . . . An Interview with Huey P. Newton (L.N.S.)," (August 21, 1970), Series 1, Box 57, Folder 8, DHPNC, 4–5.
120 Bukhari, "On the Question of Sexism within the Black Panther Party," *The War Before*. Kathleen Cleaver, "Women, Power, and Revolution," *Liberation, Imagination, and the Black Panther Party*. Regina Jennings, "Why I Joined the Party: An Africana Womanist Reflection," *Black Panther Party Reconsidered*. Tracye Mathews, "No One Ever Asks, What a Man's Place in the Revolution Is: Gender and the Politics of the Black Panther Party, 1966–1971," *Black Panther Party Reconsidered*.
121 Huey Newton, "Intercommunal Day of Solidarity" (May 5, 1971), Pacifica Radio Archives, *YouTube*, uploaded by AfroMarxist, February 12, 2022.
122 Melvin van Peebles, "Interview Re: Sweet Sweetback's Badass Song," *Reelin in the Years Productions*, April 1971.
123 Newton, "He Won't Bleed Me: A Revolutionary Analysis of Sweet Sweetback's Baadasssss Song With an Introduction by Bobby Seale," *To Die for the People*, 116.
124 Isaac Julien, "BaadAsssss Cinema," Independent Film Channel, August 2002.
125 Newton, "He Won't Bleed Me," *To Die for the People*, 118.
126 Thompson, "An Oral History with Ericka Huggins," 98.
127 Newton, "He Won't Bleed Me," *To Die for the People*, 117, 127–8.
128 Newton, *Revolutionary Suicide*, 9. Brown, *A Taste of Power*, 255.

129 Trivers, *Wild Life*, 158. In *Huey P. Newton's Family*, Lise Pearlman points to genetic evidence confirming that Walter Newton was descended from Solomon Simon. Separately, Pearlman also raises doubts about Alice Hilliard Newton's claims both that she was raped and that she was thirteen years old at the time of her son's birth in 1903. Pearlman points to documentary evidence that identifies Alice Hilliard Newton as having been born in 1885 (rather than 1889) and thereby sixteen or seventeen at the time of her sexual encounter with Solomon Simon. However, in Pearlman's effort to disprove Alice Hilliard Newton's claims, she makes no effort to account for the frequency with which documentations of birth for Black southerners in the late nineteenth century were very often erroneous and typically produced years after the fact. Pearlman also argues that "the story about Walter's father that Alice Hilliard Newton told [about being raped] distorted the truth" and suggests that their encounter(s) may have been consensual. To support this theory, Pearlman cites Walter's skepticism about his mother Alice's claim ("Walter considered his mother to bear responsibility for having a child out of wedlock") as well as the later opinions of Solomon Simon's white grandchildren that the "rape story [is] inconsistent with his character" (Pearlman, *Huey P. Newton's Family*, 10, 21–2, 25–7). Notably, although Huey Newton was aware of his father's objections to his mother Alice Hilliard Newton's claim of having been raped, he included the account in *Revolutionary Suicide* anyways.

130 "Servant of the people, Huey P. Newton Speaks at Georgia State College: February 10, 1972," Series 1, Box 58, Folder 6, DHPNC. Edited for clarity.

131 *The Black Panther*, May 13, 1972, B of the supplement.

132 Newton, "The Will to Power" (1972), Series 1, Box 48, Folders 17–18, DHPNC.

133 Newton, "Regarding the Freud and Adler Split," Series 1, Box 47, Folder 6, DHPNC. Newton and Erikson, *In Search of Common Ground*, 116.

134 Newton, "The Will to Power" (1972), Series 1, Box 48, Folders 17–18, DHPNC, 1.

135 Ibid., 11. Here is the whole quote, with the observation that Newton, while speaking, mixes up Ancient Egypt's influence on the Ancient Greeks with the historical Islamic West African empires' direct and indirect influence on medieval Europe: "The first thing with the Origin of the Family of course we give much respect to the development of the concept of the origin of the family, but it was all along the wrong historical lines, that would be more of a political kind of view than what Freud did, dealing with so many of the Greek kind of myths. I think that it was rather ethno-centric to speak of the origin of man with those particular symbols. I don't think that it fits in with the origin of man or takes under consideration probably that the first man that anthropologists recognize was born in the cradle of Africa, where of course they were not touched or influenced by the kind of Greek mythology that was concerned in Athens other than the Greek philosopher's contact with Timbuktu where they borrowed very much from the African. The underlying guilt complex as they tragically expressed, that brought about the Oedipus [complex] and so forth. We'll reject that along with rejecting the whole psycho-sexual premise that the libido is the primary driving force of man. I think that it's better understood in the will to power that was expressed by Adler and Jung

with his collective unconscious. I could buy that on a general principle line, but as far as explaining in the form of a tragedy when they become that particular, connecting it to those archetypes, we reject that."

136 Brown, *A Taste of Power*, 270–1.
137 Newton, "The Will to Power" (1972), Series 1, Box 48, Folders 17–18, DHPNC, 22. Edited for clarity.
138 Newton, *Revolutionary Suicide*, 9.
139 Ibid.
140 "3/27/70," Box 1, Folder 6, Series 1, JHBEMP. "Interview, Sept 13, 1970," Series 1, Box 2, Folder 5, JHBEMP, 41.
141 Newton, "The Will to Power: A Talk before the Southern California Counseling Center, May 20, 1972 (Draft)," Series 1, Box 48, Folders 17–18, DHPNC, 23. Newton, *Revolutionary Suicide*, 9. Pearlman, *Huey P. Newton's Family*, 66.
142 Untitled document, Series 1, Box 53, Folder 6, DHPNC, 1.
143 Newton, *Revolutionary Suicide*, 93.
144 "Interview, Sept 13, 1970," Box 2, Folder 5, JMBEMP, 24–5.
145 "June 26, 1970," Series 1, Box 1, Folder 6, JHBEMP.
146 Andrew Lester, "'This Was My Utopia': Sexual Experimentation and Masculinity in the 1960s Bay Area Radical Left," *Journal of the History of Sexuality* 29:3 (2020), 364–87.
147 Newton, *Revolutionary Suicide*, 93.
148 Ibid., 94.
149 Ibid., 95.
150 Lester, "'This Was My Utopia,'" 380.
151 Newton, *Revolutionary Suicide*, 96.
152 Untitled document, Series 1, Box 53, Folder 6, DHPNC, 5.
153 Newton, *Revolutionary Suicide*, 97.
154 Forms and Notes, Series 1, Box 38, Folder 1, DHPNC. Newton, "A Functional Definition of Politics, Revised," Series 1, Box 38, Folder 11, DHPNC.
155 Newton, "A Functional Definition of Politics, Revised," Series 1, Box 38, Folder 11, DHPNC, 6.
156 Forms and Notes, Series 1, Box 38, Folder 1, DHPNC. Newton, "Politics and Myth," Series 1, Box 38, Folder 10, DHPNC. Ama B. Biney, *Kwame Nkrumah: An Intellectual Biography*, doctoral thesis, University of London, 2007, 231.
157 Newton, "Politics and Myth," Series 1, Box 38, Folder 10, DHPNC, 3.
158 Ibid.
159 Letter, Series 1, Box 38, Folder 10. Newton, "The First Hero of Literature," Series 1, Box 38, Folder 10, DHPNC.
160 Newton, "The First Hero of Literature," Series 1, Box 38, Folder 10, DHPNC, 14.
161 Newton, "Genesis of the Homosapien: A War Story," Series 1, Box 38, Folder 13, DHPNC.
162 Newton, "Eve, the Mother of all Living," Series 1, Box 37, Folder 11, DHPNC, 2.
163 Ibid.
164 Ibid., 3.

165 Newton, "Eve, the Mother of all Living," *The Huey P. Newton Reader*, 315.
166 Ibid.
167 Ibid., 316.
168 Ibid.
169 Ibid., 313, 316.
170 Newton, "Eldridge Cleaver: He is No James Baldwin," *The Huey P. Newton Reader*, 289.
171 Catherine Clune-Taylor, "Securing Cisgendered Futures: Intersex Management under the 'Disorders of Sex Development' Treatment Model," *Hypatia* 34:4 (2019). Tamari Kitossa, ed., *Appealing Because He is Appalling: Black Masculinities, Colonialism, and Erotic Racism* (Alberta, Canada: University of Alberta Press, 2022).
172 "Huey Newton Talks to the Movement," *The Black Panthers Speak*, ed. Foner, 58–9. Interview with Burney Le Boeuf, June 2021.
173 Newton, *Revolutionary Suicide*, 279, 68, 180.
174 Matthew 19:11–12, *The New Interpreter's Study Bible: New Revised Standard Version with the Apocrypha* (Nashville: Abingdon Press, 2003).
175 Hilliard, Zimmerman, and Zimmerman, *Huey*, 199.
176 Newton, *Revolutionary Suicide*, 11. "Reporting on an Interview with Mrs. Doris Godfrey, Sister of Huey P. Newton," Series 1, Box 2, Folder 17, JHBEMP. "Interview with Lee Edward Newton, Older Brother of Huey P. Newton, November 1, 1970," Series 1, Box 3, Folder 7, JHBEMP, 26.
177 Brown, *A Taste of Power*, 243, 445.
178 Hilliard, Zimmerman, and Zimmerman, *Huey*, 199.
179 Newton, *Revolutionary Suicide*, 142.
180 Hartman, *Scenes of Subjection*, 81.
181 Curry, *The Man-Not.*
182 David Scott, "The Re-Enchantment of Humanism: An Interview with Sylvia Wynter," *Small Axe* 8 (2000), 119–207.
183 "Dhoruba Bin Wahad on Assata Shakur & Cuba" (talk delivered at City College, New York, 2013), *YouTube*, uploaded by My Name is My Name, December 7, 2016.

7 Contradictions of Power

1 C. Clark Kissinger, "Interview with Mumia Abu-Jamal," *Revolutionary Worker*, December 1994. Used with permission by Mumia Abu-Jamal.
2 Kathleen Cleaver, "Back to Africa: The Evolution of the International Section of the Black Panther Party (1969–1972)," *The Black Panther Party Reconsidered*, 244.
3 Kelley, *Freedom Dreams*, 68.
4 Robert F. Williams and Mabel R. Williams, *The Memoirs of Robert and Mabel Williams* (Chapel Hill: University of North Carolina Press, 2025), 192–205.
5 "Statement by Comrade Mao Tse-tung, Chairman of the Central Committee of the Communist Party of China, in Support of the Afro-American Struggle Against Violent Repression" (April 16, 1968), *Marxists Internet Archive*.
6 Seale, *Seize the Time*, 79–81.
7 "Eyes on the Prize II; Interview with Bobby Seale," Library of Congress.

8 Newton, *Revolutionary Suicide*, 70.
9 Hilliard and Cole, *This Side of Glory*, 224.
10 Nelson Malloy, *Out of Oakland: Black Panther Party Internationalism During the Cold War* (Ithaca: Cornell University Press, 2017), 174. Hilliard and Cole, *This Side of Glory*, 224.
11 "Know Your Enemies, Know Your Friends," *The Black Panther*, October 16, 1971, Supplement C, Series 2, Box 1275, RHR. Newton, *Revolutionary Suicide*, 349.
12 Brown, *A Taste of Power*, 295–6. "Know Your Enemies, Know Your Friends," *The Black Panther*, October 16, 1971. A copy of this article in the newspaper was shared with Toni Morrison for possible inclusion in *To Die for the People* and includes a handwritten note that reads: "Presented to Chairman Mao on National Day, Oct 1, 1971."
13 "Know Your Enemies, Know Your Friends," *The Black Panther*, October 16, 1971.
14 Newton, *Revolutionary Suicide*, 349.
15 "Interview May 6, 1972," Series 1, Box 4, Folder 2, JHBEMP, 18–19.
16 Anne-Marie Brady, *Making the Foreign Serve China: Managing Foreigners in the People's Republic* (Lanham: Rowman & Littlefield Publishers Inc., 2003), 180–2.
17 Newton, *Revolutionary Suicide*, 352. "Interview May 6, 1972," Series 1, Box 4, Folder 2, JHBEMP, 18–19.
18 "Interview May 6, 1972," Series 1, Box 4, Folder 2, JHBEMP, 28.
19 Newton, "The Will to Power," Series 1, Box 48, Folders 17–18, DHPNC, 10.
20 "Interview May 6, 1973, Series 1, Box 4, Folder 2, JHBEMP, 15–16. Newton, *Revolutionary Suicide*, 350.
21 "Black Panther Leader Huey Newton Speaks of His Meeting With Chou En-Lai, October 1971," *YouTube*, uploaded by Adeyinka Makinde, November 5, 2019.
22 Newton, "The Will to Power" (1972), Series 1, Box 48, Folders 17–18, DHPNC, 10.
23 Ibid., 13. Newton continued: "Perhaps this will be that day that I can't imagine at this time when man is not satisfied. We're striving to realize that, and then we will have universal harmony where man will be at peace with himself and will be driven by another force, and maybe that force will be only the force of man's own creative motives to create and to make that which is not and to change that which is. I can understand the Chinese because they are like our Party, they're very practical, I can imagine that if some strange mystic group arrived in the People's Republic talking about contradictions are unnecessary. So, from a practical standpoint at this time, I wouldn't take the argument too far. I was dealing strictly with abstraction." Edited for clarity.
24 Brown, *A Taste of Power*, 256.
25 "Eyes on the Prize II; Interview with Huey P. Newton," Library of Congress.
26 Newton, "A Spokesman for the People: In Conversation with William F. Buckley, February 11, 1973," *The Huey P. Newton Reader*, 279–80. When asked about Tibet, Newton said, "Well, all right then. You talk about genocide. If the Chinese were wrong then, they're in the barrel with the rest of us – with England as well as America, in your genocide against Blacks."

27 "How Does It Go with the Black Movement?," January 23, 1973, Firing Line Broadcast Records.
28 Newton, "Statement: May 1, 1971," *To Die for the People*, 57. Newton, "On the Relevance of the Church: May 19, 1971," *The Huey P. Newton Reader*, 67.
29 Huey P. Newton, "Black Capitalism Re-Analyzed," *The Black Panther*, June 5, 1971, *Alexander Street*, 13.
30 Forbes, *Will You Die With Me?*, 48–9.
31 Newton, "Black Capitalism Re-Analyzed," 14.
32 Newton and Erikson, *In Search of Common Ground*, 39.
33 Newton, "Black Capitalism Re-Analyzed," 14.
34 Ibid., 15.
35 Spencer, *The Revolution Has Come*, 149, 123–32.
36 Ibid., 120.
37 Ibid., 153. Robert O. Self, *American Babylon: Race and the Struggle for Postwar Oakland* (Princeton: Princeton University Press, 2005).
38 Newton, "Oakland: An All-American Example," Series 1, Box 38, Folder 13, DHPNC. Aaron Dixon, *My People Are Rising* (Chicago: Haymarket Books, 2012), 268–9. Brown, *A Taste of Power*. Forbes, *Will You Die With Me?*
39 Brown, *A Taste of Power*, 313.
40 Spencer, *The Revolution Has Come*, 148.
41 "A Functional Definition of Politics, Revised," Series 1, Box 38, Folder 11, DHPNC.
42 Newton, "Intercommunalism: 1974," *Viewpoint Magazine*, June 11, 2018.
43 Brown, *A Taste of Power*, 276.
44 Phone interview with Michael Fultz, January 22, 2025.
45 Newton, "The Correct Handling of a Revolution," *The Black Panther*, July 20, 1967.
46 "On the Contradictions within the Black Panther Party [CD]," March 5, 1971, prod. Bruce Soloway, Black Panther Party general collection, CD 985, FA.
47 Phone interview with George Bunchy Crear, June 18, 2025.
48 "Elbert 'Big Man' Howard Oral History Interview," Library of Congress.
49 Ollie A. Johnson III, "Explaining the Demise of the Black Panther Party: The Role of Internal Factors," *Black Panther Party Reconsidered*, 404.
50 Ibid.
51 Spencer, *The Revolution Has Come*, 156–9.
52 "Survival Programs of the Black Panther Party," *CoEvolution Quarterly*, Fall 1974. *Whole Earth Index*.
53 Spencer, *The Revolution Has Come*, 158.
54 Ibid., 195–201.
55 "Civil Rights History Project: Norma Mtume."
56 Brent, *Long Time Gone*, 123.
57 Forbes, *Will You Die with Me?*, 3.
58 Spencer, *The Revolution Has Come*, 161.
59 Phone conversation with Phyllis Jackson, January 14, 2025.
60 Ibid.
61 Brown, *A Taste of Power*, 256. "5/15/71," Series 1, Box 4, Folder 20, JHBEMP. Phone conversation with Phyllis Jackson, January 14, 2025.

62 Newton, *Revolutionary Suicide*, 209, 221.
63 Hilliard and Cole, *This Side of Glory*, 340.
64 Trivers, *Wild Life*, 150.
65 Dixon, *My People are Rising*, 246.
66 Newton, "Prison, Where is Thy Victory?" *The Black Panther*, January 3, 1970, 13.
67 Forbes, *Will You Die With Me?*, 103, 133.
68 *All Power to the People*, dir. Lee. Spencer, *The Revolution Has Come*, 168.
69 Forbes, *Will You Die With Me?*, 109.
70 Ibid., 90.
71 Hilliard, Zimmerman, and Zimmerman, *Huey*, 201.
72 Forbes, *Will You Die With Me?*, 95.
73 Newton, *War Against the Panthers*, 49, 53.
74 Ibid., 52.
75 Lance Williams, *King David and Boss Daley: The Black Disciples, Mayor Daley, and Chicago on the Edge* (Essex, CT: Prometheus Books, 2022).
76 Brown, *A Taste of Power*, 400. JoNina Abron-Ervin, *Driven by the Movement: Reports from the Black Power Era* (Chico, CA: AK Press, 2025), 68. Phone interview with Emory Douglas, June 26, 2025.
77 Phone interview with George "Bunchy" Crear, June 18, 2025.
78 Forbes, *Will You Die With Me?*, 217.
79 Errol Henderson, "Shadow of a Clue," *Black Panther Party Reconsidered*, 204.
80 Interviews with Flores Forbes, Fall 2023.
81 Forbes, *Will You Die With Me?*, 41.
82 Ibid., 2, 72. Hilliard and Cole, *This Side of Glory*, 234–5.
83 Forbes, *Will You Die with Me?*, 3.
84 Ibid.
85 Ibid., 2. "Interview, Sept 17, 1970, by Mark Lane," Series 1, Box 57, Folders 9–10, DHPNC, 92. Describing this, Newton cites Che Guevara's *Venceremos!*
86 Interviews with Flores Forbes, Fall 2023.
87 Hilliard and Cole, *This Side of Glory*, 351
88 Safiya Bukhari, "We Too Are Veterans: Post-Traumatic Stress Disorders and the Black Panther Party," *The War Before*.
89 Newton, *All Too Young*, Series 1, Box 55, Folder 3, DHPNC, 27.
90 Newton, "The Will to Power" (1972), Series 1, Box 48, Folders 17–18, DHPNC, 11.
91 *All Power to the People*, dir. Lee.
92 Newton, *All Too Young*, Series 1, Box 55, Folder 5, DHPNC, 244.
93 Brown, *A Taste of Power*, 257.
94 "Towards a Revolutionary Constitution: Black Panthers Michael Tabor and Huey P. Newton (1970)," September 4–6, 1970, WBAI September 15, 1970, *YouTube*, uploaded by Our Hidden History, October 9, 2019.
95 Newton, *Revolutionary Suicide*, 296.
96 Brown *A Taste of Power*, 282.
97 Ibid., 285.
98 Holder, "The History of the Black Panther Party, 1966–1971," 16.
99 Brown, *A Taste of Power*, 290–1.

100 Dixon, *My People are Rising*, 244.
101 Interviews with Flores Forbes, Fall 2023. Newton himself remarked in an interview with Blake, "I have a problem with people's names" ("Interview, Sept 17, 1970," Series 1, Box 2, Folder 1, JHBEMP, 26).
102 Brown, *A Taste of Power*, 256–8.
103 Document, Series 2, Box 1275, RHR. Donald Freed, *Agony in New Haven* (New York: Simon and Shuster, 1973), 184. John Peterson, "The Panthers Sheathe Their Claws," *National Observer*, February 12, 1972. Brown, *A Taste of Power*, 209, 262–4.
104 Brown, *A Taste of Power*, 299.
105 "Interview, Sept 17, 1970, by Mark Lane," Series 1, Box 57, Folders 9–10, DHPNC, 100. "How Does It Go with the Black Movement?," January 23, 1973, Firing Line Broadcast Records.
106 "Interview, Sept 17, 1970, by Mark Lane," Series 1, Box 57, Folders 9–10, DHPNC, 101.
107 "Huey Newton Speaks, July 4, 1970 by Mark Lane," Series 1, Box 57, Folder 7, DHPNC, 1.
108 "Visit w/ Huey 2/6/70," Series 1, Box 1, Folder 6, JHBEMP. See also Documents, Series 1, Box 4, Folder 7, JHBEMP.
109 Newton, *All Too Young*, Series 1, Box 55, Folder 5, DHPNC, 249. Newton, *Revolutionary Suicide*, 323–4.
110 Documents, Box 4, Folder 7, JHBEMP. Documents, Series 1, Box 4, Folder 20, JHBEMP.
111 "Ideology and Philosophy," Series 1, Box 4, Folder 20, JHBEMP.
112 Kelley and Esch, "Black Like Mao," *Afro Asia*, 126.
113 Documents, Series 1, Box 4, Folder 7, JHBEMP.
114 Newton and Erikson, *In Search of Common Ground*, 43–4.
115 "Survival Pending Revolution," June 2025, The Original Black Panther Party Museum, Oakland.
116 Brown, *A Taste of Power*, 299.
117 Don Cox, "An Insider's Take on How the Black Panther Party was Hurt by its Own Ideals," *Time*, February 13, 2019.
118 Donald Cox, "The Split in the Party," *New Political Science* 21:2 (2007), 171–6, 174–5.
119 Cox, "An Insider's Take."
120 J. Edgar Hoover, "The FBI Sets Goals for COINTELPRO," *SHEC: Resources for Teachers*.
121 Churchill and Vander Wall, *COINTELPRO Papers*, 160.
122 Spencer, *The Revolution Has Come*, 178.
123 Ibid., 183.
124 "Eliminate the Presidency," Series 1, Box 48, Folder 14, DHPNC. "Eliminate the Presidency," *The Black Panther*, August 31, 1974, *Marxists Internet Archive*. Dr. Huey P. Newton Foundation, *The Black Panther Party: Service to the People Programs*, ed. David Hilliard (Albuquerque: University of New Mexico Press, 2008).
125 "Eliminate the Presidency," Series 1, Box 48, Folder 14, DHPNC.
126 Forbes, *Will You Die with Me?*, 78–9.
127 Ibid., 93.

128 "Talking to John Seale on August 17, 1970," Series 1, Box 2, Folder 3, JHMEMP, 16.
129 Brown, *A Taste of Power*, 9.
130 "Memorandum to the file: Oct 17, 1970, On Interviewing Huey," Series 1, Box 3, Folder 1, JHBEMP.
131 Hilliard and Cole, *This Side of Glory*, 388.
132 Dixon, *My People are Rising*, 245.
133 Phone interview with George "Bunchy" Crear, June 18, 2025.
134 Brown, *A Taste of Power*, 347–52.
135 Dixon, *My People are Rising*, 244.
136 Ibid., 286.
137 Documents, Series 1, Box 39, Folder 25, DHPNC. Dixon, *My People are Rising*, 246. Newton, *War Against the Panthers*, 48.
138 Documents, Series 1, Box 39, Folder 25, DHPNC. Newton, *War Against the Panthers*, 48. "A Conversation with Huey Newton," *Oui Magazine*, March 1978, 71–2, 132–4.
139 Brown, *A Taste of Power*, 383.
140 Forbes, *Will You Die with Me?*, 149–83.
141 Anita Frankel, "'New Panthers' Face Old Problems," *Seven Days*, February 24, 1978, 7. Brown, *A Taste of Power*, 383. Hilliard, Zimmerman, and Zimmerman, *Huey*, 248.
142 Spencer, *The Revolution Has Come*, 184. Nelson, *Body and Soul.*
143 Hugh Pearson, *Shadow of the Panther* (Reading, MA: Addison-Wesley, 1994). Charles E. Jones, "Introduction," *The Black Panther Party Reconsidered*, 4.
144 Lori Robinson, "A Panther Caged By His Own Demons," *Emerge*, June 1994, 66. Emphasis added. Errol Henderson offers perhaps the most rigorous critical review of the book: Henderson, "Shadow of a Clue," *Liberation, Imagination, and the Black Panther Party.*
145 Churchill, "To Disrupt, Discredit and Destroy," *Liberation, Imagination, and the Black Panther Party*, 117.

8 Technology of Madness

1 Newton, *All Too Young*, Series 1, Box 55, Folder 3, DHPNC, 102. Used with permission by Dr. Huey P. Newton Foundation.
2 Newton, "Prison, Where is Thy Victory?" *The Black Panther*, January 3, 1970, 13. See also Newton, "Prison, Where is Thy Victory?" *To Die for the People.*
3 Blake, "Caged Panther," 248.
4 Brian P. Sowers, "Prison, Where is Thy Victory? A Black Panther Theology of Mass Incarceration," *Harvard Theological Review*, 113, 1, January 2020: 24–44.
5 Newton, "Prison, Where is Thy Victory?" *The Black Panther*, January 3, 1970, 13.
6 Ibid.
7 Ibid.
8 "Talking to John Seale on August 17, 1970," Series 1, Box 2, Folder 3, JHMEMP, 16. "Interview with Lee Edward Newton, Older Brother of

Huey P. Newton, November 1 1970," Series 1, Box 3, Folder 7, JHBEMP, 55. Phone interview with Emory Douglas, June 26, 2025.

9 Kay Boyle, "No One Can Be All Things to All People," *Evergreen* 81, August 1970, Huey Newton Collection, FA.

10 Newton, *Revolutionary Suicide*, 107.

11 Ibid., 279.

12 Ibid., 274.

13 Ibid., 282.

14 Joe Street, *Black Revolutionaries* (Athens: University of Georgia Press, 2024), 173–9.

15 Joe Street, "Shadow of the Soul Breaker: Solitary Confinement, Cocaine, and the Decline of Huey P. Newton," *Pacific Historical Review* 84:3 (2015), 333–63, 338.

16 In *Black Revolutionaries* (232 n32), Street cites considerable scholarly evidence showing that impulsive "self-directed violence," suicide, and sometimes violence towards objects are typical effects, but does not provide evidence that demonstrates clearly that a common psychological effect is impulsive violence towards other people (Stuart Grassian, "Psychiatric Effects of Solitary Confinement," *Washington University Journal of Law & Policy* 22:1 (2006); Tracy Hresko, "In the Cellars of the Hollow Men," *Pace International Law Review* 18:1 (2006); Craig Haney, "The Psychological Impact of Incarceration," From Prison to Home Conference, January 30–31, 2002; Nick de Viggiani, "Unhealthy Prisons," *Sociology of Health and Illness* 29:1 (2007). Among the cited, Haney's scholarship is the only one that identifies evidence of violent attacks on prison staff but does not specify the character of the violence).

17 Newton, "The Mind is Flesh: 1974," *The Huey P. Newton Reader*, 317.

18 Ibid., 318.

19 Ibid., 320.

20 Ibid., 322.

21 Ibid., 322–4.

22 Ibid., 325.

23 Ibid., 325–6.

24 Ibid., 326.

25 Ibid., 327.

26 Ibid.

27 José M. R. Delgado, *Physical Control of the Mind: Toward a Psychocivilized Society* (New York: Harper & Row, 1969).

28 "Jose Delgado Testimony" (1974), *Congressional Record* 26, 118.

29 Newton, "The Mind is Flesh: 1974," *The Huey P. Newton Reader*, 328.

30 Ibid., 329.

31 Ibid.

32 Armin Krishnan, *Military Neuroscience and the Coming Age of Neurowarfare* (London: Routledge, 2017), 18.

33 John Gimbel, "U.S. Policy and German Scientists: The Early Cold War," *Political Science Quarterly* 101:3 (1986), 433–51, 443.

34 Frantz Fanon, *A Dying Colonialism* (1959) (New York: Grove Press, 1965), 137. Tom O'Neill, *Chaos: Charles Manson, the CIA, and the Secret History of the Sixties* (New York: Back Bay Books, 2019), 352. Krishnan, *Military*

Neuroscience, 20. Colin A. Ross, *The C.I.A. Doctors* (Richardson, TX: Manitou Communications, 2006), 16–20. This timeline disrupts the standard view that mind control projects were initiated in response to Korean and Chinese projects.

35 Ross, *The C.I.A. Doctors*, 15, 83.

36 Zoe Colley, "Erasing Minds: Behavioral Modification, the Prison Rights Movement, and Psychological Experimentation in America's Prisons, 1962–1983," *Journal of American Studies* 57:1 (2023), 84–111.

37 Colley, "Erasing Minds," 100.

38 Ibid., 103.

39 Ibid., 104.

40 Ibid., 105.

41 Ibid.. 106.

42 Ibid., 107.

43 Nelson, *Body and Soul*, 154, 164.

44 Ibid., 155, 161, 162, 175.

45 Schreiber, *Revolution's End*, 38.

46 Ibid., 38–9.

47 Gordon Thomas, *Journey Into Madness: The True Story of Secret CIA Mind Control and Medical Abuse* (New York: Bantam Books, 1989), 264–5, as cited in Krishnan, *Military Neuroscience*, 37.

48 Nelson, *Body and Soul*, 154.

49 John D. Marks, *The Search for the Manchurian Candidate: The CIA and Mind Control* (London: Penguin Books, 1979), 201–2.

50 Schreiber, *Revolution's End*, 35–6.

51 Ibid., 35. Samuel Chavkin, *The Mind Stealers: Psychosurgery and Mind Control* (Boston: Houghton Mifflin Company, 1978), 73–4. According to Schreiber, the drugs included mescaline, quaalude, artane, and magnesium pemoline, among others. Chavkin's scholarly sources identify the use of succinylcholine.

52 Leroy F. Aarons, "Brain Surgery is Tested on 3 California Convicts," *Washington Post*, February 5, 1972.

53 Nelson, *Body and Soul*, 168. Schalk, *Black Disability Politics*, 59.

54 Krishnan, *Military Neuroscience*, 36. Peter Schrag, *Mind Control* (New York: Pantheon Books, 1978). Alan W. Scheflin and Edward M. Opton, Jr., *The Mind Manipulators* (New York: Paddington Press, 1978). Stephan L. Chorover, *From Genesis to Genocide: The Meaning of Human Nature and the Power of Behavioral Control* (Cambridge, MA: MIT Press, 1979). Ross, *The C.I.A. Doctors*, 88–9, 116, 200.

55 Nita A. Farahany, *The Battle for Your Brain: Defending the Right to Think Freely in the Age of Neurotechnology* (New York: St. Martin's Griffin, 2023), 142. R. J. R. Blair, "The Amygdala and Ventromedial Prefrontal Cortex: Functional Contributions and Dysfunction in Psychopathy," *Philosophical Transactions of the Royal Society B: Biological Sciences* 363:1503 (2008), 2557–65.

56 Hilliard and Cole, *This Side of Glory*, 365.

57 Phone interview with Emory Douglas, June 26, 2025.

58 *Eldridge Cleaver, Black Panther*, dir. Klein. See also Justin Gifford, *Revolution or Death: The Life of Eldridge Cleaver* (Chicago: Lawrence Hill Books, 2020), 261.

59 Burton, *Tip of the Spear*, 201.

60 Phone interview with Emory Douglas, June 26, 2025.
61 "Kathleen Cleaver speaking at UCLA 10/22/1971," *YouTube*.
62 Cornish Rogers, "Demythologizing Huey Newton," *Christian Century*, August 15–22, 1973, 795.
63 In scholarship, only sociologist Matthew Hughey has stated this outright (Matthew W. Hughey, "The Sociology, Pedagogy, and Theology of Huey P. Newton: Toward a Radical Democratic Utopia," *The Western Journal of Black Studies* 29:3 (2005), 652). Others seem to have suggested it (e.g. Sowers, "The Socratic Black Panther," 28–9).
64 "Tearing Out Our Thoughts," *The Black Panther*, January 6, 1973, 16–17, *Alexander Street*.
65 Schalk, *Black Disability Politics*, 63–6.
66 Pharr, *Nine Lives of a Black Panther*, 293.
67 Burton, *Tip of the Spear*, 204.
68 Newton, "The Mind is Flesh: 1974," *The Huey P. Newton Reader*, 320.
69 Burton, *Tip of the Spear*, 200.
70 Ibid., 201.
71 Ibid., 201, 207.
72 Ibid., 201–2.
73 O'Neill, *Chaos*. Describing his mental state while conducting research, O'Neill explained that, while writing the book, he often "got paranoid" and "started doubting myself," cancelling meetings and opportunities, and he had to develop techniques for combatting this: "I had a list of bullet points I'd write down on them and read to myself for encouragement" (389, 426–7).
74 O'Neill, *Chaos*, 354. Farahany, *The Battle for Your Brain*, 175. Nicholas M. Horrock, "80 Institutions Used in CIA Mind Studies," *New York Times*, August 4, 1977.
75 O'Neill, *Chaos*, 345, 360.
76 Ibid., 363
77 Ibid., 357, 354.
78 Ibid., 367. Krishnan, *Military Neuroscience*, 36.
79 O'Neill, *Chaos*, 365, 368. Krishnan, *Military Neuroscience*, 14, 17–45.
80 Ross, *The C.I.A. Doctors*, 168–74, 34–66, 150–65. Marks, *The Search for the Manchurian Candidate*, 133. Farahany, *The Battle for Your Brain*, 175–6. Krishnan, *Military Neuroscience*, 24.
81 Krishnan, *Military Neuroscience*, 21–2.
82 CIA, "Hypnotic Experimentation and Research, 10 February 1954," General CIA Records, Special Collection, August 23, 2000. Marks, *The Search for the Manchurian Candidate*, 194. Ross, *The C.I.A. Doctors*, 46. Krishnan, *Military Neuroscience*, 21–2.
83 Karen Wetmore, *Surviving Evil: CIA Mind Control Experiments in Vermont* (Richardson, TX: Manitou Communications, 2014). She writes: "It's difficult to explain the emotions that I had after learning that I had been experimented on by the CIA. After the initial shock came deep-seated feelings of fear, anger, and an almost indescribable feeling of having had the CIA traipse through my mind, doing God only knows what and leaving their footprints all over my unconscious. It was akin to a psychological rape as far as I was concerned. It took me some time to adjust to the new reality in my life and

over the next few months the fear changed into anger and then changed into a fierce determination that I would find definitive proof that the CIA had conducted MKULTRA in Vermont. The CIA entered my life as a thirteen-year-old child and their tactics shattered my life for decades after. I made a very conscious decision that I would never again be afraid of the CIA. One of the positive emotional effects that came with learning that I had been used in CIA experiments was that, for the first time since I was thirteen years old, I realized that it wasn't because of something terrible about me. It was because of the terrible things that were done to me. It was a life altering realization" (23). Notably, Wetmore has received some limited support from the office of Senator Bernie Sanders (208, 229–31).

84 Davis, *With My Mind on Freedom*, 242.
85 Ibid., 240–5.
86 Ibid., 243–4.
87 Ibid., 246.
88 "SOCDS Census Data: Output for Santa Cruz city, CA," *State of the Cities Data Systems*, accessed January 2025.
89 Emerson Murray, *Murder Capital of the World: The Santa Cruz Community Looks Back at the Frazier, Mullin, and Kemper Murder Sprees of the Early 1970s* (Scotts Valley, CA, 2021), 14.
90 Hilliard, Zimmerman, and Zimmerman, *Huey*, 208. "I. Exile," Series 1, Box 39, Folder 25, DHPNC. Brown, *A Taste of Power*, 342.
91 "I. Exile," Series 1, Box 39, Folder 25, DHPNC. Brown, *A Taste of Power*, 342.
92 Krishnan, *Military Neuroscience*, 28–30.
93 Ross, *The C.I.A. Doctors*, 120: "A March, 1996 letter from Dr. [Martin] Orne to the CIA explains that he has not yet spent all his MKULTRA money. Dr. Orne says that he understands there is no time limitation on spending the remaining funds."
94 A. J. Weberman, "Mind Control: The Story of Mankind Research Unlimited, Inc.," *CovertAction* 9, June 1980, Series VI, Mind Control: Clippings, 1975–1984, PAP, 15.
95 Krishnan, *Military Neuroscience*, Ch. 6, 116–38.
96 Farahany, "Chapter 8: Bewilderbeasts," *The Battle for Your Brain*, 170–88.
97 Ibid., 16.
98 J. A. M. Meerloo, *The Rape of the Mind: The Psychology of Thought Control, Menticide, and Brainwashing* (Cleveland, OH: The World Publishing Company, 1956).
99 Smithson, "A Visit with Huey Newton: Vacaville Prison Facility; October 17, 1968," Library of Congress.
100 Ibid.
101 Phone interview with Joe Blum, January 17, 2025.
102 Smithson, "A Visit with Huey Newton." Newton, *Revolutionary Suicide*, 269.
103 Newton, *Revolutionary Suicide*, 269.
104 Smithson, "A Visit with Huey Newton." Newton, *Revolutionary Suicide*, 268.
105 Newton, *Revolutionary Suicide*, 269.
106 Ibid., 270. Hilliard, Zimmerman, and Zimmerman, *Huey*, 161. Smithson, "A Visit with Huey Newton."
107 Newton, *Revolutionary Suicide*, 271.

108 Thompson, "An Oral History with Ericka Huggins," 89–90.
109 Hilliard, Zimmerman, and Zimmerman, *Huey*, 195
110 "The Origins of the Black Panther Party," *C-Span: American Perspectives*.
111 Hilliard, Zimmerman, and Zimmerman, *Huey*, 266–7.
112 Phone interview with John "Bunchy" Crear, June 18, 2025. Phone conversation with Phyllis Jackson, January 14, 2025.
113 Newton, *Revolutionary Suicide*, 50.
114 *All Power to the People*, dir. Lee.
115 Blake, "Caged Panther," 239.
116 "Huey Newton Speaks, July 4, 1970, by Mark Lane," Series 1, Box 57, Folder 7, DHPNC, 2.
117 Phone conversation with Phyllis Jackson, January 14, 2025.
118 Jeffries, *Huey P. Newton: Radical Theorist*, 106–7.
119 Brown, *A Taste of Power*, 9. Trivers, *A Wild Life*, 160.
120 *Huey P. Newton: Prelude to Revolution* (1971), dir. Evans. "Huey Newton: Interview from Jail," Educational Video Group, 1967, https://search.alexanderstreet.com/view/work/bibliographic_entity|video_work|2787230. "Huey P. Newton Interviewed by KTVU in Jail," Bay Area Television Archive, https://diva.sfsu.edu/collections/sfbatv/bundles/220930. "Huey P. Newton Interviewed in Jail 1968," *YouTube*, uploaded by BlackPanthersForever, March 31, 2013, https://www.youtube.com/watch?v=ymlQa-QNBRs. "Huey P Newton Interviewed in Jail (1968)," *YouTube*, uploaded by Satanico Pandemonium, May 26, 2014, https://www.youtube.com/watch?v=0_bDYXtnYKs.
121 "Huey P. Newton on the Eve of his Release (1970)," Digital Information Virtual Archive, San Francisco State University, https://diva.sfsu.edu/collections/sfbatv/bundles/228229.
122 "Huey P. Newton Speaks at a Fall 1970 News Conference," *YouTube*, uploaded by Santanico Pandemonium, July 25, 2014, https://www.youtube.com/watch?v=NplrUhW79b8.
123 "Black Panther Leader Huey Newton Speaks of His Meeting With Chou En-Lai" (October 1971), *YouTube*, uploaded by Adeyinka Makinde, November 5, 2019, https://www.youtube.com/watch?v=Djf23DyJQss.
124 "WSB-TV newsfilm clip of Huey Newton commenting on the possibility of moving the Black Panther Party headquarters to Atlanta, Georgia, 1971 September 8," Walter J. Brown Media Archives and Peabody Awards Collection, Digital Library of Georgia, https://crdl.usg.edu/id:ugabma_wsbn_wsbn38203. "WSB-TV newsfilm clip of Huey P. Newton, co-founder of the Black Panther Party for Self-Defense, at a press conference announcing the move of the Panther's headquarters to Atlanta, Georgia, 1971 September 8," Walter J. Brown Media Archives and Peabody Awards Collection, Digital Library of Georgia, https://crdl.usg.edu/id:ugabma_wsbn_wsbn64008.
125 "How Does It Go with the Black Movement?" January 23, 1973, Firing Line Broadcast Records.
126 Hilliard, Zimmerman, and Zimmerman, *Huey*, 267.
127 Jennie Rothenberg Gritz, "The Misunderstood Visionary Behind the Black Panther Party," *Smithsonian Magazine*, August 22, 2023.
128 Churchill and Vander Wall, *The COINTELPRO Papers*, 362 n129.
129 Ross, *The C.I.A. Doctors*, 161–2.

130 Brown, *A Taste of Power*, 177.
131 National Archives, "JFK Assassination Records, 2017–2018 Additional Documents Release," https://www.archives.gov/research/jfk/release-2017-2018. David J. Garrow, *The FBI and Martin Luther King, Jr.* (New York: W. W. Norton and Company, 2010). Brown, *A Taste of Power*, 94–5, 103, 365.
132 Krishnan, *Military Neuroscience*, 169.
133 "Dr. Orisanmi Burton on the Long Attica Revolt & Prisons as an Ongoing Site of War," *YouTube*, August 12, 2024, uploaded by Left of Black.
134 Newton, *War Against the Panthers*, 91–2.
135 "The Origins of the Black Panther Party," *C-Span: American Perspectives*.
136 "An Interview with Richard Helms," Center for the Study of Intelligence, May 8, 2007, https://web.archive.org/web/20100427043605/https://www.cia.gov/library/center-for-the-study-of-intelligence/kent-csi/vol44no4/html/v44i4a07p_0021.htm.
137 Newton, *War Against the Panthers*, 92. Jeremy Varon has suggested: "The whistleblowers . . . testify to the vulnerability of institutions, no matter how powerful, when subject to the moral scrutiny of insider critics" (Varon, "Winter Soldiers of the Dark Side: CIA Whistleblowers and National Security Dissent," *Whistle-Blowing Nation*, ed. Kaeten Mistry and Hannah Gurman (New York: Columbia University Press, 2020) 156).
138 Hilliard, Zimmerman, and Zimmerman, *Huey*, 212.
139 Untitled document, Series 1, Box 47, Folder 13, DHPNC, 8.
140 Anita Frankel, "'New Panthers' Face Old Problems," *Seven Days*, February 24, 1978, 9.
141 Untitled document, Series 1, Box 47, Folder 13, DHPNC, 8. "Sanctuary in Cuba," *CoEvolution Quarterly*, Fall 1977, 29.
142 Brown, *A Taste of Power*, 383.
143 Thompson, "An Oral History with Ericka Huggins," 93.
144 Brent, *Long Time Gone*, 233. Brent in fact described Newton in an identical manner each time: "His eyes were alert and intelligent" (95, 233). He also added: "After Huey left Cuba, I had no further contact with him or the Panthers. I did hear about some of his alleged misdeeds – beating up Party leaders and kicking them out of the Panthers, among other things. I hoped the stories weren't true" (236).
145 "Sanctuary in Cuba," *CoEvolution Quarterly*, Fall 1977, 27.
146 Hilliard, Zimmerman, and Zimmerman, *Huey*, 239.
147 Untitled document, Series 1, Box 47, Folder 13, DHPNC, 11.
148 Newton, *Revolutionary Suicide*, 348. "Interview May 6, 1972," Series 1, Box 4, Folder 2, JHBEMP, 25–6.
149 Spencer, *The Revolution Has Come*, 160.
150 Hilliard and Cole, *This Side of Glory*, 403.
151 Phone interview with George "Bunchy" Crear, June 18, 2025.
152 Hilliard and Cole, *This Side of Glory*, 11. Hilliard in one instance (11) said it was 1985, but at another point (403–7) suggested it was in early 1978.
153 Phone interview with Emory Douglas, June 26, 2025. Andrew Goulian et al., "A Cultural and Political Difference: Comparing the Racial and Social Framing of Population Crack Cocaine Use between the United States and France," *Harm Reduction Journal* 19:44 (2002).

154 Hilliard and Cole, *This Side of Glory*, 415.
155 Gritz, "The Misunderstood Visionary," *Smithsonian Magazine*. Thompson, "An Oral History with Ericka Huggins," 98. Flores A. Forbes, *Invisible Men: A Contemporary Slave Narrative in the Era of Mass Incarceration* (New York: Skyhorse Publishing, 2016), 64.
156 Thompson, "An Oral History with Ericka Huggins," 98.
157 Blake, "Caged Panther," 241. Newton, *All Too Young*, Series 1, Box 55, Folder 5, DHPNC, 219. Newton, *Revolutionary Suicide*, 273. Smithson, "A Visit with Huey Newton."
158 Hilliard and Cole, *This Side of Glory*, 408.
159 Ibid., 436.
160 Ibid., 428.
161 Ibid., 363.
162 Interviews with Flores Forbes, Fall 2023.
163 Hilliard, Zimmerman, and Zimmerman, *Huey*, 257.
164 Trivers, *Wild Life*, 160–1.
165 Hilliard, Zimmerman, and Zimmerman, *Huey*, 262 (according to Trivers). Brown, *A Taste of Power*. Interview with Burney Le Boeuf, June 2021.
166 Hilliard, Zimmerman, and Zimmerman, *Huey*, 262–3.
167 Ibid., 261.
168 Ibid., 194.
169 Brown, *A Taste of Power*, 447–9. Forbes, *Will You Die With Me?*, 157.
170 Forbes, *Will You Die with Me?*, 157.
171 *Comrade Sister*, prod. Jackson and Jordan.
172 Forbes, *Will You Die with Me?*, 158. Mumia Abu-Jamal recounts that, in Philadelphia, Party men were disallowed from having sex with sex workers because it was considered a "security risk" (Abu-Jamal, *We Want Freedom*, 187).
173 Newton, *Revolutionary Suicide*, 98. Among J. Herman Blake's papers is included a small set of unpublished, incomplete papers without identified authors. While it is clear that some of these – "Idealism and the Rational Method" and "Ideology and Philosophy" (Series 1, Box 4, Folder 20, JHBEMP) – were developed for use at the Ideological Institute and were composed by other Party members, two papers – "On Jealousy" (Series 1, Box 4, Folder 9, JHBEMP) and "On the Party, the Family, the Society, and the Commune" (Series 1, Box 4, Folder 10, JHBEMP; Series 1, Box 58, Folder 6, DHPNC) – appear to have been authored by Newton and composed by Blake, most likely in late 1970. They discuss the BPP's non-monogamy and child rearing. Importantly, these papers lack the distinctive designation of copyright and authorship by Newton and were clearly considered drafts. While clearly originally intended for internal Party use, the relative inconsistency of these drafts reflects that they were ultimately considered unfit for use. For more demonstration of Newton's dissatisfaction in 1970 with his incomplete analysis of the family form, see "Interview, Sept 13, 1970," Series 1, Box 2, Folder 5, JHBEMP, 64–6.
174 Spencer, *The Revolution Has Come*, 187.
175 Forbes, *Will You Die with Me?*, 159–62. Thompson, "An Oral History with Ericka Huggins," 93.

176 Thompson, "An Oral History with Ericka Huggins," 100.
177 Interviews with Flores Forbes, Fall 2023.
178 Thompson, "An Oral History with Ericka Huggins," 93.
179 Ibid., 90.
180 Ibid., 102.
181 Thomas A. Foster, *Rethinking Rufus: Sexual Violations of Enslaved Men* (Athens: University of Georgia Press, 2019), 64.
182 Ibid., 28.
183 Fanon, *Wretched*, trans. Farrington, 137.
184 Foster, *Rethinking Rufus*, 29.
185 Alcoff, *Rape and Resistance*, 12.
186 Newton, *Revolutionary Suicide*, 271–2.
187 Newton, "Thoughts on the Will to Power," Series 1, Box 40, Folder 2, DHPNC.
188 Newton, "The Will to Power" (1972), Series 1, Box 48, Folders 17–18, DHPNC, 7.
189 Ibid., 8.
190 Newton, "On Truth and Sanity," Series 1, Box 41, Folder 6, DHPNC.
191 Erika Lorraine Milam, "A Field Study of Con Games," *Isis* 105:3 (2014), 596–605. Robert L. Trivers and Huey P. Newton, "The Crash of Flight 90: Doomed by Self-Deception," *Science Digest* 90 (1982), 66–7.
192 Robert Trivers, *Natural Selection and Social Theory: Selected Papers of Robert Trivers* (Oxford: Oxford University Press, 2002), 259.
193 Thompson, "Oral History with Ericka Huggins," 98–9. Hilliard, Zimmerman, and Zimmerman, *Huey*, 289.
194 Hilliard, Zimmerman, and Zimmerman, *Huey*, 280. Gritz, "The Misunderstood Visionary," *Smithsonian Magazine*.
195 Hilliard, Zimmerman, and Zimmerman, *Huey*, 279.
196 Jonathan M. Metzl, *The Protest Psychosis: How Schizophrenia Became a Black Disease* (Boston: Beacon Press, 2009).
197 "Understanding Psychosis," NIH Publication 23-MH-8110, National Institute of Mental Health, https://www.nimh.nih.gov/health/publications/understanding-psychosis.
198 Metzl, *The Protest Psychosis*, 198.
199 Micha Frazer-Carroll, *Mad World: The Politics of Mental Health* (London: Pluto Press, 2023).
200 Jess Whatcott, *Menace to the Future* (Durham, NC: Duke University Press, 2004).
201 Ellen Barry, "Under an L.A. Freeway, a Psychiatric Rescue Mission," *New York Times*, October 20, 2024.
202 Pickens, *Black Madness :: Mad Blackness*, 4.
203 Thompson, "Oral History with Ericka Huggins," 99.
204 Fanon, *Wretched*, trans. Farrington, 121.
205 Fanon, "Medicine and Colonialism," *A Dying Colonialism*, 134.
206 Ibid., 135.
207 Ibid., 141–2.
208 Ibid., 141.
209 Ibid., 140–1. Olanzapine, quetiapine, and lurasidone, for instance.

210 Ibid., 145.
211 Newton, "A Citizen's Peace Force," Series 1, Box 47, Folder 23, DHPNC, 3, 6, 3. Published in '*Crime and Social Justice: A Journal of Radical Criminology* 1 (1974).
212 Newton, "A Citizen's Peace Force," 3.
213 Ibid., 9.

9 Life of the Mind, Politics of the Street

1 Huey Newton and Ericka Huggins, *Insights & Poems* (San Francisco: City Lights, 1975), 18. Used with permission by Dr. Huey P. Newton Foundation.
2 Nick Mitchell, *Discipline and Surplus: Black Studies, Women's Studies, and the Dawn of Neoliberalism* (forthcoming).
3 Newton, "The Will to Power" (1972), Series 1, Box 48, Folders 17–18, DHPNC, 24. Edited for clarity.
4 "Huey Newton Gets his PhD," *San Francisco Chronicle*, June 16, 1980, 22.
5 Newton, "Merritt Lecture Series 1–3: A Primary Introduction to Phenomena (Lecture 1)," Series 1, Box 59, Folder 4, DHPNC.
6 Letter, Series 1, Box 37, Folder 1, DHPNC, 2.
7 Ford, "Hounded," *Hip Santa Cruz 6*, 217–8, 236. Ford interviewed former UCSC professors and administrators Paul Lee (his uncle), Page Smith, Noel King, Ralph Abraham, Burney Le Boeuf, Robert Trivers, Hayden White, Billie Harris, and former BPP members and supporters William Moore, Johnny Chesko, and Bert Schneider. Ford's account is the most rigorous text currently available on Newton's experiences at Santa Cruz.
8 Interview with City on the Hill Press, Series 1, Box 37, Folders 8–10. "Huey Newton Gets his PhD," *San Francisco Chronicle*. Letter, Series 1, Box 4, Folder 17, JHBEMP.
9 Documents, Series 1, Box 39, Folder 2, DHPNC.
10 Documents, Series 1, Box 37, Folders 8–9, DHPNC.
11 Interviews with Flores Forbes, Fall 2023.
12 Letter from Charles Garry to Newton, Series 1, Box 37, Folder 10, DHPNC.
13 Documents, Series 1, Box 38, Folders 2–3, DHPNC. Letter from Lewis Keizer, Series 1, Box 37, Folder 10, DHPNC.
14 Letter (March 12, 1974), Series 1, Box 37, Folder 10, DHPNC.
15 Letter to Page Smith, Series 1, Box 37, Folder 10, DHPNC.
16 "Huey Newton Gets his PhD," *San Francisco Chronicle*. Hilliard, Zimmerman, and Zimmerman, *Huey*, 251.
17 "Instructor Narrative Evaluation, Winter 1978," Series 1, Box 39, Folder 21, DHPNC.
18 Ford, "Hounded," 217.
19 Trivers, *Natural Selection and Social Theory*, 259.
20 Milam, "A Field Study of Con Games," 601.
21 "Instructor Narrative Evaluations, Fall 1977," Series 1, Box 39, Folder 21, DHPNC.
22 "Instructor Narrative Evaluations, Spring 1978," Series 1, Box 39, Folder 21, DHPNC.

23 Ford, "Hounded," 220.
24 Ibid., 231.
25 Ibid., 233.
26 Ibid., 232. Moore later said: "I know there were other incidents that Huey was involved with . . . those I wasn't there for. This one I was there. I saw how people reacted – I watched it in the newspaper . . . I found that if the rest of these stories that are in a negative light are as bullshit as this one then I got real serious doubts about the other [charges]" (235).
27 Hilliard, Zimmerman, and Zimmerman, *Huey*, 261.
28 Letter, Series 1, Box 46, Folders 1–3, DHPNC.
29 Phone interview with Barry Katz, July 2021.
30 Documents, Series 1, Box 39, Folder 14, DHPNC.
31 Documents, Series 1, Box 42, Folders 6–9, DHPNC.
32 Ford, "Hounded," 216–19.
33 Letter from Hayden White (April 18, 1980), Series 1, Box 46, Folders 1–3, DHPNC.
34 Documents, Series 1, Box 39, Folder 3 and 5, DHPNC.
35 Phone interview with Barry Katz, June 2021.
36 Email conversation with Richard Mahon, March 2025. Phone interview with Diane Lebow, March 2025.
37 Diane Lebow remarked also on the prevalence of acute sexism among some of the male faculty at the time.
38 Documents, Series 1, Box 39, Folder 6, DHPNC.
39 Conversation with Robert Meister, December 2023.
40 Forter and Pulcrano, "Newton Presents his Philosophy," June 8, 1978, *City on a Hill Press*, Series 1, Box 39, Folder 19, DHPNC. Specifically, Newton was hopeful that Derrida's *Of Grammatology* could serve as a first-year text and common language in the department ("Course and Instructor Evaluation Form" for Course 203-C with Dr. E. Donato, Box 39, Folder 21). See also Newton, "De-constructing the Object," Series 1, Box 41, Folder 6, DHPNC.
41 Newton, *War Against the Panthers*, 8–9.
42 Ford, "Hounded," 214.
43 Ibid., 216–17.
44 "Huey P. Newton at New York Community College" (November 19, 1970), Series 1, Box 57, Folder 12, DHPNC, 26.
45 Newton, "Vanguard of the People's Struggle," *Off the Pigs*, 224.
46 Newton, *Revolutionary Suicide*, 353.
47 Newton, "The Mind is Flesh: 1974," *The Huey P. Newton Reader*, 330.
48 Newton and Erikson, *In Search of Common Ground*, 35.
49 Newton, *Revolutionary Suicide*, 359.
50 Newton and Huggins, *Insights & Poems*, 16.
51 Newton, *Revolutionary Suicide*, 353.
52 Romy Opperman, "We Need Histories of Radical Black Ecology Now," August 3, 2020, *Black Perspectives*, African American Intellectual History Society.
53 Kathryn Yussof, *A Billion Black Anthropocenes* (Minneapolis: University of Minnesota Press, 2018).
54 Newton, "Dialectics of Nature: 1974," *The Huey P. Newton Reader*, 311.

55 "The Whole World Revolution Will Be Kicked off . . . An Interview with Huey P. Newton (L.N.S.)" (August 21, 1970), Series 1, Box 57, Folder 8, DHPNC, 6.
56 "Interview, Sept 17, 1970, by Mark Lane," Series 1, Box 57, Folders 9–10, DHPNC, 123–4.
57 Document, Series 1, Box 39, Folder 26, DHPNC.
58 Newton, "The Roots of Existential Philosophy in Western Thought" (1978), Series 1, Box 42, Folders 6–8, DHPNC, 1, 5.
59 Ibid., 1, 3–4.
60 Ibid., 17–18.
61 Fanon, *Wretched*, trans. Farrington, 314.
62 Newton, "The Roots of Existential Philosophy in Western Thought," 5, 11.
63 Ibid., 5.
64 Newton, "Rise of a Non-Aristotelian System (with Introduction)" (1977), Series 1, Box 40, Folder 1, DHPNC, 9.
65 Ibid., 13.
66 Ibid., 2.
67 Ibid., 9.
68 Ibid., Intro-2.
69 Ibid., Intro-3.
70 Ibid., 9.
71 Ibid., 12.
72 Ibid.
73 Trivers and Newton, "The Crash of Flight 90: Doomed by Self-Deception?" *Science Digest* 90 (1982), 66–7.
74 Trivers, *Natural Selection and Social Theory*, 257.
75 Trivers and Newton, "The Crash of Flight 90: Doomed by Self-Deception?" *Natural Selection and Social Theory: Selected Papers of Robert Trivers*, 296–71, 263.
76 Hilliard, Zimmerman, and Zimmerman, *Huey*, 256. Ford, "Hounded," 238–9. Contract, Series 1, Box 46, Folder 9, DHPNC.
77 Robert Trivers, *Deceit and Self-Deception: Fooling Yourself the Better to Fool Others* (London: Penguin, 2013).
78 Trivers and Newton, "The Crash of Flight 90," *Natural Selection and Social Theory*, 268.
79 Trivers, *Deceit and Self-Deception*, 253.
80 Newton, "Proposed Book on Deceit and Self-Deception," Series 1, Box 50, Folder 11, DHPNC, 9.
81 "Interview, Sept 17, 1970, by Mark Lane," Series 1, Box 57, Folders 9–10, DHPNC, 103–4.
82 Newton, "Speech at Boston College," *To Die for the People*, 20.
83 Hilliard and Cole, *This Side of Glory*, 171.
84 "Convention on the Prevention and Punishment of the Crime of Genocide," UN General Assembly resolution 260 A (III), December 9, 1948.
85 Clayborne Carson, *Malcolm X: The FBI File* (New York: Skyhorse Publishing, 1991).
86 "International Tribunal Finds U.S. Guilty of Crimes Against Humanity," *Workers World*, November 1, 2021.

87 Phone interview with Emory Douglas, June 26, 2025.
88 "December 28, 1986," *The Last Speeches of Huey P. Newton, with presentations by Omali Yeshitela* (Oakland, CA: Burning Spear Publications, 1990), 1. See also "Images of Black Men in America," *People are Talking*, January 15, 1988, *YouTube*, uploaded by Reelblack One, June 2, 2020.
89 Matthew W. Hughey, "The Pedagogy of Huey P. Newton Critical Reflections on Education in His Writings and Speeches," *Journal of Black Studies* 38:2 (2007).
90 Newton, "New Educational Models," Series 1, Box 40, Folder 10, DHPNC, 11.
91 Hilliard, Zimmerman, and Zimmerman, *Huey*, 195.
92 Thompson, "An Oral History with Ericka Huggins," 94.
93 Hilliard, Zimmerman, and Zimmerman, *Huey*, 276–7, 281.
94 "Huey Newton Gets his PhD," *San Francisco Chronicle*, June 16, 1980, 22.
95 Newton, "New Educational Models," 6.
96 Ibid., 6.
97 Ibid., 16.
98 Ibid.
99 Newton, "Utopia: Universal Life Energy" (1974), Series 1, Box 39, Folder 1, DHPNC, 5.
100 Newton, "De-constructing the Object" (1978), Series 1, Box 41, Folder 6, DHPNC, 2.
101 Newton, "Utopia: Universal Life Energy," 11.
102 "Huey P. Newton at New York Community College" (November 19, 1970), Series 1, Box 57, Folder 12, DHPNC, 10.
103 Newton, "Georgia State College," Series 1, Box 58, Folder 6, DHPNC.
104 Newton and Erikson, *In Search of Common Ground*, 33, 109–10.
105 Newton, *Revolutionary Suicide*, 178.
106 Vincent W. Lloyd, *Religion of the Field Negro* (New York: Fordham University Press, 2018), 191.
107 Newton, "The Son of Man" (1973), Series 1, Box 38, Folder 11, DHPNC.
108 Newton, "'Second Isaiah' and the Mystery of the Servant" (1974), Series 1, Box 37, Folder 11, DHPNC.
109 Conversation with historian of religion Nathaniel Deutsch, Summer 2021.
110 Document, Series 1, Box 2, Folder 7, DHPNC. Ford, "Hounded," 258. Dwight N. Hopkins, *Black Faith and Public Talk: Critical Essays on James H. Cone's Black Theology and Black Power* (Waco, TX: *Baylor University Press*, 2007), 91.
111 Richard Baker, "Introduction," Newton and Huggins, *Insights & Poems*. Michael Rogers, "Some Quiet Hours with Huey Newton," *Esquire*, May 1, 1973.
112 Application, Series 1, Box 46, Folder 8, DHPNC.
113 Letter, Series 1, Box 46, Folders 1–3, DHPNC.
114 Document, Series 1, Box 2, Folder 6, DHPNC.
115 Brown, *A Taste of Power*, 345.
116 Gritz, "The Misunderstood Visionary," *Smithsonian Magazine*.
117 Ford, "Hounded," 243–50.
118 Ibid., 244.

119 Trivers, *Wild Life*, 164. At the level of phenomena, the spiritual and the technological can be difficult to parse.
120 bell hooks, *All About Love: New Visions* (New York: HarperCollins, 2001), 225–6. Even dreams can be colonized.
121 Newton, *All Too Young*, Series 1, Box 55, Folder 5, DHPNC, 251.
122 Pearlman, *Huey P. Newton's Family*, 206.
123 Trivers, *Natural Selection and Social Theory*, 259–60. "Huey P. Newton at New York Community College" (November 19, 1970), Series 1, Box 57, Folder 12, DHPNC, 25.
124 Abu-Jamal, "The Genius of Huey P. Newton," *Prison Radio*.
125 Falk Huettig and Ramesh K. Mishra, "How Literacy Acquisition Affects the Illiterate Mind: A Critical Examination of Theories and Evidence," *Language and Linguistics Compass* 8:10 (2014), 401–27. Eleonore H. M. Smalle, et al., "Literacy Improves Short-Term Serial Recall of Spoken Verbal But Not Visuospatial Items: Evidence from Illiterate and Literate Adults," *Cognition* 185 (2019), 144–50.
126 Phone conversation with Phyllis Jackson, January 14, 2025.
127 Hilliard, Zimmerman, and Zimmerman, *Huey*, 277.
128 Ibid., 276.
129 Brown, *A Taste of Power*, 256.
130 "Huey Newton Speaks, July 4, 1970, by Mark Lane," Series 1, Box 57, Folder 7, DHPNC, 2.
131 Interview with Burney Le Boeuf, June 2021.
132 Newton, *Revolutionary Suicide*, 49.
133 Ibid., 49. Hilliard, Zimmerman, and Zimmerman, *Huey*, 203. "David Hilliard: Oct 9, 1970," Series 1, Box 2, Folder 11, JHBEMP, 16. According to Pearlman, Newton learned this from his brother Melvin (*Huey P. Newton's Family*, 205).
134 Seale, *Seize the Time*, 18.
135 Forbes, *Will You Die with Me?*, 277.
136 Hilliard, Zimmerman, and Zimmerman, *Huey*, 203.
137 Brown, *A Taste of Power*, 239–40.
138 Ibid., 313.
139 Ibid., 253.
140 Robin D. G. Kelley, "What Did Cedric Robinson Mean by Racial Capitalism?" *Boston Review*, January 12, 2017.
141 Newton, *Revolutionary Suicide*, 60–6. "Interview, Sept 17, 1970, by Mark Lane," Series 1, Box 57, Folders 9–10, DHPNC. "July 2, 1970," Series 1, Box 1, Folder 6, JHBEMP. Newton was recruited by Maurice Dawson.
142 Cedric Robinson, *The Terms of Order: Political Science and the Myth of Leadership* (1980) (Chapel Hill: University of North Carolina Press, 2016), 49–54, 51.
143 Ibid., 33.
144 Ibid., 67.
145 Ibid., 61.
146 Ibid., 39. Emphasis added.
147 Ibid., 69.
148 Ibid., 67.

149 "Angela Davis on Feminism, Communism and Being a Black Panther During the Civil Rights Movement" (May 2018), Channel 4 News, *YouTube*, uploaded May 25, 2018.
150 Newton and Erikson, *In Search of Common Ground*, 141.
151 Newton, "Hidden Traitor Renegade Scab: Eldridge Cleaver" (1972), Series 1, Box 50, Folder 3, DHPNC.
152 Hilliard, Zimmerman, and Zimmerman, *Huey*, 281.
153 Gritz, "The Misunderstood Visionary," *Smithsonian Magazine*.
154 Phone interview with Emory Douglas, June 26, 2025.
155 Hilliard, Zimmerman, and Zimmerman, *Huey*, 281. "Lonely Death: Family, Friends Mourn Huey Newton," *The Tribune*, August 24, 1989, Series 1, Box 5, Folder 8, JHBEMP. Pearlman, *Huey P. Newton's Family*, 490.
156 Clarence Johnson and Lori Olszewski, "Friends Say Huey Newton Had Financial Problems," *San Francisco Chronicle*, August 24, 1989.
157 Hilliard, Zimmerman, and Zimmerman, *Huey*, 282.
158 Johnson and Olszewski, "Friends Say Huey Newton Had Financial Problems," *San Francisco Chronicle*, August 24, 1989.
159 "Convicted Bank Robber and Reputed Cocaine Dealer Tyrone Robinson," *San Francisco Chronicle*, August 29, 1991, A12, Huey Newton Collection; Pearlman, *Huey P. Newton's Family*, 495.
160 Conversation with Xavier Buck, June 12, 2025.
161 Ibid. Pearlman, *Huey P. Newton's Family*, 495.
162 Churchill and Vander Wall, *The COINTELPRO Papers*, 417 n89.
163 Ibid., 418 n90.
164 Peter Fimrite, "Huey Newton Murder Trial Set to Begin," *San Francisco Chronicle*, August 24, 1991, Huey Newton Collection, FA.
165 Johnson and Olszewski, "Friends Say Huey Newton Had Financial Problems," *San Francisco Chronicle*, August 24, 1989. Pearlman, *Huey P. Newton's Family*, 493–4, 503.
166 Johnson and Olszewski, "Friends Say Huey Newton Had Financial Problems."
167 Hilliard and Cole, *This Side of Glory*, 9. Pearlman has perceptively pointed this out (*Huey P. Newton's Family*, 512–14.
168 "Huey P. Newton," National Archives Website.

Appendix: The Intellectual Legacy of Huey P. Newton

1 Newton, "Eclipse of Community: The Making of the English Working Class," Series 1, Box 38, Folder 9, DHPNC, 17. Used with permission by Dr. Huey P. Newton Foundation.

Index